Anatomy of a Home Studio

How Everything *Really* Works,
From Microphones to MIDI

by Scott Wilkinson

Foreword by Mark Isham

Edited by Steve Oppenheimer

6400 Hollis Street
Emeryville, CA 94608

©1997 Scott Wilkinson

06 05 04 03 02 01 00   6 5 4 3 2

Library of Congress Catalog Card Number: 97-073718

Book design, layout, and cover art: Linda Gough

Edited by: Steve Oppenheimer
Technical graphics: Chuck Dahmer

Production staff
Mike Lawson: publisher, Lisa Duran: editor, Randy Antin: editorial assistant, Don Washington:
operations coordinator, Teresa Poss: administrative assistant, Ellen Richman: production director,
Sherry Bloom: production assistant

"Hearing Preservation" section of Chapter 4 co-written by Joanna Cazden.
"Guitar Controllers" section of Chapter 8 co-written by Scott Summers.
"Tracking" section of Chapter 22 co-written by Neil Brighton.
Photo in cover collage used with permission from Coda Music Technology, Inc.

6400 Hollis Street
Emeryville, CA 94608
(510) 653-3307

Also from EMBooks:
Making the Ultimate Demo
Tech Terms: A Practical Dictionary for Audio and Music Production
Making Music With Your Computer

Also from MixBooks:
The AudioPro Home Recording Course, Volumes 1 and 2
I Hate the Man Who Runs This Bar!
How to Make Money Scoring Soundtracks and Jingles
The Art of Mixing: A Visual Guide to Recording, Engineering, and Production
500 Songwriting Ideas (For Brave and Passionate People)
Music Publishing: The Real Road to Music Business Success, Rev. and Exp. 4th Ed.
How to Run a Recording Session
Mix Reference Disc, Deluxe Ed.
The Songwriters Guide to Collaboration, Rev. and Exp. 2nd Ed.
Critical Listening and Auditory Perception
Keyfax Omnibus Edition
Modular Digital Multitracks: The Power User's Guide
Concert Sound
Sound for Picture
Music Producers
Live Sound Reinforcement

Also from CBM Music and Entertainment Group:
Recording Industry Sourcebook
Mix Master Directory
Digital Piano Buyer's Guide

MixBooks is a division of Cardinal Business Media Inc.

Printed in Auburn Hills, Michigan

ISBN 0-918371-21-X

Contents

vi

FOREWORD

vii

ACKNOWLEDGMENTS

viii

INTRODUCTION

1

PART 1: FUNDAMENTALS

Chapter 1
Musical Physics 2
Acoustics
Tuning and Temperaments

Chapter 2
Synthesis 9
Sample-Based Subtractive
Physical Modeling

Chapter 3
Basic Electrical Concepts 21
Electrical Concepts
AC Power and Grounding

Chapter 4
Decibels 30
Electrical Decibels
Acoustic Decibels
Hearing Preservation

Chapter 5
Digital Audio 40
Basic Concepts
Dithering

49

PART 2: MIDI

Chapter 6
Basic MIDI 50
MIDI Messages
MIDI Implementation Charts
Multitimbral MIDI

Chapter 7
Sequencing 61
Standard MIDI Files
General MIDI

Chapter 8
Alternate Controllers 77
Guitar Controllers
Percussion Controllers
Wind Controllers

Chapter 9
Advanced Topics 87
Bank Select
MIDI Processing
MIDI Machine Control
System Exclusive

101

PART 3: COMPUTERS

Chapter 10
Computer Applications 102
Hard-Disk Recording
Editor/Librarians
Notation
Music Education

Chapter 11
SCSI 116

123

PART 4: IN THE STUDIO

Chapter 12
Audio Connections 124
Analog Connections
Digital Connections

Chapter 13
Input Devices 130
Microphones
Direct Boxes

Chapter 14
Tape Decks 138

Chapter 15
Signal Routing 146
Mixers
Patch Bays

Chapter 16
Output Devices 154
Power Amplifiers
Monitors

163

PART 5: EFFECTS

Chapter 17
Basic Effects 164
Reverb
Delay
Pitch Shifting

Chapter 18
Modulation Effects 173

Chapter 19
Equalization 176
Spectral Enhancers

Chapter 20
Dynamics Processing 183

Chapter 21
Other Effects 188
Noise Reduction
3-D Processing

195

PART 6: TIPS, TRICKS, AND TIDBITS

Chapter 22
Recording Technique 196
Tracking
Mixdown
Premastering

Chapter 23
Manufacturer Mumbo Jumbo ..204
Alphanumeric Soup
Tower of TechnoBabel

211

INTERNET GLOSSARY

217

INDEX

Foreword

There is perhaps no other artistic activity in life that has undergone such a transformation due to technological advance than music. I look back at that day in fourth grade when I raised my hand and signed up for trumpet in the grade school band. Little did anyone imagine what other areas of study would eventually be required for a career in music.

The musician, both amateur and professional, has always had tools of their trade to contend with, the technology of their particular instrument, whether it be piano or washboard. With the advance of electronic technology into the world of music, we have seen a gradual change that has enhanced the musician's life tremendously but also added a large, complex subject to be studied and understood. All musicians today have access to a level of technology that is truly marvelous and potentially overwhelming. However, it is often difficult to keep up with a subject that is literally advancing in sophistication by the hour.

Basics are essential to keeping up, and here we have a book that presents the fundamental concepts of electronic music and the recording arts in a well-organized, well-defined way. It's a perfect textbook for those who wish to use this technology to help make music, from amateur musicians who want to set up their own home studio to seasoned professionals; it even cleared up a misunderstanding I had about the MIDI protocol.

In an activity in which the last thing you need to be worrying about is the technical side of things, where the true ideal is an environment in which you can focus purely on creative and aesthetic questions, a solid and thorough knowledge of the technology you're using is essential. This book delivers that.

—MARK ISHAM

A veteran of the music world for nearly 25 years as both a recording artist and a composer, Mark Isham has received a Grammy Award for his work as a solo artist; written scores for over 40 feature films, including *Kiss the Girls, Quiz Show, The Net, Nell, Short Cuts,* and *Never Cry Wolf;* earned both an Academy Award nomination and a Grammy nomination for the soundtrack to *A River Runs Through It;* won the Los Angeles Film Critics Award for Best Score for *The Moderns;* recorded with the Rolling Stones, Joni Mitchell, Bruce Springsteen, Toots Thielemans, and Robbie Robertson; and received an Emmy Award for his theme song to *EZ Streets.*

Acknowledgments

Few books are completely solitary endeavors, and this one is no exception. I am deeply indebted to many people who have helped me write complete and correct descriptions of all the various aspects of music technology. In particular, I want to thank everyone who has checked these words for technical and factual accuracy. This group includes representatives of many (if not most) hardware and software companies in the electronic-music industry. There are too many of these fine folks to thank individually, but I thank them nonetheless.

In addition, many experts contributed extensive research information, which helped make this book as complete and useful as possible. In alphabetical order, they include Bruce Bartlett, Neil Brighton, Bobby Brim, Bill Calma, Rick Cannata, Julian Colbeck, Gary Davis, John Eargle, Mike Eneboe, Steve Fisher, Peter Freeman, Jim Furman, Dennis Goettsch, Steve Gorney, Paul Ierymenko, Bob Katz, Frank Kelly, Ken Keyes, Keith Klawitter, Bob Lee, Ed Long, John Magnussen, Michael McFall, Chris Meyer, John Meyer, Bob Moses, Dave Murphy, George Petersen, Ken Pohlmann, Dale Roche, David Roudebush, Rod Squire, John Subbiondo, Scott Summers, Matt Suzuki, Tom White, Tran Whitley, and Bill Whitlock.

I would like to extend special thanks to several people for their efforts on behalf of this book: Mike Lawson, general manager of Mix Bookshelf; Michael Molenda, editor in chief of *Electronic Musician* magazine; and John Pledger, publisher of *EM*, who provided me with the opportunity to create the book.

Joe Humphreys, editorial assistant for *EM*, who was instrumental in establishing a coherent computer archive of the magazine's past issues and helping me retrieve the files I needed.

Linda Gough, the art director for this project, who designed a wonderful cover and turned my text files and disparate graphics into a beautiful book.

Lisa Duran, my editor at MixBooks, who remained ever cheerful and upbeat while coordinating the editing and production of the book amid frequent revisions from me.

Chuck Dahmer, who produced most of the technical diagrams used throughout the book. I greatly appreciate his artistic excellence and endless patience with my requests to retrieve "just one more diagram" from his archives.

Steve Oppenheimer, who did a careful technical edit of all my "From the Top" and "Square One" articles for *EM* and then edited them all over again as sections of this book. His diligent attention to detail contributed greatly to the accuracy of the result.

Joanna Cazden, my wife and partner in life and music, whose love and support never wavered during the stress of finishing the book. As an *EM* author herself, she also offered many excellent editorial comments that provided a very helpful perspective.

Robert and Jean Wilkinson, my parents, from whom I inherited my love of music and all things technical. Thanks for letting me play with that Wollensack tape recorder as a kid!

Introduction

Like many of you reading this book, I have always been fascinated by music technology. This fascination began with the technology of wind instruments, particularly brass instruments, which I began to play in the fourth grade. As I graduated from trumpet to trombone and tuba, I also developed an intense interest in electronics. I listened to early synthesizer pioneers, such as John Eaton playing the Syn-Ket, and experimented with an old Wollensack tape recorder my parents used to document their musical performances.

After enrolling at the University of California at Santa Cruz as a physics major, I quickly found the electronic-music lab, which included a TEAC 3340 4-track tape deck and a Moog modular suitcase synthesizer. I was in heaven. I stayed up way too late on innumerable nights recording tape-delay loops and creating new patches on that old Moog synth, oblivious to any discomfort in the windowless, concrete, basement studio. One of the most exciting moments came when I discovered how to play melodies with a fixed-frequency sawtooth waveform passing through a voltage-controlled bandpass filter. This produced a "harmonic" scale, which was very cool.

After graduating from UCSC (and hanging around Santa Cruz for a while playing for passing change on the Pacific Garden Mall with the Flying Karamazov Brothers), I spent several years at the California State University at Northridge studying music. This time, I gravitated toward the computer-music lab, which included a handmade prototype of the New England Digital Synclavier. I even got to disassemble and clean the hard disks (which were 15-inch platters that held a whopping 1.5 megabytes!) in honest-to-goodness "clean rooms," where I was clad in a white paper hat, mask, lab coat, and booties.

My first professional job in the MI (musical-instrument) industry was working as a product specialist at Roland Corp. US, where I fielded questions from users of Roland products. This led me to realize just how confusing and intimidating technology had become for a majority of musicians; most of the questions I was answering were extremely basic, and I was answering them over and over again. ("What's this Middy thing, and where do I plug it into my stereo?")

When I started working as a journalist in the field, I wanted to continue demystifying the basic concepts of electronic music, so I began writing a regular column for beginners, first in *Music Technology* magazine and later in *Electronic Musician*. After six years, I realized that my *EM* columns covered most of the basics, so I decided to compile them into the book that you now hold in your hands.

I have tried to keep the information presented here as general as possible, using specific hardware and software products primarily as examples. Of course, these products change very quickly; many of the tools used today were unheard of only five years ago, and devices that were hot items back then are now gathering dust in the closets of those who could afford to upgrade them. However, the underlying concepts on which these products are based do not change so rapidly. As a result, the product references in this book will certainly become obsolete soon after it is published, but they will continue to ably illustrate the concepts that I expect to remain valid for some time.

This isn't to say that new products and technologies aren't exciting. After all, there is no cure for technolust; no matter how much gear you have, you always want the Next Big Thing. Even after many years in this business, I still salivate over new products. For example, when I first played the Yamaha VL1 with a MIDI woodwind controller, I was astounded at its expressive response to my breath, far surpassing any sample-playback synth in this regard. I had to have one, even though it cost thousands of dollars at the time (and even though I knew the VL1's physical-modeling synthesis would be used in subsequent generations of less-expensive instruments).

The tools of electronic music stand ready to take us into the new millennium with ever more powerful capabilities that can greatly streamline and even stimulate the creative process. But all this power is useless without the guiding light of human knowledge and intention. Not only must you have something musical to express, you must know how to make the most of the technology in order to bring your dreams into reality. Once you do, your music will have a showcase from which to shine.

Fundamentals

Chapter 1: Musical Physics
Acoustics
Tuning and Temperaments

Chapter 2: Synthesis
Sample-Based Subtractive
Physical Modeling

Chapter 3: Basic Electrical Concepts
Electrical Concepts
AC Power and Grounding

Chapter 4: Decibels
Electrical Decibels
Acoustic Decibels
Hearing Preservation

Chapter 5: Digital Audio
Basic Concepts
Dithering

Musical Physics

Anyone reading this book is probably involved with sound in one way or another. After all, sound is the most fundamental building block of music. Most people can subjectively describe a sound as loud or soft and specify a pitch as high or low, and it's relatively easy to distinguish between a violin and a trombone. But what are the physical characteristics of sound that cause these perceptions?

If you've never been exposed to the fundamental principles of sound, take heart: they're easy to understand. In this chapter, you'll learn about the physical phenomena associated with sound as well as some basic terms used to describe its properties.

ACOUSTICS

Sound begins when something vibrates. For example, this something can be a woodwind reed, brass player's lips, guitar string, or speaker cone. For now, I'll use the example of a drum, but the principles are the same for all sound sources.

When you hit a drum, the drum head vibrates. This motion imparts a certain amount of energy to the air molecules immediately adjacent to the drum head, momentarily creating a region of higher than normal air pressure as the head moves outward.

However, air is elastic, which means it tends to return to its normal pressure if it's not constrained. The energy imparted by the vibrating head must go somewhere, so it moves on to the neighboring air molecules a bit farther from the head. These molecules then become momentarily compressed with higher-than-normal pressure.

This starts a chain reaction in which a region of air is compressed and then returns to its normal pressure, passing the energy of the compression to the adjoining region. It is important to understand that the air molecules themselves do not travel along with the region of high pressure; they vibrate in their own vicinity, somewhat like walking in place. It is the *energy* that travels outward from the source.

Meanwhile, the drum head moves inward, creating a momentary region of lower-than-normal pres-

sure adjacent to its surface. This region also moves away as the drum head pushes outward again and creates another temporary region of high pressure. This process repeats itself as long as the drum head continues to vibrate, causing alternating regions of high and low air pressure to expand and move away from the drum.

All sound sources vibrate in some manner, causing a similar pattern of expanding high- and low-pressure regions. This pattern is called a sound wave. Again, it's important to remember that the air molecules themselves do not travel along with the sound wave, as many people mistakenly believe. Individual air molecules vibrate in their own vicinity as the air pressure around them changes. It is the *pattern* of high and low pressure that travels, or propagates, outward from the source (see Fig. 1-1).

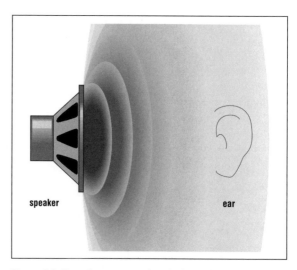

speaker   ear

Figure 1-1. Sound waves consist of alternating areas of high and low air pressure that propagate from a vibrating speaker cone or other acoustic source through the air to our ears.

Wave Terms

If you measure the air pressure at a particular point in space, you will find that it alternates between slightly higher than normal and slightly lower than normal as a sound wave passes by. This is often depicted in a graph of the pressure as it changes over time (see Fig. 1-2a).

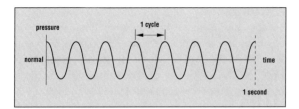

Figure 1-2a. Frequency of a sound wave. In this example, the frequency is 7 cycles/second, or 7 Hz, which means that each cycle takes ¹/₇ second to complete.

The variation of pressure from its maximum value to its minimum value and back to its maximum value is called one cycle of the sound wave. The number of cycles through which the pressure fluctuates in one second is called the frequency. As you might guess from this definition, frequency is measured in cycles per second. In honor of the contributions to the study of sound by the German physicist Heinrich Hertz, cycles per second are also called hertz (abbreviated Hz).

As human beings, we are unable to perceive a sound wave with a frequency of 7 Hz, as shown in Fig. 1-2a. Theoretically, the lowest frequency that we can detect is 20 Hz; the highest is 20,000 Hz, or 20 kilohertz (abbreviated kHz). In musical terms, this is a range of about ten octaves. As we grow older, the upper end of this range drops; most adults have an upper limit of about 14 to 15 kHz or so.

What we perceive as musical pitch is determined primarily by frequency. For example, the note A above middle C that is normally used to tune an orchestra is at a frequency of 440 Hz. As the frequency increases, we describe the note as being higher in pitch. The lower the frequency, the lower the pitch.

The speed at which a sound wave travels through a particular medium depends on the elastic properties and density of the medium; as the density decreases, the speed of sound increases. Typically, we are most interested in the speed of sound in the air under what are called the standard conditions (i.e., sea-level air pressure and a temperature of about 70° Fahrenheit or 21° Celsius). Under these conditions, the speed of sound is approximately 1,130 feet/second. However, as the temperature increases, the density decreases because the pressure remains constant if it is not completely confined. As a result, the speed of sound increases with temperature.

The speed of sound is very different in other media. For example, the speed of sound in fresh water at the standard temperature is 4,856 feet/second. This might seem odd considering that the density of water is much higher than air, but water is incompressible, whereas air is highly compressible. This property is related to the elasticity of the medium, which also affects the speed of sound. The elasticity of water causes the speed of sound to be much greater than it is in air, even though the density of water is greater than air. Interestingly, the speed of a sound wave does not depend on its frequency; all frequencies travel at the same speed through a given medium.

The physical distance between one area of maximum pressure and the next (or between one area of minimum pressure and the next) is called the wavelength. This can be depicted in a graph of the air pressure as it changes over distance (see Fig. 1-2b).

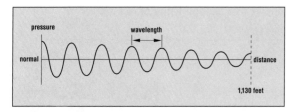

Figure 1-2b. Wavelength of a sound wave. As in Figure 1-2a, the frequency is 7 Hz, which means that the wavelength (in air) is 161.4 feet.

Wave Math

The frequency, wavelength, and speed of a sound wave are related. Using a simple formula, it's possible to calculate the wavelength of a sound wave if you know the frequency, and vice versa. The formula is:

wavelength = speed of sound/frequency

Let's try this formula on the lowest frequency that humans can perceive. At 20 Hz (assuming that the sound wave is traveling in air under standard conditions):

wavelength = 1,130/20 = 56.5 feet.

At the highest frequency detectable by humans:

wavelength = 1,130/20,000 = 0.0565 feet = 0.678 inches.

So the wavelengths of sounds we can hear range from over 56 feet to about two thirds of an inch.

This formula can also be expressed as follows:

frequency = speed of sound/wavelength

This explains why the pitch of wind and brass instruments is a bit flatter when they are first played than after they have warmed up. The temperature of the air in the instrument rises as it is played, so the speed of sound increases as the player's breath warms the air within. As the speed of sound increases, so does the frequency, which determines the pitch.

Another important characteristic of sound waves is the difference between the highest and lowest values of air pressure. This difference is called the amplitude, and it determines the volume or intensity of the sound. The greater the amplitude, or the greater the difference between the highest and lowest pressure in the wave, the louder the sound.

In Fig. 1-2c, you'll notice that the amplitude decreases as you move away from the source. This is because there is a fixed amount of energy carried in a sound wave. As the wave travels away from the source, it expands in a more or less spherical pattern, similar to a balloon being blown up.

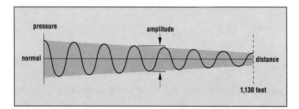

Figure 1-2c. Amplitude of a sound wave. As in Figures 1-2a and 1-2b, the frequency is 7 Hz. Notice that the amplitude decreases as you get farther away from the source, even though the wavelength and frequency remain unchanged.

A light bulb, which gives off a fixed amount of light, provides another analogy. The light from the bulb travels in all directions at once. As you move farther away from the bulb, the light appears to get dimmer. The bulb is producing a constant amount of light, but less of it is getting to your eye as you move farther away.

Sound works in a similar way. The sound source is producing a constant amount of sound, but less of it gets to your ear as you move farther away. Specifically, sound follows the inverse-square law, which states that the amplitude of a sound wave is inversely proportional to the distance from the source. For example, the amplitude of a sound wave at a distance of ten feet from the source is one quarter of the amplitude at a distance of five feet. This relationship often does not hold true in an enclosed space, where sound waves reflect from walls, ceilings, and floors.

Amplitude is specified in several ways; the most common is a unit of measurement called the sound-pressure level decibel. I'll go into more detail about decibels later in Chapter 4. For now, suffice it to say that humans can distinguish between about 250 different levels of amplitude, from the softest audible sound to a level that's painful to hear.

Waveforms

If you examine exactly how the pressure changes over the cycle of a sound wave, you can describe its waveform. Does the pressure suddenly switch from low to high and back again or does it change gradually up and down? Does it rise steadily from low to high, then suddenly drop to low before repeating the cycle? Does it change erratically with no apparent pattern?

Fig. 1-3 illustrates some of the common waveforms that older analog synthesizers produce (which I'll explore in more detail in Chapter 2). As you can see, these waveforms are relatively simple. The waveforms produced by most acoustic musical instruments are far more complex. Even so, a waveform must be periodic (that is, it must repeat itself with a constant frequency) in order to exhibit a recognizable pitch.

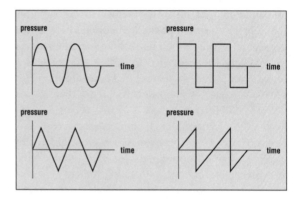

Figure 1-3. Four common synthesizer waveforms: sine, triangle, square, and sawtooth. These graphs represent the way in which the air pressure changes during several cycles.

Almost 200 years ago, the French mathematician Jean Baptiste Joseph Fourier discovered that any waveform can be distilled into a series of sine waves, which are the simplest possible waveforms. These sine waves exhibit different frequencies and amplitudes, and they are collectively known as the harmonic spectrum of the waveform. Individually, they are called harmonic components. The harmonic spectrum is normally depicted in a bar graph that reveals the frequency and amplitude of each component (see Fig. 1-4). The component with the lowest frequency is called the fundamental.

The harmonic components of a complex waveform can be any frequency, but most waveforms with a recognizable pitch consist of components that are whole-number multiples of the fundamental frequency. For example, if the frequency of the fundamental is 100 Hz, the frequencies of the higher components would be 200 Hz, 300 Hz, 400 Hz, and so on. This special type of harmonic spectrum is known as the harmonic or overtone series.

Although many people use the terms "harmonic" and "overtone" interchangeably, they are not exactly synonymous. Harmonics include all harmonic components, even the fundamental, whereas overtones include only the components above the fundamental, not the fundamental itself. For example, the second harmonic is the same as the first overtone. Fig. 1-4 is an example of a harmonic series.

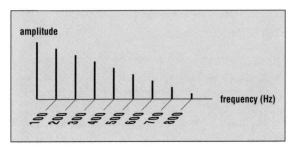

Figure 1-4. The harmonic spectrum of a sawtooth waveform. Each line represents one of the sine wave components. The horizontal position of each line indicates its frequency and the height indicates its amplitude relative to the other members of the spectrum.

Most musical instruments are especially resonant at certain frequencies, which are called formants. For example, the human vocal tract exhibits a formant at about 500 Hz, but trained singers can produce another formant at 2 to 3 kHz; this is known as the singer's formant. These frequencies are particularly pronounced in the spectrum of the instrument's sound regardless of the note being played. As a result, the shape of the harmonic spectrum changes as different notes are played.

TUNING AND TEMPERAMENTS

Anyone who works with synthesizers knows there is an infinite number of pitches between two notes separated by an octave. All you have to do is move the pitch wheel.

It seems strange, then, that Western music uses only twelve pitches. These twelve pitches—which are repeated in each octave—are the basic foundation of everything from high-art music (what most people mistakenly call "classical") to pop music. And guess what? Except for octaves, none of the intervals and chords played with these pitches are precisely in tune! We normally don't notice that our music is minutely out of tune, because we have become accustomed to these twelve pitches over the last 200 years.

To play intervals and chords that *are* in tune, the precise pitches of many notes must be shifted slightly from their normal frequencies. Microtuning is the term used to describe these tiny frequency adjustments. Trained singers, wind-instrument players, and

fretless stringed-instrument players constantly perform these shifts to produce intervals that are as in-tune as possible. On the other hand, keyboards, fretted strings, and mallet percussion instruments can play only fixed frequencies and therefore are never perfectly in tune.

Why did Western music settle on a set of notes that are always out of tune? How can electronic musicians overcome the tyranny of this limited palette of pitches? To answer these questions, we must understand the nature of musical intervals and what it means to be in tune.

Tuning Intervals

All notes are defined by their pitch, which corresponds directly to their fundamental frequency. Intervals consist of two notes sounding simultaneously or sequentially, while chords consist of several simultaneous intervals. The relationship between these notes is often expressed as the ratio of their frequencies. In the interval of an octave, for example, the frequency of the higher note is exactly twice the frequency of the lower note. The ratio of the two frequencies is 2:1.

Intervals with ratios of two whole numbers are called pure intervals. The common pure intervals include the octave (2:1), perfect fifth (3:2), perfect fourth (4:3), major third (5:4), and major second (9:8). Of course, there are many other intervals, but some of them can be one ratio or another depending on the tuning system (more on this in a moment). For example, the ratio of a minor second is 16:15 in one tuning system and 17:16 in another system.

Other tuning systems—including the one used in all of Western music today—use intervals that cannot be expressed as ratios of two whole numbers. Such intervals are called impure, and their ratios are called irrational. These intervals are impossible to represent with whole-number ratios, so a different interval-measuring system was developed.

The octave was divided into 1,200 equal intervals called cents, which lets us measure pure and impure intervals in the same way. For example, the pure major third is approximately 386 cents, while the impure major third used in Western music is exactly 400 cents. As a result, modern major thirds are sharp with respect to the pure variety.

All music students encounter the Circle of Fifths in their studies (see Fig. 1-5). This graphic includes all twelve notes in the standard Western tuning system in a sequence of perfect fifths. In this tuning system, the circle closes on itself, because B# is just a different name for C. These notes are called enharmonic equivalents. However, if you use pure perfect fifths in this exercise, the final B# is 23.46 cents higher than the starting C (discounting octaves). Under these conditions, the Circle of Fifths becomes a Spiral of Fifths.

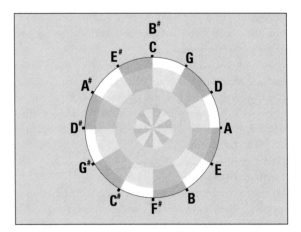

Figure. 1-5. The Circle of Fifths becomes a spiral if you use pure perfect fifths. The final B# is 23.46 cents higher than the starting C (discounting octaves).

This discrepancy is known as the Pythagorean comma, named after the ancient Greek scholar Pythagorus, who did a lot of fundamental research into musical intervals. Because most tuning systems are octave-based (i.e., they include a set of pitches that repeat in each octave), the Pythagorean comma must be placed somewhere in the scale to preserve the pure octave. Exactly how this is done is the art of creating a tuning system.

Tuning Systems

To construct a tuning with nothing but pure intervals, you must specify each interval individually. This is generally called just intonation (see Fig. 1-6). Each interval with the root sounds perfectly in tune. However, like most scales other than the common Western tuning, the notes in just intonation are not equally spaced. As a result, you can only play in the key defined by the root note and a few closely related keys. For example, in just intonation with a root of C, the major third from C to E is 386 cents, but the major third from B to D# is 428 cents (42 cents sharp with respect to a pure major third). So if you play in the key of C everything sounds fine, but modulating to the key of B sounds terrible.

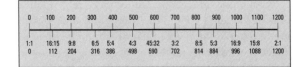

Figure 1-6. In just intonation, each interval with the root of the scale is pure. The scale above the line is the familiar 12-tone equal temperament.

One of the earliest tunings that can play in different keys is called meantone temperament (see Fig. 1-7). The word "temperament" refers to the fact that some or all of the intervals are tempered, or adjusted, from their pure forms to allow performances in different keys. In meantone temperament, some of the perfect fifths are shortened slightly to accommodate the comma. However, they are not shortened by the same amount, so some keys sound distinctly better than others.

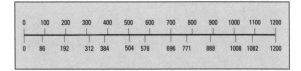

Figure 1-7. Meantone temperament is one of the first attempts to create a 12-tone tuning that could modulate into different keys. It was not entirely successful.

By the beginning of the 18th century, Western music was becoming more complicated and modulating into increasingly distant keys. Many musicians and theorists devised various temperaments to allow modulation into any key. Among the most successful of these pioneers was Andreas Werckmeister (see Fig. 1-8), whose temperaments were used by J. S. Bach and others. The notes were still not equally spaced in the scale, so each key had a distinct character. In fact, Bach wrote *The Well-Tempered Clavier* to demonstrate the character of each key in a temperament.

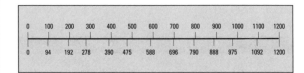

Figure 1-8. Andreas Werckmeister created many temperaments, including this one, which is now called Werckmeister III.

During the same period in history, other musicians experimented with equal temperament, in which the twelve notes were equally spaced within the octave. This "equality" is achieved by shortening each perfect fifth in the Spiral of Fifths by about 2 cents, making each one exactly 700 cents. The interval between consecutive notes in the scale is exactly 100 cents, which collapses the Spiral into the Circle of Fifths.

With this compromise, you can play in any key with equal ease. Each key sounds identical, with no change in character from one to another. Unfortunately, they also sound equally out of tune. Compared to their pure forms, perfect fifths are 2 cents narrow, major thirds are 14 cents wide, and minor thirds are 16 cents narrow. The other intervals are similarly out of tune with their pure forms.

There are other scales of equal steps that come closer to producing pure intervals. Some musicians divide the octave into 19, 31, or 53 equal steps, which include many almost-pure intervals. Wendy Carlos has taken a slightly different approach. She has assembled a series of equal steps that don't repeat in each octave. Her alpha scale (see Fig. 1-9) includes steps of 78 cents each. This tuning produces very pure thirds, fourths, fifths, and minor sevenths, although there is no pure octave.

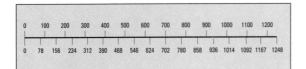

Figure 1-9. Wendy Carlos' alpha tuning uses equal steps of 78 cents. This tuning produces perfect fifths and fourths, major and minor thirds, and minor sevenths that are very close to pure in any key.

As Western musicians were converging on 12-tone equal temperament, the rest of the world was using many different tunings, some of which survive to this day. The musics of Indonesia, India, Asia, and the Middle East sound exotic and foreign because they are based on different intervals than Western music. For example, Indonesian music primarily uses one of two scales: Pelog and Slendro (see Fig. 1-10).

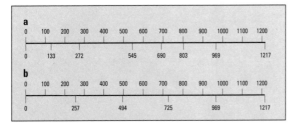

Figure 1-10. Indonesian music uses two main scales: Pelog (a) and Slendro (b). These tunings probably arise from the harmonics of the gong and struck-bar instruments used to play them.

Tuning Synths

One of the main reasons to adopt 12-tone equal temperament is the historical tendency toward music that is intended to be played on a keyboard and that modulates into widely diverse keys. With early tunings that are highly key-dependent, you must retune any keyboard instrument each time you play in a different key. As you might imagine, this is not something you'd want to do with a harpsichord or acoustic piano

in the middle of a piece of music. Equal temperament eliminates this requirement, so it found favor among Western musicians.

Of course, retuning digital synthesizers is very easy. All it takes is the appropriate software to recalibrate the oscillators to produce any set of frequencies you desire. The first widely available synth to offer this capability was the Yamaha DX7II. Since then, many electronic-keyboard manufacturers have included the ability to use tunings other than equal temperament.

Most of these instruments—which include models from E-mu, Korg, and Kurzweil—can retune only the twelve notes in an octave, and these tunings are repeated in all octaves. For key-dependent tunings, you can usually specify the desired root note. In a few instruments, you can retune each note in the entire MIDI range independently. This capability lets you construct larger tunings, such as 53-tone equal temperament or the Indian 22-note scale from which ragas are derived.

Synths with alternate tunings can't usually share their tuning data with dissimilar instruments or retune on the fly, so the MIDI Tuning Standard (MTS) was developed by Robert Rich and Carter Scholz and added to the official MIDI specification. This standard includes two major parts: bulk dumps and single-note retuning. The standard outlines the messages by which an instrument can be retuned during a performance. The specified resolution is 0.0061 cent, which is fine enough for most researchers and musicians.

Using Tunings

There are many ways to use alternate tunings, particularly with synths. Early and ethnic music can be played with greater authenticity, and you can achieve better consonance in all forms of music—particularly if you don't modulate into widely divergent keys. Even if you do modulate, you can often change tunings at the same time. For example, you might create two synth patches with the same sound and different tunings, such as just intonation in the keys of C and B, and select the patch that is tuned to the key you are playing in at any particular moment.

Another important application of microtuning is education. If you're a music teacher, you can impart a greater sense of historical perspective to your students by playing music from different periods and locations with appropriate tunings. For example, try playing a sequence with equal temperament followed by the same sequence in just intonation. The difference is startling. You can also explore the world of sound and acoustics with greater ease and precision.

Using alternate tunings has never been easier, thanks to modern music technology. Hopefully, manufacturers will continue to offer this capability in their instruments and include support for MTS. MTS brings microtuning into the MIDI fold and provides musicians with even greater resources for composition and experimentation. After all, if we don't push the musical envelope, who will?

CHAPTER 2

Synthesis

The primary reason I became interested in electronic music is synthesis, the creation of musical audio signals with electrical circuits. I've always found it fascinating to use the principles of acoustics to create sounds as well as analyze them. In addition, you can warp those principles in the electronic domain, creating sounds that do not exist in the acoustic world.

Synthesizers create, or synthesize, waveforms by electronically generating, combining, and manipulating harmonics in different ways. The earliest synthesizers included many separate sine-wave oscillators, which are electronic circuits that produce an alternating electric current in the shape of a sine wave. When the outputs of these oscillators are combined, the result is a complex waveform. This process is called additive synthesis because harmonic components are added together.

As oscillators became more sophisticated, they were able to produce complex waveforms with many harmonic components, such as the triangle, square, and sawtooth waveforms depicted in Fig. 1-3. (Sine waves have no harmonic components except themselves.) A technique called subtractive synthesis passes these complex waveforms through a filter, which is a circuit that removes certain harmonic components from the waveform.

A third technique for synthesizing complex waveforms is called frequency modulation or FM synthesis. In this process, the frequency of one oscillator is varied, or modulated, by another oscillator. The relationship between the frequencies and amplitudes of the two signals determines which harmonic components are present in the resulting waveform. FM synthesis was made popular by Yamaha in its DX7 and subsequent family of instruments.

SAMPLE-BASED SUBTRACTIVE

Most modern synths are subtractive: an oscillator generates a signal that is sent through a filter to alter its waveform, after which it passes through an amplifier to control its volume (see Fig. 2-1). The oscillator signal is typically supplied by PCM sampled waveforms

and digitally constructed synth waveforms, such as sawtooth, triangle, and pulse, which are stored in ROM and/or RAM computer memory.

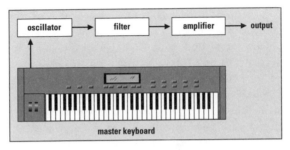

Figure 2-1. Basic synth architecture. The oscillator produces a waveform at a pitch that is controlled by the keyboard. This waveform is sent through the filter, which changes the harmonic spectrum by removing certain harmonics and boosting others depending on the type of filter, the cutoff frequency, and the resonance. The amplifier determines the final volume of the sound.

The final sound is determined by the values of a large number of parameters, which I'll get into shortly. Taken together, these parameter values constitute a patch, program, voice, or tone, depending on the nomenclature adopted by a particular manufacturer. (See "Tower of TechnoBabel" in Chapter 23 for more on this.) When referring to a generic set of parameters that synthesize a sound, I prefer the term "patch," because it harkens back to the days when sounds were synthesized by connecting the outputs and inputs of electronic modules—particularly oscillators, filters, and amplifiers—with patch cords.

In addition to using computer memory to store PCM waveforms, most modern synths also include memory to store different patches, which lets you call up a wide variety of sounds at the touch of a button. Many synths can store hundreds of patches, and they are shipped from the factory full of sounds called presets, which have been created by experts on each particular instrument.

In many cases, some or all of these sounds are stored in ROM memory, which can't be changed; what you hear is what you get. In other cases, some or all of the factory patches are stored in RAM, which can be changed by the end user. This lets you program your own sounds, either by tweaking the factory presets or starting from scratch.

Polyphony and Multitimbral Capability

There are two fundamental concepts that limit the performance of all synthesizers. The first is polyphony, which is the maximum number of notes the synth can play simultaneously. Polyphony is determined by the total number of oscillators in the synth, and it can be affected by the way a patch is organized. For example, a patch might use two oscillators for every note, which reduces the maximum number of simultaneous notes in half.

As a result, polyphony is often specified by the number of voices that can be played at once, which usually corresponds to the number of oscillators in the instrument. (This use of the word "voice" should not be confused with the same word when it is used as a synonym for the word "patch.") Modern instruments offer up to 64 or more voices of polyphony. However, if an instrument with 64 voices of polyphony and a patch uses two oscillators to play each note, the maximum number of simultaneous notes is 32.

The other concept with which you should be familiar is multitimbral capability. Unlike older instruments, modern synths can actually play several different patches simultaneously. There are many applications for this capability, such as layering several patches together much like combining oscillators in a single patch. In this application, the patches all sound together, creating a massive sound. (There are other applications of this capability, which I'll discuss in Chapter 6.)

However, it's important to remember that this technique also reduces the polyphony of the instrument. For example, if a synth provides 64-voice polyphony and some of its patches use two oscillators for each note, a layered sound that includes two of these patches can play only sixteen notes at a time.

One of the best ways to become familiar with the process of synthesis is to try changing the parameters of a factory preset. This is the approach I'll take as I discuss the various parts of a modern synthesizer.

Oscillators

One of the most basic parameters is the waveform produced by the oscillator. By changing this selection, you can create an entirely new sound instantly. Of course, the new sound might be better or worse than the original, but it's important to try different waveforms to discover their contribution to the sound.

If you want to improve a factory preset without radically changing it, try different waveforms from the same family. For example, there probably are several bass waveforms to try in a bass patch; one of them might sound more to your liking than the one in the preset. You also might try a synth waveform such as triangle or sawtooth in place of a sampled acoustic sound.

As mentioned earlier, most modern synths have the ability to combine two or more oscillators in a single patch, although this usually reduces the polyphony of the instrument. This architecture often includes the entire signal path, letting you combine two or more oscillator/filter/amplifier groups. In other cases, the signals from two or more oscillators are sent through a common filter/amplifier path.

Combining different waveforms in a single patch provides an almost unlimited potential for interesting sounds. You can also assign the same waveform to several oscillators and detune them slightly for a chorusing effect. Detuning can be effective with different waveforms as well. Try transposing one of the oscillators up or down by a larger interval, such as a fifth, to create a parallel harmony; transposing one oscillator by an octave creates a fatter sound.

The frequency of the oscillator can be modulated using various control sources. Perhaps the most common controller is a synth's built-in keyboard; playing different notes on the keyboard tells the oscillators what frequency to play. The frequencies of the oscillators in synths without built-in keyboards (i.e., MIDI sound modules) are controlled by external controllers, which I'll discuss in Chapter 8. In addition, the frequencies of the oscillators can be controlled by a wide variety of other sources, which I'll get to later in this section.

Filters and Amplifiers

As mentioned earlier, a filter removes certain frequencies from the harmonic spectrum of the oscillator's waveform. Some synths let you select the type of filter through which the oscillator's signal will pass. By changing the filter type, it is possible to create wildly different sounds from the original. The most common type is the lowpass filter, which allows frequencies below a certain threshold to pass unaltered while reducing or eliminating higher frequencies. Similarly, a highpass filter attenuates frequencies below the threshold and allows higher frequencies to pass.

The most common filter tweak is changing the threshold frequency, which is called the cutoff frequency. Lowering the cutoff frequency of a lowpass filter lets fewer high harmonics through, making the sound duller, while raising it makes the sound brighter. Raising the cutoff frequency of a highpass filter trims off the low and mid frequencies, producing a thin sound, while lowering it lets more of the sound through.

A bandpass filter lets through only a specified range (band) of frequencies, rejecting all others (see Fig. 2-2). The cutoff frequency is at the center of the band and is more properly called the center frequency. Changing the center frequency affects the character of the sound in different ways, depending on the initial waveform. In addition, it might be possible to broaden or narrow the range of the frequencies passed; this range is called the bandwidth.

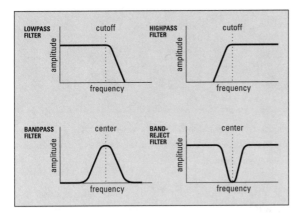

Figure 2-2. Filter behavior can be represented graphically. A lowpass or highpass filter lets frequencies on one side of the cutoff frequency pass through unaltered, while attenuating frequencies on the other side. A bandpass filter only lets through frequencies within a defined range around the center frequency, while a band-reject filter attenuates the frequencies near the center frequency.

A band-reject filter is the opposite of a bandpass filter; it passes everything *but* a specified range of frequencies around the center frequency. The most common kind of synthesizer band-reject filter is a notch filter, which stops a very narrow band of frequencies.

In analog synthesizers, most filters include a parameter called resonance or Q. Increasing the resonance value amplifies the frequencies near the filter's cutoff or center frequency, regenerating them in a feedback loop. This produces a peak in the filter's response close to the cutoff frequency (see Fig. 2-3). In a notch filter, increasing the resonance narrows the notch.

With most resonant filters, you can increase the resonance so much that it goes into self-oscillation, creating its own waveform at the cutoff frequency. Until recently, the digital filters found on most modern synths had no resonance, but many now offer a resonance parameter.

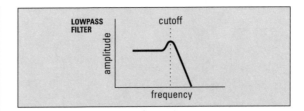

Figure 2-3. A lowpass filter with a high resonance value.

The amplifier controls the volume of the sound, usually after the signal leaves the filter. The only direct control parameter is the level, which determines the maximum volume of the sound. This parameter is useful when mixing two or more sounds in a single patch, as you can balance their levels to taste. It's also useful when certain waveforms and/or filter settings result in an overall level that's too hot.

Modulators

Sounds that maintain a constant volume over the course of each note quickly become boring. The same holds true for oscillators and filters that don't change during each note. As a result, a variety of modulators are applied to the oscillator, filter, and amplifier to modulate, or change, their characteristics over time.

Modulators come in two varieties: automatic and manual. As you might imagine, automatic modulators do their thing automatically; they are often triggered by the start of each note. Manual modulators are controlled by the player during performance. These modulators are instrumental in bringing expression to electronic music.

Automatic Modulators

There are two automatic modulators that are universally applied to all types of synthesis: envelope generators (EGs) and low-frequency oscillators (LFOs). The signals from EGs and LFOs are programmed by the sound designer and sent to the control inputs of the oscillator, filter, and amplifier (see Fig. 2-4). These signals automatically control the behavior of the oscillator, filter, and amplifier over each note. In some cases, their effects are quite immediate and subtle, while in others they are slower and more pronounced.

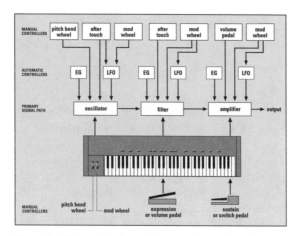

Figure 2-4. The architecture of many modern synths includes the primary signal path from an oscillator through a filter to an amplifier. These components are controlled by various automatic and manual modulators.

All acoustic sounds have a beginning, middle, and end. They start from silence and vary in loudness until they return to silence. The profile of this behavior is called the sound's amplitude envelope. For example, a piano note reaches its maximum loudness very quickly and decays slowly until the key is released, after which the sound falls to silence almost immediately (see Fig. 2-5).

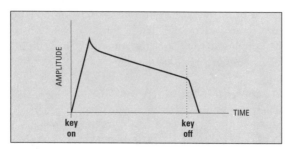

Figure 2-5. The amplitude envelope of a note played on a piano.

In synthesizers, this fundamental aspect of all musical sounds is simulated with an envelope generator. By applying the output of an EG to the amplifier at the end of the primary signal path, the volume of each note follows the preprogrammed profile determined by the EG parameter settings. As each key on the keyboard is pressed, the EG output goes from a value of zero up to a certain level, after which it varies according to the parameter settings and falls to silence in a user-specified length of time after the key is released.

Modern EGs let you specify the rate at which the envelope moves from one level to the next, as well as the levels themselves. For example, Fig. 2-6 illustrates an EG with four rates and four levels, all of which are specified by the programmer. The first rate deter-

mines the attack time of the sound from the moment a key is pressed until the first level is reached. The second rate determines the time it takes to reach the second level, while the third rate determines how long it takes to reach the third level. The EG stays at the third level until the key is released, after which it moves to the fourth level in the time determined by the fourth rate. The fourth level almost always is set to zero; otherwise, the sound never completely fades away.

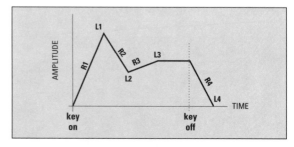

Figure 2-6. A typical synth EG provides four rates and four levels. Once it is reached, the third level remains constant until the key is released.

As you can see in Fig. 2-7, this type of envelope generator can simulate a piano envelope quite effectively. The attack rate is quite fast, quickly raising the signal to a high level, followed by a short, slightly slower decay to simulate the initial "spike" in a piano envelope. The third rate is slow to simulate the slow decay as the key is held down; the third level is set to zero in case the player holds the key until the note disappears completely. If you let go of the note prior to reaching level 3, the EG skips to rate 4 and level 4. The fourth rate relatively quickly leads to a fourth level of zero after the key is released.

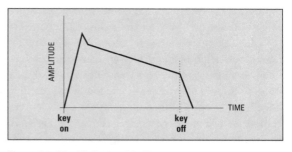

Figure 2-7. The EG depicted in Fig. 2-6 can be used to simulate a piano envelope quite accurately.

It's important to note that even though levels 3 and 4 are both zero, the sound level does not rise between them and fall again. A sound simply follows the appropriate path to zero depending on where in the envelope you take your finger off the key.

Of course, electronic sounds can be modified to resemble nothing in the acoustic world. For example, if you have a piano sound with an envelope like Fig. 2-7, you might slow down the first and fourth rates and increase the third level to equal the second level to create a sustaining, spacey "piano pad" sound.

Most modern synths include several EGs, one of which can be applied to the filter. This changes the timbre over time by modulating the filter's cutoff frequency in the same way that the amplitude envelope modulates the sound's volume. Find a preset with a timbre that changes radically during the course of a note; such presets often have the word "sweep" in their names. Take a look at the EG settings, then try changing the attack time and other parameters to get a feel for the effect of a filter EG.

Another EG often is applied to the frequency of the oscillator. Unlike the amplifier or filter EGs, which output values between zero and a maximum level, the pitch EG varies between negative and positive values, with zero in the middle (see Fig. 2-8). This allows the pitch EG to vary the frequency of the oscillator above and below its nominal (in-tune) value.

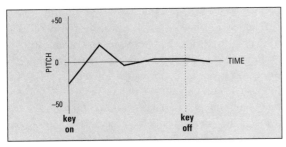

Figure 2-8. A pitch EG controls the frequency of the oscillator. In this example, the frequency can be shifted by as much as 50 cents above or below the nominal pitch.

Typically, the pitch EG is used to vary the pitch of the oscillator by small amounts to simulate the small pitch variations in the attack portions of many acoustic-instrument sounds. However, you might want to experiment with larger variations to create a wild, pitch-sweeping effect.

LFOs

LFOs are most often used to simulate vibrato by applying a slow, regular control signal to the pitch of the oscillator. This signal varies the pitch up and down slightly a few times per second. By applying an LFO to the amplifier, the volume of the sound is slowly modulated up and down, creating a tremolo effect. When it's applied to a lowpass filter cutoff, an LFO creates a "wah-wah" effect.

There are three major LFO parameters: the first is called frequency, rate, or speed; and the other two are depth and waveform. The frequency of an LFO is usually between 0.1 and 10 Hz (vibrato rates are in

the 4 to 7 Hz range), although some LFOs offer much higher frequencies. If your LFO has a large frequency range, increase the frequency into the audible range above 20 Hz and apply it to the oscillator. This is a crude form of FM synthesis that results in distinctly different timbres as you play different notes on the keyboard.

The depth parameter determines how much effect the LFO has; in essence, this is the amplitude of the LFO. At low depth values, the pitch, cutoff, or volume vary less radically than at high depth values. (Some instruments also include EG depth parameters that determine how much the EG affects the component it's controlling.)

The LFO waveform determines the exact pattern of the modulation (see Fig. 2-9), which allows many different effects. The sine and triangle waveforms normally simulate vibrato and tremolo. Apply a square or sawtooth waveform with a high depth value to the oscillator in a brass patch for European and American siren sounds, respectively. A mechanical, random sound is achieved using the sample-and-hold waveform to modulate the filter cutoff and/or oscillator frequency.

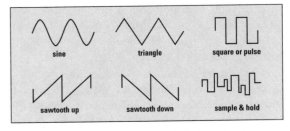

Figure 2-9. Common LFO waveforms include sine, triangle, square or pulse, sawtooth up, sawtooth down, and a random sample-and-hold.

Manual Modulators

Manual modulators are manipulated in real time to change the sound of a synth as you play. The most common manual modulator is the keyboard, which controls the frequency of the oscillators to produce different pitches as different keys are played. (Any source of MIDI note data, such as a MIDI guitar or wind controller, plays an equivalent role; see Chapter 8 for more.) However, there is much more potential for control under those keys. For example, many instruments let you apply the key number to the filter cutoff with a parameter called key follow. As you play higher notes, the sound gets brighter.

The initial volume of each note is determined by the velocity with which the key is pressed on most synths; the faster the keystroke, the louder the sound. But velocity can control a variety of other parameters, too. For example, velocity can control the filter cutoff in many synths using a parameter called velocity follow (often referred to as modulating with velocity). This lets you brighten the sound as you play louder notes.

A parameter called EG velocity sensitivity is used to scale the EG levels according to the velocity of the keystrokes; the greater the velocity, the higher the levels. As you increase the EG velocity sensitivity, this effect becomes more pronounced.

These three parameters—key follow, velocity follow, and EG velocity sensitivity—are often applied to the filter in brass, string, and some woodwind patches. As you play higher and louder, the timbre changes radically, simulating the behavior of acoustic instruments. Try adjusting these parameters in a brass or string patch to balance their effect. Then, take them to their extreme values and play high and low notes with different velocities just to hear what happens.

Most modern keyboards are sensitive to aftertouch (also called pressure). After the initial keystroke, extra pressure can be applied to the key with your finger. The amount of extra pressure is used to control many different parameters. For example, aftertouch changes the timbre of the sound if it's applied to the filter, or it bends the pitch if applied to the oscillator. Aftertouch can also control the LFO. Greater pressure increases the depth of the LFO signal, resulting in a more pronounced vibrato, tremolo, or other LFO-triggered effect.

On the far left of most electronic keyboards are two wheel controllers: the pitch-bend wheel and modulation wheel. On some instruments, particularly those made by Roland and Korg, these wheels are replaced by a joystick or other device that moves in two directions independently.

The function of the pitch-bend wheel should be obvious: it modulates the frequency of the oscillator up or down as the wheel is moved away from its spring-loaded center position. The maximum range (plus or minus) over which the pitch can be modulated is called the pitch-bend range. This range usually is set from ±1 to 12 semitones, allowing the pitch to be "bent" as much as one octave up or down from the nominal pitch. On a lead-guitar patch, try setting the pitch-bend range to one or two semitones, which is as far as many guitarists bend the pitch in most circumstances. A wider range is harder to control precisely, particularly in the heat of live performance.

The mod wheel is an all-purpose manual controller. It can be applied to virtually any parameter on most synths. For example, the mod wheel is often used to control the filter cutoff. This lets you brighten or dull the sound by moving the mod wheel. Like aftertouch, the mod wheel can control the LFO depth, as well. Moving the mod wheel away from the

"zero" or "off" position increases the LFO's depth. If you check out several patches on your synth, you'll find this is one of the most common applications for the mod wheel. Many newer instruments also offer sliders that can be assigned to control a wide variety of different sound parameters, including attack time (an EG parameter), filter cutoff, and volume.

Two types of pedals can be plugged into the back of most keyboard instruments: expression and switch pedals. Expression pedals, often called modulation pedals, serve the same function as the mod wheel and sliders and can be applied to almost any parameter. In particular, expression pedals are often applied to the amplifier for overall volume control or the filter for timbral control. They can also bring in the LFO. Some musicians modify their expression pedals by spring loading them, which makes the pedal a good substitute for aftertouch or the pitch-bend wheel (though you only can bend in one direction).

Switch pedals are most commonly used to sustain a sound after releasing a key, much like the sustain pedal on a piano. (In this situation, the EG behaves as if the key is still depressed until the pedal is released.) However, these pedals can also be used in many other ways. For example, you often can program a synth to call up a different patch by stepping on a switch pedal. Some synths let you create a customized "chain" of patches that are called up sequentially each time the pedal is pressed, which is great for live gigs in which you need a certain set of sounds in a certain order.

In addition, you often can engage portamento with a switch pedal. This causes the synth to glide smoothly between notes instead of changing abruptly as different notes are played. The time it takes to glide from one note to the next is determined by the portamento time parameter.

There are plenty of situations in which you need both hands for playing. For example, you might need to play a comping or lead part with the right hand and a bass part with the left hand. In these situations, pedals, aftertouch, key following, and velocity following are particularly useful, because you can't manipulate the pitch-bend wheel or mod wheel. Keep this in mind when tweaking patches intended for live use.

Programming

In the early days of electronic music, most performers also were sound programmers. Synths didn't have patch memory, so synthesists had to create their own sounds before performing or recording. Often, electronic performers hired sound programmers to assist them in the studio and onstage.

With the advent of patch memory (not to mention more complicated instruments), these two roles began to diverge. Today, few performers create their own synth patches or hire sound programmers; instead, they use factory presets, buy third-party patches, and settle for an undistinguished sonic signature.

There's no doubt that sound programming is highly intimidating, even for seasoned pros. Nevertheless, it can be one of the most rewarding aspects of synthesis, as it helps you develop a unique sound that sets you apart from the crowd. Best of all, it's easier than you might think. You need not start from scratch, staring at a blank display waiting for inspiration to strike. The factory presets provide an excellent starting point for sonic exploration.

First and foremost, don't be afraid to enter the Edit mode of your synth and muck around with parameter values. You can't damage the instrument; at worst, you'll lose some of the factory presets. This is unlikely, however, since most synths include memory protection that you must intentionally disable in order to save any sounds. Even if you do save a new sound in the memory location of a factory preset, many instruments have the presets backed up in ROM and let you recall them by reinitializing the memory. (This often wipes out any new sounds you may have stored there, however.) To be safe, save the factory presets to another medium—a RAM card or cartridge, internal floppy disk, external data-storage device, or computer running a patch-librarian program—before you begin to create your own sounds.

It's a good idea to use a patch-editor program when developing sounds (see Chapter 10). No matter how large the display on a synth might be, a computer screen is larger, which makes it far easier to see what you're doing.

Modern synths usually include two basic operational modes that go by different names: Voice, Single, or Play mode and Performance, Multi, or Combi mode. In Voice/Single/Play mode, a single patch is played across the entire keyboard. In Performance/Multi/Combi mode, several patches are assigned to different regions of the keyboard. This mode is used to layer several patches together for a bigger overall sound. It can also be used for playing multiple parts at once (say, a bass part with the left hand and a pad or lead sound with the right hand) and for multitimbral sequencing with each patch responding to a different MIDI channel (see Chapter 7).

Each of these operational modes has a corresponding Edit mode in which parameter values are set to achieve a certain result. If you're not using a computer-based patch editor, start from the desired operational mode and press the Edit button on the synth's front panel to enter the corresponding Edit mode. Once in the desired Edit mode, you probably need to navigate through several "pages" of parameters. These pages are usually organized in a more or less logical manner, grouping related parameters together.

In the Performance/Multi/Combi Edit mode, try layering entirely different patches or several detuned copies of the same patch. Transposing one or more patches is quite effective, as well. Try assigning one patch across the entire keyboard while another patch is active only in one part of the keyboard. For example, you might want to assign a string section sound to the entire keyboard while a flute sound is active only in the upper third.

As you progress, you will develop the ability to predict the effect your actions will have on the sound. You can foster this ability by using the Edit/Compare button found on many synths. After changing one or more parameter values, pressing this button restores the original values and lets you hear the sound as it was before your changes. Pressing it repeatedly toggles between the edited and unedited sounds. Use this button often.

The possibilities seem endless, but they aren't as daunting as you might think. With a little knowledge and some common sense, you can learn to create sounds that will set you apart.

PHYSICAL MODELING

On a crystal blue California spring day in 1975, I sat at the kitchenette counter in my apartment near the famous Santa Cruz Beach Boardwalk, poring over my research thesis. This was my last assignment as a physics undergrad, and it was almost finished. My topic was the acoustics of woodwind instruments. I was into making bamboo flutes and shakuhachis and had decided to kill two birds with one stone: finish my degree and improve my flute-making with a little acoustical theory. The math was hairy, but after a while it began resonating in my head, just like the instruments it described.

During that same year, I was also studying electronic music with Gordon Mumma, who had worked with John Cage and Merce Cunningham. The electronic-music lab at UCSC was equipped with an old, monophonic Moog suitcase synth. It made some great sounds, but it was hardly capable of what I had in mind. I dreamed of using the mathematics in my thesis to electronically simulate the sound of acoustic instruments.

Almost twenty years later, my dream finally became reality. The mathematical descriptions, or models, of musical-instrument acoustics are being used to generate and control reasonable facsimiles of instrumental sounds in real time. This form of virtual reality, called physical modeling, requires immense computational horsepower, which has been unavailable in commercial products—until now.

Resonance Review

To understand physical modeling, you must understand how acoustic instruments work. Anything that vibrates exhibits resonance, which is the tendency to vibrate at particular frequencies called modes. All musical instruments exhibit resonance modes that depend on several factors.

For example, each string on a violin, guitar, or piano vibrates at several specific frequencies, which are determined by the length, thickness, and tension of the string. A wind instrument consists of a tube enclosing a column of air that vibrates at frequencies determined by the length and cross-sectional shape of the tube, as well as the type of mouthpiece: single reed (clarinet, saxophone, etc.), double reed (oboe, bassoon, etc.), lip reed (all brasses), or air jet (flute, recorder, etc.). The resonance modes of percussion instruments depend on the material and shape of each vibrating surface, as well as where the surfaces are fixed to the frame.

The resonant-mode frequencies correspond to the harmonic spectrum of the instrument, and the amplitude of each harmonic is determined in part by the material from which the instrument is made. For example, a silver flute has a different harmonic spectrum than a wooden flute. This is due to the fact that different materials absorb and reflect different amounts of energy at different frequencies.

To produce a sound with a musical instrument, you must start the appropriate part vibrating by applying energy to the system. A momentary impulse, such as striking a piano string, plucking a guitar string, or hitting a drum, starts the vibration, which might include several resonant modes simultaneously. This vibration then diminishes to silence if no further energy is applied.

To maintain a constant vibration, you must continue to pump energy into the system by blowing into a wind instrument, bowing a string, and so on. Amazingly, the steady flow of breath or movement of a bow is converted into a pulsed air stream or vibrating string. This is too complicated to explain in detail here; suffice it to say that the mouthpiece or bow interacts with the resonant modes of the air column or string to produce a standing wave. (A standing wave occurs when sound waves are reflected back and forth along the same path, interacting with each other to create stationary zones of high and low amplitude.) This standing wave normally includes several partials arising from the resonant modes, which are an important part of the instrument's timbre.

Wind instruments of a fixed length, such as a bugle, can normally play only the notes in the harmonic series. To play a chromatic scale, there must be some way to make the length of the instrument shorter or longer, which shifts the resonant modes up or down, respectively. Woodwind instruments do this with tone holes, which effectively change the length of the instrument as they are opened and closed. Brass instruments physically add lengths of tubing as different combinations of valves are depressed. The trombone changes its length directly by moving the slide. String instruments shift their resonant modes by changing the vibrating length of the string with a finger or the tension of the string with a tuning peg.

Although most wind and string instruments can shift their resonant modes by changing the effective length of the vibrating part, there are certain resonant frequencies that remain fixed no matter what else is going on. These frequencies, called formants, are mainly determined by the overall shape of the instrument, which doesn't change as different notes are played. As we'll see in a moment, formants are among the most distinguishing characteristics of physical modeling.

The behavior of a musical instrument is extremely complex, but it does succumb to analysis. Physical properties (reed stiffness, bore shape, string tension, etc.) and the way different parts of the instrument interact to produce sound can be described mathematically. The resulting equations are daunting, but they provide invaluable insight into the nature of musical sound. With the recent improvement in computer processing power and speed, these equations can now be used to simulate the instruments they represent in real time.

Modeling Clay

Unlike most forms of music synthesis, physical modeling does not use oscillators, filters, amplifiers, envelope generators, or LFOs, at least not as primary sound sources and modifiers. Instead, the mathematical description of an instrument's acoustic behavior is programmed into a digital signal processor (DSP). The DSP then churns out numbers based on this description and sends them to a digital-to-analog converter (DAC). Notes are typically triggered with MIDI Note On/Off messages and modulated with MIDI Control Change and other continuous messages.

One of the primary reasons that real-time physical modeling has been unavailable until now is the limitations of DSP hardware. Historically, DSPs have been unable perform the required calculations fast enough. At best, you could feed the appropriate data into a computer and go to lunch while it crunched the numbers, after which you could play the sound. If you wanted to make any tweaks to the sound, you had to wait through yet another round of compilation.

In addition, general-purpose DSPs, such as the Motorola DSP56000 series, are not optimized for the required operations. As a result, several companies have developed custom DSPs optimized for physical modeling. Others are using the latest generation of generic DSPs, which have achieved much higher speeds in the last couple of years.

Physical modeling exhibits several distinguishing characteristics. For one thing, modeling systems tend to offer much more expressive capability with MIDI continuous control than most forms of synthesis, particularly sample-based synthesis. For example, blowing harder into a breath controller can cause a wind-instrument model to jump resonant modes, just like its acoustic counterpart. Different articulations, such as legato and slurring, are much easier to achieve with a modeled sound, as well. The model responds like an acoustic instrument, whereas a sample plays exactly the same way every time. (It is possible to coax some expression out of sample-based synths; see Chapter 6.)

However, models are often not as accurate as samples in their re-creation of acoustic sounds. As complex as it is, the math is usually a simplified approximation; the actual behavior of an acoustic instrument is more subtle and individual than the math can generally describe. In addition, the computational requirements are still too intense to construct completely accurate models in real time with current commercial hardware.

As a result, there is a tradeoff between samples and models. Samples are recordings of acoustic sounds, so each note is a more accurate representation than the corresponding modeled note. But samples are less accurate than modeled sounds when played in phrases, because the behavior of a model is closer to that of an acoustic instrument.

One of the best ways to suggest the behavior of acoustic instruments is to model formants. With samples, the recorded formants are transposed along with the rest of the sound as you play different notes. With physical models, however, the formants can remain fixed as you play different notes.

Another important difference is that mathematical descriptions generally take up less memory than digital-audio recordings, so modeling systems usually require less memory than sample-based synths. In addition, "macro" parameters are relatively easy to design. As you change one aspect of the model—say, the "material" out of which the virtual instrument is made—a whole host of low-level parameters automatically change as a result.

Finally, physical modeling lets you create hybrid sounds by combining the characteristics of two or more acoustic instruments, which can lead to entirely new and useful sounds. However, many combinations of physical elements, such as reeds and bores, do not result in a desirable sound, and some do not make any sound at all. Acoustician Arthur Benade calls these silent instruments "tacet horns."

Yamaha VL1

The first company to introduce a commercial product based on physical modeling is Yamaha. The VL1 (see Fig. 2-10) is the first product to use the company's Virtual Acoustic Synthesis (VAS) technology, which has been under development since 1986. One result of this effort is a custom DSP chip optimized for physical modeling. The VL1 is designed around a woodwind model, the specifics of which are encoded in ROM.

Figure 2-10. The Yamaha VL1 is the first product to use the company's Virtual Acoustic Synthesis modeling technology. It is intended to play lead lines and solos with a maximum polyphony of two notes.

The VL1 is intended to play lead lines and solos (VL stands for "Virtual Lead"). As a result, it has a maximum polyphony of two notes. Of course, this design is also a result of limited processing power.

Like most modeling systems, the VL1 offers a high degree of expressive capability. Many of its parameters—such as Embouchure, Tonguing, Scream, Breath Noise, and Growl—can be controlled with any continuous message. Most of the factory sounds are designed to respond to Breath Controller messages in ways similar to acoustic wind instruments. For example, if you blow very softly while playing a sax note, you hear the air noise with no pitch. As you blow harder, the model begins oscillating. If you continue to blow harder, the model jumps to the next resonant mode.

In order to avoid tacet horns, the VL1 provides integrated, preset models that represent various combinations of reeds, bodies, and bells. The models also include several guitars, basses, and bowed strings.

Korg *SynthKit*

Korg is another company hard at work developing physical modeling technology. Their efforts center on a Macintosh program called *SynthKit,* written for the purpose of internal research and development. This software is a synthesis construction kit, similar to Digidesign's *TurboSynth* but with a lot more real-time control capabilities.

Like other construction-kit programs, you start by creating an algorithm consisting of functional blocks, which are connected in various ways (see Fig. 2-11). The blocks pertaining to physical modeling include hammer, reed, bow, bore, and glottal-pulse models. As you assemble the algorithm, you can construct a control panel to address only those parameters you select (see Fig. 2-12).

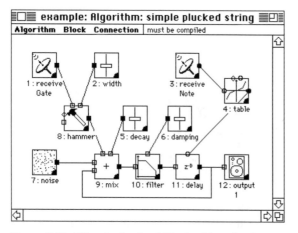

Figure 2-11. This simple *SynthKit* algorithm simulates a plucked string. Each block includes one or more inputs (open squares on the left of the block), outputs (solid squares on the right), and control inputs (open squares on the top). Each block can also be named; the number preceding the name indicates the order of operation in the compiled code.

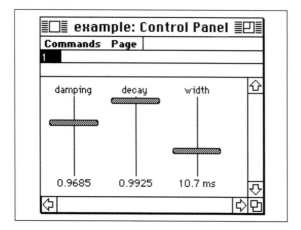

Figure 2-12. Any control sliders that are placed in a *SynthKit* algorithm can appear in the control panel. These sliders can be moved as notes are played to "voice" the algorithm.

After the algorithm is complete, it is compiled into DSP code, which is downloaded into one of several DSPs, including the Motorola 56000, Texas Instruments 57000, or a custom chip. Part of the code, such as LFOs and activities that don't happen all the time, can be specified to run in the host Macintosh to reduce the processing demands on the DSP. You can then trigger and control notes via MIDI in real time as you modify the algorithm from the onscreen control panel.

At present, *SynthKit* is used mostly with Digidesign audio cards, such as Audiomedia III. The current system provides from one to eight voices of polyphony, depending on the complexity of the algorithm.

The program also includes functional blocks for oscillators, filters, and other synthesis elements. These elements can be combined with the modeling blocks in many ways to create hybrid algorithms. The power of this approach is obvious, and the algorithms developed with *SynthKit* have appeared in such products as the Prophesy and Z1 synthesizers.

CCRMA Waveguide

At Stanford University's Center for Computer Research in Music and Acoustics (CCRMA, pronounced "karma"), associate professor Julius Smith has been working on a type of physical modeling called waveguide synthesis. This approach models a physical waveguide, or transmission line, which is any path along which a wave can travel undistorted. Examples include fiber-optic cables, microwave transmitters, and even certain aspects of room acoustics. The most important characteristic of a waveguide is its length, which must be significantly greater than its other dimensions.

Strings and air columns in musical instruments make great waveguides. They can be simulated by replacing the physical transmission lines with delay lines. As a wave travels from one end of an instrument to the other, it is delayed by the time it takes to traverse the distance. In wind instruments, it is reflected back and forth along the bore. As the effective length of a bore or string is changed to produce different notes, the instrument acts like a variable-length, bidirectional delay line.

Smith began his research by simulating a bowed string, which can be modeled as two waveguides, one on either side of the bow. He then moved on to the clarinet, when he was joined by graduate student Perry Cook. Cook continued the clarinet work and soon added trombone and vocal models to their repertoire. By that time, Smith was head of signal processing for NeXT, so they used a NeXT computer with its built-in 56000 for their simulations (see Fig. 2-13). Their models were typically between 1- and 18-voice polyphonic, depending on the complexity of the model.

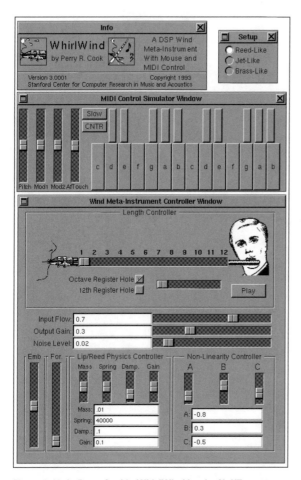

Figure 2-13. In Perry Cook's *WhirlWind* for the NeXT computer, any wind instrument can be modeled, including brass, reed, air-jet, and any hybrid in between. The onscreen controls let you "construct" the instrument by specifying the relevant parameters.

This work resulted in a synthesis and MIDI-processing software package called *Music Kit,* created primarily by David Jaffe and Julius Smith, which eventually made its way back to CCRMA, where Smith, Jaffe, Nick Porcaro, Pat Scandalis, Scott Van Duyne, Tim Stilson, and others refined it further and added a graphical front end called *SynthBuilder.* Like *Synth-Kit, SynthBuilder* is an object-oriented, graphical environment in which discrete modules can be combined to generate and process MIDI and digital-audio data, with an emphasis on waveguide modeling. As of this writing, a spin-off company, Staccato Systems, is working on a commercial version of *SynthBuilder* for the Apple Rhapsody and Microsoft Windows platforms.

Silicon Sound Reson8

Another approach to physical modeling was originally conceived at the Institut de Recherche et Coordination Acoustique/Musique (IRCAM), in Paris, about ten years ago. Called resonant synthesis, this technique models the resonant behavior of an instrument, rather than its physical behavior. Resonant synthesis begins by analyzing the sonic behavior of various musical instruments, then simulating this behavior without worrying about the physics.

Adrian Freed, now director of systems and software development at the University of California, Berkeley, Center for New Music and Audio Technologies (CNMAT, pronounced "senmat"), and Marie-Dominique Baudot, now president of Silicon Sound, built a box called the Reson8 and developed an editing environment to implement IRCAM's resonant models in real time. The Reson8 includes eight 56000s tied together on a high-speed bus. This box is custom-made by Silicon Sound for researchers and well-heeled musicians. It connects to a Macintosh with an add-on card and uses Opcode's *Max* for its front end.

The main goal is to generate as many resonances as possible. The Reson8 can re-create between 400 and 800 resonances, depending on the sample rate. For a low note on a piano, you need 300 to 400 resonances to make it sound convincing. These include the resonances associated with the string, the thud of the key, and sympathetic resonances of other strings (see Fig. 2-14). The important point is that you can simulate an instrument's complexity without knowing how it works internally.

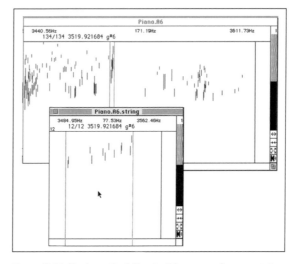

Figure 2-14. Each vertical line in this screen from a custom resonance editor for the Reson8 represents one resonance in a piano when G#6 is played. The horizontal axis is frequency, the vertical axis is amplitude, and the length of each line corresponds to the decay rate. The small region between the dotted cursor lines, which is magnified in the inset window, depicts the G#6 strings themselves. The low-frequency resonances to the left of the region represent the hammer thud, while the high-frequency resonances to the right represent the sympathetic vibrations of the higher strings.

One advantage of this approach is the ease with which hybrid models can be constructed. Once you have the resonance information for various instruments in the same form, you can easily combine it in different ways. This is more difficult with waveguide models, in which the pieces interact quite differently, making it hard to build models in between. The resonance model forces everything into the same format.

Another advantage is data reduction. For example, it takes only three numbers to represent a resonance: amplitude, frequency, and decay rate. For a piano with 300 resonances, that's a mere 900 numbers.

The Dreamer Wakes

Almost twenty years have passed since that day in Santa Cruz, California, when I dreamed of using the mathematical models in my physics thesis to electronically emulate acoustic-instrument sounds. It seems that others had the same dream, which is finally a reality thanks to their dedication, ingenuity, and hard work.

Physical modeling holds great promise for increasing the expressive potential of electronic music, answering one of the biggest complaints about the medium. It brings us one step closer to closing the gap between electronic and acoustic performance, so that both might be integrated into a seamless musical whole for all to enjoy.

CHAPTER 3

Basic Electrical Concepts

In order to understand how various types of audio equipment work, you must first understand the basic electrical and mathematical concepts that underlie their operation. These concepts are important for a number of reasons. For example, manufacturer specs mean nothing without them. (Some specs mean nothing anyway, but that's another story.) In addition, the concepts are essential to understanding decibels (I'll discuss these in detail in Chapter 4).

ELECTRICAL CONCEPTS

Most audio signals consist of electrons flowing through a conductor, such as a copper wire. This flow of electrons is called a current. The amount of current is measured in units called amperes, or amps (abbreviated A), after French physicist Andre Ampere, and it is represented by the letter I in electrical equations.

There are two types of current: direct and alternating. Direct current (DC) flows steadily in one direction through a conductor; alternating current (AC) changes direction in the conductor at various frequencies. Analog audio signals are alternating currents with waveforms and frequencies that correspond to acoustic sounds. These audio signals are called analog because the waveform of the current is analogous to the acoustic waveform it represents.

An electromotive force (EMF) causes current to flow. This name makes sense when you think about it: EMF is a force that causes electrons to move. EMF is more commonly called voltage, which is measured in units called volts, after Italian physicist Alessandro Volta, and is abbreviated V. It is represented by the letters V or E in electrical equations. Voltage is produced in many different ways, such as chemical reactions in a battery.

One helpful analogy is to think of voltage as the height of a hill. Because there is a difference in height between the top and bottom of the hill, a ball rolls down the hill under the influence of gravity. When the ball is at the top of the hill, it is said to have potential energy; that is, it has the potential to move down the hill. As it rolls down the hill, the potential energy is converted into kinetic energy, the energy of motion.

In this analogy, the hill has a top and a bottom at different heights, and the ball moves from one to the other. The same is true for voltage and current. Any voltage source has two poles, and electrons flow from one to the other. There is a potential difference between these poles. The greater the difference, the greater the potential for moving electrons. However, this potential can't be fulfilled until the two poles of the voltage source (which correspond to the top and bottom of the hill) are connected by an electrical conductor. If you connect the poles in this way, you create a circuit, or closed loop, through which the current flows.

One common voltage source is a battery, which has positive and negative poles. If you connect a conductor to these poles, electrons flow from the negative pole to the positive pole. If you've ever played with magnets, you know that opposite poles attract and similar poles repel each other. The same is true for electrons, which are negatively charged. They are repelled by the negative pole of a battery and attracted to the positive pole.

Because a battery's voltage produces a direct current, its voltage is specified in units of VDC. If the poles of a voltage source alternate (as they do in a power outlet in the wall, for example), the current changes direction periodically, and the voltage is specified in VAC.

Measuring the voltage from a battery or other DC source is easy. Returning to the hill analogy, the higher the hill, the more potential energy the ball has. The voltage produced by a battery is analogous to the height of the hill: the more voltage, the more potential it has for moving electrons. To measure the voltage of a battery, simply attach the two leads from a voltmeter to the poles and read the voltage.

Measuring alternating voltages is not quite so straightforward. You could simply measure the highest voltage level as it varies up and down, but what if this peak level changes from one cycle to the next as it does at the output of most audio equipment? Taking the average of several peaks is better, but engineers have devised an even better way to measure alternating voltages: root mean square (RMS).

First, you measure the instantaneous voltage value at many points during one complete cycle. (This is similar to digital audio recording, which I'll cover in Chapter 5.) Then, you square each voltage value (i.e., multiply the value by itself). Next, calculate the average of these squared values and take the square root of this average. If the voltage variation takes the form of a sine wave (as the voltage from a wall outlet does), the calculation becomes simpler: multiply the peak value by 0.707.

This is relatively complicated, but it yields a voltage value that is meaningful, even in the face of different peak levels over time. Of course, anyone who wants to measure an alternating voltage simply connects a voltmeter to the poles of the voltage source. The voltmeter does all the squaring and averaging, giving you a readout in VRMS or VAC.

Impedance

In virtually all electrical circuits, there is some opposition to the flow of current. Even copper wire opposes the flow of current to some degree. (The only exception is a circuit made with superconducting material, which exhibits practically no opposition to current. Of course, as of this writing, superconductors don't exist outside of the laboratory!)

The opposition to direct current is called resistance. It is measured in units called ohms after German physicist Georg Ohm, and it is abbreviated with the Greek letter omega (Ω). Resistance is represented by the letter R in electrical equations. The opposition to alternating current is called impedance, which is also measured in ohms, but it's represented by the letter Z in electrical equations. Impedance is the sum of any DC resistance and the reactance of the circuit, which is measured in ohms and represented by the letter X in electrical equations. (Actually, reactance includes two parts: capacitive and inductive reactance.) Among other things, reactance depends on the frequency of the alternating current.

Resistance and reactance are often depicted on an XY coordinate graph, and the total impedance is the vectorial sum of these values. In such graphs, the vectorial sum of X (reactance) and Y (resistance) values is often labeled Z, hence its use to represent impedance.

The impedance of a circuit determines the load it places on the voltage source. If the circuit's impedance is high, it doesn't let much current flow, which places little demand on the voltage source to move electrons. A high impedance is said to present a small load to the voltage source. However, if the impedance is low, the circuit doesn't resist the flow of current, which places greater demand on the voltage source to move electrons. A low impedance is said to place a large load on the source. As you can see, impedance and load are inversely related; if the impedance is high, the load is small, and vice versa.

In all audio connections, there are two points of impedance you should be aware of: the output impedance of a source device and the input impedance of a destination device. In general, the lower the input impedance, the greater the load on the source device. As a result, a destination device's input impedance should be at least ten times the output impedance of the source device.

The output impedance of most professional microphones is low, generally in the range of 150 Ω, so mic preamps should have an input impedance of about 1.5 kΩ. (Some mic preamps have an input impedance as high as 10 kΩ, but the range from 1.5 to 3 kΩ is more typical.) Line-level devices, such as synths, also exhibit low output impedances in the 50 to 100 Ω range, and they operate well with any input impedance above 1 kΩ. (Older synths and some consumer hi-fi equipment are often in the 100 Ω to 1 kΩ range, which requires an input impedance in the 1 to 10 kΩ range.)

The output impedance of an electric guitar depends on the pickup design, the settings of the volume and tone controls, and the frequency being produced. When the volume knob is turned up (which is usually the case), the guitar's output impedance is typically 3 to 10 kΩ at low frequencies and 100 to 500 kΩ at 10 kHz. When the volume is down, the output impedance is more constant, but it still varies by a factor of ten from low to high frequencies.

In addition, guitars are very sensitive to the input impedance of an amp or direct box (see Chapter 13); the higher the input impedance, the better the frequency response. Typical guitar amps have an input impedance in the 1 megaohm (MΩ) range, which gives you a high-frequency response up to 20 kHz with single-coil or humbucking pickups; low-impedance pickups provide even more high-frequency response.

The relationship between voltage, current, and impedance is defined by Ohm's Law, which was derived by Ohm in the early nineteenth century. This law can be stated in three different but equivalent ways:

$$V = I \times Z$$

$$I = V/Z$$

$$Z = V/I$$

Among other things, Ohm's Law clarifies the concept of load. Take a look at the first form of the law. If the voltage remains constant, the current is high if the impedance is low and vice versa.

Power

Another common electrical quantity is power, which measures how much "work" can be done by a given voltage and current through a given impedance. It is represented by the letter P in electrical equations, measured in units called watts after Scottish engineer James Watt, and abbreviated W. DC electrical power is defined by Joule's Law, which is named after British physicist James Joule:

$$P = V \times I$$

If the voltage and current alternate, as in an audio signal, so does the power. As a result, alternating power is often expressed in watts RMS. This should be familiar to anyone who has shopped for a power amplifier. Joule's Law is slightly different for AC circuits:

$$P = K \times V \times I$$

K is a constant called the power factor, which depends on the reactance of the circuit. It's value is always between +1 and -1.

Here's another analogy that helps illustrate these concepts. Imagine a water tower with a pipe and a valve that lets the water flow from the tank and turn a water wheel (see Fig. 3-1). The distance between the tank and the water wheel corresponds to voltage; the higher the tank above the wheel, the more potential there is for the water to flow. Of course, the flow of water through the pipe corresponds to current.

The valve can be opened to different degrees, letting more or less water through. As you might guess, this corresponds to impedance. The water turns the water wheel, which allows the wheel to perform work (e.g., grinding flour). This corresponds to power. As you can see, if the valve is mostly closed (impedance is high), little water flows (current is low), and the wheel does little work (power is low). On the other hand, if the valve is mostly open (impedance is low), lots of water flows (current is high), and the wheel can do lots of work (power is high).

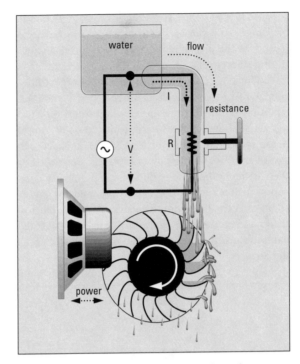

Figure 3-1. This mechanical water system is analogous to a simple electrical circuit. The height of the water tank above the water wheel corresponds to voltage, and the flow of water through the pipe corresponds to current. The valve offers resistance to the flow of the water, which corresponds to impedance, and the wheel turns as the water falls on it, which corresponds to power.

AC POWER AND GROUNDING

Electronic musicians should be intimately familiar with AC power; after all, it is required by most of the equipment we use to make music. However, most of us are woefully uninformed about this critical subject, which can lead to all sorts of problems, from mysterious hums in the audio to outright electrocution. Clearly, it's important to understand AC power if you want to create a clean audio signal and remain alive long enough to enjoy the fruits of your labor.

The information presented here will help you understand AC power, but be forewarned: you should have a professional electrician make any significant changes in your home's electrical system. Mucking around with household current can be very dangerous, so leave it to a pro.

Down to Basics

The electrical signal that reaches your home from the power company is an alternating current (AC) with a sinusoidal waveform. In this country, the signal's frequency is 60 Hz (in Europe, it's 50 Hz), which is very tightly controlled to a tolerance of 0.01%. Many time-based devices are designed to sync to this frequency because it is so stable. However, it is also in the audible range, so it can be heard if it gets into an audio path. (On the plus side, it makes a very nice B-natural tuning reference!)

The power signal arrives at your home with a voltage of 240 VAC. Once this signal reaches the distribution point in your home, it is divided into two signals of about 120 VAC each, which are 180° out of phase with each other (see Fig. 3-2). The exact voltage of these signals is not as carefully controlled as the frequency, because conditions at the power company can fluctuate as the overall demand for power changes. A few heavy-duty appliances, such as electric stoves and clothes dryers, use the entire 240 VAC signal, but most powered items use one of the 120 VAC signals.

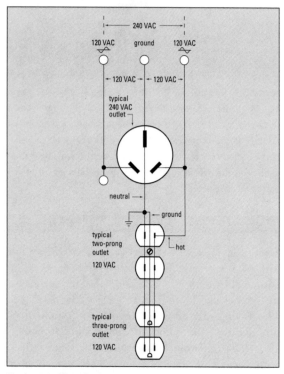

Figure 3-2. Electrical power enters your home as a 240 VAC sine wave, which is divided into two 120 VAC sine waves that are 180° out of phase with each other.

The distribution point is normally a metal box with fuses or circuit breakers arranged in two vertical rows. Each row distributes one of the two 120 VAC signals to the outlets and light fixtures in your home. Typically, each distribution point in the box sends power to several outlets and light fixtures, such as those found in a particular room.

In addition, each fuse or circuit breaker limits the amount of current that can be drawn from all the outlets and fixtures it feeds. This limit is typically 15 or 20 amps. If the combined current exceeds this limit, the fuse or circuit breaker "blows," disconnecting the power from all its outlets and fixtures. This prevents the wires in your walls from overheating and possibly causing a fire.

Speaking of the wires in your walls, the 120 VAC signal is sent to each outlet through a single wire called the hot wire. Of course, all outlets have at least two holes; newer outlets are "polarized," and the hot wire is connected to the smaller hole on the right of the outlet to make sure that the device's hot wire is connected to the correct hole.

When you plug something into an outlet, the power signal flows from the hot wire through the device and back out to the other hole (which is the larger one on the left of a polarized outlet). This other hole is connected to the neutral wire, which goes back to the breaker box, where it is connected to a ground point. Because the power signal makes a round trip from one of the distribution points and back to the ground point in the breaker box, it is said to complete a circuit. Each distribution point is often called a circuit, as well.

Ground represents 0 VAC, and it is often established by connecting the ground point in the breaker box to the cold-water plumbing in your home. Some homes use plastic plumbing, in which case one or more metal (preferably copper or copper-clad) stakes are driven into the ground on which your home is built and the ground point is connected to it. This approach, which is often used in professional studios, is commonly referred to as a true earth ground. (I'll return to this point in a moment.) Basically, the ground provides an infinite sink for electrons, which always take the easiest path to ground they can find. Once the power signal leaves the device, it makes a beeline to ground via the neutral wire.

Three-prong outlets include a separate ground hole and ground wire, which is sometimes called the safety ground and is also connected to the ground point. The safety ground provides protection in case the hot lead is accidentally connected to the chassis of the device being powered, which is called a short circuit. If this happens in a device with a 2-prong plug, and you are touching the chassis, you become the current's path to ground, which could give you a real jolt. With a 3-prong plug, however, the current has a much easier path to ground, which protects you from electrocution.

It is so important to keep these wires straight that a convention has been established in the electrical industry. The insulation of the neutral wire is white, while the ground wire in a 3-prong outlet is either green or has no insulation at all. The insulation of the hot wire is any color other than white or green, with black being the most common.

The Right Stuff

Appliances that include motors, such as air conditioners, dishwashers, and refrigerators, can sometimes put a momentary strain on the side of the circuit-breaker box to which they are connected when the motor turns on. It's best to make sure the outlets in your studio are connected to the other side of the box from any such appliances. Otherwise, the power might fluctuate when these appliances start their motors, which can cause problems with studio equipment (e.g., it can scramble the memory of synths and other devices).

It's relatively easy to determine which side of the box your studio outlets and other appliances are connected to. First, make sure any computers and music gear are turned off and unplugged. Next, plug in several radios or lights around your home and turn them on. Then, trip each circuit breaker in the box and see which radios and/or lights turn off. Make a note of which breakers affect which outlets.

If necessary, have an electrician reconfigure the breaker box so that heavy-duty, nonmusical appliances are on one side and the studio outlets are on the other side. However, this might not be possible, because the electrical load on both sides should be relatively equal.

By the way, if you notice that the lights dim momentarily when a major appliance such as the air conditioner or refrigerator turns on, call an electrician ASAP. This symptom generally indicates either that you have a fault in the neutral or one of the hot legs is not properly connected.

For maximum isolation, have an electrician establish a completely separate electrical service and ground for the studio outlets. In particular, the electrician can create a true earth ground using a dedicated grounding rod. This can be expensive, but it is the only way to be completely sure that other appliances in your home won't affect the studio equipment.

Another thing to consider is the total amount of power drawn by all the equipment in your studio to make sure it isn't overloading the circuit to which it's connected. This is relatively easy to determine; most pieces of electronic-music equipment specify the amount of power they require (in watts) on the back plate or in the technical specifications of the manual. However, the limit of most circuit breakers is specified in amps, which relates to current.

Fortunately, the voltage remains relatively constant at 117 to 120 VAC, so it's possible to convert watts to amps. Recall Joule's Law:

$$P = V \times I$$

This law can also be stated:

$$I = P/V$$

Apply this formula to the power rating of each piece of equipment to determine the amount of current it draws. For example, suppose a synthesizer draws 90 watts. If the voltage is 120 VAC:

$$I = 90/120$$
$$I = 0.75 \text{ amps}$$

Add up all the current requirements for all the gear in your studio to determine if the circuit can safely deliver the current you need to run the studio. If not, have an electrician install a higher-amp circuit for the studio. Fortunately, most electronic-music equipment doesn't need much power. Tape decks, power amps, and mixers require the most, but even so, most home studios can easily run from one 20-amp circuit as long as there is nothing else on the same circuit. Keep studio lighting and ventilation fans on a separate circuit.

It is extremely important to test the outlets in your studio. If an outlet is a 3-prong design, use an AC outlet analyzer, which is available at Radio Shack and other electronic-parts stores. This will reveal if the hot, neutral, and ground wires are properly connected (see Fig. 3-3). In some cases, the polarity of the hot and neutral connections is reversed, which can create a shock hazard and increase noise in the audio signal. In addition, the ground hole might not be connected to anything, which creates a potential shock hazard and defeats surge and spike protection. These problems should be corrected by an electrician.

If the outlet is a 2-prong design, use a neon circuit tester (also available at Radio Shack and elsewhere) to test the ground. Touch one lead of the tester to the metal screw that secures the cover plate and insert the other lead into hot-wire slot of the socket, which is the smaller slot of a polarized outlet. (Make sure the screw isn't covered with paint.) If the tester glows, the ground is okay. Unfortunately, the cover-plate screw is often not connected to ground. In this case, do the right thing: don't even bother grounding the old outlet but have an electrician install a properly grounded 3-prong outlet.

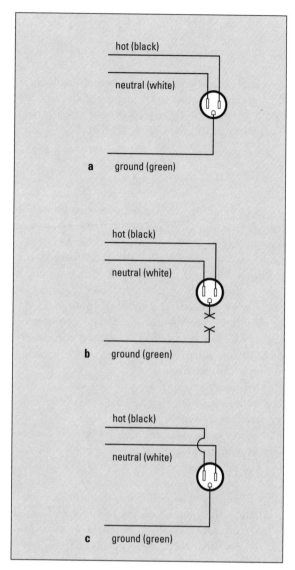

hot (black)

neutral (white)

a   ground (green)

hot (black)

neutral (white)

b   ground (green)

hot (black)

neutral (white)

c   ground (green)

Figure 3-3. In a properly wired 3-prong AC outlet (a), all three conductors are connected and color-coded. In some cases, the ground is disconnected (b) and/or the hot and neutral wires are reversed (c).

If you must connect a 3-prong plug to a 2-prong outlet—and the only excuse for this is that you are playing a live gig and are stuck with the venue's lame power system—make sure the cover-plate screw is connected to ground and use a 3-to-2-prong adapter that includes a ground lug on a short wire protruding from the plug (see Fig. 3-4). Connect the lug to the cover-plate screw to assure proper grounding.

Figure 3-4. Use a 3-to-2-prong adapter only if the outlet face-plate screw is connected to ground.

The Inside Story

Most of the problems caused by AC power in the studio arise because of improper grounding among the various pieces of equipment. Ideally, the chassis of each piece of equipment is connected to the ground of its power supply's input, which should be connected to the safety ground wire in a 3-conductor power cord. However, this connection sometimes comes loose, or the grounding for the unit was poorly implemented to start with.

To verify this connection, use an ohm meter to check the resistance between the ground prong of the power plug and the metal case of the equipment. (Make sure to touch an unpainted part of the case.) If the resistance is high, the connection between the chassis and the ground prong is broken or inadequate, in which case you should take the equipment to a repair facility and have it fixed.

Audio Enters the Picture

Every piece of AC-powered equipment includes a power supply that accepts 120 VAC and converts it into a DC voltage, typically ±15 VDC. The power supply might be internal or external (e.g., wall wart or lump-in-the-line). In either case, there is a ground point at 0 VDC between +15 and -15 VDC. This is called the signal ground, because it is normally connected to the ground conductor of the audio cables that carry audio signals from one device to another.

Like 2-conductor power cords, unbalanced analog audio cables include two conductors: hot and shield. The shield forms a concentric tube around the central hot wire and is attached to the signal grounds of the devices it connects. Balanced audio cables include three conductors: hot, cold, and shield. The hot and cold wires both carry the audio signal 180° out of phase with each other, and the shield is connected to the signal ground. (I'll discuss balanced and unbalanced audio connections in greater detail in Chapter 12.) In many devices, the signal ground is also connected to the chassis ground, which can cause problems (more in a moment).

Ideally, these cables carry only the audio signal. In the real world, however, extraneous signals sometimes get into them. This can occur when a current in an audio device's AC ground is generated by the device's impedance to the power signal. In this case, the signal in the power ground appears in the signal ground because they are connected through the chassis.

Another common means by which extraneous signals enter the audio path is a process called induction. All current produces a corresponding electromagnetic field that radiates from the conductor carrying the current. Conversely, a radiant electromagnetic field can induce current in a nearby conductor. As a result, unwanted signals can be induced into the audio cable. Balanced cables are much less susceptible to induced noise because of the 180° phase relationship between the two signal-carrying wires.

The main sources of this induced signal are radio-frequency interference (RFI) and electromagnetic interference (EMI). RFI is caused by radio stations, cell phones, and other sources of radio energy that is transmitted through the air. EMI is caused by any nearby current-carrying conductor, such as power cords, large transformers, or electromagnetic coils (e.g., in televisions and computer monitors). When these signals are induced into the audio cables, they can become an audible part of your audio.

Thrown for a Loop

RFI and EMI are aggravated by the presence of ground loops, which are formed when your equipment is connected to ground through more than one path. This is especially problematic with 2-conductor power cords and audio equipment in which the signal ground is connected to the chassis ground.

For example, consider two pieces of equipment that are plugged into different wall outlets and connected together with an audio cable (see Fig. 3-5). Each device has its own ground connection through its power cord, but each unit is also connected to the other's ground through the shield of the audio cable, which is connected to the chassis of both devices. As a result, ground loops can act as antennas that pick up RFI and EMI, causing a current in the ground line that can get into the audio signal via the signal ground.

One way to reduce ground loops is to connect all equipment and outlet grounds to a single ground point, such as a grounding stake, using ground wires that are as short as possible. However, this is not always practical.

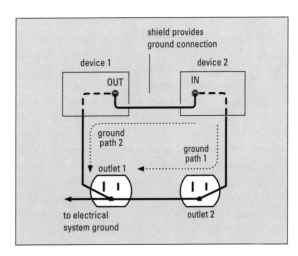

Figure 3-5. When two audio devices are powered from different outlets and connected by an audio cable, they have two different paths to ground, which forms a ground loop. Only the ground paths for device 2 are shown here; device 1 has two similar paths.

Many people are tempted to use a ground lifter (such as a 3-to-2 AC adapter without the ground lug) on one of the AC power cords; some people go so far as to remove the ground prong from a 3-prong plug. In this case, both devices see only one path to ground —one through its own power cord and the other through the audio cable's shield to the first device's ground. But this is very dangerous and not recommended because it eliminates the inherent shock protection offered by grounding. A safer alternative is to plug two devices that might form a ground loop into the same outlet, which shortens the ground wire between them (see Fig. 3-6).

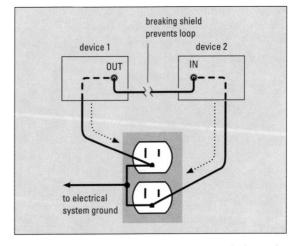

Figure 3-6. Plugging both devices into the same duplex outlet helps reduce ground-loop problems. Disconnecting the signal ground from the chassis ground with a ground-lift switch also helps.

Some equipment includes a ground-lift switch, which disconnects the signal ground from the chassis ground and eliminates the path to ground through the AC power cord. This is equivalent to using a ground lifter, but it's much safer. Using ground-lift switches is a trial-and-error process; in general, most or all of these switches should be in the lifted position, but you must determine the best configuration for your studio by trying different combinations.

Another way to eliminate ground loops is to disconnect the cable shield at one end of an audio cable. This is called a telescoping shield, and it only works with balanced audio cables; both conductors of an unbalanced audio cable must be connected at both ends for the signal to flow. You can buy such cables or make them yourself. In general, the shield's connection should be broken at the end that goes to an audio input.

Yet another method of breaking ground loops is to use audio isolation transformers (also called iso transformers), which are available from Furman, Jensen, Ebtech, and others. Audio iso transformers pass the audio signal from their input (called the primary) to their output (called the secondary) by induction, which requires no direct electrical connection. (see "Direct Boxes" in Chapter 13 for more on transformers.) This effectively isolates the audio signal from the rest of the electrical system.

Iso transformers can also be used on the power line. For example, MidiMotor makes a rack-mountable box called the Hum Buster that isolates several AC outlets using power iso transformers.

Ground loops can form when the chassis of your rack-mounted gear are electrically connected in some way. This commonly occurs in a rack when the metal faceplates of different modules come into contact. It can also occur because the metal rack ears of each device are electrically connected by the metal mounting rails of the rack itself. In these cases, each device has its own ground connection, and it's also connected to the chassis ground of the other devices.

To prevent ground loops in racks, make sure the faceplates do not touch each other and use nylon washers on the front and back of the rack ears when attaching devices to the rack with metal screws. To be extra safe, use nylon washers with a sheath that fits into the devices' mounting holes to prevent any metallic contact between the rack ears and mounting rails via the mounting screws. Some people even build their own racks with wooden mounting rails to avoid ground loops.

To reduce EMI from power cords, it's very important to keep audio cables as far away from them as possible. Use cable ties to bundle power cords on one side of a rack and audio cables on the other side.

Power Management

Despite all the precautions you might take to prevent grounding problems, the AC signal from the wall can fluctuate due to circumstances beyond your control. These fluctuations include surges (temporary increases in the voltage) and spikes (momentary but huge increases in the voltage) from lightning and other sources. The voltage can also drop dramatically in a brownout or disappear altogether in a blackout.

If your gear experiences these conditions, it could be damaged; at the very least, it could operate improperly and its effective lifetime could be shortened. In addition, the power signal, which should be a nice, clean sine wave, can be polluted with noise from RFI/EMI and other sources before it reaches your home, and this noise can get into the audio signal path.

Fortunately, you can protect yourself from most of these problems with various power-management devices. These devices typically include several AC outlets, which can be used to power an entire rack. More expensive units often include several types of protection and are available in rack-mount cases.

The simplest form of protection is a surge/spike protector. Many power strips include this type of protection, which is provided in two ways. Transverse-mode rejection guards against spikes between the hot and neutral lines, and common-mode rejection protects against spikes between the hot or neutral line and ground. Make sure the surge/spike protector you use has both types. Surges and spikes can also travel along telephone wires, and some protectors include phone jacks in addition to AC outlets.

Many power strips include RFI/EMI filtering, which is also called line conditioning. This uses a low-pass filter with a cutoff above 60 Hz that redirects higher-frequency signals to ground before they get to your equipment. The result is a clean sine-wave power signal. However, these filters can generate extraneous currents in the ground when used with a standard 120 VAC power source.

One solution to this problem is called balanced power, which is used in products from Equi=Tech, Furman, MidiMotor, and others. In this scheme, the hot and neutral wires from a balanced power supply each carry a power signal of 60 VAC instead of 120 and 0 VAC, respectively, and these signals are 180° out of phase with each other (see Fig. 3-7).

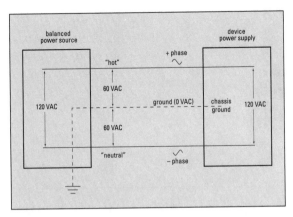

Figure 3-7. A balanced-power system divides the 120 VAC from the wall into two 60 VAC sine wave signals that are 180° out of phase with each other. Any EMI from this type of power system is effectively canceled out.

This resembles the way 240 VAC is divided into two 120 VAC lines in your home as well as the operation of balanced audio cables. The total voltage between the "hot" and "neutral" wires is still 120 VAC, so the equipment works fine, but any current in the ground is canceled out. In addition, radiated EMI from the two conductors cancel each other out, effectively eliminating any induced EMI from the power cord.

The next step up in power management is a voltage regulator (also called a line regulator or stabilizer), which are available from companies such as Furman, Juice Goose, and Tripp Lite. A voltage regulator attempts to maintain a constant output voltage to each outlet in spite of varying input voltage from the wall. Most can provide a steady 117 or 120 VAC as long as the input voltage remains in the range of approximately 90 to 130 VAC. (Some regulators can deal with input voltages up to 300 VAC.) If the voltage rises above the unit's maximum input range, it should trip an internal circuit breaker to prevent damage.

A voltage regulator can be very helpful in the event of a short brownout (also called a sag), but it can't protect against a long voltage drop below the unit's minimum input or a complete blackout. For this, you need an uninterruptable power supply (more in a moment). In most cases, the regulator's outlets are rated for a given amount of power, so make sure you match the power requirements of each device with the appropriate outlet.

The only protection against complete blackouts is an uninterruptable power supply (UPS). This device includes a battery that kicks in if the power drops too low or disappears completely, preserving the data in your computer and synth/sampler RAM and giving you time to save your work and safely shut everything down. (The exact amount of time before failure varies depending on the UPS and the load,

but usually you get at least ten minutes.) Some units, such as models from American Power Conversion (APC) and Furman, also have surge/spike protection, RFI/EMI filtering, and voltage regulation.

The most important factor is the time it takes the UPS to detect a power loss and switch over to the battery. The combined detection/switching time should be under 10 ms. Some systems even include computer software (such as APC's *PowerChute Pro*) that monitors and tests the UPS and allows you to schedule computer shutdowns to conserve power.

Power management is of critical importance in any studio if you want to minimize hums, buzzes, and other noise from creeping into your audio signals. Armed with a solid grounding in the principles of AC power, you can now start to clean up your audio act.

CHAPTER 4

Decibels

Y ou probably have some notion that decibels are used to measure signal levels. However, most people don't understand exactly what decibels are or how they are used in the world of audio devices. Even audio professionals are often a bit fuzzy about the precise nature of decibels.

This is understandable; decibels can be quite confusing. There are many different types of decibels, and manufacturers use them in their specs with reckless abandon, which adds to the confusion. To clear away the fog surrounding this essential concept, we must start with some basic math.

Exponents

Exponents and logarithms frighten many people thanks to poor math teachers in high school, but they're really not all that complicated. Exponents provide a way to simply and elegantly represent the result of multiplying the same number together several times. For example, consider the following equation:

$$2 \times 2 \times 2 \times 2 \times 2 = 2^5 = 32$$

In this example, the "2" is called the base and the "5" is called the exponent.

Exponents can help us express very large numbers with relatively few digits. For example, $10,000,000 = 10^7$. You can even use fractional exponents. For example, $5^{2.3} = 40.52$. In fact, you can make a graph of the relationship between exponents and the value they generate for a given base (see Fig. 4-1[a]).

Exponents can also help express mathematical formulas more elegantly. For example, let's take a look at the DC form of Joule's Law again.

$$P = V \times I$$

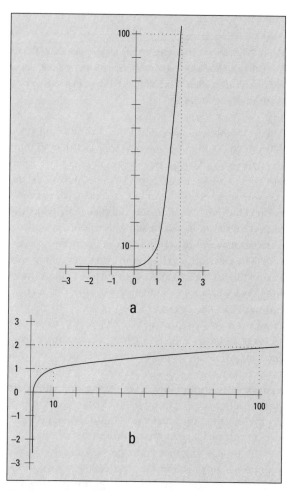

Figure 4-1. If you raise a specific number to different exponents, the result grows quickly as the exponent increases (a). In this case, $y = 10^x$. On the other hand, if you take the log of different numbers, the result grows very slowly as the initial numbers increase dramatically (b). In this case, $y = \log x$. Notice that the graph in (b) resembles the graph of an audio compressor's performance.

From Ohm's Law, we know that $I = V/R$. If we substitute V/R for I in Joule's Law, we get:

$$P = V \times (V/R) = (V \times V)/R = V^2/R$$

We can make a similar substitution for V, which is equal to I x R:

$$P = (I \times R) \times I = (I \times I) \times R = I^2 \times R$$

Now, we have three equivalent expressions of Joule's Law:

$$P = V \times I$$

$$P = V^2/R$$

$$P = I^2 \times R$$

Logarithms

Logarithms (or logs) are simply the opposite of exponents. In sound applications, the base is assumed to be 10, and logs are defined as follows:

$$\text{If } a = 10^b \text{ then } b = \log a$$

This is difficult to put into English, but I'll give it a try. Logarithms identify the exponent (b) to which you would raise 10 to obtain the number you are taking the logarithm of (a).

For example, $100 = 10^2$, so log 100 = 2. This also works with fractional exponents. For example, $20 = 10^{1.301}$, so log 20 = 1.301. If you create a chart of the relationship between various numbers and the logs of those numbers, you see that this graph is identical to the exponent graph flipped across a diagonal (see Fig. 4-1[b]). To calculate logs, it's best to use a calculator with a log function.

Logs help us manipulate large numbers more easily. They also help us manipulate large ranges of numbers, which is why they are used in decibels: audio signal levels encompass a *very* large range of possible values. In fact, logs act like "mathematical compressors." Just as an audio compressor accepts a large range of input levels and outputs a smaller range of levels (which I'll explain more fully in Chapter 20), logarithms accept a large range of numbers and return a much smaller range of numbers. The graph in Fig. 4-1(b) even resembles the graph of a compressor's input vs. output.

Now that we've covered the concepts of voltage, current, impedance, and power in Chapter 3 and exponents and logarithms in this chapter, we can turn our attention to decibels. I'll start with electrical decibels, after which I'll apply the same principles to acoustic sounds.

The following information is pretty dense. At first, it might seem highly theoretical, but have patience; I'll include some practical examples after we've covered some basic concepts.

Define Your Terms

Many people use the term decibel as if it were an absolute unit for measuring the amplitude of electrical audio signals. However, this is not correct. When used with electrical audio signals, decibels express the *ratio* of two values.

Scientists at Bell Labs invented a unit of measurement to compare two power values and named it the Bel in honor of Alexander Graham Bell. By definition,

$$\text{Number of Bels} = \log (P_1/P_0)$$

P_1 and P_0 are quantities of power in watts, and P_0 is usually a reference power value to which another power value (P_1) is compared.

There are several reasons to work with the log of a power ratio instead of the ratio itself. As mentioned in the previous section, logs help us work with large ranges of numbers more easily, and audio ratios can encompass a very large range. For example, the ratio of the loudest sound we can stand to the softest sound we can hear is approximately one trillion to one. Logs act as "mathematical compressors," reducing a large range of values to more manageable proportions.

In addition, the sensitivity of human hearing to amplitude is generally logarithmic. We perceive equal changes in the *percentage* of amplitude, not in amplitude itself. For example, if one sound appears to be twice as loud as another sound, the actual amplitude of the louder sound is over three times the amplitude of the softer sound, not twice the amplitude, as you might expect. This is why logarithmic potentiometers are used in most audio gear instead of linear pots.

As it turns out, Bels "compress" power-ratio values too much to be useful in audio circuits. As a result, audio engineers use the decibel, which is equal to one tenth of a Bel (i.e., there are ten decibels to a Bel) and is abbreviated dB. By definition,

$$\text{Number of decibels} = 10 \log (P_1/P_0)$$

Decibels are often plotted on a graph with dB on the X axis and the power ratio from which they arise on Y axis. As you can see in Fig. 4-2, this can be done in two ways. If the graph uses a linear scale, the curve is relatively complex and takes ten times as much physical space to represent the ratio 100:10 as it does for the ratio of 10:1, even though both ratios are equivalent. You would need a very large piece of graph paper to represent a ratio of 1,000,000,000,000:1!

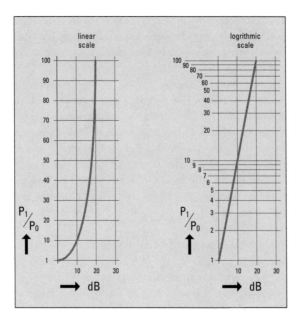

Figure 4-2. If you graph decibels with respect to the corresponding power ratios using a linear scale (left), each increase of 10 dB takes up ten times more vertical space. However, if you use a logarithmic scale (right), each increase of 10 dB takes up the same vertical space, and the curve becomes a straight line.

However, if you use a logarithmic scale, the curve becomes a straight line, and all equivalent ratios (e.g., 100:10 and 10:1) occupy the same physical space on the graph. This makes it easy to see that a difference of 10 dB is the same percentage of change in the power ratio regardless of the actual power values. It also makes it easier to chart large ranges of numbers in less physical space.

Voltage and Current

Decibels are also used to compare voltage values, especially with circuits that exhibit high impedance and let little current flow. However, the equation is slightly different. Without going into the mathematical derivation, the formula for voltage-referenced decibels is:

$$\text{Number of decibels} = 20 \log (V_1/V_0)$$

By the same reasoning, we can apply the same equation to current.

$$\text{Number of decibels} = 20 \log (I_1/I_0)$$

However, decibels are rarely applied to current. If a circuit draws more than a negligible current from a voltage source, units of power are used instead. If a circuit draws very little current (i.e., impedance is high, load is small), volts are used.

Power to the Decibel

There are several standard reference values to which power and voltage are compared using decibels (see table, "The Decibel Zoo"). Unfortunately, this leads to much confusion. Remember that all voltage in audio equipment is based on alternating current and measured using the RMS method.

As mentioned earlier, power-referenced decibels are used for circuits that draw a significant amount of current from the voltage source. If the measured power is equal to the reference power ($P_1 = P_0$), the difference is 0 dB. In other words, 0 dB is the reference level.

$$10 \log (P_1/P_0) = 10 \log 1$$
$$= 10 \times 0$$
$$= 0 \text{ dB}$$

If the measured power is twice the reference value ($P_1 = 2P_0$), the difference is about 3 dB.

$$10 \log (P_1/P_0) = 10 \log 2$$
$$= 10 \times 0.301$$
$$= 3.01 \text{ dB}$$

If the measured power is ten times the reference value ($P_1 = 10P_0$), the difference is 10 dB.

$$10 \times \log (P_1/P_0) = 10 \log 10$$
$$= 10 \times 1$$
$$= 10 \text{ dB}$$

The most common power-referenced decibels are denoted dBm, and the reference power value (P_0) is 1 milliwatt (mW), or 0.001 watt. In other words,

$$0 \text{ dBm} = 1 \text{ mW}$$

This type of decibel is handy when talking about small but significant power values, such as those that exist in most professional audio equipment. In fact, dBm is typically used to specify the nominal signal level in professional gear, which I'll discuss shortly.

High-Voltage Decibels

Voltage-referenced decibels are used when a circuit draws negligible current from the voltage source (i.e., when the impedance is high and the load is small). This applies to most consumer and semipro gear, including synthesizers. The reference level is still 0 dB. However, if the measured voltage is twice the reference value ($V_1 = 2V_0$), the difference is 6 dB, not 3 dB as in power-referenced decibels.

$$20 \log (V_1/V_0) = 20 \log 2$$
$$= 20 \times 0.301$$
$$= 6.02 \text{ dB}$$

If the measured voltage is ten times the reference value ($V_1 = 10V_0$), the difference is 20 dB.

$$20 \log (V_1/V_0) = 20 \log 10$$
$$= 20 \times 1$$
$$= 20 \text{ dB}$$

One common type of voltage-referenced decibel is denoted dBu. The "u" stands for "unloaded," which refers to the very small load that high-impedance circuits present to the voltage source. The reference voltage for dBu is 0.775V. In other words,

$$0 \text{ dBu} = 0.775V$$

Perhaps the most common type of voltage-referenced decibel is denoted dBV, for which the reference voltage is 1V. In other words,

$$0 \text{ dBV} = 1V$$

This type of decibel is generally used to measure the signal level in consumer and semipro gear. (See table "dBV vs. dBm/dBu" to compare these types of decibels.)

You might occasionally come across a similar decibel designation (dBv) that is completely equivalent to dBu. Don't let the "v" fool you; it is not the same as dBV. This type of decibel is not used much today.

Volume, Level, and Gain

Among the many terms that are tossed around when discussing audio systems, perhaps the most misused are volume, level, and gain. All three words have something to do with the amplitude of an AC electrical signal, and they also relate to decibels, but their precise meaning is not clear to many people who use them with reckless abandon.

Volume is often used to describe acoustic sound intensity or the amplitude of an AC electrical signal. Technically speaking, however, volume is defined as power, and it is typically applied to the output of a power amplifier. If you turn up the volume, you are increasing the power output in watts.

Many people use the word level in conjunction with voltage or power values (e.g., "the power level is so many watts" or "the voltage level is so many volts"). However, level is defined as the magnitude of a quantity with respect to a particular reference value. (Sound familiar?) As a result, this word is correctly used only in conjunction with decibels. For example,

the audio signal level in professional audio equipment is expressed in dBm, which is referenced to 1 mW.

Gain is defined is several different ways, which doesn't help matters any. Unless otherwise specified, it is usually assumed to refer to the change in a signal's power and is measured in decibels. In this case, there is no standard reference value. Instead, the gain compares the signal's power values before and after the change. For example, if a signal's power increases by a factor of two, the gain is 3 dB.

It's All Relative

The concept of gain brings up another application of decibels: they are often used to compare two voltage or power values without respect to a standard reference level. When decibels are used to relate two arbitrary values in this way, they are expressed in dB without a modifier (such as "m" or "V") because they use no standard reference. This approach is typically used to describe the change in a signal that is altered by adjusting a control. For example, you might manipulate an equalizer control to reduce the level of a signal by 3 dB.

In addition, it doesn't matter whether power or voltage values are being compared; the number of decibels remains the same in either case. If you change the power flowing through any circuit with a given impedance, the voltage also changes, but by a different factor than the change in power. The factor by which the power changes is the square of the factor by which the voltage changes. For example, if the power increases by a factor of 4, the voltage increases by a factor of 2 (the square root of 4). This is due to the fact that power is proportional to the square of the voltage, as revealed in Joule's law:

$$P = K \times V \times I$$

$$= K \times V^2/Z$$

Remember that K is a constant that depends on the reactance of the circuit, and it can be ignored for our purposes. Of course, V is voltage, I is current, and Z is impedance.

THE DECIBEL ZOO	
Type of Decibel	**Standard Reference**
dBm	1 milliwatt
dBu	0.775 volts RMS
dBV	1 volt RMS

Practical Examples

At this point, let's look at a few practical examples. You've probably seen frequency-response specifications, which identify the range of frequencies that a piece of audio gear can effectively pass from its input to its output at a given gain. For example, a piece of gear might have a frequency response of 50 Hz to 18 kHz, ±3 dB. This means that all frequencies between 50 Hz and 18 kHz will pass from the input to the output with no more than 6 dB of variation in gain (3 dB above the nominal level and 3 dB below nominal) from one frequency to another.

Equalizers include one or more boost/cut controls that amplify or attenuate different ranges, or bands, of frequencies, which I'll cover in more detail in Chapter 19. For example, many EQs boost or cut the frequencies in each band by ±12 dB. At maximum boost (+12 dB), the signal's power in that frequency band is increased by a factor of sixteen, and the voltage is increased by a factor of four.

Another characteristic of most audio gear is the signal-to-noise ratio (which is often abbreviated S/N). This is the difference in decibels between the nominal signal level and the noise floor of the equipment. For example, in many analog tape decks, the noise floor is 45 to 65 dB below the nominal signal level, which corresponds to 0 on the tape deck's volume unit (VU) meters.

You can record signals at a level as much as 5 dB above the nominal level on an analog tape deck, which determines the dynamic range of the deck. By definition, dynamic range is the difference in decibels between the maximum undistorted signal level and the noise floor. In this example, the dynamic range is 50 to 70 dB.

DBV VS. DBM/DBU

dBV	Volts RMS	dBm (into 600 Ω) or dBu
+6.00	2.000	+8.2
+4.00	1.600	+6.2
+1.78	1.228	+4.0
0.00	1.000	+2.2
-2.20	0.775	0.0
-6.00	0.500	-3.8
-8.20	0.388	-6.0
-10.0	0.316	-7.8
-12.0	0.250	-9.8
-12.2	0.245	-10.0
-20.0	0.100	-17.8

ACOUSTIC DECIBELS

As mentioned earlier, decibels are also applied to the amplitude of acoustic sounds. As with their electrical counterparts, however, acoustic decibels are often used without a good understanding of exactly what they are and to what they are referenced, which leads to some confusion.

What's in a Name?

As you'll recall from the previous section, there is a difference between the terms volume, level, and gain with respect to electronic audio signals. There is also a difference between the terms power, intensity, and loudness when referring to acoustic sounds. Acoustic power is the total energy radiating from the source per second, which is expressed in units of watts (W). For example, a clarinet generates a peak power output of 0.05W, while a trombone can put out over 6W of power.

Intensity is the amount of power that reaches a given surface area (say, one square meter) located a given distance from the source. It's typically measured in watts/square meter (W/m²). As a sound wave expands away from the source, the total power it carries is distributed across an increasingly larger surface area. As a result, the amount of power in a given area decreases as you get farther from the source. This is one reason sounds get softer as you move away from the source.

The term loudness refers to our perception of intensity. In this context, it should not be confused with the Loudness control on many stereo systems, although that control's function is related to how we perceive intensity.

Perceptual loudness depends on a number of factors, including the amplitude of the eardrum's oscillation, the amount of noise-induced hearing loss, and the subject's age. In addition, each person's evaluation of loudness can differ depending on the ambient noise to which they are accustomed; one person's soft is another person's loud. This makes loudness difficult to quantify. Nevertheless, many people have been tested, and the results have been averaged to form a pretty good picture of loudness (more in a moment).

Of course, there are limits to the acoustic intensity we can perceive. For most people with normal hearing, the softest detectable sound has an intensity of 10^{-12} W/m²; the loudest sound most people can tolerate without pain has an intensity of 1 W/m². These values differ by a factor of one trillion, which illustrates just how sensitive the human hearing system is. This range is too large for practical purposes, so the logarithmic decibel scale comes to the rescue once again.

Pressure Tactics

The next acoustical term to consider is sound pressure. This is the force per unit area (e.g., force per square centimeter) that vibrating air exerts against the elastic resistance of an eardrum or microphone diaphragm. It is measured in units called dynes/cm² or Newtons/m². (The latter units are also called Pascals.)

Sound pressure is analogous to electromotive force pushing electrons against the impedance of a circuit. As a result, sound pressure is treated like voltage and uses the "20 log" formula for decibels, which express the sound pressure level (SPL) and are denoted dB SPL.

As you'll recall, most types of decibels are measured with respect to a reference level, which is called "0 dB," and dB SPL is no exception. However, the reference value for dB SPL is more difficult to define than it is for other types of decibels. The reference value is the softest level at which a young person with undamaged hearing can detect a sound in the ear's most sensitive frequency range (1 to 4 kHz). As mentioned earlier, this corresponds to an intensity of 10^{-12} W/m², which is equivalent to 0.0002 dynes/cm². In other words,

$$0 \text{ dB SPL} = 0.0002 \text{ dynes/cm}^2$$

Now that 0 dB SPL is established, the amplitudes of various acoustic sounds can be measured with respect to this reference level (see table, "How Loud is Loud?").

Interestingly, if we perceive one sound as being twice as loud as another, the difference between them is actually 10 dB, not 6 dB as you would expect from the math, because perception is subjective. In fact, this is another reason that Bels are divided into decibels: one Bel (ten decibels) represents a doubling of perceived loudness according to the average response of many test subjects.

Perceived Reality

One of the most interesting aspects of the human hearing system is the fact that we are not equally sensitive to all frequencies. If you had a sound system that could reproduce all audible frequencies with the same SPL, the low frequencies would seem softer than the midrange. Conversely, if a low frequency and a midrange frequency seem equally loud, the SPL of the low frequency is greater than the SPL of the midrange. We are also less sensitive to high frequencies, although to a lesser extent. In other words, the human hearing system does not exhibit a flat frequency response.

In 1933, the quest to quantify loudness led two Bell Labs researchers, Harvey Fletcher and W.A. Mun-

son, to examine the hearing system's frequency response by playing sine waves at different frequencies for a large number of people. They measured the SPL of each tone and correlated it with the test subjects' indication of equal loudness with respect to a 1 kHz tone at a fixed SPL. The averaged results of their research are depicted in equal-loudness curves (also known as Fletcher-Munson equal-loudness contours; see Fig. 4-3). Keep in mind that these curves apply to pure sine-wave tones, and musical sound is much more complicated. Nevertheless, the curves give you a general idea of the human hearing response, which is useful.

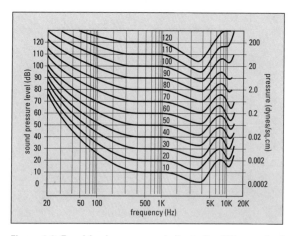

Figure 4-3. Equal-loudness curves indicate the SPLs required for different frequencies to sound equally loud to most people with normal hearing. Each curve is identified by the SPL at 1 kHz, which is also known as the phon of the curve.

Each curve indicates the SPL required for different frequencies to seem equally loud to most people with normal hearing. As you can see in Fig. 4-3, low frequencies must be delivered at a higher SPL to sound as loud as midrange frequencies. For example, a tone at 50 Hz must be over 40 dB SPL to sound as loud as a 1 kHz tone at 10 dB SPL. Interestingly, as the overall SPL increases, the equal-loudness curves flatten out a bit, which could be one reason why sound engineers often monitor at such high levels.

Each equal-loudness curve is identified by the SPL at 1 kHz. This is also known as the phon of each curve. For example, the 30-phon curve in Fig. 4-3 indicates the SPL required for all frequencies to sound as loud as 1 kHz at 30 dB SPL.

Because the human hearing system does not exhibit a flat frequency response, meters that measure SPL are normally calibrated to compensate, especially in the low frequencies. This compensation is called weighting, and it results in readings that correspond to our perception of loudness. If we hear different frequencies as being equally loud, the meter will register them as equally loud, even though their SPLs are different.

There are three major types of weighting: A, B, and C (see Fig. 4-4). With A weighting, the meter is much more sensitive to low frequencies than it is to the midrange. In fact, the response of A weighting is roughly the inverse of the 40-phon equal-loudness curve, which makes it ideal for relatively low levels. As mentioned earlier, the equal-loudness curves flatten out at high SPLs, so B and C weighting don't compensate as much as A, making them better suited to metering high-level sounds. If you see a spec such as "dB SPL (A weighted)" or "dB (A)," it means that the measurement was taken with an A-weighted SPL meter.

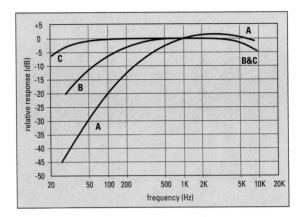

Figure 4-4. Weighting in SPL meters compensates for the fact that human hearing does not exhibit a flat frequency response. A weighting is used for relatively low SPLs, while B and C weighting is used for high SPLs, where the human frequency response is flatter.

HOW LOUD IS LOUD?	
dB SPL	Typical Source
140	.45 caliber Colt pistol (25 feet)
130	threshold of pain
120	studio monitor level, rock music (10 feet)
110	studio monitor level, film scoring (20 feet)
100	loud classical music
90	heavy street traffic (5 feet)
80	cabin of commercial jet (cruising)
70	passenger compartment of car on freeway
60	average conversation (3 feet)
50	average suburban home (night)
40	quiet auditorium
30	quiet whisper (5 feet)
20	very quiet recording studio
10	rustling leaves
0	threshold of hearing

Unfortunately, current trends in music and technology include an increasing risk of permanent hearing loss due to prolonged exposure to extremely loud sounds. In the movie *This Is Spinal Tap,* Nigel Tufnel proudly displays an amp that "goes to 11, which is 1 louder than 10, isn't it?" This satire reflects a trend in our society: music is getting louder all the time.

Of vital importance to all musicians, hearing is something we must understand and protect. Once the ability to hear is gone, it's gone for good. The only way to prevent hearing loss is to educate yourself about the dangers of continued exposure to loud sound and make some common-sense changes. In order to prevent hearing loss, we first need to understand how the auditory system works.

The Three Ears

The human auditory system consists of three areas: the outer, middle, and inner ears (see Fig. 4-5). As a sound wave passes through each area, the signal is processed, altered in intensity and/or spectrum, and analyzed.

The outer ear consists of the visible flap on the side of your head (called the pinna), an irregular bowl-shaped depression called the concha (where those funky airline headphones fit), and the ear canal, which ends at the tympanic membrane, or eardrum. These structures help us localize sound and act as resonators, boosting the incoming signal by as much as 25 dB.

The translucent, semi-elastic eardrum forms a complete seal at the end of the ear canal. Beyond it is the middle ear, which contains three tiny bones known as the ossicle chain. The first bone is called the malleus, or hammer, which is attached to the eardrum. As the eardrum vibrates, so does the malleus, which moves the next bone in the chain called the incus or anvil. The incus then moves the final bone, which is called the stapes, or stirrup. The stapes is attached to another flexible membrane called the oval window at the entrance to the inner ear.

In essence, the middle ear matches the mechanical impedance between the eardrum, which vibrates in air, and the oval window, which moves fluid. Infections, arthritis, or other conditions impairing the middle ear can lead to hearing losses of up to 50 dB. These are called conductive losses and are often correctable with medical treatment.

The inner ear is filled with electrically charged fluid. Its structures include the spiral-shaped cochlea (pronounced "COKE-lee-a") and the semicircular canals that help us maintain postural balance. As the stapes bone rocks across the oval window at one end

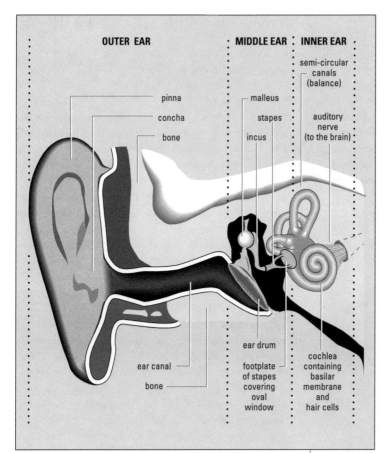

OUTER EAR | MIDDLE EAR | INNER EAR

pinna
concha
bone
malleus
stapes
incus
semi-circular canals (balance)
auditory nerve (to the brain)

ear drum
footplate of stapes covering oval window
ear canal
bone
cochlea containing basilar membrane and hair cells

Figure 4-5. The human auditory system is divided into three main areas: the outer, middle, and inner ears.

of the cochlea, its vibration is transmitted to the cochlear fluid.

Within the entire length of the cochlea is a coiled, semi-stiff structure called the basilar membrane, which picks up the vibratory waveform from the surrounding fluid. Different frequencies cause different regions of the membrane to vibrate; if several frequencies are present at once, several different regions of the basilar membrane vibrate simultaneously.

Sitting along length of the basilar membrane is the delicate organ of Corti, which contains millions of microscopic, hair-like cells connected to receptive ends of the auditory nerve. As different sections of the basilar membrane vibrate, the hair cells in those areas are stimulated, which causes electrochemical changes in the corresponding nerve endings. These auditory-nerve signals then travel to the brain.

The end of the basilar membrane nearest to the middle ear, at the base of the cochlea, responds to the highest frequencies, while the far end (known as the apex) is sensitive to the lowest frequencies. Thus, the hair cells at the base, middle, and apex of the cochlea transmit high-, medium-, and low-frequency components of the signal to the brain, respectively. In

fact, the auditory nerve is actually a bundle of individual fibers in which information about different frequencies is already sorted and organized. The cochlea acts like a finely tuned spectrum analyzer, responding to the harmonic components in the incoming signal.

Big Bang

After long and repeated exposure to extremely loud sounds, the hair cells in the cochlea lose their ability to respond to vibratory stimulation. Electron-microscope photographs reveal damaged hair cells that are collapsed and in disarray; the respective nerve endings receive no stimulation. The subsequent hearing loss is called sensory-neural loss, which is cumulative, permanent, and irreversible.

This damage occurs with long-term exposure to levels of 90 dBA and above; as a result, it is also called noise-induced loss. The Occupational Safety and Healthy Administration (OSHA) defines "long-term" as eight hours per day for ten years. However, the higher the sound level, the sooner the effect accumulates. The OSHA standard cuts the safe exposure time in half for every 5 dB above 90 dB SPL. In other words, 95 dB is considered safe for 4 hours, 100 dB is safe for 2 hours, 105 dB is safe for 1 hour, 110 dB is safe for

Warning Signs

There are several distinctive warning signs that accompany noise-induced hearing loss. Some of these symptoms are temporary at first, lasting a few hours to a few days. However, these conditions can become permanent if left unattended.

1. Ringing in the ears, which is technically called tinnitus (pronounced "TIN-ni-tus").
2. Sounds are muffled, which is known as a temporary threshold shift (TTS).
3. Speech is difficult to understand, especially in a noisy environment.
4. Some sounds at moderate levels seem very loud. This is called hyperacusis, or hypersensitivity. For example, writing on a pad of paper might sound like Niagara Falls. This condition can be mistaken for exceptional hearing, but it is a sign of damage.

half an hour, and 115 dB is safe for only 15 minutes. Rock concerts at sustained levels well above 100 dB can easily last three hours or more.

Typically, noise-induced hearing loss is not flat. It shows up first as a characteristic "notch" around 3 to 4 kHz, later spreading to include the 6 to 8 kHz range (see Fig. 4-6). Unfortunately, these deficits usually appear gradually, making them especially insidious. In addition, many of the symptoms are temporary at first, which makes them easy to disregard until repeated exposure makes then permanent (see sidebar "Warning Signs").

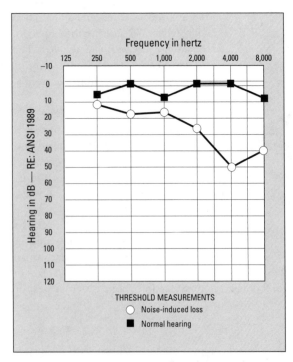

Figure 4-6. A hearing test produces an audiogram such as this one. Unlike most audiograms, this one includes two measurements: typical readings for normal and noise-damaged hearing.

Gotta Have It
If you've spent any time at all in a professional recording studio, you know that engineers often monitor at extremely high levels. The most common reason for this dangerous behavior is the desire to hear more detail in the music, which may have some basis in fact, considering that the equal-loudness curves are flatter at high levels. Another important consideration is the emotional, and even physical, impact of the music, which is especially true of heavy metal and grunge bands.

The problem of monitoring at high levels applies even more strongly to live performance. Unfortunately, the gradual nature of noise-induced hearing loss can cause engineers to push the volume levels to compensate for their own unrecognized injury. Some engineers boost the high-end EQ for the same reason, which not only changes the sound for the audience, but could also result in further hearing damage for the engineers.

Just Do It
In cases of permanent hearing loss, the only way to restore some of the lost sound is to get a hearing aid. However, even though hearing aids help to some degree, they can never fully replace the user's former aural acuity.

Clearly, the best medicine for hearing loss is to prevent it in the first place. Wearing ear plugs is an excellent starting point. Generic plugs of rubber, foam, or wax can be found in most drug stores, and closed headphone-type protectors intended for recreational gun use are often available in sporting goods stores. These products are rated by their attenuation abilities, which typically range from 6 to 40 dB.

For musicians, most of these products suffer the drawback of distorting the perceived frequency spectrum, usually cutting the high end dramatically. Fortunately, several custom-made ear plugs attenuate the entire spectrum more equally. For example, the West-one ER-15 and ER-25 cut by 15 or 25 dB, respectively. These plugs must be custom-molded to each person's ears by an audiologist or hearing-aid dispenser. They're also more expensive than the generic models, but the benefits could well outweigh the cost.

Testing, Testing, 1, 2, 3

If you work with loud music on a regular basis, consider it part of your professional routine to get your hearing tested annually. Ask your regular physician for a referral or contact any hospital or hearing clinic. Tests at audiology training clinics at universities might be lower in cost.

Tell the examiner you are a musician, and ask to be tested with high-frequency equipment. (Many audiometers only test up to 8 kHz; others go up to 12 kHz. Very few go all the way up to 20 kHz.) If your hearing is normal, you'll have a valid baseline for future comparisons. This could be important legally if your hearing worsens and you are no longer able to work.

If you suspect you have a hearing loss, don't panic. Ignoring or denying the problem won't make it go away. Hearing aids can help, and it's never too late to protect the hearing you have left.

Other common-sense precautions include taking quiet breaks during loud sessions and avoiding exposure to non-musical sources of noise such as motorcycles and firearms. If possible, monitor performance, recording, and playback at comfortable, rather than damaging, levels. Remember, you are protecting others in the studio as well as yourself.

CHAPTER 5

Digital Audio

S ound is an acoustic phenomenon. The changing air pressure that pushes and pulls on our eardrums varies smoothly rather than jumping discretely from one pressure to another. With electrical audio signals, the voltage in a cable varies smoothly in a way that mimics the changing air pressure of the sound represented by the signal. The signal's changing voltage is analogous to the changing pressure of the sound it represents, hence the term "analog."

Recently, however, the recording landscape has been altered dramatically. Audio signals are now commonly stored and transmitted as digital information. This offers several advantages over analog audio. For example, there is virtually no loss of audio quality when you make copies of the data. In addition, it is much easier to edit and assemble digital audio information. Finally, there is no tape noise when recording digital audio.

Fortunately, the same basic principles apply to all forms of digital audio recording, storage, and playback. This includes samplers, digital tape decks, hard-disk recorders, and CDs. As a result, the following section applies equally to all these types of digital audio equipment.

BASIC CONCEPTS

Humans use ten digits (0 to 9) to express all numbers; this is called the decimal number system. The decimal system probably arose because we have ten fingers (which are also called digits). To express numbers larger than 9, we combine two or more digits. For example, with two decimal digits, we can express 100 numbers from 0 to 99. With three decimal digits, we can express 1,000 numbers from 0 to 999.

Computers use only two digits: 0 and 1. This is called the binary number system, and binary digits are called bits (short for Binary digITS). Like humans, computers combine two or more bits to express larger numbers. For example, with two bits, you can express four numbers: 00, 01, 10, and 11. With three bits, you can express eight numbers, from 000 to 111.

Are you starting to see a pattern here? The pattern is this:

Number of numbers you can express = $2^{(\text{number of bits})}$

So, if you have eight bits, you can express 2^8 = 256 numbers from 00000000 to 11111111; with sixteen bits, you can express 2^{16} = 65,536 numbers.

Computers almost universally combine eight bits into a group called a byte. A group of four bits is half a byte, which is called a nibble. These days, most computers also work with larger groups of bits called words, which typically include 16 to 32 bits.

A/D Conversion

The starting point of most digital audio systems is an analog audio signal from a microphone or other analog source. (Some systems can generate digital audio from scratch without an analog source, but I'm going to put this idea aside for now.) The goal is to convert the analog audio signal into a series of discrete digital numbers that a computer can deal with.

A sample-and-hold circuit measures, or samples, the instantaneous voltage, or amplitude, of an analog audio signal and holds that value until an analog-to-digital converter (ADC) converts it into a binary number, which is called the quantization value (see Fig. 5-1). The sample-and-hold circuit then reads the next instantaneous amplitude and holds it for the ADC. This occurs many times per second as the signal's instantaneous voltage rises and falls. As a result, the smoothly varying analog waveform is converted into a series of "stair steps" (see Fig. 5-2).

In some systems, the lowest possible instantaneous amplitude is represented by a string of zeros, and the highest possible instantaneous amplitude is represented by a string of ones. In other systems, a string of 0s represents the middle of the possible amplitudes. Values with a zero as the first bit represent amplitudes above the middle (positive), while values with a one as the first bit represent amplitudes below the middle (negative). This is called two's-complement representation, which allows for positive and negative numbers.

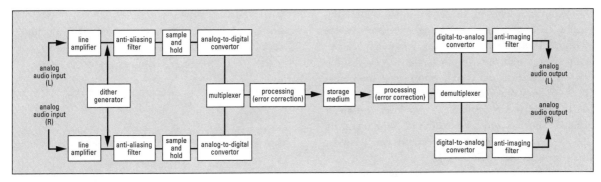

Figure 5-1. All digital-audio systems include these basic components. (Courtesy Ken C. Pohlmann)

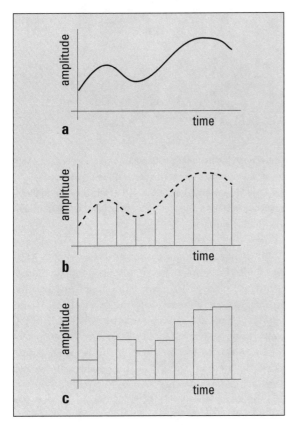

Figure 5-2. The instantaneous amplitude of an analog waveform (a) is measured many times per second by a sample-and-hold circuit (b), resulting in a stair-step representation (c). (Courtesy Ken C. Pohlmann)

Stereo signals are converted separately and then multiplexed, or combined, into a single stream of binary numbers. The numbers representing the right and left channels are interleaved, or alternated, in the stream.

One of the most common techniques for encoding each instantaneous amplitude is pulse-code modulation (PCM). Each bit is a code for an electrical or optical pulse: 1 = high-level pulse, 0 = low-level pulse. For example, if an instantaneous amplitude is repre-

sented by the binary number 1101, four pulses are sent: high, high, low, high. The rate at which the measurements are taken and the number of bits used to represent each measurement are the two most fundamental concepts in digital audio.

Sampling Rate

The rate at which the instantaneous-amplitude measurements are taken is called the sampling rate, and the time between measurements is called the sampling period. The more often measurements are taken, the higher the frequency that can be accurately represented (see Fig. 5-3). However, more measurements require more digital storage (which I'll discuss in more detail shortly).

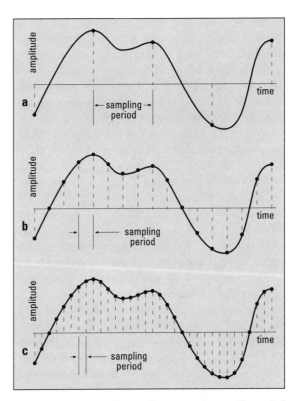

Figure 5-3. As the sampling rate increases, the sampling period decreases, and more of the high harmonics in the original signal are accurately represented. (Courtesy Ken C. Pohlmann)

If the frequency of the analog signal is low compared with the sampling rate, you get an accurate representation of the signal. If the frequency of the signal is over half the sampling rate, however, some weird things start to happen (more in a moment). The frequency that corresponds to half the sampling rate is called the Nyquist frequency after American engineer Harry Nyquist. For example, if the sampling rate is 48 kHz (48,000 measurements per second), the Nyquist frequency is 24 kHz.

The Nyquist frequency is the maximum audio frequency that the system can accurately represent and reproduce. This defines the audio bandwidth of the system. For example, if the sampling rate is 48 kHz, the system can represent and reproduce audio signals at frequencies from 0 to 24 kHz. In other words, the audio bandwidth of the system is 24 kHz.

By contrast, the digital bandwidth of the system is the maximum number of bits per second it can transmit or receive. For example, if the maximum sampling rate is 48 kHz, and each instantaneous-amplitude measurement is represented with sixteen bits, the digital bandwidth is 48,000 x 16 = 768,000 bits per second, or 768 kbps. In a stereo system, this digital bandwidth would double to 1.536 megabits per second (Mbps).

When digitizing a signal whose frequency is greater than the Nyquist frequency, you run into a problem called aliasing. In this case, the measurements of instantaneous amplitude don't accurately reflect the shape of the original signal's waveform (see Fig. 5-4). The measurements are taken at disparate points along the waveform. When these measurements are reconstructed into an analog signal, the reconstructed signal has a lower frequency than the original. (In fact, several alias signals appear above and below the original frequency.)

As a precaution against aliasing, the input signal is usually sent through an anti-aliasing filter before it reaches the sample-and-hold circuit (see Fig. 5-1). This lowpass filter blocks any frequencies that are greater than the Nyquist frequency of the system while passing all frequencies below the Nyquist limit. The slope of the filter is very steep, which leads many people to call it a brickwall filter.

All audio CDs use one sampling rate—44.1 kHz—which is also common among samplers, hard-disk recorders, digital multitracks, and DATs. This rate was adopted as a standard because its Nyquist frequency is 22.05 kHz, which is just above the top of the human hearing range. As a result, all frequencies we can hear are accurately represented. However, there is much debate in the audio industry about whether or not overtones above 20 kHz make an audible contribution to the entire signal. In fact, some DATs are

now available with a sampling rate of 96 kHz to address this issue. Most consumer DAT machines sample at 48 kHz, and most professional systems offer both 48 kHz and 44.1 kHz sample rates.

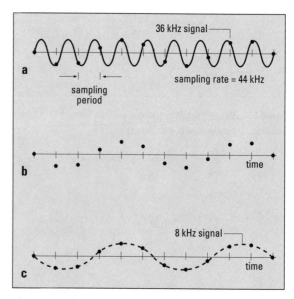

Figure 5-4. If the frequency of the input signal is more than half the sampling rate, a lower-frequency alias signal appears. In this example, the sampling rate is 44 kHz and the input signal's frequency is 36 kHz. The resulting alias signal is 8 kHz. (Courtesy Ken C. Pohlmann)

As you might expect, a sound sampled at 22 kHz uses half the storage space required by the same sound sampled at 44 kHz. Therefore, multimedia producers generally use sampling rates of 11 kHz or 22 kHz to reduce storage requirements, CD-ROM access time, and, in the case of Internet-based products, download time. Because of the reduced bandwidth dictated by the Nyquist frequency, however, lower sample rates yield lower audio quality.

In many samplers and hard-disk recorders, it's possible to use different sampling rates. For example, you might sample the lowest notes of a bass at 11 kHz; there are probably no overtones above 5.5 kHz, so you don't lose anything by sampling these notes at a lower rate, and you conserve sample memory. Higher notes can be sampled at 44.1 kHz and combined with the low notes to form an entire bass patch in a sampler.

In some systems, the input is sampled at a higher rate than will be used to reproduce the signal; this is called oversampling. As you might imagine, this increases the Nyquist frequency and reduces aliasing. After the signal has been sampled, a digital filter removes any frequency components above the final Nyquist frequency, and the data is output at the final (lower) sampling rate.

Resolution

The number of bits used to represent each instantaneous measurement is called the resolution or word length. The greater the resolution, the more accurately each measurement is represented (see Fig. 5-5). However, the more bits you use, the greater the storage requirements.

The resolution determines the number of steps between the lowest and highest instantaneous amplitude the system can represent. With 16-bit resolution, there are 65,536 steps between the lowest and highest amplitudes. This defines the dynamic range of the system. Theoretically, the dynamic range of a 16-bit system is 96 dB, but various factors reduce this figure to about 90 dB for practical purposes. Higher resolutions mean more steps and correspondingly higher dynamic ranges.

The most common resolution for professional digital audio is 16 bits, but 8-bit audio is often used for multimedia applications for the same reason that lower sampling rates are used: the file size is reduced by half. Multimedia sound designers usually have to strike a balance between resolution (8-bit or 16-bit) and sampling rate (11 kHz or 22 kHz).

Many professional digital audio products use 18-bit D/A converters, but that doesn't mean they necessarily record 18-bit audio; products such as the Alesis ADAT XT use 18-bit converters but record 16-bit audio. (I'll explain the reason for using higher-resolution converters in a moment.) Some professional systems actually record at 18-bit or 20-bit resolution, and a few even record at 24 bits.

You must be extremely careful not to exceed a digital recording system's maximum input-signal level. If the instantaneous amplitude of the input signal rises above the highest point that can be represented by the binary numbers, the digitized signal will be clipped (i.e., the top of the waveform will be chopped off, forming a horizontal line). This makes a very unpleasant noise. Unlike analog recorders, the input-signal level must not exceed 0 on the VU meter of a digital recorder in order to avoid clipping. Some digital recorders actually calibrate the 0 VU point a few dB below the actual clipping point so users can exceed this level without clipping as if they were using an analog recorder.

On the other hand, the hotter the recorded signal (i.e., the greater the input level), the more bits

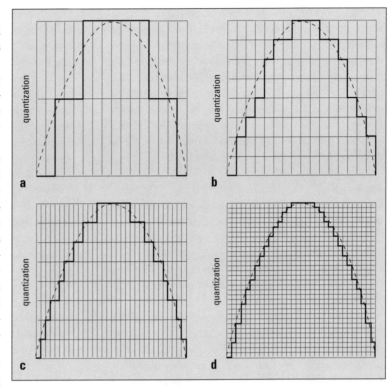

Figure 5-5. If the resolution is low (a), the signal is poorly represented with large stair steps. If you increase the resolution (b), the approximation is more accurate. If you increase the sampling rate (c) and the resolution (d) even more, the approximation is very close to the original waveform. (Courtesy Ken C. Pohlmann)

are used to represent it. If you record a signal whose level is the maximum possible short of clipping, you will use every available bit of the system's resolution. But if the input signal is at a lower level, fewer bits are used to represent it. This means you might not be using all sixteen bits in a 16-bit converter. (I'll return to this concept in the section on dithering.) To ensure full 16-bit recording, some 16-bit recording devices have 18- or 20-bit A/D converters. That way you can run a hot enough signal to record with 16-bit resolution while still having some headroom left over to protect against digital clipping.

No matter how many bits are used to represent each instantaneous measurement, the representation is not always completely accurate. In most cases, the actual measurement value must be rounded to the nearest binary number. This is called quantization, and the difference between the actual measured amplitude and the quantization value is called quantization error.

Quantization error can lead to audible quantization noise, which is particularly apparent in signals of low amplitude because only a few bits are used to represent the entire signal. As a result, you should try to keep the input signal's overall amplitude as close as possible to the maximum level that the system can accommodate.

The most common solution to quantization noise is called dithering. In this process, a small amount of noise is added to the input signal before it is measured and quantized (see Fig. 5-1). This randomizes the quantization error, reducing its audible effect. For this reason, it is particularly important to apply dither to minimize audible artifacts that arise when the resolution of a digital-audio signal is reduced, which is a common procedure in multimedia titles. I'll dig into dithering in more detail later in this chapter.

Storage

Once the signal has been digitized into a stream of binary numbers, it is stored in one medium or another. Common media include magnetic tape or disk, optical disc, RAM, and ROM. At a sampling rate of 44.1 kHz and a resolution of sixteen bits, digital audio data consumes over 5 MB per minute for a monaural file or 10 MB per minute for a stereo file.

To reduce storage requirements, you can reduce the sampling rate and/or resolution, but this also reduces audio quality. Another option is called compression, which is often used in multimedia titles, Web audio, and some professional applications. In this process, the digital audio data is compacted to reduce storage requirements. There are many types of digital compression, which can be divided into two broad categories: lossy and lossless.

With lossy algorithms (e.g., MPEG, ADPCM, and μ-Law [pronounced "myu-law"]), parts of the signal are discarded in order to compress the remainder. Lossy compression schemes are designed to lose information that, in theory, represents sound we wouldn't hear anyway due to masking and other psychoacoustic effects. However, the lost information is gone forever, and you can, in fact, hear the difference. While this might be marginally acceptable for a few multimedia applications (e.g., Web-based games) where high-fidelity playback is not expected, it simply won't do for professional audio recording. The advantage of lossy compression is that it provides the greatest storage reduction, generally by as much as 4:1, 5:1, and even more. In other words, a given amount of compressed digital-audio data requires ¼ or ⅕ as much storage as the original data.

Lossless compression discards no data. Instead, it depends on identifying and marking redundant data. In effect, programs such as Aladdin Software's *StuffIt* remove redundant instances of data and replace them with markers, which take up much less space than the data itself. If you have lots of redundant data, as in your average word-processing file or bitmapped graphic, these programs can dramatically reduce file size. When the file is expanded, the program follows the markers to replace redundant data with no loss.

But most digital audio files are densely packed with data in which redundancies are not obvious and not easily identified by standard file-compression algorithms. As a result, compressing audio files with, say, *StuffIt* or *PKZip* doesn't save much space.

Recently, however, several lossless audio-file compression programs for the Mac and Windows have arrived. These programs operate much like *StuffIt*, *DiskDoubler*, and *PKZip* in that they look for redundancies in a file. But unlike regular file-compression programs, these new audio compactors use algorithms specifically designed to find and eliminate nonlinear redundancies in audio files, which makes a huge difference. Although lossless compression retains all the information in a file, the storage reduction is not as dramatic as with lossy compression.

D/A Conversion

To play a digital-audio signal, it must be converted back into analog form. After some error correction, the digital signal is sent to a digital-to-analog converter (DAC). If it's a stereo signal, it is first demultiplexed to separate the right and left channels (see Fig. 5-1).

The analog output of the DAC still has a stair-step shape, which introduces high-frequency artifacts into the signal. In addition, the process of digitization creates images of the original waveform's harmonic spectrum centered at multiples of the sampling rate. For example, if the sampling rate is 44.1 kHz, images of the original spectrum appear centered at 88.2 kHz, etc. You might think that there is no need to bother with these images, which lie outside the human hearing range. However, these frequencies can cause audible problems in other audio components. And if the sampling rate is relatively low (e.g., 11 kHz), the images can be audible.

To solve both problems, another brickwall low-pass filter, called an anti-imaging filter, is traditionally placed after the DAC to remove any sonic components above the Nyquist frequency and smooth out the stair steps (see Fig. 5-1). These days, many systems use a digital anti-imaging filter before the DAC, which reduces the phase anomalies that are so problematic with analog brickwall filters.

In many modern systems, a digital filter uses oversampling to create a smoother, more accurate output. In this process, the filter interpolates between the original sample points.

Low-Bit Systems

Although many systems use sixteen bits or more to represent each instantaneous measurement, another approach is gaining popularity. This approach is called low-bit conversion because it uses only a few bits, sometimes even a single bit, to represent the audio signal.

How is this possible? Consider the following analogy. Traditional digital-audio systems are like a row of sixteen light bulbs, each controlled by its own switch. There are 65,536 possible on/off combinations, which determine the brightness in the room. Room brightness is analogous to the instantaneous amplitude of an audio signal. However, each bulb has a different inherent brightness, which introduces error into the system. This is analogous to the error introduced by high-bit converters.

You can also control the brightness in the room with a single light bulb by switching it on and off at a high rate. The brightness is determined by how long the light is on relative to how long it is off. This is analogous to a 1-bit converter. When the instantaneous amplitude is high, the converter sends mostly ones; when the amplitude is low, the converter sends mostly zeros. Low-bit converters are inherently more accurate than high-bit converters, but their sampling rate must be much higher than high-bit designs.

One way to use fewer bits is called differential coding. This technique is based on measuring the difference between one instantaneous amplitude and the next rather than the amplitudes themselves. It generally requires fewer bits to accurately represent the differences, which are smaller than the actual amplitudes. For example, delta modulation quantizes the difference (which is often represented by the Greek letter delta) between consecutive amplitudes.

A more sophisticated variation is called delta-sigma modulation. (This is sometimes called sigma-delta modulation, although some audio professionals make a distinction between these terms, using them to describe slightly different techniques.) This process takes the difference (delta) between the current instantaneous amplitude and the integral of the quantized previous difference. (Integrals are mathematical operations related to sums, and sums are often represented by the Greek letter sigma.) Delta-sigma converters provide excellent sound quality at a lower price, which is why they are used so much these days.

Digital-audio systems are difficult to design and build, but the basic concepts are relatively easy to understand. Once you grasp these concepts, you can optimize your use of samplers, DATs, digital multitracks, and hard-disk recorders and enjoy high-quality audio for relatively low monetary investment. In addition, digital products always improve their performance while falling in price, so the future looks bright for all forms of digital audio.

Although dithering might seem to be a relatively minor part of a digital audio system, it's of critical importance if you want to maximize the sound quality, and it's misunderstood even by many professionals.

Recall that when an analog signal (an electrical voltage that varies over time) is directed to the input of a digital audio system, an ADC measures the instantaneous voltage level of the signal many times per second (typically 44,100 or 48,000 times per second). Each measurement is then represented by a binary number (the quantization value) that includes a fixed number of bits. The number of bits in the quantization value is called the resolution of the system.

But what about if the instantaneous voltage falls between two consecutive quantization values (e.g., between 1010101010101010 and 1010101010101011)? In most cases, the system uses the quantization value that is closest to the actual voltage (see Fig. 5-6), which is similar to rounding a fraction to the nearest whole number. This happens more often than not in digital audio systems because the chance that a voltage corresponds exactly with a quantization value is very small. After all, there is an infinite number of voltages between any two consecutive quantization values. This is one of the fundamental differences between analog and digital audio.

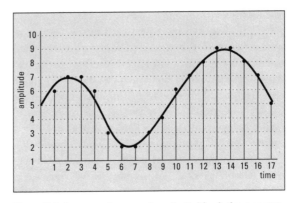

Figure 5-6. As an analog waveform is digitized, the measurement of each voltage value is rounded to the nearest quantization value, causing quantization error and distortion. (Courtesy Ken C. Pohlmann)

This rounding process results in an inaccurate representation of most measured voltages, which can lead to audible distortion and noise. One of the most common solutions to this problem is called dither. But before I can explain what dither is, you must first understand the nature of the distortion caused by the rounding process.

In a Dither

As described previously, the difference between the actual voltage and the nearest quantization value is called quantization error, and it leads to an often audible artifact called quantization noise or quantization distortion. This artifact manifests itself in several different ways, depending on the situation.

In part, quantization distortion depends on the resolution of the system. The greater the number of bits used to represent each voltage measurement, the smaller the interval between consecutive quantization values, and the less the measured value must be rounded. This means less quantization error and therefore less quantization distortion. Each added bit of resolution lowers quantization noise by 6 dB. However, simply adding more bits to a system's resolution becomes cost-prohibitive after a certain point.

Quantization distortion also depends on the input signal itself. With high-level signals, quantization distortion is random and resembles white noise. However, it is rarely objectionable (or even perceptible) with high-level signals, as with most music.

With low-level signals (including low-level harmonics in otherwise high-level signals), quantization distortion is more problematic. These signals have a small amplitude; i.e., the voltage varies over a narrow range of values. As a result, only a few quantization values are used to represent the entire signal. To put it another way, low-level signals only use a few bits of the system's resolution.

This leads to greater quantization distortion because most of the measured voltages are rounded to only a few quantization values. In this case, the digital waveform doesn't look much like the original analog waveform. This type of quantization distortion is often called granulation noise, because of its "gritty" quality. In extreme cases, a sine wave can become a square wave, or it might even disappear completely.

Unlike many digital audio systems, the system depicted in Fig. 5-7 always rounds upward to the nearest higher quantization value. If the sine-wave voltage crosses a single quantization value and never reaches the adjacent values, all voltages above the center value are rounded up to the next higher value, while all voltages below the center value are rounded up to the center value, which produces a square wave output (see Fig. 5-7 [a, b]). If the voltage remains within the boundaries of two consecutive quantization values, all voltages are rounded up to a single value, which results in no output at all (see Fig. 5-7 [c, d]).

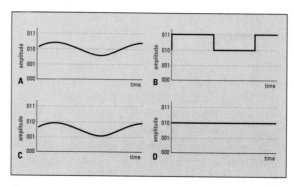

Figure 5-7. In the digital audio system represented here, all voltage values are rounded up to the next higher quantization value. If a low-level input sine wave crosses a single quantization value (a), it is digitized into a square wave (b). If the input sine wave stays within the boundaries of two consecutive quantization values (c), the digitized output does not oscillate at all (d). (Courtesy Ken C. Pohlmann)

If a low-level sine wave is distorted into a square wave in this manner, it exhibits its own set of harmonics that extend well beyond the Nyquist frequency of the system. All digital audio systems include a lowpass filter at the input that removes any overtones above the Nyquist frequency to prevent aliasing. However, the harmonics arising from quantization distortion appear after the anti-aliasing filter, so the filter cannot prevent aliasing in this case. If these harmonics are near the sample rate, a chirping effect called bird singing or birdies can be heard.

Dither Thou Goest

Oddly, one of the best solutions for quantization distortion is to add a small amount of analog white noise to the input signal before it is digitized. This added noise is called dither.

Take a look at Fig. 5-8, in which dither has been added to the sine-wave signals from Fig. 5-7. The added dither noise causes the waveform to jump around the nominal voltages of the original sine wave, although the overall shape of the original signal is retained (see Fig. 5-8 [a, c]). As a result, the dithered input signal comes close to different quantization values much more often than the original sine wave does, and the digitized square wave jumps between quantization values more often. In fact, the output is no longer a square wave; it's a rectangle or pulse wave in which the pulse width changes from cycle to cycle. This is called pulse-width modulation (PWM).

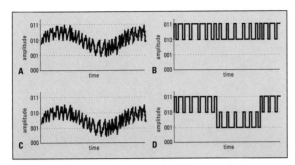

Figure 5-8. If the sine waves in Fig. 5-7 are dithered by adding white noise (a and c), the pulse width of the digitized rectangle wave varies according to the shape of the original sine wave (b and d). The original sine wave is reconstructed from this pulse-width modulated waveform by a lowpass filter, and we perceive it as a sine wave. (Courtesy Ken C. Pohlmann)

In Figures 5-8 [a, b], notice that when the overall shape of the dithered waveform is near its crest or peak, the PWM wave spends most of its time at the upper quantization value. The PWM wave does spend short periods of time at the lower quantization value when the dither noise is at one of its low points. Conversely, when the overall shape of the dithered waveform is near its trough, the PWM wave spends most of its time at the lower quantization value with only short periods at the higher value when the dither noise is at one of its peaks.

Between the overall peaks and troughs of the dithered input waveform, the PWM wave spends different amounts of time at the upper and lower quantization values. To put it another way, the pattern of changes in the pulse width over time corresponds to the overall shape of the original input waveform. This statement is critical for understanding the effect of dither, so let me repeat it: *the pattern of changes in the pulse width over time corresponds to the overall shape of the original input waveform.*

When the PWM wave is converted into an analog signal by a DAC, it proceeds through a lowpass filter just before the final output. This filter removes the high-frequency harmonics that arise from the small stair steps in the waveform introduced by the digitization process. Removing these harmonics smoothes out the waveform, returning it to its original shape.

In addition, the output filter offers an added bonus: it reconstructs the original low-level sine wave from the PWM wave as depicted in Fig. 5-8. This reconstructed sine wave includes a bit of white noise that was not present in the original input, but this is a small price to pay for recovering a low-level signal that would have otherwise been very distorted or lost altogether.

It is also helpful to consider the resulting harmonic spectrum of dithered and undithered inputs. As mentioned earlier, when an undithered, low-level

signal is digitized, it can become a square wave, which introduces its own harmonics (see Fig. 5-9 [a]). If the original signal is dithered, these harmonics are eliminated at the cost of a bit of white noise (see Fig. 5-9 [b]). In other words, dithering actually removes the distortion harmonics rather than simply masking them. Amazingly, dithering lets digital audio systems represent signals with amplitudes that are less than the minimum quantization interval.

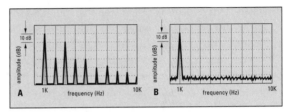

Figure 5-9. In this example, a low-level, undithered sine wave with a frequency of 1 kHz is digitized, and quantization distortion produces additional harmonics (a). Dithering the input removes the distortion harmonics but adds some white noise (b). (Courtesy Ken C. Pohlmann)

Dithering Down

Dither can also be applied to a signal after it has been digitized; this is called redithering to distinguish it from input dithering. Redithering is usually performed when reducing the number of bits used to represent the signal. In this case, the process is often called dithering down.

For example, many professional recording studios record with 20-bit resolution to improve the dynamic range of the recording and reduce quantization noise. However, these signals must eventually end up with 16-bit resolution to accommodate the CD format. In addition, just about any type of digital signal processing (DSP) results in data words that are longer than original samples in order to maintain the accuracy of the computations. These data words must be returned to their original resolution at some point, which means reducing the number of bits in each word.

Of course, you could simply delete the extra bits; this is called truncation. But this is generally considered unsatisfactory because of the potentially audible artifacts it creates. A much better solution is to add random numbers to the longer data words and then truncate to the desired resolution. These random numbers should have a resolution equal to the number of extra bits you want to remove. For example, if you want to convert from 20-bit to 16-bit words, add random 4-bit values to the 20-bit words and truncate to 16-bit resolution.

As a result of this process, the least significant bit (LSB) of the final 16-bit words switches its value from 0 to 1 and back in a pattern that represents the information from the extra bits, much like the changing pulse width of a digital PWM signal represents the shape of the original, dithered analog waveform as described earlier.

As before, dithering down adds a bit of white noise to the final signal, which is pervasive throughout the audible frequency range. This noise is often compensated for by shifting it to regions of the audio spectrum to which the human auditory system is less sensitive. This process is called noise shaping, and it is accomplished by controlling the pattern in which the value of the LSB switches from 0 to 1 and back.

The total power of the noise is not reduced (there is no such thing as a free lunch!), but it is restricted to a limited frequency range, typically above 10 kHz. The amplitude of the noise in this region is greater than the original white noise, but our hearing system is less sensitive to it, so we don't perceive it as well. The noise in the frequency range to which we are most sensitive is greatly reduced, which means we perceive less noise overall.

Understanding dither is very important for all electronic musicians, who use digital audio systems more and more with each passing year. Multimedia producers must often create several versions of sound files in various formats, and each file might have a different sample rate and resolution. Many digital audio programs offer dithering options for just these purposes. Dithering is also important when performing almost any computational processing on a digital audio file.

To dig deeper into the concepts of digital audio, check out *Principles of Digital Audio,* Third Edition, by Ken C. Pohlmann, published by McGraw-Hill.

P a r t

2

MIDI

Chapter 6: Basic MIDI
MIDI Messages
MIDI Implementation Charts
Multitimbral MIDI

Chapter 7: Sequencing
Standard MIDI Files
General MIDI

Chapter 8: Alternate Controllers
Guitar Controllers
Percussion Controllers
Wind Controllers

Chapter 9: Advanced Topics
Bank Select
MIDI Processing
MIDI Machine Control
System Exclusive

Basic MIDI

Anyone reading this book has probably heard of MIDI (pronounced "MID-ee"). MIDI has been around for over ten years, but many people still don't understand exactly what it is or why it's useful. So let's take the whole concept of MIDI from the top.

MIDI stands for Musical Instrument Digital Interface. A well-accepted technical specification, its purpose is to allow electronic instruments and computers from different manufacturers to be connected so they can share a common language that describes how each instrument is played during a performance. The spec is maintained by the MIDI Manufacturers Association (MMA) in the U.S. and everywhere else in the world except Japan, where the development of MIDI is overseen by the Japanese MIDI Standards Committee (JMSC).

In, Out, and Thru

Information about a musical performance is encoded in a set of MIDI messages that represent various performance gestures and other musical events. These messages are carried over a MIDI cable from the device that generates them to one or more devices that respond to them. Both ends of a MIDI cable terminate with the same type of connector, called a 5-pin DIN (see Fig. 6-1). This connector was selected because it's a standard configuration that is readily available.

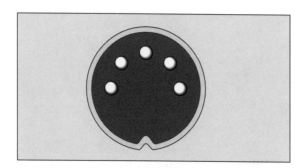

Figure 6-1. MIDI cables terminate at both ends with a 5-pin DIN plug. The notch at the bottom ensures that the connector fits properly into the socket.

The instrument that generates these messages is called the master or instrument controller, while the instrument that receives them is called a slave. To convey the messages, one end of the MIDI cable is connected to the MIDI Out jack on the master, and the other end is connected to the MIDI In jack on the slave (see Fig. 6-2). All MIDI devices include one or both of these connectors. Unlike many computer protocols, MIDI is unidirectional; messages flow in one direction within a MIDI cable.

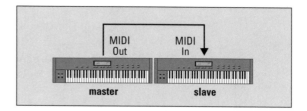

Figure 6-2. The MIDI Out from the master instrument controller is connected to the MIDI In of a slave using a MIDI cable.

Every time you play a note, release a note, step on the sustain pedal, change patches, move the pitch wheel, or make any performance gesture on the master controller, a corresponding message is generated, which travels along the MIDI cable. When the slave receives the message, it responds as if its own controls had been manipulated directly (that is, if the channels on the master and slave have been set correctly; more in a moment). For example, if the message says, "Play middle C," the slave plays middle C just as if that note had been played on its own keyboard. The note continues to play until the slave receives another message that says, "Release middle C."

Many MIDI devices include another jack on the back panel labeled MIDI Thru. Messages received at the MIDI In jack are split: one copy of the message stream enters the slave, which responds in the normal manner, while the other copy is diverted to the MIDI Thru jack, which sends it on to the next connected slave. This is called a daisy chain (see Fig. 6-3).

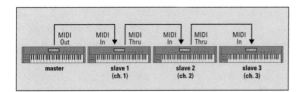

Figure 6-3. Several MIDI instruments can be connected using the MIDI Thru jack; this is called a daisy chain.

Aside from master controllers and slaves, there are two more basic types of MIDI devices you should be aware of: sequencers and processors. As I'll discuss in Chapter 7, sequencers record MIDI messages from a controller and let you edit them and send them to the various devices in your system. I'll also discuss MIDI processors, which include computer MIDI interfaces, later in this chapter and in Chapter 9.

MIDI MESSAGES

When MIDI was first developed, its messages were designed to represent keyboard gestures because virtually all synthesizers were keyboard-based. Since then, other types of instruments, such as guitars, drums, and wind instruments, have been adapted to use MIDI (see Chapter 8), but the messages retain their keyboard orientation (see table, "MIDI Messages").

Among the most common MIDI messages are Note On and Note Off. As you might imagine, these messages represent a note being played and released. MIDI includes code numbers for 128 chromatic notes (numbered 0 to 127), which exceeds the range of a piano and was deemed sufficient for most musical situations. Each Note On and Note Off message indicates which note is played or released.

These messages also include the Velocity with which the note is played or released. As discussed in Chapter 2, most modern electronic keyboards measure the speed with which each key is depressed. The measured speed is converted into a Velocity value that is included in each Note On message; such keyboards are said to be Velocity-sensitive. Some keyboards also measure the speed with which each note is released; this Velocity information is included in each Note Off message. MIDI provides 128 Velocity values (0 to 127).

Note On Velocity is typically used to control the initial volume of each note and often controls other parameters as well. Note Off Velocity is sometimes used to modify parameter values, but many controllers do not generate Note Off Velocity. Interestingly, a Note On with zero Velocity is equivalent to a Note Off. Velocity is one of the many ways MIDI facilitates musical expression, which I'll discuss in greater detail later in this chapter.

Also recall from Chapter 2 that many electronic keyboards measure the amount of pressure (also called aftertouch) applied to a key after it has been depressed. This information is encoded in a MIDI message called Pressure or Aftertouch, and such keyboards are said to be Pressure- or Aftertouch-sensitive.

Actually, there are two types of Aftertouch messages: Channel Pressure and Polyphonic or Poly Pressure. Channel Pressure is by far the more common type. If you hold more than one note at a time, the key under the greatest pressure determines the value of the Aftertouch message. Keyboards with Polyphonic Pressure generate independent Aftertouch messages for each key. It is very expensive to include separate pressure sensors for each key, so Poly Pressure is not often implemented. Aftertouch messages provide another means of expression via MIDI.

The position of a keyboard's pitch wheel is represented by a MIDI message called Pitch Bend, which is great for emulating the effect of bending guitar notes, sliding trombones, and so on. Similarly, the mod wheel's position is represented by the Modulation message. This message is often used to control the amount of LFO vibrato or brighten the tone by increasing the filter cutoff frequency.

Modulation is one of a set of 128 messages called the Control Change (CC) messages, which represent most of the expressive potential of MIDI (see table, "Control Changes"). The CC messages are divided into two main categories: continuous and switched. The continuous CCs represent performance gestures that encompass a range of values, such as Modulation, Volume (which represents the main volume of the sound), and Pan (which represents the pan position of the sound in the stereo field).

The switched CCs represent gestures that are either on or off. For example, when you step on a keyboard's sustain pedal, the instrument generates a Sustain On message; when you release the sustain pedal, the instrument generates a Sustain Off message.

As you'll recall from Chapter 2, most synths include memory for storing different patches. When you select a patch, the instrument generates a Program Change message encoded with the number of the selected patch. Program Change messages can only deal with patch numbers from 0 to 127; if an instrument has more memory locations than this, an extra message called Bank Select must also be used to represent the selected patch (see Chapter 9).

Changing Channels

The MIDI messages I've described so far include a code number called the channel; in fact, they are collectively known as the Channel Voice messages because they are used to control an instrument's voices on a particular channel. The master transmits these messages on any one of sixteen user-specified channels, and each slave is set to receive on one of these channels. Sequencers and many master controllers can transmit messages on several channels simultaneously. All slaves in the system receive all messages, but they ignore all messages that are not encoded with the channel number to which they are set to respond.

This is quite similar to broadcast or cable television. The signals from many stations are transmitted through the air or along the cable simultaneously and into your house. However, your TV ignores all of them except the channel to which it is tuned. Similarly, MIDI slaves ignore any messages they receive except those encoded with the channel number to which they are set.

For example, refer to Fig. 6-3. Slave 1 is set to receive on channel 1, slave 2 is set to channel 2, and slave 3 is set to channel 3. If you set the master to transmit on channel 1 and play the keyboard, slave 1 responds; slaves 2 and 3 receive the messages but ignore them. If you change the master's transmit channel to 3, slave 3 responds while slaves 1 and 2 ignore the messages and remain silent. Of course, you can create huge layered sounds by setting all slaves to the same channel. Up to sixteen instruments can be independently controlled in this way. (Some MIDI messages are intended for the entire system and do not include a channel number; more in a moment.)

Unlike television, most MIDI devices have the ability to respond to all channels at once. This ability depends on the Omni mode setting within the device. If Omni mode is on, the instrument responds to messages on any channel; if Omni mode is off, the instrument responds only to messages on the channel to which it is set. Omni mode is useful if you want to connect two instruments and layer their sounds without having to set matching channels, but it is turned off most of the time.

A La Mode

Omni On and Off are two of eight Channel Mode messages. Technically, these are part of the CC messages, but they serve a different purpose; instead of representing expressive gestures, the Channel Mode messages control a device's response to the Channel Voice messages.

Other Channel Mode messages include Mono On and Poly On. As you might imagine, Mono On causes the receiving device to play monophonically (i.e., one note at a time), and Poly On causes the device to play polyphonically. Along with Omni On and Off, these messages define four operating modes

for all MIDI devices (see table, "MIDI Modes").

Occasionally, a MIDI device will play a note in response to a Note On message, but it fails to receive or recognize the corresponding Note Off, which results in stuck notes. In this case, All Notes Off (ANO) is a handy Channel Mode message that tells the receiving device to release all notes that are currently sounding on the channel encoded in the ANO message. (Omni On/Off, Mono On, and Poly On also behave as ANO messages, turning off all sounding notes.)

The ANO message is often sent on all sixteen channels when you press the panic button on a device. However, not all MIDI devices respond to this message, so a well-designed panic button should also send individual Note Off messages for all 128 notes on all sixteen channels. All Sound Off is a similar Channel Mode message, but it shuts off all sound immediately; ANO allows the programmed envelopes to finish their release cycle.

Most panic buttons also send the Reset All Controllers message, which resets Pitch Bend, Aftertouch, and all CCs to their nominal values. In most cases, the default value is zero; Pitch Bend is reset to its middle value.

The remaining Channel Mode message is called Local Control. This message controls the Local status of the receiving device. When Local is on, the device's keyboard (or other controller) is directly connected to its internal sound engine, which responds to the keyboard, wheels, pedals, and other physical controllers. If Local is off, the internal sound engine does not respond to the instrument's physical controllers. In both cases, the instrument sends the appropriate MIDI messages when its controllers are manipulated.

At this point, you might be asking yourself, "Why would you want to disconnect an instrument's keyboard from its own internal sound engine?" In most cases, you wouldn't. However, it is often advantageous when you are sequencing (see Chapter 7).

A slave will only respond to Channel Mode messages that are sent on the device's basic channel, which can only be changed from the device's front panel or by sending it the appropriate SysEx message (more in a moment). In addition, a master controller only sends Channel Mode messages on its basic channel.

Bits and Bytes

Because MIDI is a digital standard, its messages are encoded into bytes. With only one exception that I'll discuss shortly, all MIDI messages include a well-defined (and small) number of bytes. The first byte of all messages is called the status byte, which identifies the message type. Any subsequent bytes in the message are called data bytes, which represent the appropriate value(s) of the message. For example, a Note On message includes a status byte (which identifies the message as a Note On and includes the channel number) and two data bytes. The first data byte specifies the note to be played, and the second data byte specifies the Velocity.

How does a MIDI device distinguish between status and data bytes? Simple. The first bit in a status byte is always 1, and the first bit in a data byte is always 0. This leaves seven bits in each byte to encode the message. Recall from Chapter 5 that the number of bits in a binary number determines the number of different things it can represent according to the following formula:

$$\text{Number of things it can represent} = 2^{(\text{number of bits})}$$

With seven available bits, each byte can represent $2^7 = 128$ different things. As a result, there are 128 chromatic notes in MIDI, which are specified in the first data byte of a Note On and Note Off message. Similarly, there are 128 Velocity values, which are encoded in the second data byte of these messages.

As mentioned earlier, the status byte of all Channel messages includes the channel on which the message is sent, and MIDI provides sixteen channels. This requires four bits, which leaves only three bits to encode the message type. As a result, there can be only eight different types of Channel messages, which seems pretty skimpy when you consider how many different performance gestures are possible.

Fortunately, the designers of MIDI solved this problem with the Control Change messages. All CC messages use the same status byte and include two data bytes. The first data byte specifies the type of CC represented by the message (e.g., Volume); this is sort of a "pseudo" or secondary status byte. The second data byte includes the value of the message (e.g., the Volume value).

Because the first data byte doesn't have to include channel information, it can represent 128 different types of CC messages. The first 120 CCs (0 to 119) represent many different continuous and switched gestures, such as Modulation, Volume, Pan, and Sustain; the last eight CCs (120 to 127) are the Channel Mode messages.

As you might surmise by now, the second data byte in a CC message can encode 128 different values, which normally works well. (In fact, this is overkill for the switched CCs, which need only two values to represent On and Off.) However, there are some situations in which you might want greater continuous resolution. To provide this extra resolution, the first 32 CCs (numbers 0 to 31) can be used as the most significant byte (MSB) of a longer message; CCs 32 to 63 can be used as the least significant byte (LSB) in conjunction with the first 32 to provide 14-bit resolution. Unfortunately, "MSB" and "LSB" are also used to mean "most significant bit" and "least significant bit," which can lead to some confusion.

Although Pitch Bend is not a CC message, it always uses two data bytes (MSB and LSB) to provide fourteen bits of resolution. This ensures that the pitch bends smoothly with no "stairstep" or "zipper" effect. As a result, the range of Pitch Bend values extends from 0 to 16,383, and 8,192 is the center (no bend) value.

Changing the System

So far, I've been discussing MIDI messages that include a channel code and are therefore intended only for those devices that are set to the same channel. However, there are additional messages that are intended for all devices in the system, so they have no channel code in their status bytes. These are the System messages, which are divided into three categories: System Exclusive, System Common, and System Real Time.

Although MIDI is designed to be a common language that all electronic musical instruments can understand regardless of their manufacturer, the designers of MIDI decided it was important to be able to encode information that is unique to each instrument, such as exactly how the instrument generates its sound. Among other applications, this would allow any instrument to send and receive its unique information to and from a computer (see Chapters 9 and 10). For now, suffice it to say that this information is encoded in System Exclusive (SysEx) messages.

Because SysEx messages include information that is unique to each instrument, there is no way to predict how long they will be. Unlike all other MIDI messages, SysEx messages can be hundreds or even thousands of bytes long. As a result, a special message called End of Exclusive (EOX) has been defined that identifies the end of a SysEx message. Technically, EOX is one of the System Common messages, although it is used only at the end of SysEx messages.

The other System Common messages include Tune Request, which was important in the days of analog synthesizers because their oscillators could easily drift out of tune. However, it isn't used much today because of the stability of digital oscillators. If a sequencer can hold several songs in its memory, the Song Select message selects the song you want to play. The Song Position Pointer message identifies where you are in the song at any given time.

Another important System Common message is MIDI Time Code (MTC) Quarter Frame, which represents the passage of time in hours, minutes, seconds, film or video frames, and quarter frames. It is sent four times per frame as the music is playing to synchronize sequencers, drum machines, and other time-based devices (see Chapter 7). Additional MTC messages are encoded as Universal SysEx (discussed shortly).

All System Real Time messages consist of a single status byte and no data bytes. The most common System Real Time messages are Start, Stop, Continue, and Timing Clock. As you might guess, the Start message tells a sequencer to start playing from the beginning of the selected song, and Stop tells it to stop playing. Continue tells the sequencer to play the song from the point at which it was last stopped. Timing Clock (also called MIDI Clock or simply Clock) is sent 24 times per quarter note by the master sequencer to synchronize other time-based devices. Unlike MTC, MIDI Clock does not represent the passage of absolute time—it is referenced to the tempo of the music—so it can't be used to tell devices where to start.

Another System Real Time message called Active Sensing is sent by many master devices about three times per second. Slave devices use this message to make sure they are still connected to a master device; if they stop receiving Active Sensing messages, they assume the connection has been broken and turn off all sounding notes. This is very handy in live situations if someone accidentally trips over a MIDI cable and disconnects it while notes are sounding.

The last System Real Time message is called System Reset, As its name implies, this message causes all devices in the system to revert to their default conditions. This is useful in the event of a power failure or other catastrophe that might scramble the brains of the devices in your system.

Expanding Universe

One of the beautiful things about MIDI is its expandability. The original designers knew they couldn't think of every possible application, so they left certain messages undefined to accommodate future additions. For example, there are several CC messages that remain undefined as of this writing, and many useful CC messages have been added to the spec since its inception. In addition, there are two undefined System Common messages and two undefined System Real Time messages as of this writing.

Another way to increase the expandability of MIDI is to let manufacturers apply certain CC messages to any parameters they wish within their instruments. This might seem to defeat the entire purpose of MIDI, but if the number of such messages is limited, the application of MIDI can be expanded without sacrificing its standardization.

The CC messages that have been set aside for this purpose are the General Purpose Controllers, Sound Controllers, Registered Parameter Numbers, and Non-Registered Parameter Numbers. There are eight General Purpose controllers, which manufacturers are free to use in any way they wish. For example, an instrument with a special, user-definable joystick or slider might use one of the General Purpose controllers to represent its movement. Four of the General Purpose controllers include an MSB and LSB, and the other four include only an MSB.

Of the ten Sound Controller CC messages, the first five include default definitions, but manufacturers are not required to implement them. These defaults are Sound Variation (used to select alternate versions of sounds during a performance), Timbre (an absolute controller for parameters that affect timbre), Brightness (a relative controller to increase or decrease the current level of harmonics), and Attack and Release Time (which affect envelopes).

The function of Registered Parameter Numbers (RPNs) must be agreed upon by the MMA and JMSC. As of this writing, there are five defined RPNs: Pitch Bend Sensitivity, Fine Tuning, Coarse Tuning, Tuning Program Select, and Tuning Bank Select. (The last two RPNs select alternate tunings stored in an instrument's memory; see Chapter 2.) The use of Non-Registered Parameter Numbers (NRPNs) is entirely up to the manufacturer.

Like many other CC messages, RPNs and NRPNs include an MSB and LSB. However, these messages work a bit differently than the other Control Changes. For example, suppose you want to send the RPN MSB for Pitch Bend Sensitivity. The status byte indicates that the message is a CC, the first data byte indicates that it's an RPN MSB, and the second data byte indicates that it's the Pitch Bend Sensitivity message. How do you specify the actual value of the Pitch Bend Sensitivity? CC messages include only two data bytes, which are used up indicating the type of RPN MSB.

To specify the actual Pitch Bend Sensitivity value, you must send another CC message: Data Entry, Data Increment, or Data Decrement. If a device receives an RPN or NRPN message, nothing changes until it subsequently receives one of these messages, which sets the value of the specified parameter.

As mentioned earlier, System Exclusive (SysEx) messages are normally used to represent the unique aspects of a device. However, several SysEx messages have been standardized to represent various additions to the MIDI Specification. Collectively, these are called Universal System Exclusive messages, and they come in two forms: Real Time and Non Real Time.

The Real Time Universal SysEx messages repre-

Type of Message	Status Byte (hex)	Number of Data Bytes	Meaning or Value of Data Byte 1	Meaning or Value of Data Byte 2
Channel Voice				
Note Off	8n	2	Note #	Velocity
Note On	9n	2	Note #	Velocity
Poly Pressure	An	2	Note #	Value
Control Change	Bn	2	Control #	Value
Program Change	Cn	1	Program #	
Channel Pressure	Dn	1	Value	
Pitch Bend	En	2	Value LSB	Value MSB
Channel Mode				
Local Control On/Off	Bn	2	7A	00/7F
All Notes Off (ANO)	Bn	2	7B	00
Omni Off	Bn	2	7C	00
Omni On	Bn	2	7D	00
Mono On (Poly Off)	Bn	2	7E	00
Poly On (Mono Off)	Bn	2	7F	00
System Common				
MTC Quarter Frame (Different types of this message represent hours, minutes, seconds, and frames)	F1	1	Message Type (3 bits) and Value (4 bits)	
Song Position Pointer	F2	2	Value LSB	Value MSB
Song Select	F3	1	Song #	
Undefined	F4			
Undefined	F5			
Tune Request	F6	0		
End Of Exclusive (EOX)	F7	0		
System Real Time				
Timing Clock	F8	0		
Undefined	F9			
Start	FA	0		
Continue	FB	0		
Stop	FC	0		
Undefined	FD			
Active Sensing	FE	0		
System Reset	FF	0		
System Exclusive				
Bulk Dump, Sample Dump, Parameter Values, etc.	F0	can have any # of data bytes		

sent events that must occur at specific times, such as starting a tape deck or turning on a spotlight at the correct moment during a performance. These messages are organized into several application-specific groups, including MIDI Show Control (for controlling curtains, hydraulic risers, lighting, and other live-show events), MIDI Machine Control (for controlling various devices in the studio, such as tape decks, VCRs, etc.), real-time pitch changes in the MIDI Tuning Standard, and MIDI Time Code cueing, among others.

Of course, Non-Real Time Universal SysEx mes-sages represent events that do not need to occur at specific times, such as data dumps. For example, most MIDI devices can dump the entire contents of their memory (or a portion of it) over MIDI to another device, such as a computer, which is how editor/ librarians work (see Chapter 10). In addition, the MIDI Sample Dump Standard represents digital audio samples in a standard format and lets devices share this sample data over MIDI. Non-Real Time Universal SysEx is also used to dump MIDI Tuning Standard data, represent certain non-real time aspects of MIDI Time Code (such as punch-in and

CONTROL CHANGES		
CC Number (First Data Byte)		**Control Function**
Decimal	**Hex**	
0	00	Bank Select MSB
1	01	Modulation
2	02	Breath Controller
3	03	Undefined
4	04	Foot Controller
5	05	Portamento Time
6	06	Data Entry MSB
7	07	Channel Volume
8	08	Balance
9	09	Undefined
10	0A	Pan
11	0B	Expression Controller
12-15	0C-0F	Undefined
16-19	10-13	General Purpose Controllers 1-4
20-31	14-1F	Undefined
32	20	Bank Select LSB
33-37	21-25	LSB for CCs 1-5
38	26	Data Entry LSB
39-63	27-3F	LSB for CCs 7-31
64	40	Damper Pedal (Sustain)
65	41	Portamento On/Off
66	42	Sostenuto
67	43	Soft pedal
68	44	Legato Footswitch
69	45	Hold 2
70	46	Sound Controller 1 (default: Sound Variation)
71	47	Sound Controller 2 (default: Timbre/Harmonic Intensity)
72	48	Sound Controller 3 (default: Release Time)
73	49	Sound Controller 4 (default: Attack Time)
74	4A	Sound Controller 5 (default: Brightness)
75-79	4B-4F	Sound Controllers 6-10 (no defaults)
80-83	50-53	General Purpose Controllers 5-8
84	54	Portamento Control
85-90	55-5A	Undefined
91	5B	Effects 1 Depth
92	5C	Effects 2 Depth
93	5D	Effects 3 Depth
94	5E	Effects 4 Depth
95	5F	Effects 5 Depth
96	60	Data increment
97	61	Data decrement
98	62	Non-Registered Parameter Number LSB
99	63	Non-Registered Parameter Number MSB
100	64	Registered Parameter Number LSB
101	65	Registered Parameter Number MSB
102-119	66-77	Undefined
120-127	78-7F	Channel Mode messages

punch-out points), request identification information from a device, and activate or deactivate a synth's General MIDI mode (see Chapter 7).

There's much more to learn about MIDI, and we'll continue to explore it throughout this part of the book, but you should now have a basic understanding of how it works. This information will help you keep up with the dizzying pace of technological development as electronic music races into the next century. In the meantime, remember that all this technology has only one purpose: to make music. MIDI is your servant, not the other way around. Keep that in mind the next time you feel intimidated by the next technological wonder.

MIDI MODES	
Mode 1	Omni On/Poly
Mode 2	Omni On/Mono
Mode 3	Omni Off/Poly
Mode 4	Omni Off/Mono

MIDI IMPLEMENTATION CHARTS

MIDI has standardized the way electronic musical instruments communicate performance gestures such as playing a note, moving a slider, or stepping on a sustain pedal. But even though all MIDI devices use the same message to represent a particular gesture, there is nothing that says every device must send or recognize all MIDI messages. Some messages are irrelevant to certain devices; for example, a sound module with no keyboard should recognize the Sustain message, but it has no reason to send that message. The specific set of messages that a device sends and recognizes is called its MIDI implementation.

Instrument manufacturers created a standardized form for presenting a device's MIDI implementation called, logically enough, a MIDI Implementation Chart. Usually located in the back of the owner's manual, this one-page chart offers a relatively straightforward, though very condensed, outline of the device's MIDI capabilities.

On the Charts

As I discuss MIDI implementation charts, I'll refer to a typical chart (see Fig. 6-4). At the top is the name of the product and possibly the version number of the chart or product and a brief description of the type of product.

The majority of the chart is taken up by four columns. The first column is labeled Function; it includes a list of the various types of MIDI messages. The next two columns are labeled Transmitted and Recognized. These columns indicate whether each

MIDI Implementation Chart

Manufacturer:
Young Chang

Digital Synthesizers

Model: K2000

Dated: 12 / 6 / 91
Version: 1.0

FUNCTION		TRANSMITTED	RECOGNIZED	REMARKS
Basic Channel	Default	1	1	Memorized
	Changed	1 – 16	1 – 16	
Mode	Default	Mode 3	Mode 3	Use Multi mode for multi-timbral applications
	Messages			
	Altered			
Note Number			0 – 127	0 – 11 sets Intonation Key
	True Voice	12 – 120	12 – 127	
Velocity	Note ON	O	O	
	Note OFF	O	O	
After Touch	Keys	X	O	
	Channels	O	O	
Pitch Bender		O	O	
Control Change		O 0 – 31 (32 – 63 LSB) 64 – 95	O 0 – 31 32 – 63 (LSB) 64 – 95	Controller assignments are programmable
Program Change		O 1 – 999	O 1 – 999	Standard and custom formats
	True #	0-127	0 – 127	
System Exclusive		O	O*	
System Common	Song Pos.	X	X	
	Song Sel.	X	X	
	Tune	X	X	
System Real Time	Clock	O	O	
	Messages	X	X	
Aux Messages	Local Control	X	X	
	All Notes Off	O	O	
	Active Sense	X	O	
	Reset	X	X	

Notes

* Manufacturer's ID = 07
Device ID: default = 0;
programmable 0 – 127

O = Yes
X = No

Mode 1: Omni On, Poly
Mode 2: Omni On, Mono
Mode 3: Omni Off, Poly
Mode 4: Omni Off, Mono

Figure 6-4. The MIDI Implementation Chart of the Kurzweil K2000. (Courtesy Kurzweil)

type of MIDI message is transmitted and recognized by the device. The fourth column is labeled Remarks, which includes notes and additional information.

As you can see, the Kurzweil K2000 transmits and recognizes messages on all sixteen MIDI channels. The two categories of basic channels, Default and Changed, are relics from the early days of MIDI, when the default channel of an instrument was recalled every time the power was turned on. The "Changed" channels could be set on the instrument, but often remained active only until the power was turned off. In the case of the K2000, any channel can be memorized as the default power-up channel independently for transmission and recognition, and these can be changed to any other channel at any time.

The K2000 transmits MIDI note numbers 12 to 120 from its 5-octave keyboard and recognizes 12-127 note numbers from a remote source. "True Voice"

indicates the actual range of pitches that the instrument can sound. Note numbers 0 to 11 select the root note for alternate tunings (see Chapter 1).

The "O" in the columns next to Velocity indicates that the K2000 sends and recognizes the Velocity value in Note On messages; Note Off Velocity is also recognized. The K2000 does not send Polyphonic Aftertouch (called "Keys" here), but it does recognize this message. It also transmits and recognizes channel aftertouch and Pitch Bend messages.

The next function lists all Control Change messages transmitted and/or recognized by the instrument. The K2000 sends and recognizes Control Changes 0 to 95. It can also send and receive Program Changes 0 to 127 and receive Kurzweil-specific non-MIDI Program Changes 1 to 999.

In terms of System messages, the K2000 sends and recognizes SysEx, but it doesn't send or recognize Song Position Pointer, Song Select, or Tune Request. It sends and recognizes Clock but no other System Real-Time message. In addition, it doesn't send or recognize Local Control or Reset messages. However, it does send and recognize All Notes Off; and it recognizes Active Sensing, although it doesn't send this message.

The Kurzweil K2000

You should now be able to evaluate the MIDI implementation of just about any device at a glance by looking in the back of the manual. Armed with this knowledge, you can judge for yourself whether an instrument can do what you want it to do, MIDI-wise. The ability to read and understand MIDI implementation charts is a valuable skill for any MIDI musician.

MULTITIMBRAL MIDI

People always seem to pine for the good old days, but I prefer the present, particularly when it relates to technology. For example, I remember the bad old days of MIDI, when you needed a separate keyboard or sound module for each instrumental sound in a sequenced score. Each one was assigned to a different MIDI channel so they could play independent musical parts. This wasted a lot of studio space and required a lot of techno-spaghetti to cable it all together.

These days, most keyboard and rackmount synths and samplers are multitimbral, which means they can play several independent instrumental parts on different MIDI channels. Many of these devices also include an internal sequencer and effects processor. By using these elements together, you can often sequence an entire score with a single instrument. Sounds like the good new days to me.

Multitimbral Madness

A multitimbral keyboard or sound module functions as if there are several synths within one physical device (see Fig. 6-5). Each "virtual" synth within the unit responds to MIDI messages on a separate MIDI channel. For example, if the device can support sixteen independent parts, it is said to be 16-part multitimbral.

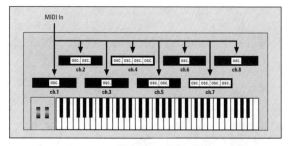

Figure 6-5. This multitimbral synth is 8-part multitimbral and 32-voice polyphonic. The programs in the setup use one, two, or four oscillators; if each part plays one note, sixteen voices of the total polyphony are used up.

Of course, these multitimbral devices can also play one sound at a time like the synths of old; this is often called Program mode. In this mode, which you typically use to play a piano patch or other single program, the device responds to messages on only one MIDI channel.

If you are sequencing several different parts, you typically enter Multi or Combi mode, in which different patches are assigned to different channels. With a sequencer, you can record and play back MIDI messages on different channels, and each program in the multitimbral setup responds to these messages independently. In most cases, you can send a Program Change message to one of these virtual instruments and change its sound without affecting the other programs in the setup. However, some older multitimbral synths change the entire setup in response to a Program Change.

You can also use Multi mode to layer several sounds across the keyboard, or split the keyboard to play different sounds in different key ranges. For example, you might assign a bass part to the left half of the keyboard and a piano sound to the right half. These layered or split sounds can be on the same MIDI channel or on different channels. Some instruments let you layer and split two or more sounds in Program mode; you can then layer these compound programs in Multi mode, which results in incredibly rich, fat sounds. However, this also seriously reduces the available polyphony (discussed shortly).

Things can get really crazy when you combine several multitimbral synths into a large system. MIDI specifies sixteen channels, which lets you control up to sixteen physical or virtual devices independently from one MIDI cable. With a multiport MIDI interface connected to your computer, you can break the 16-channel barrier. For example, you can combine four 16-part multitimbral synths and a computer with a multiport interface that includes four MIDI In and Out ports. By using software that lets you separately address each port of the interface (most medium-to-high-level sequencers do these days), you can control 64 separate MIDI channels and play 64 different parts!

Poly Want a Cracker

Imagine you're sequencing a song on a multitimbral synth, with a piano part, bass part, drums, etc. After recording a few parts, you notice some of the parts are not playing properly, and you can't hear all the notes you originally recorded. The problem you've run into is the brick wall of polyphony.

As discussed in Chapter 2, each note you play engages one or more oscillators. All synths have a fixed number of oscillators within them, which determines the polyphony of the device. However, the polyphony is the maximum *total* number of notes the entire device —including all multitimbral parts—can play simultaneously. If a synth with 32-voice polyphony uses two oscillators in each patch, it can play only sixteen notes at the same time. In addition, if a 2-oscillator piano patch in a 32-voice synth plays a 5-note chord, the other patches in the setup must share the 22 remaining voices while that piano chord is sounding (see Fig. 6-5). As soon as the piano chord is released, however, those oscillators are free to be used by other patches on other MIDI channels.

Liberal use of the sustain pedal on one or more parts also reduces the polyphony for other instruments in the setup. If you hold the sustain pedal and play the same note five times, you'll use up five notes of the total polyphony (or more, if the program uses multiple oscillators), though you hear only one note playing.

Ensoniq's TS-10 synth offers 32 voices and supports twelve multitimbral parts.

Voice allocation distributes a multitimbral synth's available polyphony among the various virtual instruments in a setup. Early devices, such as the Yamaha TX81Z, used fixed voice allocation; you had to specify how many notes were assigned to each patch in the setup. For example, you might assign one note to the bass part, four notes to the piano, etc. Unfortunately, the TX81Z had only 8-note polyphony, so this assignment wasn't easy.

Modern multitimbral synths use dynamic voice allocation, which automatically assigns notes to the parts as needed. Even so, it's easy to run out of notes when sequencing complex music. Many instruments use a scheme called last-note priority to decide which notes to cut off if the polyphony is exceeded. In this case, the last note to start has priority over the notes that started before it; the first in a series of sustained notes is generally the first to be cut off if the polyphony is exceeded.

In some instruments, such as the Roland JV and Sound Canvas lines, you can reserve a number of notes for one or more parts; this assures a minimum number of notes played by that part will not be cut off. If the polyphony is not exceeded, notes are assigned dynamically. Essentially, this is a combination of fixed and dynamic voice allocation. Those parts without reserved notes are the first to be cut off if necessary. Of course, you can't reserve more notes than the total polyphony of the device.

Effective Outputs

Most multitimbral synths include one or two effects processors that provide reverb, delay, chorus, flanging, and other effects (see Part 5). Each program includes its own effects settings. However, if you record one part into a sequencer, then record another part, you might be surprised to find the first part's effects have changed to those of the second part. This can be a real problem because many programs rely heavily on their effects settings; if you change the effects, the sound of the patch might suffer considerably.

For multitimbral sequencing, you generally use a global effects setting that applies to all parts. In many synths, you can control the depth of effect applied to each part (this is similar to the aux-send controls in each channel of a mixer; see Chapter 15), but the type of effect is the same for all parts. Some effects algorithms split the processor into two independent effects that can be applied to two different parts. For example, members of the Korg 01/W family include two such processors, allowing up to four independent effects for different parts (see Fig. 6-6). More recently, insertion effects were added to some multitimbral synths, such as the Yamaha MU80, which can be applied to a single instrument in the setup.

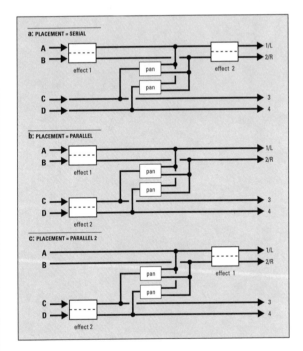

Figure 6-6. The Korg 01/W offers three effects configurations and four audio outputs. Each processor can be split to apply different effects to different parts, each of which are assigned to signal path A, B, C, and/or D. In all three configurations, any parts assigned to C and D can be mixed via the pan controls with paths A and B; this sends all parts to the main outputs if the auxiliary outputs are not used.

These days, all synths have two main audio outputs: stereo right and left. Many multitimbral instruments also include two, four, or eight additional outputs. Typically, rack-mount sound modules have more of these auxiliary outputs than their keyboard siblings. The signal from each part in a setup can be routed to one or more of these outputs.

The outputs are integrated with the effects processors in several selectable configurations (see Fig. 6-6). In some configurations, several outputs bypass the effects altogether; this lets you send some of the parts to an external processor. Of course, this also requires more inputs on your mixer. If you have no extra mixer inputs, you can send all the parts to the main outputs.

Multitimbral synths and samplers have brought a new era of cost effectiveness to the MIDI studio. You can now realize entire orchestrations with a single device that costs no more than single-timbre instruments did when they were new. All it takes is a little understanding, and you will be well on your way to creating your next magnum opus.

CHAPTER 7

Sequencing

Sequencing is probably the most common application of MIDI. Perhaps you've read something about sequencing or watched someone do it, but you still don't understand the details of the process. Even if you own a MIDI keyboard and sequencer, you might be unable to learn sequencing fundamentals from their user's manuals. (This isn't surprising, since many product manuals are incomprehensible even to seasoned veterans.)

Tape Decks vs. Sequencers

Conceptually, sequencing is similar to multitrack tape recording. In fact, sequencers can be thought of as MIDI recorders. With sequencing, as you play a keyboard or other MIDI instrument, your performance is recorded into a sequencer. After recording, you can play back your performance and listen or record additional parts. However, unlike a tape recorder, the sequencer does *not* record the actual sounds that you produce on the instrument.

This point is so important, it deserves an example. Let's say you play a MIDI keyboard and record your performance into a sequencer. As you record, the patch on the keyboard is a string sound. After the recording, you change the patch on the keyboard to a flute sound and play the sequence back. The part you just recorded is played back faithfully, but with the flute sound instead of the string sound.

This occurs because sequencers record the MIDI messages that are sent from the instrument as you play: messages such as Note On, Note Off, Pitch Bend, Aftertouch, Sustain, and so on (see Chapter 6). In the previous example, the sequencer simply recorded the messages generated by the keyboard as you played. (If you want, you could have the sequencer record a Program Change message, which would reset the synthesizer to the sound of your choice.)

The messages generated by a MIDI instrument are carried along a MIDI cable from the instrument to the sequencer, which is nothing more than a computer dedicated to the task of recording, storing, and manipulating a sequence, or list, of MIDI messages (hence the name "sequencer"). When you play back the recording, the sequencer sends the MIDI messages back to the instrument, which responds by playing the part as if you were playing the instrument directly.

Theoretically, the timing of the MIDI messages as they are played back corresponds exactly with the timing of the messages as they were recorded. However, all computers have a finite timing resolution that limits how accurately they can represent the timing of events. As a result, all sequencers have a resolution that determines how accurately they can reproduce the timing of sequenced MIDI events. This resolution is specified in pulses per quarter note (ppqn). (Pulses are sometimes called ticks.) Early sequencers had a resolution of 96 ppqn, but modern sequencers have a resolution of 480 ppqn or more, which lets them reproduce the timing of sequenced events much more accurately.

Similarities and Differences

The conceptual similarity between sequencers and tape decks can be seen in the main controls found on most sequencers, which are Play, Record, Stop, Pause, Fast Forward, and Rewind. Also, most sequencers can record on more than one track, letting you record one part and then record another part while listening to the one you previously recorded.

However, the differences outweigh the similarities. As stated before, sequencers do not record sound at all. (Digital audio sequencers integrate MIDI and hard-disk recording; see Chapter 10.) In addition, the "transport" is instantaneous. Unlike a tape deck, pressing the Rewind button takes you to the beginning of the sequence instantly. Many sequencers have more tracks than the most expensive tape decks (sometimes hundreds of tracks).

Sequencers let you change the tempo of a song while recording or playing back without affecting the pitch of the music. This can be handy if you can only play certain passages slowly; simply record at a slower tempo and speed it up for playback. It also lets you establish a tempo map, which automatically changes the tempo as you specify during the song.

A primary advantage of sequencers is their editing capabilities. Compared to magnetic tape, editing on a sequencer is far easier and more precise and comprehensive. Many people claim that sequencers offer the same advantages over tape decks that word processors offer over typewriters, which is true in many respects. Although sequencers can't manipulate sound directly, they can manipulate the MIDI messages in an entire performance, a single track, or even a single note with a wide variety of editing techniques such as cut-and-paste, transposition, and many others, which will be discussed later in this chapter. (The hard-disk recording function of a digital audio sequencer lets you edit digital audio files in a similar manner; see Chapter 10.)

On a tape deck, the "memory" is a reel of tape. The length of the tape determines the maximum length of the material that can be recorded. In a sequencer, the memory is RAM (Random Access Memory), which also determines the length of the material that can be recorded. Unlike tape, the capacity of which is measured in minutes, sequencer memory is measured by the number of events or notes that it can accommodate, regardless of their length. When comparing the capacity of different sequencers, it's important to remember that a "note" consists of two MIDI events: Note On and Note Off. If the capacity of a sequencer is specified as a number of events, the note capacity is probably half that amount.

Another distinction between tape decks and sequencers is the difference between tracks and MIDI channels. As discussed in Chapter 6, most MIDI messages are sent on one of sixteen channels. This means that up to sixteen independent, polyphonic parts can be carried on one MIDI cable.

A track on a tape deck usually holds only one musical part, unless you "bounce" (mix and re-record) several recorded tracks onto a single track. However, a track in a sequencer can include musical parts on any or all of the sixteen MIDI channels, meaning that up to sixteen different parts can occupy a single track. Essentially, each track in a sequencer provides sixteen "virtual tracks" that correspond to the sixteen MIDI channels. Typically, each musical part in a sequence is played on its own separate MIDI channel.

In a sequencer, you also can bounce parts on one channel or track to other tracks. However, unlike an analog tape deck, the sound quality never degrades because the sound comes from the instrument itself as it is played by the sequencer. When you bounce parts from one track to another on an analog tape deck, you lose some sound quality in the process. (This is not true of digital audio recorders.)

Equipment

Now that some of the basic concepts are out of the way, it's time to deal with equipment requirements for MIDI sequencing (see Fig. 7-1). First in the chain is some sort of MIDI controller, such as a keyboard, MIDI guitar, MIDI wind instrument, or drum pads (see Chapter 8). This is the device that you actually play, sending MIDI messages to the sequencer.

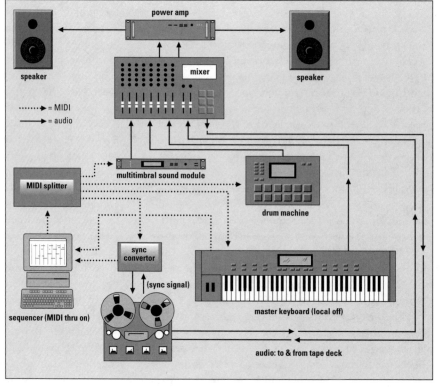

Figure 7-1. A simple sequencing system. The computer implies a software sequencer, but it could just as well be a hardware sequencer. If it is a computer, the MIDI splitter should be a multiport MIDI interface for the computer. You must switch the connection on the sync converter's MIDI In from the sequencer's MIDI Out to the keyboard's MIDI Out in order to sequence additional parts while synched to tape.

Next in line is the sequencer itself, which comes in several forms: stand-alone, integrated, and software. Stand-alone sequencers are basically computers dedicated solely to sequencing. They are generally small and portable, making them good for gigs and tours. However, they often have a small display and are not easily updated with new features. Also, the less expensive models might not even have permanent storage in the form of a floppy disk drive.

Integrated sequencers are built into keyboard workstations. These function identically to stand-alone sequencers but don't require a physical connection between the keyboard and sequencer. All communications are handled internally.

Software sequencers are programs written for one of the common general-purpose computers such as the Apple Macintosh or Windows-based PCs (see Chapter 10). These sequencers offer a larger display (the computer screen), easily installed updates, permanent disk storage, and more sophisticated features. Of course, they are usually less portable than hardware sequencers (unless you are fortunate enough to own a laptop computer with a MIDI interface). Many current products in this category are actually digital audio sequencers, which integrate hard-disk recording with MIDI sequencing.

All sequencers fall into one of two basic categories (although many include aspects of both): linear and pattern-oriented. Linear sequencers provide the closest analogy to tape decks—several tracks on which you record different parts from the beginning of the song to the end. Pattern-oriented sequencers follow a drum-machine analogy: you record short patterns that are later strung together to form a whole song.

At the other end of the sequencing chain, you need a MIDI sound module that will respond to the MIDI messages sent from the sequencer. This sound module might be incorporated into the keyboard or other MIDI instrument used to send data to the sequencer, or it could be an external unit. In either case, the most cost-effective type of sound module is one that is multitimbral, which means that it can play several different parts on different MIDI channels with different sounds at the same time (see Chapter 6). It often takes only one such sound module to play an entire song.

Whether you use a workstation or separate units, you also need a sound system of some sort to hear what you're doing. This might be a simple pair of headphones or a mixer with an amplifier and a pair of speakers (see Part 4).

System Design

Fig. 7-1 provides an example of a typical MIDI sequencing system. The keyboard includes its own internal, single-timbre sound module, which is set to receive on MIDI channel 1. The external sound module is multitimbral, capable of producing up to eight different sounds on channels 2 through 9. The other elements of the system include a drum machine (set to receive on channel 10), the sequencer itself, and a sound system.

As you can see, the MIDI Out from the keyboard is connected to the MIDI In of the sequencer, and the MIDI Out from the sequencer is connected to the MIDI Ins of the keyboard, sound module, and drum machine using a MIDI splitter, patch bay, or Thru box. You could also connect the MIDI Thru of one device into the MIDI In of the next if you don't have a Thru Box. If the sequencer is computer-based, a better alternative would be to use a multiport MIDI interface, to which you would connect the MIDI Ins and Outs from each device.

Most sequencers include a function called Thru or Echo that determines whether or not the incoming MIDI messages will be sent right back out in addition to being recorded. Turning this function on lets you hear an external sound module or drum machine respond as you play on the keyboard and record into the sequencer. The MIDI messages are sent from the keyboard into the sequencer and on to the sound module.

However, if you play the keyboard's internal sound generator from the keyboard, and the sequencer's Thru function is on, MIDI messages will be sent from the instrument to the sequencer and right back to the instrument again. At best, this will result in each note being played twice—once by you and once by the sequencer as the MIDI messages are reflected back to the instrument—which will cut the polyphony of the instrument in half. At worst, the result will be stuck notes (notes that don't turn off) and other weirdnesses associated with MIDI feedback loops.

To avoid these problems, turn the sequencer's Thru function off when recording the keyboard's own part. However, it is often preferable to turn the keyboard's Local function off instead. This prevents the keyboard from triggering its own sound generator, but it doesn't interfere with the MIDI messages it generates. You can play on the keyboard, and the internal sound engine responds only to MIDI messages from the sequencer.

Recording and Playback

The two basic types of sequence recording are real-time and step-time. Real-time sequencing resembles audio tape recording: after some preliminary setup, simply press Record and start playing.

All sequencers provide some sort of metronome for real-time sequencing. The metronome establishes the tempo and provides a reference for your performance. The sound of the metronome might be generated within the sequencer itself as a sort of click, or it might be sent at regular intervals from the sequencer as a MIDI Note On message on one MIDI channel. This message is meant to be played by an external sound module, typically a drum machine set to something like a rim-shot or sidestick sound. Most devices and programs let you specify a count-in, which plays the metronome for a number of bars before the sequencer starts recording.

If the song you want to sequence is too difficult for you to play at its intended tempo, you can slow down the metronome until you can play it easily. If you tried to do this with a tape recorder, the performance would sound much higher in pitch when you played it back at the right speed. However, a sequencer can change the speed of playback without changing the pitch because it's recording a sequence of MIDI messages rather than actual sounds. The messages specify the pitch of the notes while the sequencer controls how quickly they are sent to the instrument that's playing them.

Once you've recorded one part, you can record additional parts in a process called overdubbing. The sequencer plays the part you previously recorded while recording the new part (see "Real-Time Sequencing" sidebar). If your sequencer has many tracks, you might try recording the different drum and percussion parts (kick, snare, hi-hat, etc.) on separate tracks so that you can easily edit them separately.

Referring to Fig. 7-1, let's say the keyboard's internal sound module is set to play a piano sound on MIDI channel 1. Remember to turn the keyboard's Local function off and the sequencer's Thru function on. (This might not apply if you're using a workstation.) The multitimbral sound module is set to play a bass sound on channel 2, a rhythm-guitar sound on channel 3, a lead-synth sound on channel 4, a punchy horn sound on channel 5, and an additional bass sound on channel 6. The drum machine will play the drum part on channel 10. For now, the drum machine acts like a passive sound module producing drum sounds without using its internal drum programming capabilities. Its part will be recorded into the sequencer along with all the other parts.

Step-time sequencing differs from real-time sequencing in that each note or chord is recorded one at a time without playing to a metronome. This lets you record parts that are impossible to play otherwise. However, it also results in a very machine-like recording. This is a tedious job at best (see "Step-Time Sequencing" sidebar), but it does provide a means to record musical ideas that are too difficult to play in real time.

Real-Time Sequencing

1. On the sequencer, select real-time recording and set the tempo and time signature you wish. Remember that, if necessary, you can set a slower tempo for recording than the song will be played at. You can also specify different time signatures at different points in the song.

2. Set the count-in so that you know when to start. A typical count-in is two bars long.

3. Decide which part you want to record first. Many people record the drum part first so that they have a sense of the "groove" when recording the other parts. Others prefer to record the piano part first to get a sense of the whole song. You might want to record a condensed piano version of the whole song even if such a part won't be in the final recording. You can play subsequent parts to this piano reference and delete it later.

4. On the keyboard, set the MIDI transmit channel to match the instrument you've selected. Referring to Fig. 7-1, if it's the piano part, set MIDI transmit channel 1; if it's the drum part, set channel 10.

5. Play a few notes on the keyboard to ensure the MIDI messages are getting to the right sound module. If not, make sure that the sequencer's Thru is on and the controller's Local is off.

6. On the sequencer, select the track on which you wish to record the part, enable its Record function, and press Record.

7. After the count-in, play the selected instrument's part.

8. After the part is recorded, press Stop.

9. Press Rewind and disable the track's Record function.

10. Press Play to hear the part you just recorded.

11. To overdub the next part, press Stop and Rewind. Select the next part to record and follow steps 4 through 9. Repeat these steps until all parts are recorded.

Editing

As mentioned earlier, one of the main advantages of sequencing over tape recording is editing. If you make a few mistakes, many types of editing functions available on most sequencers let you fix them. These functions can be applied to an entire song, sections of a song (such as the chorus), individual tracks, sections of tracks (such as bars 9 to 16), MIDI channels, specific note ranges (such as C4 to B4), types of events (such as MIDI Volume messages), and even single events (such as a single note). Typically, you simply select the event, section, or type of message you want to edit and apply the desired editing function.

For example, you can transpose the selected notes up or down by semitones. The events in the selected range can be channelized to a different MIDI channel and shifted forward or backward in small increments of time, which changes the feel of the part. The selected range of events also can be merged with other events, which is useful for combining tracks in a manner similar to "bouncing" tape tracks. Unlike bouncing, however, merging results in no degradation of signal quality, and messages on different MIDI channels can coexist in a single track.

Another important editing function is cut-and-paste. As its name implies, most sequencers let you cut or copy a section of the song or a track and paste it elsewhere in the song. For example, you can record a repeating background part only once and then copy and paste it throughout the song. This is not unlike the cut-and-paste function found in most word processors.

The events in a sequence can be displayed in a variety of ways, providing a visual representation of the music and letting you select the events you want to edit. Because of their small displays, hardware sequencers only offer an event list that presents the events in a list of numbers. This lets you change a single note or other event such as a Program Change quite easily, but it's cumbersome if you're trying to change a stream of CC messages. Most hardware sequencers also offer the ability to select a specific type of event in a specific section of a song or track (or on a specific MIDI channel) for more global editing such as transposition.

Software sequencers often include event-list editing, but they usually offer graphic editing, as well (see Fig. 7-2). Thanks to a large computer screen, many events can be displayed at once. This display can take the form of a strip chart much like a piano roll, and some programs also can display the data as standard musical notation. A graphic editor also lets you draw continuous CC messages, such as Modulation, on the screen with a mouse or other pointing device. In the case of programs that offer several different editing modes, it's important to remember that you're always working with the same musical information. The different modes simply provide different ways of looking at and working with the musical data.

Step-Time Sequencing

1. Select the part you wish to record and set the keyboard's transmit channel accordingly.
2. On the sequencer, select step-time recording, select the track on which you wish to record, enable its Record function, and press Record.
3. On the sequencer, select the duration value (whole note, eighth note triplet, etc.) for the first note or chord.
4. On the keyboard, play the first note or chord. You needn't play any particular rhythm or duration. The sequencer simply records the note or chord you play and assigns the specified duration to it.
5. On the sequencer, select the duration value for the next note or chord and play it on the keyboard.
6. Repeat step 5 until the entire part is recorded.
7. On the sequencer, press Rewind and disable the track's Record function.
8. Press Play if you want to hear the part you just recorded. You might have to exit step-time mode and adjust the tempo setting.
9. Select the next part to record and follow steps 1 through 8. Repeat these steps until all parts are recorded.

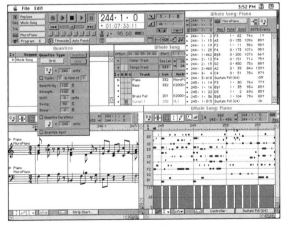

Figure 7-2. Opcode's *Studio Vision Pro* lets you edit in an event list, piano-roll graphic window, or standard musical notation.

Quantization

One of the most important editing functions is quantization, which lets you clean up sloppy rhythms in several different ways. Basically, it shifts each selected event to coincide with the nearest user-specified rhythmic position. It's usually applied to notes, but it can be applied to other MIDI messages in some sequencers.

For example, let's say you apply quarter-note quantization to all the notes in a particular track. If a note starts right on a quarter-note position (beat 1, 2, 3, etc.), it is left alone. However, if the note starts slightly ahead of a quarter-note position, it is shifted back to coincide with that position. Similarly, a note that starts a bit late is shifted forward. This helps clean up slightly sloppy playing, but notes that are far off the mark might get shifted to an unintended position (see Fig. 7-3).

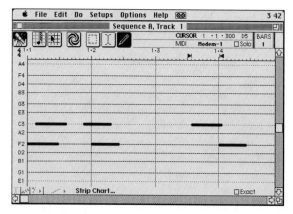

Figure 7-3. In this example, the C3 eighth notes are not quantized while the F2 eighth notes were played with the same rhythm and quantized to quarter note resolution. In both cases, all notes are supposed to start on consecutive beats. Notice that the first note was played a bit late and the second note was played a bit early, but both were shifted to their correct positions. The third note was played so late that it was shifted to beat four instead of beat three.

Quantization is almost always applied to Note On events. It can also be applied to Note Off events, although this sometimes changes the duration of the notes, and the result sounds like it was entered in step time. Most sequencers offer the option to preserve the performed duration of quantized notes by shifting Note Off events by the same amount as the Note On events.

In general, you should use a quantization value equal to the shortest note in the section to be quantized. If you have alternating triplet and duplet figures, you should quantize each figure separately. This is a tedious chore, but quantizing eighth-note triplets into straight eighth notes destroys the triplets.

In early sequencers, quantization was an all-or-nothing proposition; the selected notes were shifted to coincide exactly with the nearest specified rhythmic position. However, the quantization function in modern sequencers includes a variety of parameters that let you apply partial quantization to improve the rhythmic accuracy of the part while retaining some of the human feel in the performance.

For example, a strength parameter lets you specify how far each note should be shifted; if you specify a strength of 50%, the selected notes will be shifted halfway toward the quantized rhythmic position from their current location. Sensitivity lets you specify which events are shifted. If a note falls within a user-specified distance from the nearest quantization position, it is not shifted; if it falls outside this range, it is shifted.

The swing parameter shifts a string of notes with equal durations so that they correspond to a swing style. In swing jazz, for example, a string of eighth notes is played "long-short-long-short," etc. The relationship between the long and short durations can be specified with the swing parameter; a value of 75% means that a pair of eighth notes will be played as a dotted eighth-sixteenth pair, which emulates the Lawrence Welk style of swing. A value of 66% turns a pair of eighth notes into a quarter-eight triplet, which corresponds to a more modern style of swing.

The quantization function in many sequencers also includes a randomization parameter, which randomly shifts the selected events away from the specified rhythmic position within a user-specified range to simulate the inaccuracy of human performance. However, most skilled musicians aren't randomly inaccurate, they are consistently inaccurate, perhaps pushing or dragging the beat. As a result, randomization is not generally satisfying.

Quantizing to an absolute rhythmic position is often called grid quantization. However, many sequencers now offer an alternative called groove quantization. Instead of shifting events to a rhythmic position, groove quantization uses a previously recorded performance as its rhythmic reference. This shifts the quantized events to match the rhythmic "groove" of the reference performance. The rhythmic reference can be extracted from a sequenced part or a digital audio recording, and many sequencers include many groove templates to use in your music.

It's important to recognize when and where quantization should and shouldn't be applied. If you quantize everything, your music will sound mechanical and uninteresting (unless you're into techno, trance, and similar forms of music, in which case it will sound mechanical and interesting). My preference is to quantize as little as possible, but there are situations in which it helps the overall sound. For example, the kick drum and bass parts should be dead-on together, especially on the downbeats, so it might be a good idea to quantize these parts. On the other hand, a lead solo should not be quantized; the juxtaposition of a quantized rhythm section and fluid solo can be quite exciting.

In the sidebar "Sequence Editing," several basic editing functions are illustrated with specific examples. It assumes that several parts already have been recorded on several tracks. Although this procedure probably doesn't apply directly to your own editing needs, it should give you an idea of how to edit your own songs.

Synchronization

Up until now in this discussion of sequencing, the drum machine has been used as a passive sound module and its parts have been recorded into the sequencer along with everything else. But what if you've already programmed some great patterns or songs into the drum machine and you want to use them as is? How do you synchronize its performance with the sequencer so that the drum patterns play in time with the sequencer?

As it turns out, this is relatively easy (see sidebar, "MIDI Synchronization"). The drum machine is placed into external-sync mode, and the sequencer sends System Real-Time messages to it. As discussed in Chapter 6, these messages include Start (which tells the drum machine to start playing from the beginning of the selected pattern or song), Clock (which is sent 24 times per quarter note and therefore defines the tempo), Stop (which tells the drum machine to stop playing), and Continue (which tells the drum machine to start playing from the point at which it was stopped). Another real-time message is Song Position Pointer, which tells the drum machine where to start playing if you jump to another part of the song. (Unfortunately, not all drum machines respond to Song Position Pointer.)

This approach saves memory that could be used to record the drum parts, which is important in small-capacity hardware sequencers. It also lets you use the drum machine as a "groove" metronome, which is more inspiring than a simple click.

While sequencing is invaluable for recording electronic instrumental parts, it can't handle vocals or acoustic instruments. Of course, digital audio sequencers can record acoustic parts (see Chapter 10). Alternatively, if you have a sampler, such as a Kurzweil K2000 or E-mu Emulator-series instrument, you can sample short vocal phrases and trigger them from a MIDI sequencer.

If you want to record acoustic parts on a multitrack tape deck, you must synchronize the sequencer to the tape deck (see "Tape Synchronization" sidebar).

With an analog tape deck (and in some cases, a digital tape deck), a sync signal is recorded on the last track of the multitrack tape (e.g., track four, eight, or sixteen).

One type of sync signal that is rarely used today is called FSK (Frequency Shift Keying). This signal consists of two alternating frequencies recorded onto the tape from the sequencer. The rate at which they alternate is determined by the tempo of the sequence. As shown in Fig. 7-1, this is accomplished with an extra device called a sync converter that takes the MIDI Clock messages from the sequencer and converts them into an FSK signal. This signal is recorded (or striped) onto the tape by playing the entire song in the sequencer, which means that the length of the composition must be decided and at least some of the parts must be sequenced before the sync signal is recorded. The recorded FSK signal is then played back and converted into MIDI Clocks for the sequencer, which is placed in external-sync mode like the drum machine in the previous procedure. Some

Sequence Editing

1. To transpose the horn part up an octave, select the track on which the part was recorded and apply an upward transposition of twelve semitones.

2. To layer the bass part with the other bass sound on channel 6 in the multitimbral sound module, select the bass track, copy it, and paste it to an empty track. Now select the new track and assign it to channel 6.

3. To shift the snare-drum part slightly behind the beat, select the snare track and shift backward by several clock pulses. Listen to the result and adjust until it sounds right.

4. To quantize the kick-drum and bass parts (assuming that the parts have no triplets and notes no shorter than sixteenths), select the appropriate tracks and apply sixteenth-note quantization. You might have to adjust some notes individually if they are too far from their intended rhythmic positions.

5. Once the drum tracks are edited to your satisfaction, you can merge them together. Select one track as the final merged drum track and merge the other drum tracks into it. You might have to do this one track at a time.

6. Your solo lead line is perfect except for one wrong note. Select the note and change its pitch to correct the error.

sequencers provide a direct FSK input and output, eliminating the need for a separate sync converter.

The advantage of FSK is that it's inexpensive. The drawback is that there is no way to start the tape in the middle of a song and have the sequencer "chase" to that location. With regular FSK, the sequencer simply starts at the beginning, no matter where you are on tape. An enhanced FSK signal called Smart FSK includes positional information that allows the use of Song Position Pointer for this purpose.

Nowadays, a type of sync signal called SMPTE time code is used far more often than FSK. Developed by the Society of Motion Picture and Television Engineers, this sync signal represents the passage of time in hours, minutes, seconds, frames (which reflects its film and video origins), and bits. (SMPTE time code uses 80 bits to represent each time value, including hours, minutes, seconds, and frames. Therefore, each frame is specified with 80 bits, and many SMPTE devices can work at the bit level.) SMPTE time code allows sequencers to start playing at any point in the song based on the tape's position.

SMPTE time code was originally developed to synchronize film and video, which run at different standard frame rates. For example, film runs at 24 frames per second (fps) throughout the world, but video is a different story. In Europe and elsewhere, video runs at 25 fps. In the early days of black-and-white television, video in the U.S. ran at 30 fps; current color video runs at 29.97 fps.

This fractional frame rate causes some problems. In the U.S., video frames are numbered from 0 to 29. Although the frame rate is 29.97 fps, SMPTE time code still counts 30 frames as one second. As a result, SMPTE time slowly starts to lag behind real time (as measured by a clock on the wall) at a rate of about 3.6 seconds per hour.

One solution to this problem is to skip a frame once in a while so that SMPTE time remains in sync with real time. This process is called drop frame, or simply drop. Specifically, drop-frame SMPTE skips frame numbers 0 and 1 at the beginning of every minute that is not a multiple of 10. If all frame numbers are used, it is called non-drop frame, or non-drop. In general, musicians who are not scoring film or video soundtracks don't need to worry about this; just use 30 fps non-drop SMPTE time code.

Typically, a type of sync converter called a SMPTE generator/reader is required to use SMPTE with sequencers. (These devices are often built into multiport MIDI interfaces.) However, the procedure is slightly different. For example, you generally specify a frame rate and type (drop or non-drop) and stripe SMPTE time code for the entire length of the tape. This can be done before any parts are sequenced because the time code represents absolute time rather than relative time. For each song, you specify the SMPTE time value (called the SMPTE offset) at which the song begins. (Make sure that the sequencer is set to the same frame rate as you used when striping the time code on tape.)

In addition, SMPTE time code is typically converted into MIDI Time Code (MTC) instead of Clock messages within the converter. MTC was added to the System Common messages to represent the passage of absolute time in MIDI systems, just like SMPTE time code does in film and video systems. As such, it represents time in hours, minutes, seconds, frames, and quarter frames, so it's easy to convert between SMPTE and MTC.

Tape Synchronization

1. Place the sequencer in Master or Internal sync mode.
2. On the tape deck, enable the Record function on the sync track.
3. Press Play on the sequencer. (Some sequencers have a separate Stripe command that performs this task.)
4. On the tape deck, adjust the input level for the sync track to read between 0 and +3.
5. Press Stop on the sequencer and then Rewind.
6. On the tape deck, press Record.
7. On the sequencer, press Play.
8. When the song is finished, wait a few extra seconds and press Stop on the tape deck.
9. Press Rewind on the sequencer and the tape deck.
10. If you have an outboard synchronizer (as opposed to a SMPTE generator/reader that is built into your MIDI interface), disconnect the sequencer's MIDI Out from the sync converter's MIDI In and connect the keyboard's MIDI Out to the sync converter's MIDI In. This lets you sequence additional parts while the sequencer is synched to the tape.
11. Place the sequencer in External or MIDI sync mode and press Play or Record.
12. On the tape deck, disable the Record function on the sync track and press Play. The sequencer will start playing.
13. You can now record any acoustic parts on the other tape tracks along with the sequenced parts. You also can record new parts into the sequencer.

Now that you have a basic understanding of the fundamentals of sequencing, try it for yourself. There's no substitute for the teacher of experience. And remember: The tools of electronic music exist to help us develop our ideas, not to intimidate us into creative stagnation. So go on, show them who's the boss around your studio!

MIDI Synchronization

1. On the sequencer, set the sync mode to Master or Internal.
2. On the drum machine, set the sync mode to Slave, MIDI, or External.
3. On the drum machine, select the pattern or song you wish to play with the sequencer. You can automate this on some machines by sending a Program Change message from the sequencer. You insert this event at the beginning of the sequence.
4. Press Play on the drum machine. It won't start playing; instead, it's put into a mode that waits for a Start message from the sequencer.
5. Press Play or Record on the sequencer. The drum machine will start playing in sync with the sequencer.
6. Press Stop on the sequencer. The drum machine will stop with the sequencer. Pressing Continue on the sequencer would start the two again from the stopping point.

STANDARD MIDI FILES

Although sequencers are great for recording, editing, and playing MIDI performances, they have one drawback: Files recorded in one sequencer generally cannot be used in another sequencer. Each sequencer uses its own file format, which is mutually incompatible with the file formats of other sequencers.

Fortunately, a solution to this problem has been developed and adopted into the official MIDI spec: Standard MIDI Files (SMFs). If a sequence is saved as an SMF, it can be opened by any sequencer that supports this standard file format. This means musicians can share sequences, even if they use different sequencers on different computers. One musician might record the basic rhythm tracks into a Macintosh sequencer and send the file to a collaborator, who then records the lead lines and solos on a Windows-based machine.

Chunky Soup

An SMF represents one or more sequences, which can include multiple channels of MIDI data on one or more tracks. The sequence data is divided into sections called chunks. The first chunk is called the header, which includes information about the entire file, such as the file's format (more in a moment), the number of tracks, and the rhythmic resolution (which is also called the division) in pulses per quarter note (ppqn) or SMPTE frame rate and pulses per frame.

Following the header are track chunks, which represent the sequence tracks and contain the actual MIDI data and other information. Track chunks can include three kinds of events: MIDI Channel messages (such as Note On, Pitch Bend, and Sustain Pedal), SysEx events (which can be of virtually any length), and meta-events (which are non-MIDI events; more in a moment).

Each event in a track chunk is preceded by a delta-time value, which specifies the amount of time since the previous event. This value insures that each event is sent at the proper moment. Delta-time is expressed in pulses as specified in the header's division parameter.

All chunks begin with a type and length parameter. The type parameter specifies whether it's a header or track chunk, and the length parameter specifies the number of bytes in the chunk. The maximum length for each chunk is over 268 MB, which is larger than most sequences ever get.

Formats

All SMFs conform to one of three formats: Type 0, 1, or 2. Type 0 files contain a single track, which can include data on multiple MIDI channels (see Fig. 7-4 [top]). This is the most easily interchangeable format; it is often used with simple MIDI file players, such as the Yamaha MDF2.

Type 1 files contain one or more tracks that are played simultaneously. Unlike Type 0 files, each track includes data on only one MIDI channel (see Fig. 7-4 [bottom]). This is the most common format for multitrack sequencers. In fact, most modern sequencers can save and open Type 0 and 1 SMFs. If you save a multitrack sequence as Type 0, all tracks are merged into one multichannel track.

Type 2 files contain one or more tracks that are played sequentially, one after the other. This is useful for sequencers that chain several independent patterns together into an entire song, which is similar to the way in which many drum machines operate. This format is rarely used; a few sequencers can read Type 2 files, but I know of none that save sequences in this format.

Meta-Events

As mentioned earlier, SMFs can include non-MIDI events, which are called meta-events. Like chunks, meta-events start with a type and length designator, followed by the actual data. Meta-events can be up to 268 MB in length, which is far more than any current application requires.

```
┌─────────────────────────────────────────┐
│▤▤▤▤▤▤▤▤    Seq A: SMF Type 0    ▤▤▤▤▤▤▤║⬆│
├─────────────────────────────────────────┤
│SYNC  Speed      OFFSET  00:00:00:00.00 ▲│
│  •  │  │Meter  4/4  │Seq Len│  Start    │▓│
│  •  │  │Tempo  42.00│  71   │  1 .0     │▓│
├─────────────────────────────────────────┤
│ RecMuteSolo      Loop Length  Instrument │
│1 ▷│ │  │All Tracks    │ 71  │Multi      │▓│
│2 •│ │  │  (empty)     │     │           │ │
│3 •│ │  │  (empty)     │     │           │ │
│4 •│ │  │  (empty)     │     │           │ │
│5 •│ │  │  (empty)     │     │           │ │
│6 •│ │  │  (empty)     │     │           │ │
│7 •│ │  │  (empty)     │     │           │ │
│8 •│ │  │  (empty)     │     │           │ │
│9 •│ │  │  (empty)     │     │           │ │
│10•│ │  │  (empty)     │     │           │ │
├─────────────────────────────────────────┤⬇│
│TRACK 1 │PLAY □Atks ♪│□Durs ♪│SHIFT    │▣│
│        │QUANTIZE  ♩ │    ♪  │     0   │  │
└─────────────────────────────────────────┘
```

```
┌─────────────────────────────────────────┐
│▤▤▤▤▤▤▤▤    Seq B: SMF Type 1    ▤▤▤▤▤▤▤║⬆│
├─────────────────────────────────────────┤
│SYNC  Speed      OFFSET  00:00:00:00.00 ▲│
│  •  │  │Meter  4/4  │Seq Len│  Start    │▓│
│  •  │  │Tempo 120.00│  71   │  1 .0     │▓│
├─────────────────────────────────────────┤
│ RecMuteSolo      Loop Length  Instrument │
│1 •│ │  │A. Guitar     │ 71  │MIDI File-1 │
│2 •│ │  │Slide Jazz    │ 71  │MIDI File-2 │
│3 •│ │  │Chords        │ 71  │MIDI File-3 │
│4 •│ │  │Country       │ 71  │MIDI File-4 │
│5 •│ │  │Whammy        │ 71  │MIDI File-5 │
│6 •│ │  │Jazz          │ 71  │MIDI File-6 │
│7 •│ │  │Lead 1        │ 71  │MIDI File-7 │
│8 •│ │  │Ghost         │ 71  │MIDI File-8 │
│9 •│ │  │Ghost         │ 71  │MIDI File-9 │
│10▷│ │  │Drums         │ 68  │MIDI File-10│
├─────────────────────────────────────────┤⬇│
│TRACK 10│PLAY □Atks ♪│□Durs ♪│SHIFT    │▣│
│        │QUANTIZE  ♩ │    ♪  │     0   │  │
└─────────────────────────────────────────┘
```

Figure 7-4. Type 0 SMFs (top) include multiple channels of MIDI data in one track. In contrast, Type 1 SMFs (bottom) include multiple tracks, each with data on one MIDI channel.

The SMF specification allows up to 128 different types of meta-events, of which fifteen are currently defined. This leaves the door open for future development, which is one of MIDI's greatest strengths. Sequencers are not required to support all types of meta-events, but they should gracefully ignore any meta-events they don't support.

Many of the defined meta-events accommodate text within the SMF. There are several specific types of text events, including Copyright Notice, Sequence/ Track Name, and Instrument Name. In addition, the Marker event lets you insert text that identifies different sections of the music (e.g., "Verse 1," "Chorus,"

"Bridge"), and the Cue Point event lets you notate onscreen action that corresponds with a musical moment in a film or video score (e.g., "car crashes into wall" or "door opens").

Sequence Number, which is used mainly in Type 2 SMFs to identify different patterns in a song, is another meta-event. It can also be used to distinguish between several Type 0 or 1 SMFs transmitted as a single file. As you might surmise, the End of Track event identifies the end of a track chunk, and Set Tempo specifies the tempo in microseconds per quarter note. The SMPTE Offset event specifies the SMPTE time at which a track chunk is to start; in Type 1 files, it must be stored with the tempo map in the first track.

Two fundamental meta-events, Time Signature and Key Signature, are particularly critical for opening SMFs in notation programs (see Chapter 10). There is also a meta-event called Sequencer Specific. This is the "SysEx" of SMFs; it represents information specific to a particular sequencer.

Among the new meta-events being developed is the Lyric event, which represents each syllable of the lyrics with a separate event. Others include Audio events, which represent audio data from a digital audio sequencer, and Output Port, which identified the MIDI or audio port destination for a track.

Cross-Platform Transfers

The entire *raison d'être* of SMFs is to allow sequences to be shared among different sequencers and computer platforms. However, opening an SMF on a computer other than the type that created it is not always as easy as you might think. Most of the issues concern opening PC files on the Mac, so we'll focus on that first.

A Macintosh equipped with a 1.44 MB (high-density) floppy-disk drive can recognize floppy disks and files from a PC by adding a system extension. If you have System 7.0 or later, for example, you can use Apple's PC Exchange Control Panel to mount PC disks and make them look and operate like Mac disks. Users of System 6.0.7 or later can use a third-party product such as Software Architects' *DOS Mounter 95*, which lets you access a variety of DOS and Windows media, including removables, and offers several handy bells and whistles. Mac veterans might recall mounting PC disks or Apple II disks (really!) on the Mac using *Apple File Exchange*, but that program is outdated.

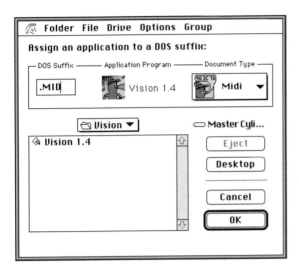

Figure 7-5. The PC Exchange control panel's Add dialog box lets you specify the Mac application that will open a PC SMF and the type of document it will be, which correspond to the Creator and File Type parameters.

After the Mac recognizes the disk, you must change the File Type and Creator of SMFs that originated on a PC before they can be opened by a Mac program. There are several ways to accomplish this. PC Exchange can be set up to change these parameters as it copies an SMF (identified by a ".MID" extension) from a PC disk to a Mac disk. In the control panel's Add dialog box, you specify the application that will open the file (which establishes the Creator parameter) and the Document (File) Type (see Fig. 7-5).

ResEdit, another commonly available utility, can also be used to change the File Type and Creator of an SMF (see Fig. 7-6). It's important to open a copy of the file you wish to tweak with *ResEdit* rather than the original to avoid any possible corruption of the data. Select Get Info from the File menu. In the Get Info dialog box, change the File Type to "Midi" (be sure to type an upper-case "M" and lower-case "idi").

The Creator can be any four capital letters. For consistency, you might specify the same Creator code used by the manufacturer of your software. For example, Mark of the Unicorn's *Performer* uses the Creator code MOUP, and Opcode uses OPCD. In *ResEdit*, open a copy of any file created by the software you want to use and note the Creator code used by that software. Alternatively, you could use "MIDI" as a generic Creator code; just make sure it's all capital letters in this case.

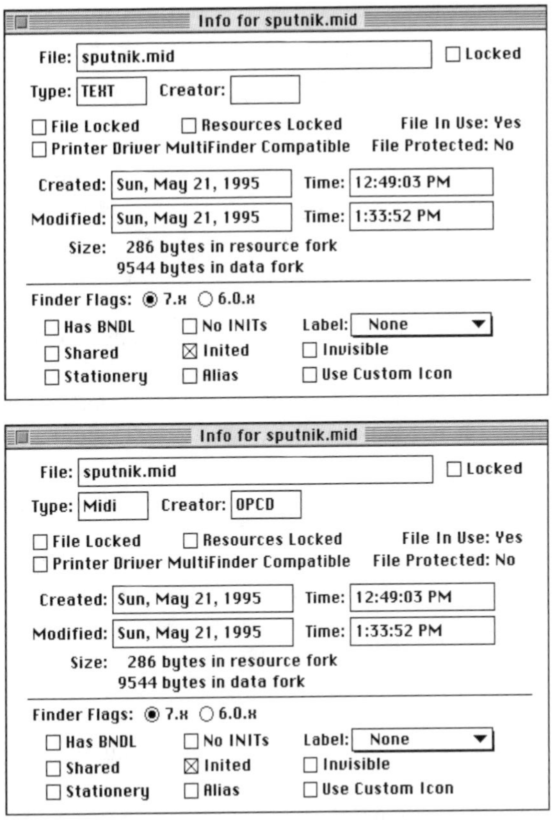

Figure 7-6. If you open a PC SMF in *ResEdit* on a Mac, the File Type and Creator typically look like those in the upper window. Change these fields to look like the lower window before opening the file in a Mac program.

A shareware utility called *Midi Typer* offers a slick way to make these changes; simply drag one or more SMF icons (or folders or even entire disks) onto the *Midi Typer* icon and you're done; the files can now be opened with the Mac program you specify. *Midi Typer* is available on various BBSs and Internet sites, or you can e-mail the author, Peter Castine, at pcastine@prz.tu-berlin.de.

Opening a Mac-created SMF on a PC is much easier, especially if the person with the Mac is considerate enough to copy the file onto a DOS-format floppy disk. If you then rename the file with a DOS-style name (up to eight characters followed by a 3-character extension), most PC programs should be able to open the file. Life will be much easier if you use a standard 3-character extension such as .MID.

To mount a Mac-format floppy disk directly on your PC, you need a third-party application. Software Architects' *Here & Now* essentially does for PC folks what *DOS Mounter 95* does for Mac users: it seamlessly reads Mac files on virtually any type of media. Another possibility is *MacOpener* from Data Viz.

If your transfer needs are simple, you also might want to check out shareware programs, such as *Trans-*

mac, which can be found on the World Wide Web. *Transmac* has a file-size limit of 1.4 MB, but that's more than enough to handle an SMF.

Transfer Issues

If you want to transfer a file from one sequencer to another, you might be tempted to connect them via MIDI and simply play the file on the source machine while recording on the destination machine. However, this can cause some problems.

For example, if the sequence includes a tempo map, this information is not sent via MIDI in real time. If you slave the destination to the source and perform a real-time transfer, the music won't play back correctly on the destination machine, which uses its own specified tempo, not the tempo map of the original sequence. If you don't synchronize the machines during the transfer, the music will play properly, but it will no longer correspond to the original bar lines. To avoid these problems, save the file as an SMF and open it on the destination machine.

Occasionally, transferring SMFs between platforms does not go as smoothly as expected, however. You may encounter a few quirks that require you to experiment a bit. One important issue to keep in mind is rhythmic resolution. If you record an SMF with a high resolution (e.g., 480 ppqn) and open it in a program that doesn't support resolutions that high, some events might be moved, destroying the rhythm. Most sequencers can accommodate 192 ppqn resolution, so that's a safe choice.

The issue of resolution is particularly important for Pitch Bend messages. If you record Pitch Bend messages with high resolution and then play them back with low resolution, several messages are likely to be moved to the same clock pulse. In this case, the last Pitch Bend message to be played might not be at the nominal value, which would affect the tuning of the following notes.

Another potential anomaly might appear when a sequencer tries to convert between Type 0 and Type 1 SMFs. If you load a Type 0 file (single track with multiple channels) into a multitrack sequencer that can accommodate only one channel per track, it must separate the file's channels onto separate tracks. Most sequencers can do this.

The Roland MC-50 mk II and Super MRC sequencer systems accept Type 0 or 1 SMFs, but they have only eight tracks. If the SMF includes more than eight channels, all channels between 9 and 16 are assigned to track 8, which could be confusing. Roland's MV-30 sequencer/sound module has sixteen tracks, but it only uses tracks 9 through 16 for SMFs.

Although the Roland Sound Brush is no longer manufactured, there are many of these SMF players

in the field. If you have one, keep in mind that it can play Type 0 or Type 1 files, but no more than sixteen tracks; if the file includes more than sixteen tracks, it won't play. The Sound Brush also has trouble playing files that are close to this limit, so it's better to use Type 0 files with this device.

In addition, the Sound Brush and most Roland General MIDI products that include a disk drive can accommodate only double-density (720 KB) disks. However, the newer XP-50 and XP-80 can accept high-density (1.44 MB) disks. When in doubt, use double-density disks to store SMFs.

A New Industry

In addition to helping musicians share their musical files, SMFs have spawned an entirely new industry. A number of companies create complete SMFs of popular tunes, which are primarily marketed for karaoke but can also be used for rehearsal and on gigs. Any musical part in the tune can be muted, which lets you play along on the instrument of your choice. Other companies produce rhythm loops and other musical phrases in various styles. These SMFs can be used to inspire your own creative juices or enhance existing tunes; they can also be used as groove-quantization templates.

Of course, SMFs can be used with any synthesizer or sound module, but the patches in a particular device's memory might not match the instruments intended by the creators of the sequence. For this reason, most commercial SMFs are designed for General MIDI sound modules (discussed later in this chapter).

Standard MIDI Files are great for anyone who wants to share their music with other electronic musicians. They also allow commercial music to be distributed in a new way. (In Japan, people buy SMFs for dedicated MIDI players that include their own multitimbral sound module. These SMFs serve the same function as CDs, except for the fact that you can reorchestrate and otherwise tweak the music.) With a little understanding, you can use SMFs to create and/or preserve your music for generations to come.

GENERAL MIDI

MIDI is a great benefit to musicians everywhere because it lets computers and electronic instruments from different manufacturers share information about what to play and how to play it. In addition, computers can be used to record, edit, and play sequences of MIDI messages on various sound modules.

However, sharing sequences between systems can be problematic. Standard MIDI Files (SMFs) allow most sequencers to read and play sequences from different systems, but how does the composer know what instruments are included in someone else's system? Suppose you try to create a sequence that has a piano part, and the desired piano sound in your synth is called up with Program Change 13 on channel 5. How do you know this Program Change will call up a piano patch in the instrument assigned to channel 5 in another MIDI system?

The answer is, you don't. Program Change 13 might call up a flute, synth pad, or any other type of sound in the instrument assigned to channel 5 in another system. This patch would then be used to play the piano part, which might be interesting but would not be what you intended.

Fortunately, an addition to the MIDI Specification called General MIDI (GM) solves this problem. (The complete name of this addition is "General MIDI Level 1"; a Level 2 spec is in the works. For now, I'm referring to Level 1.) GM defines minimum performance criteria and standard Program Change and drum-note maps for sound modules. Any synth that conforms to these criteria can be used to play a GM sequence with the correct sounds.

GM is primarily concerned with how a device responds to MIDI messages, so it applies equally to sound modules, keyboard synths with internal sound engines, sound cards, motherboard audio circuitry, and software synths. Of course, any sequence that is intended for GM instruments must send messages that conform to these criteria, as well.

Minimum Specs

To be certified as a GM synth, an instrument must meet certain minimum performance criteria. First, a GM synth must include a standard set of 128 instrumental patches that are called up with a standard set of Program Change messages (see table, "GM Sound Set"). In addition, it must include at least one drum kit with 47 percussion sounds assigned to a fixed set of MIDI note numbers (see table, "GM Percussion Map").

Even though all GM synths include the same set of sounds, they are not all created equal. In fact, some musicians object to the wimpy quality of many GM sounds. One reason many GM synths sound wimpy is that they were created to emulate the original Roland Sound Canvas module, which replaced the Roland MT-32 as a *de facto* standard for computer-based music-playback applications, such as game music. Many commercial SMFs that implement GM were also originally designed with Sound Canvas playback in mind.

But the first Sound Canvases sounded wimpier than the professional synths a lot of musicians use, and their patches were set at very conservative output levels in order to ensure consistent SMF playback. In fact, if you boost the levels of the GM patches in some synths, you might be surprised at how much better they sound. Today, there are several GM synths that sound quite good without editing and can be used in fully professional situations.

In order to play complete arrangements, a GM synth must be 16-part multitimbral; i.e., it must be able to respond to messages on all sixteen channels at once. The drum kit is played on channel 10. All other instruments can be played on any channel except 10, and no other instrumental sounds can be played on channel 10.

This channel assignment arises from tradition. In the early days of MIDI, Roland used channel 10 for drum parts, and Yamaha used channel 16. Channel 10 probably became the GM drum channel because Roland products, particularly the MT-32, were very popular in the computer sound market. In addition, Roland contributed heavily to the original GM proposals.

A GM synth must be capable of 24-voice polyphony. These voices can be allocated to musical parts in one of two ways. All 24 voices can be dynamically allocated among the melodic and percussion instruments, or sixteen voices can be dynamically allocated among the melodic instruments with eight voices reserved for percussion.

The use of controllers is also standardized. A GM synth must respond to Velocity, Channel Pressure, and Pitch Bend as well as Control Changes (CCs) 1, 7, 10, 11, 64, 121, and 123. These correspond to Modulation, Volume, Pan, Expression, Sustain, Reset All Controllers, and All Notes Off. In addition, it must recognize Registered Parameter Numbers (RPNs) 0, 1, and 2, which correspond to Pitch Bend Sensitivity, Fine Tuning, and Coarse Tuning. When a GM synth powers up, the default conditions for each channel are:

Pitch Bend = 0
Pitch Bend Sensitivity = ±2 semitones
Channel Pressure = 0
Modulation = 0
Volume = 100
Pan = 64 (center)
Expression = 127
Sustain = 0 (off)

Although they aren't detailed in the GM spec, Data Entry messages (CC 6 and 38) also must be implemented in order to change RPN values. In addition, there are a number of other recommendations that are not officially required by GM Level 1—they were decided upon after the Level 1 spec was finalized—but will be required for Level 2 compatibility.

GM SOUND SET

PC#	INSTRUMENT	PC#	INSTRUMENT	PC#	INSTRUMENT	PC#	INSTRUMENT
	PIANO		**BASS**		**REEDS**		**SYNTH EFFECTS**
1	Acoustic Grand	33	Acoustic	65	Soprano Sax	97	Rain
2	Bright Acoustic	34	Electric (Finger)	66	Alto Sax	98	Soundtrack
3	Electric Grand	35	Electric (Pick)	67	Tenor Sax	99	Crystal
4	Honky Tonk	36	Fretless	68	Baritone Sax	100	Atmosphere
5	Electric Piano 1	37	Slap Bass 1	69	Oboe	101	Brightness
6	Electric Piano 2	38	Slap Bass 2	70	English Horn	102	Goblins
7	Harpsichord	39	Synth Bass 1	71	Bassoon	103	Echoes
8	Clav	40	Synth Bass 2	72	Clarinet	104	Sci-Fi
	CHROMATIC PERCUSSION		**STRINGS**		**PIPE**		**ETHNIC**
9	Celesta	41	Violin	73	Piccolo	105	Sitar
10	Glockenspiel	42	Viola	74	Flute	106	Banjo
11	Music Box	43	Cello	75	Recorder	107	Shamisen
12	Vibraphone	44	Contrabass	76	Pan Flute	108	Koto
13	Marimba	45	Tremolo Strings	77	Blown Bottle	109	Kalimba
14	Xylophone	46	Pizzicato Strings	78	Shakuhachi	110	Bagpipe
15	Tubular Bells	47	Orchestral Strings	79	Whistle	111	Fiddle
16	Dulcimer	48	Timpani	80	Ocarina	112	Shanai
	ORGAN		**ENSEMBLE**		**SYNTH LEAD**		**PERCUSSION**
17	Drawbar	49	Strings 1	81	Square	113	Tinkle Bell
18	Percussive	50	Strings 2	82	Sawtooth	114	Agogo
19	Rock	51	Synth Strings 1	83	Calliope	115	Steel Drums
20	Church	52	Synth Strings 2	84	Chiff	116	Wood Block
21	Reed	53	Choir Aahs	85	Charang	117	Taiko Drum
22	Accordion	54	Voice Oohs	86	Voice	118	Melodic Tom
23	Harmonica	55	Synth Voice	87	Fifths	119	Synth Drum
24	Tango Accordion	56	Orchestra Hit	88	Bass+Lead	120	Reverse Cymbal
	GUITAR		**BRASS**		**SYNTH PAD**		**SOUND EFFECTS**
25	Acoustic (Nylon)	57	Trumpet	89	New Age	121	Guitar Fret Noise
26	Acoustic (Steel)	58	Trombone	90	Warm	122	Breath Noise
27	Electric (Jazz)	59	Tuba	91	Polysynth	123	Seashore
28	Electric (Clean)	60	Muted Trumpet	92	Choir	124	Bird Tweet
29	Electric (Muted)	61	French Horn	93	Bowed	125	Telephone Ring
30	Overdriven	62	Brass Section	94	Metallic	126	Helicopter
31	Distortion	63	Synth Brass 1	95	Halo	127	Applause
32	Guitar Harmonica	64	Synth Brass 2	96	Sweep	128	Gunshot

Some synths include a GM mode in addition to an individual mode that exceeds the GM spec. This lets you use GM when necessary and the full capabilities of the instrument in other situations. In this case, you can activate GM mode from the front panel or send a GM On message, which is a Universal System Exclusive (SysEx) message. To return to the device's individual mode, you simply push the appropriate button on the front panel or send a GM Off message. This process can be automated by sending the GM On or Off message at the beginning of a sequence.

Extended Systems

As with most things in this business, as soon as GM was established, there were those who felt it was too limited. In particular, Roland and Yamaha have extended the basic GM specs to create their own

"supersets" of GM, which are open specs that can be used by other manufacturers and software developers. Both supersets are fully compatible with GM, so synths that implement them can play GM sequences with no problem.

As you might expect, both systems include more than the basic 128 instrumental sounds and one drum kit, so they use Bank Select in addition to Program Change (see Chapter 9). Of course, the basic 128 patches and 47 drum sounds are available, and devices that conform to one of these supersets can be placed in a strict GM mode by sending a GM On message.

Roland's system is called GS, which is rumored to stand for General System, but the company claims it means nothing at all. GS calls for a minimum of 226 instrumental sounds and can accommodate up to 16,384 patches using Bank Select MSB. In addition, a

Note#	Drum Sound	Note#	Drum Sound	Note#	Drum Sound
35	Acoustic Kick	51	Ride Cymbal 1	67	High Agogo
36	Kick 1	52	Chinese Cymbal	68	Low Agogo
37	Side Stick	53	Ride Bell	69	Cabasa
38	Acoustic Snare	54	Tambourine	70	Maracas
39	Hand Clap	55	Splash Cymbal	71	Short Whistle
40	Electric Snare	56	Cowbell	72	Long Whistle
41	Low Floor Tom	57	Crash Cymbal 2	73	Short Guiro
42	Closed Hi-Hat	58	Vibraslap	74	Long Guiro
43	High Floor Tom	59	Ride Cymbal 2	75	Claves
44	Pedal Hi-Hat	60	Hi Bongo	76	Hi Wood Block
45	Low Tom	61	Low Bongo	77	Low Wood Block
46	Open Hi-Hat	62	Mute Hi Conga	78	Mute Cuica
47	Low-Mid Tom	63	Open Hi Conga	79	Open Cuica
48	Hi-Mid Tom	64	Low Conga	80	Mute Triangle
49	Crash Cymbal 1	65	High Timbale	81	Open Triangle
50	High Tom	66	Low Timbale		

GS device can include up to 128 drum/percussion kits, each with up to 61 sounds.

GS supports twenty different CCs, which allows a great deal of expressive control, and patches can be extensively edited using Non-Registered Parameter Numbers (NRPNs) and SysEx. Optional effects include reverb and chorus, which most GS synths have.

Several companies, especially sound-card manufacturers, have adopted GS as their playback standard. Among these companies is Microsoft, which will include a GS software synth in the next release of Windows.

Yamaha's extended GM system is called XG for eXtended GM. XG is an even larger superset than GS; for example, it specifies a minimum of 480 instrumental sounds and can accommodate over 2 million thanks to the use of Bank Select MSB and LSB. It also specifies a minimum of nine drum kits, each with up to 72 sounds, and two sound-effects kits.

Yamaha's **MU80** sound module employs the company's **XG** superset of General **MIDI**, which adds more sounds, more controller assignments, and extensive patch-editing capabilities.

XG also implements a wide range of CCs and patch-editing capabilities, and it requires a minimum of three effects processors: reverb (eight types, minimum), chorus (eight types, minimum), and "Varia-tion" (35 types, minimum), which includes a wide variety of effects. The reverb and chorus are applied globally to all channels according to each channel's send level, and the Variation effect can be applied globally or inserted into one channel. All three effects can be used simultaneously and controlled in real time, and a graphic EQ on the final output is optional.

Finally, an XG instrument can optionally include a stereo analog input to digitize one or two audio signals, process them with the internal effects, and mix them with the synth sounds. This is a very powerful system that is implemented in many Yamaha products, including a software synth to be bundled with Dell and Gateway computers, as well as products from Staccato Systems and Mediatrix.

Applications

Of course, the most obvious application of GM and its variants is exchanging sequence files between various systems. This is especially important if you are composing music for multimedia titles and games, which can use GM SMFs with sound cards and sound modules to provide consistent musical soundtracks. This method requires much less data overhead than even the most heavily compressed digital audio. In addition, GM SMFs can be downloaded from the Internet in much less time than audio files, and they can even play in real time while you're logged on. In fact, GM has fostered an entire industry that creates SMFs of popular songs primarily for karaoke but also for use in rehearsal and performance. These mostly consumer-oriented applications have largely driven the GM market.

Having a common sound map is also useful for collaborating composers; you can quickly sketch arrangements with a GM instrument and send them back and forth for tweaking, after which you can replace some or all of the sounds with custom patches from non-GM synths.

GM is ideal for studying arrangements (assuming the person who created them did an accurate job) because you know which part is which. You can also mute any musical part and play along in music-minus-one fashion. Both of these applications are very useful for music education.

GM is the missing link for interchanging SMFs. Without it, your carefully constructed song might sound like caterwauling when played on a different system. With it, your music will sound more or less as you intend it to when played on any GM synth anywhere in the world.

CHAPTER 8

Alternate Controllers

As mentioned in Chapter 6, MIDI was designed around the keyboard paradigm. At that time, electronic musical instruments were universally controlled by keyboards. Since then, however, players of other types of instruments have wanted to get in on the MIDI act, and enterprising engineers have worked hard to oblige them. As a result, a number of alternate controllers are now available, allowing guitarists, drummers, and wind players to join the MIDI band. (MIDI violin controllers also exist, and except for bowing, they work in much the same way as guitar controllers.)

Before we get into these alternate controllers, however, I'd like to discuss some of the common characteristics of keyboard master controllers, which I have not described elsewhere in this book. Unlike keyboard synths and samplers, master controllers normally do not include their own internal sound engine (although an optional sound engine can be added to a few models). Their primary purpose is to control external MIDI sound modules.

One of the most immediately apparent characteristics of keyboard controllers is their action, which determines how the keys feel when you play them. Less expensive and smaller controllers use an unweighted action, which feels like an organ or synthesizer keyboard. A semi-weighted action exhibits more resistance than an unweighted keyboard and feels more "substantial." Larger 88-key controllers often use a weighted action, which tries to duplicate the feel of an acoustic-piano keyboard. Action is the most personal aspect of a controller; if you're a trained keyboard player, some actions feel good and others feel bad.

Any keyboard master controller worth its salt is sensitive to both Velocity and Aftertouch. (More expensive models might even be sensitive to Poly Aftertouch.) You can often tailor the feel of the keyboard to your playing by using the instrument's available Velocity and Aftertouch curves (see Chapter 6).

Keyboard master controllers offer a variety of MIDI capabilities that you can configure in different ways, and these configurations can usually be saved as programs in the controller's user memory. One of the most important capabilities is called zoning. The keyboard on many master controllers can be divided into as many as eight or more zones that send MIDI messages on different channels. These zones can often overlap if you want, which lets you layer two or more sounds in a section of the keyboard.

When you save a program with zones, you can often assign different Program Changes and CC values to each zone. When you recall that program from memory, the assigned Program Changes and CC values are automatically sent to the external sound modules set to the zones' channels. This lets you automatically configure your system by recalling a program on the master controller. In addition, you can manually send individual Program Changes on any channel.

Keyboard master controllers provide a variety of physical controllers to manipulate the sound of external sound modules. Of course, no self-respecting master controller would be caught dead without pitch and modulation wheels (or their equivalent, such as the combo pitch/modulation joystick on many Korg and Roland products). In addition, many master controllers include several rear-panel jacks for footswitches and continuous foot controllers; some also include an extra modulation wheel. The messages sent by these footpedals (and the wheels) are often user-definable.

Some master controllers also include several user-definable sliders and buttons on the front panel, which lets you control many different parameters in the external sound modules. Another type of controller that was popular on pre-MIDI synths and is regaining popularity these days is the ribbon controller, which consists of a flat ribbon on the front panel. As you slide your finger along the ribbon, it sends a user-definable CC message.

Advanced keyboard controllers often provide controller mapping, which lets you reassign each controller message to a different type of message. For example, if the continuous foot pedal is normally assigned to send Volume messages and you need it to send Breath Controller in an isolated situation, you can change the assignment temporarily with a controller map.

Some keyboard controllers let you create a chain of Program Changes that are sent sequentially each time you step on a footswitch. This is great for live gigs in which you know the order of patches you want to recall in the external modules.

Finally, a few keyboard controllers include buttons to control a sequencer. As you might imagine, these buttons are usually labeled Start, Stop, Pause, Record, Fast Forward, and Rewind. This lets you control an external sequencer from the controller, which is particularly useful if you use a sequencer onstage.

GUITAR CONTROLLERS

Guitar players seem to have all the fun. They get to flail around in front of the band, howl with feedback, and smash their instruments. But there is a limit to what they can do. For one thing, their sound palette is somewhat restricted. Sure, they can use all sorts of processors to tweak their sound a million different ways, but you almost always know it's a guitar. If only they could access the unlimited sonic potential keyboard players have enjoyed for years, they'd have it all.

Indeed, they can have it all. MIDI guitar controllers allow guitarists to play synths and samplers. However, it's not as simple as connecting the MIDI Out from a guitar controller to the MIDI In on a synth. MIDI guitars have their own rules. In addition, many guitarists have not worked with MIDI sound sources, and the learning curve can be frustrating.

Many guitar controllers include their own dedicated sound module, which makes them relatively easy to play right out of the box. (These products are generally known as guitar synthesizers to distinguish them from guitar controllers without their own sound engine.) But owners of these all-in-one models eventually want to play external MIDI sound modules and record performances into a MIDI sequencer from their guitar controller.

On the Right Track
Perhaps the most important aspect of guitar synths and controllers is tracking. The primary element of tracking is the speed with which a note is recognized and transmitted to a connected synthesizer. However, tracking is more than pure speed. It also refers to the ability to accurately reproduce guitar-playing techniques, such as slides, string bends, vibrato, hammer-ons, pull-offs, and whammy-bar tricks. Tracking also includes the accurate reproduction of dynamics, which are critically important to expressive guitar playing.

There are two primary types of guitar controllers: fretboard controllers and standard guitars equipped with a special pickup and a pitch-to-MIDI converter. By avoiding the constraints of standard guitars, several manufacturers have developed unique and interesting fretboard controllers, such as the Suzuki Unisynth and Starr Switch Ztar, which have no strings at all. Other designs, such as the Beetle Quantar and Yamaha G10 (see Fig. 8-1), use ultrasonic scanning to detect the pitch of each vibrating string. Some controllers, such as the Synthaxe, Stepp, Zeta Mirror 6, and Peavey CyberBass (see Fig. 8-2), use detectors in the frets and elsewhere to determine which pitches are being played.

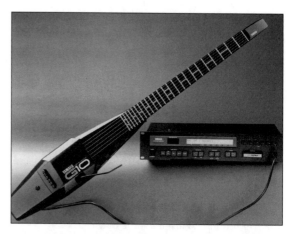

Figure 8-1. The Yamaha G10 uses ultrasonic scanning to detect the vibration frequency of each string.

Figure 8-2. The Peavey CyberBass includes detectors in each fret to determine the pitches you play.

These dedicated controllers are often better at telling a synthesizer what notes to play, because they don't suffer from the delays inherent in pitch-to-MIDI conversion (discussed shortly). However, they are not real guitars, so they don't play like real guitars, and conventional guitar techniques are sometimes impossible. As a result, many players are not willing to learn these instruments, and many fretboard controllers have been discontinued.

Standard guitars can also control synthesizers by installing a special hex pickup, which includes six independent magnetic-field or piezo poles that detect the vibration of each string. This information is sent to a pitch-to-MIDI converter, which then sends the appropriate MIDI messages to any connected synthesizer. Many companies have used this approach, including Casio, Gibson, Ibanez, IVL, Korg, Ovation/Takamine/Charvel, Passac, Photon, Lyrrus, Roland, and New England Digital. Unfortunately, as with fretboard controllers, many of these products are no longer available.

In fact, Roland and Yamaha are among the few viable guitar-controller companies left these days. The Roland GK-2A (see Fig. 8-3) is a magnetic-field hex pickup that can be mounted on your favorite electric or steel-string acoustic guitar without damaging the surface. If you want to control synths with a nylon-string acoustic guitar, you need a piezo hex pickup that is mounted on the bridge to detect the strings' mechanical vibrations. A company called Godin makes a custom nylon-string guitar with such a pickup.

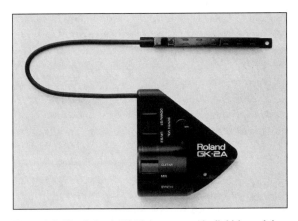

Figure 8-3. The Roland GK-2A is a magnetic-field hex pickup that can be mounted on any electric or steel-string acoustic guitar.

Yamaha's hex pickup is the G1D, which is used in conjunction with their pitch-to-MIDI converters. As of this writing, the company's newest converter is the G50, which detects pitch, picking position (proximity to the pickup), and amplitude envelope. In addition, you can split the strings horizontally based on pick position or vertically into two sets of strings; of course, you can play each string on a different channel, as well. The G50 also includes an analog audio input, which is converted to MIDI messages by the pitch-to-MIDI converter.

Blue Chip is another notable company in this regard. This company makes the Axon NGC 77 guitar-

to-MIDI converter, which uses the Roland GK-2A pickup. (Blue Chip makes their own hex pickup, the AIX-101, which is fully compatible with the GK-2A, and a version for bass guitars, the AIX-102.) The Axon uses neural-network technology to improve the tracking characteristics of its MIDI conversion, which is notoriously slow in most such devices (more in a moment). It also detects pick position in three different zones, and it lets you define string-zone boundaries at any fret and between any two strings. All these zones can control a different channel.

Roland also makes guitar synthesizers, such as the GR-30 and VG-8 (which is really more of a signal processor). These devices can be played with a Godin acoustic guitar or any steel-string guitar with a GK-2A pickup. In this case, the signals from the pickup are not converted into MIDI messages. Instead, they control the synth directly, which results in less tracking delay (more in a moment). In addition, the patches in the Roland GR and VG synths are optimized for guitar control, making them easier to play right away. Of course, these devices also include a MIDI Out jack, which lets you play external synths from the controller.

The biggest advantage of pitch-to-MIDI technology is that it works on any standard guitar. This results in a more natural feel and tracks guitar nuances such as bends and vibrato better than dedicated controllers. However, using a real guitar also has some disadvantages when controlling MIDI devices, particularly tracking delay.

Delayed Gratification

No matter which pitch-to-MIDI system you use, tracking delay is inevitable. This delay is the time between the moment you pluck a string and the moment the synth makes a sound in response. There are three contributing factors to tracking delay: the time it takes to determine the pitch of the note, the time it takes to convert this information into a MIDI message, and the time it takes the receiving synth to respond to the message and make a sound.

The first factor is limited by physics. As a string vibrates, the pitch-to-MIDI converter takes at least one complete cycle to determine its frequency. For example, an open A string on a guitar vibrates at 220 Hz, so each cycle takes about 4.5 milliseconds (ms) to complete. The Roland GR guitar synths take one full cycle to determine the pitch; older pitch-to-MIDI converters require two full cycles.

As mentioned earlier, the Blue Chip Axon uses neural-network technology to address this problem in a different way. The Axon "learns" to recognize the transient characteristics of your playing style, which makes the configuration and setup process very important. Two dedicated processors have been "taught" the initial attacks of all the notes that a guitar or bass can output. The processors then compare the input from your guitar with their library of attack transients, which enables the unit to recognize the pitch much more quickly than normal pitch-to-MIDI conversion.

Once the frequency is known, it must be converted into a MIDI message, using several more milliseconds. Dedicated controllers that use buttons, ultrasonic scanning, or fret detectors exhibit no delay in this process, because the converter knows which note is being fretted before the string is plucked.

After a MIDI message is generated, it takes time to travel from the controller to the synth. For example, each Note On message takes 0.768 ms to transmit, so a 6-note chord takes about 4.5 ms. If you include Pitch Bend messages, this delay increases even further. Once the synth receives a message, more time is taken to process it and make a sound. For example, the E-mu Proteus takes 4 ms to respond to a single Note On message, while the Yamaha DX7 takes about 6 ms. If you call up a complex, multilayer patch that uses a lot of the synth's oscillators and play a 6-note chord on six different MIDI channels, it can take an instrument, such as the Korg M1 or Roland JD-990, as much as 20 to 30 ms to respond completely.

These final transmission and processing delays are common to all MIDI devices, but keyboard players are used to them; guitarists might have some trouble adjusting at first. With some practice and minor modifications to your playing technique, however, you can become accustomed to these delays.

In addition, you must learn to play each sound for what it is. For example, don't strum a saxophone sound. Try to think like a player of the instrument you are emulating. In addition, you must generally play slightly ahead of the beat to compensate for delays. Don't lay back!

MIDI Out

All MIDI guitar controllers send Note On and Note Off messages. Velocity information is derived from the initial amplitude of the string's vibration. However, no information about the string's amplitude envelope is transmitted, so the controller sends a Note Off message when the vibration falls below a certain amplitude threshold. Of course, you can stop a note by damping the string, but if you let it ring, the controller will eventually send a Note Off whether you want it to or not. (Dedicated controllers without strings don't suffer from this problem.)

If the pickup is set to a low sensitivity, or it is too far from the strings, notes played on the guitar might not be detected. Even if they are detected, they don't last long. To increase the time a note can last, you must increase the sensitivity of the pickup. However, if you set the sensitivity too high, the controller will transmit lots of unwanted "ghost" notes at high Velocities. The proper setting usually transmits notes in the upper part of the Velocity range (the average value is around 100), and you must also find the appropriate Velocity curve in the receiving synth (discussed shortly).

Guitar controllers also transmit Pitch Bend messages to convey string bends, vibrato, slides, hammer-ons, and pull-offs. However, guitars have six strings, each of which can be bent independently. Moving the pitch-bend wheel on a keyboard normally bends all sounding notes by the same amount.

As a result, most guitar controllers transmit in one of two modes: Poly and Mono. In Poly mode, all six strings transmit on the same MIDI channel. As long as you play single-note lines, Pitch Bend messages are sent as usual. But as soon as you play two or more notes simultaneously, most controllers stop transmitting Pitch Bend messages. Otherwise, the receiving synth would sound out of tune under a barrage of conflicting messages.

In Mono mode, each string's note and Pitch Bend messages are sent on a separate MIDI channel. You can still play chords in Mono mode, but this takes up several channels in the receiving synth. However, the controller plays like a normal guitar as long as the receiving synth is programmed to respond accordingly (more in a moment).

Another important controller parameter is pitch-bend range. Most synths have a maximum bend range of twelve semitones (one octave), while most guitars can bend as much as two octaves by sliding up and down the neck. It's important to set the controller's bend range to the same value as the synth's to avoid sounding out of tune. If you are playing a patch that uses no pitch bend, turn the controller's bend range off (set it to zero); this is sometimes called Chromatic mode.

It certainly helps if the controller can transmit other messages, such as Program Change. This lets you select a synth patch from the controller itself, which is mighty handy.

MIDI In

When selecting an appropriate synthesizer to use with a MIDI guitar controller, there are several things to consider. First, it must be able to respond on six MIDI channels at once. This is not a problem if you have a recent model that offers at least 6-part multitimbral operation (see Chapter 6). Some older monotimbral synthesizers, such as the Roland D-50 and Oberheim Matrix series, can play the same patch monophonically on six consecutive channels if they are set to

MIDI Mode 2 (Omni On/Mono; see Chapter 6). However, they still don't work as well as modern, multitimbral synths.

The second critical feature is a maximum pitch-bend range of at least twelve semitones; 24 is even better. In many synthesizers, this is a global parameter for the entire unit, but in some cases, the bend range is memorized with each patch. It might take a while to adjust this parameter for every patch in the unit, but the flexibility it offers is well worth the time.

The synthesizer should also offer programmable Velocity curves. At the least, it must have several pre-set curves. Select or program a curve in which the upper part of the Velocity range controls the widest possible range of volume levels.

Some synths offer two special response modes, which are often called Solo and Legato. In Solo mode, the synth plays only one note at a time. If you can assign Solo mode to each part in a multitimbral synth, it will respond to a guitar controller more like a real guitar. In this case, the controller should also be set to its Mono mode, which sends messages from each string on its own MIDI channel.

If the synth is in Legato mode and it receives two Note On messages without an intervening Note Off, it turns off the first note and plays the second note, but it does not retrigger the envelope generator. This lets you play smoothly from one note to the next without hearing the programmed attack. (If it receives the first note's Off message before the second note's On, it behaves just like Solo mode.) Legato mode helps the synth respond well to different playing techniques, such as neck slides, hammer-ons, and pull-offs. It also helps differentiate various articulations.

Using a MIDI guitar or fretboard controller requires a solid understanding of the controller's capabilities as well as the capabilities of the responding MIDI sound module. There are also a number of variables unique to these controllers. Of course, the electronic-instrument market has more keyboardists than guitarists, so most synths are designed to work with a keyboard. However, this isn't a problem if you take the time to learn everything you can about the gear you use.

PERCUSSION CONTROLLERS

You've probably heard some variation of the old joke by now: "The band has three musicians and a drummer." But despite their much-maligned reputation, drummers *are* musicians in every sense of the word. Unfortunately, they don't get to explore the realms of melody or harmony as often as other musicians; their gig's in the rhythm department.

MIDI was created to connect keyboards, but it also offers drummers the opportunity to control synthesizers and samplers, freeing them to play melodies and harmonies. MIDI percussion controllers expand the drummer's horizons to include all aspects of music-making and bring them into the computer age of sequencing, sampling, and synthesis.

Electronic Pads

MIDI percussion systems perform the same function as MIDI keyboards: striking a pad sends a Note On message to a MIDI sound-making device. A typical system consists of three basic components: trigger pads, a trigger-to-MIDI converter, and one or more MIDI sound modules.

MIDI drum pads resemble rubber practice pads. Underneath the rubber surface is a sensor that detects when the pad is hit and generates an electrical voltage, with an amplitude corresponding to the strength of the hit.

There are two types of sensors used in MIDI drum pads: piezo triggers and force-sensing resistors (FSRs). Piezo triggers are about the diameter of a quarter and are glued to the underside of the rubber in the middle of the pad (see Fig. 8-4). They get their name from the piezoelectric effect, in which a quartz crystal under sudden compression generates an electrical voltage. The harder the hit, the greater the voltage.

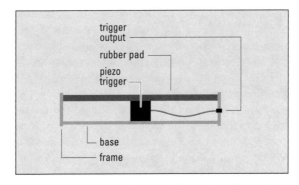

Figure 8-4. A piezo trigger is mounted beneath a rubber pad and connected to the trigger output. When the pad is hit, the trigger generates a voltage that is sent from the trigger output to a trigger-to-MIDI converter.

FSRs consist of two pieces of plastic film that are coated with electrically conductive ink. Like piezo triggers, the harder they are hit, the more voltage they generate. FSRs are more sensitive than piezo triggers, and they generate a continuous voltage that changes with the pressure. This lets you trigger the pad with varying force; the resulting voltages can be used to control different parameters of the sound.

Trigger-to-MIDI Converters

When you hit a pad or acoustic drum sensor (discussed shortly), it generates a voltage. But this voltage must be changed into MIDI note messages to trigger a sound from the MIDI sound source. So the voltage from each sensor, called the trigger signal, is sent to its own input on a trigger-to-MIDI converter. The converter sends MIDI messages to one or more sound modules, which respond by playing the specified notes. Any MIDI sound source will work, allowing drummers to play melodies and harmonies with synths and samplers.

When setting up the converter, you assign specific MIDI note numbers to each trigger input. The converter uses these instructions to determine which MIDI notes to send when signals arrive at the trigger inputs. When you strike a pad, the converter measures the voltage of the incoming trigger signal and sends the appropriate Note On message with a Velocity value. As the strength of the hit increases, so do the voltage and the corresponding Velocity value. Some converters also send Aftertouch or Modulation messages in response to varying pressure on a pad with an FSR sensor.

Unlike keyboard players, drummers can't sustain a note by holding down a key; they must accept the fixed, rapid decay of virtually all percussive sounds.

Using a trigger-to-MIDI converter, however, drummers can play sounds that don't decay until a Note Off message is received. In order to avoid sustaining notes indefinitely, most converters include a gate time setting. This function automatically sends a Note Off message to the triggered source after a specified period of time.

Some pads have distinct areas that send different voltages, which you can route to separate inputs on the converter to trigger different notes. For example, the pad itself might trigger a snare drum sound, while its rim triggers a rim shot.

More sophisticated trigger-to-MIDI converters can send different notes depending on the strength of the hit. For example, hitting the pad softly might play a brushed snare sound, while hitting it harder plays a sharp, sticked snare sound. This is called Velocity switching. A related feature is Velocity mixing, in which harder hits add different sounds to a soft base sound. Velocity switching and mixing also can be applied to MIDI channels: a hard hit sends the same Note On message as a soft hit, but the note is sent on a different channel. Using this feature, a soft hit could play a flute sound on one sound module on channel 1, while a hard hit adds or switches to a trumpet sound on channel 2.

Types of Drum Controllers

There are three basic types of drum controllers: integrated controllers, individual pads, and acoustic drum triggers. Integrated controllers include eight to twelve pads in a single case, along with an internal trigger-to-MIDI converter. This lets you control any MIDI sound source without any additional gear. These units typically include a number of trigger inputs that let you add external pads or acoustic drum triggers to the system. The internal converter takes care of the note assignments and velocity conversion for internal and external pads. Some integrated controllers, such as the Roland SPD-8, also include an internal drum sound module (sometimes called a drum brain) that is controlled by its own pads.

Integrated controllers are available in two configurations: drums and mallets. In the drum configuration, the pads are arranged in a rectangle or some other shape. The Roland SPD-8 and PAD-80 provide eight square pads in two rows of four, while the E-mu drumKAT offers ten pads in a pattern that resembles a silhouette of Mickey Mouse ears (see Fig. 8-5). For xylophone or marimba players, mallet controllers such as the E-mu malletKAT offer rectangular pads in a standard keyboard arrangement. These controllers often can be expanded by adding one-octave extension units, letting you create a mallet instrument of up to ten octaves.

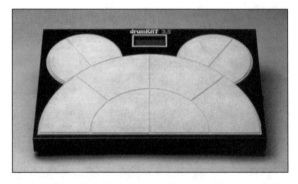

Figure 8-5. The E-mu drumKAT provides ten pads arranged in a mouse-ears-like pattern.

Some integrated controllers and trigger-to-MIDI converters include a special input jack for a momentary footswitch such as a keyboard sustain pedal. Pressing the switch cuts off one sound as it plays another sound. This is generally used with open and closed hi-hat sounds to simulate the effect of playing an open hat on an acoustic drum set and quickly closing it with the pedal.

Individual pads are mounted on a drum rack or set of drum stands to form part or all of a drum set. Each pad has one or more trigger outputs that connect to the trigger inputs of a trigger-to-MIDI converter or integrated controller using standard audio cables with ¼-inch jacks. These pads are available in several forms, including snare, tom, and cymbal pads such as the Roland PD series (see Fig. 8-6) and kick-drum triggers such as the Roland KD-7. Other companies such as Drum Workshop and E-mu also offer kick-drum triggers.

Figure 8-6. The Roland PD drum pads combine to form an entire drum set.

Acoustic drum triggers are mounted directly on acoustic drums rather than using rubber pads. These piezo triggers are taped, clamped, or glued onto the head, rim, or shell of each drum in the set. As a drum is hit, the trigger sends a corresponding voltage to the trigger-to-MIDI converter. Head-mounted triggers are attached to the head near the rim and work best on the snare and high toms. Shell-mounted triggers are usually attached to the shell near the upper rim and work best on low toms and kick drums.

Unfortunately, acoustic triggers are prone to accidental or false triggering from adjacent drums or vibrations in the drum rack. Sometimes a drum head vibrates long enough to activate its trigger twice. There are several ways to address these problems. For instance, Drum Workshop offers a line of active triggers, which are electronically optimized for snares, toms, and kicks. They are mounted on the inside of the shell, which minimizes false triggering.

Another problem with acoustic triggers is the fact that their voltage levels often do not match well with the trigger inputs of some converters. Trigger Perfect offers acoustic triggers with an adjustable output voltage, which goes a long way toward solving this problem.

Putting It Together
You can combine any or all of the different types of drum controllers into a MIDI drum system (see Fig.

8-7). This lets you add pads to your system as budget and space permit. Many drummers combine MIDI drum controllers with acoustic drums and cymbals to form a hybrid drum set.

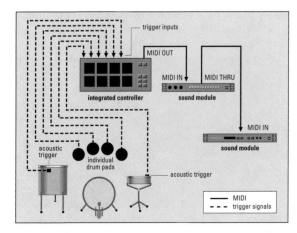

Figure 8-7. Individual pads and acoustic triggers connect to the trigger inputs of an integrated controller, which sends MIDI messages to a MIDI sound module.

Like MIDI keyboard, guitar, and woodwind controllers, electronic drum pads feel different than their acoustic counterparts, and it takes some practice to get used to them. But the rewards are great: drummers can use MIDI to play melody, harmony, and rhythm with equal ease, dispelling the myth that they aren't really complete musicians.

WIND CONTROLLERS

Although MIDI was developed to represent keyboard performance gestures, it has been adapted to let guitars, drums, and even violins control MIDI sound modules. Wind instruments and vocals, however, pose special problems. Their expressive characteristics are difficult to represent with MIDI messages. For example, a breath-controlled *sforzando-piano-crescendo* is a common wind-instrument technique in which a note is attacked with a loud volume and immediately dropped to a soft volume, followed by a slow increase to a loud volume again. This is not a common keyboard technique, however, and thus difficult to represent in keyboard-oriented MIDI terms.

In spite of these difficulties, there are two different types of products that let wind players and vocalists control MIDI instruments: wind controllers and pitch-to-MIDI converters (PMCs). With these devices, wind players and singers can apply the expressive techniques they have so carefully cultivated to an infinite palette of electronic sounds and record their performances into a sequencer.

Background

Wind controllers are designed to imitate acoustic wind instruments. They consist of two basic elements: the instrument controller itself and an interface unit (see Fig. 8-8). The instrument controller usually resembles a clarinet or straight saxophone with one or more keys for each finger.

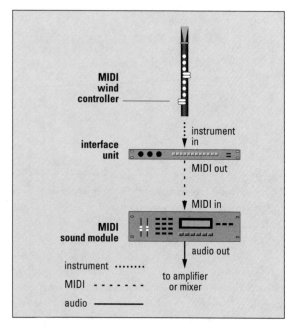

Figure 8-8. In a wind controller system, the instrument controller connects to the interface unit, which sends MIDI data to a sound module and/or sequencer. The sound module is sometimes integrated into the interface unit. A PMC is essentially identical with the exception of a microphone or transducer instead of an instrument controller.

Notes are fingered much like their acoustic counterparts, although there are some significant differences. For example, each note is fingered identically in each octave, and there are several octave keys under the left thumb instead of just one. Also, there are many more alternate fingerings than you find on acoustic instruments, which can be very convenient once you learn them.

The mouthpiece of the instrument controller often looks like that of a sax or clarinet. There's even a reed in some cases. Of course, the reed doesn't vibrate; instead, it usually sends Pitch Bend messages when it is bitten, simulating the effect of biting an acoustic reed.

Breath resistance is another important factor. Some controllers, such as the Yamaha WX11, let your breath flow through the instrument, which feels much more natural than controllers that let no air through them at all. However, controllers that let no air through, such as the Akai EWI, offer the opportu-

nity to play phrases of any length without running out of air; simply breathe through your nose while maintaining pressure in your mouth and a tight seal around the mouthpiece. (If you circular breathe, you can achieve the same effect on controllers that let your breath through.)

The instrument controller is usually connected to the interface unit with a special cable. The interface unit receives signals from the instrument and converts them into MIDI messages, which are sent to any MIDI sound source and/or sequencer (see Fig. 8-8). In some cases, the interface unit includes its own sound module.

Wind controllers make no sound of their own. When you play, the only sound you hear is made by the sound module, which is great for headphone listening and acoustic isolation. Also, wind controllers offer a much wider pitch range than acoustic instruments. Up to eight octaves or more can be played and no octave is more difficult to play than any other. However, wind controllers do not feel or play the same as their acoustic counterparts. They must be approached and learned as new instruments that happen to have similarities to familiar instruments.

Pitch-to-MIDI converters (PMCs) can be used by wind players or vocalists to control MIDI instruments with their familiar axe. Like wind controllers, PMCs have two basic elements: a microphone, transducer, or other pickup and an interface unit. The microphone or transducer picks up a signal which is sent to the interface unit. The interface determines the pitch and volume of the input note and converts this information into MIDI messages, which are then sent to a sound module.

There is an inherent delay (and often inaccuracies) in the conversion process, and the acoustic sound is always present. The pitch range is limited to the acoustic norm, with the exception of the inevitable transposition function in the interface unit, and the extreme limits of the range are no easier to play. On the other hand, there is no need to learn a new instrument, so the learning curve usually is much shorter.

MIDI

All wind controllers and PMCs send Note On/Off messages and most send Velocity as determined by the initial breath pressure or volume of each note. (As I'll explain in a moment, there are good reasons for sending a fixed, maximum Velocity value for each note from a wind controller or PMC.) In addition, Pitch Bend is universal to all wind controllers and PMCs. As mentioned earlier, some wind controllers send Pitch Bend in response to biting the "reed," while others provide a wheel or rocker under the right thumb for this purpose.

Because acoustic wind instruments and the voice can produce a more or less continuous range of pitches, PMCs send Pitch Bend with every note. The initial frequency of each note is analyzed, and the note number of the closest MIDI note is used in the resulting Note On message. The Note On is followed by Pitch Bend messages that adjust the pitch to match the frequency of the input note. Unless you play or sing pitches very accurately, this can lead to an enormous number of Pitch Bend messages, so many units let you turn Pitch Bend off. The tradeoff is that you can't swoop or slide into pitches as you would acoustically, and you might trigger more wrong notes.

Changing breath pressure during a note to vary its timbre and volume is a fundamental characteristic of all wind instruments and vocals. Wind controllers and PMCs send one or more continuous controller messages in response to this technique. The most common messages include Aftertouch, Volume, Modulation, and Breath Controller. These messages change the output of the sound module by opening filters, increasing amplification, etc.

Note On Velocities based on initial breath pressure can lead to problems when combined with Volume messages. If a Note On has a low Velocity value, it will remain soft no matter what the subsequent Volume values are. As a result, it is usually better to keep the Velocity fixed at its maximum value (127) and control the volume of each note with Volume messages.

Wind controllers and PMCs take the place of keyboard controllers in the MIDI system of a wind player or singer, so they should have master controller features. One common feature is transposition, which lets you transpose the Note On/Off messages up or down by semitones or octaves. This is handy for musicians that normally play transposing instruments such as sax or clarinet. It can also be used to play a piece in a difficult key signature while using the fingerings of an easier key.

An important variation of transposition is harmonization, in which the interface unit generates one or more notes to accompany the notes you play. Although they are not all available on all controllers and PMCs, there are three basic types of harmonization: hold, chord or parallel, and programmable or intelligent harmonization. In Hold mode, you play one or more notes while pressing a switch on the controller or stepping on a footswitch. After releasing the switch, the notes you played are sustained while you play new notes over them, which simulates the effect of a bagpipe. In Chord or Parallel mode, each note you play is accompanied by other notes at fixed intervals. For example, this lets you play parallel major, minor, or dominant chords. With programmable har-

monization, you can preprogram a different chord to be played for each note in the chromatic scale. In each case, the harmonization usually is enabled and disabled with a switch.

Unfortunately, most wind controllers and PMCs lack other master controller features such as comprehensive and flexible patch change capabilities. These capabilities can be added with a MIDI fader/switch box or footboard, which sends Program Change and other messages. Footboards come in two varieties: those with a merging MIDI In and those without (see Fig. 8-9). These devices are very handy for live performance.

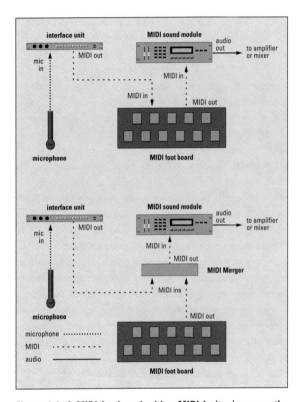

Figure 8-9. A MIDI footboard with a MIDI In (top) merges the data from the interface unit with its own Program Change and other messages. A MIDI footboard without a MIDI In (bottom) must use an external MIDI merger.

Other master controller features missing from most wind controllers and PMCs include zoning, controller mapping, Aftertouch curves, and other advanced functions. These functions can be added with a MIDI processor (see Chapter 9).

For example, you might use a MIDI processor to fix all Note On Velocities at 127, add Breath Controller messages to the Volume messages generated by the wind controller or PMC, and layer or switch between different sound modules on different MIDI channels, depending on the pitch and volume range in which you play. If you do use a MIDI processor in conjunction with a footboard, it should be placed immediately after the interface unit and before the footboard to prevent the processor from unintentionally filtering messages from the footboard.

Patches and Glitches

The nature of the patches you play with a wind controller or PMC is vital to a good sound. The most expressive patches are those that sustain at full level throughout the duration of the note and respond to Aftertouch or Breath Controller messages in a meaningful way, such as changing the timbre and volume of the note.

The attack setting also is critical. If it's too slow, the delay between your attack and the start of the note is intolerable. If it's too fast, another problem called glitching rears its ugly head. For wind controllers, moving from one note to the next as you play sometimes requires several fingers to press or release their keys at the same time. As your fingers move to press or release the keys, they often do not make or break their contact at precisely the same moment. The minute differences between the contacts are interpreted as separate notes by the sound module. This results in several very quick "glitches" between the notes you intended to play. PMCs have a similar problem when the pitch-bend function is disabled.

Glitching can be reduced by developing the best possible technical accuracy in fingering and articulation. Playing notes with a detached articulation also reduces glitching, which is nearly impossible to achieve while slurring. Some controllers include a special sensitivity control that lets you specify the minimum duration of a transmitted note. Adjusting the attack of the sound you are controlling is also very helpful.

Many wind controller and PMC users disable the LFO in the patches they play. This lets them produce vibrato, tremolo, or wah-wah effects with their breath or jaw as they would on an acoustic instrument.

MIDI wind controllers and PMCs have brought the unlimited range of sounds from today's synthesizers and samplers to wind players and vocalists. The development of these controllers provides new opportunities in the fields of live performance, sequencing, and composition. Creative wind players and vocalists can now extend the boundaries of their craft as they explore new musical dimensions.

CHAPTER 9

Advanced Topics

Once you understand the basic concepts of MIDI, you can dive into its more advanced aspects. There are many such advanced topics, of which I discuss four in this chapter. This information gets pretty dense, so it's not for the faint of heart. I present it here for those who have a taste for the technical side of MIDI.

Of particular importance is the section on Bank Select. Although this is a standard MIDI message, different manufacturers implement it differently, which causes many headaches among electronic musicians. The Bank Select section will help you sort out this tricky topic, which has become increasingly important with the advent of synthesizers that include hundreds or even thousands of patches.

BANK SELECT

In the early days of synthesizers, patches were stored as hand-drawn diagrams on sheets of paper. You had to draw where the patch cords went and write down the settings of the front-panel controls. As digital technology was incorporated into synths, these connections and settings could be stored in computer memory.

By the time MIDI was introduced, most synths had enough memory for no more than 64 patches, and you could recall these patches remotely by sending Program Change messages from another device. The Program Change message can call up 128 different patches, which was deemed sufficient at the time.

Of course, the 128-patch limit was exceeded shortly thereafter, and now synths have enough memory for hundreds or even thousands of sounds. However, Program Change messages can address only 128 of them, so a way around this limitation had to be found.

Basic Banking

The solution adopted by the MIDI Manufacturers Association was to organize patches into banks of up to 128 and add a new message to the MIDI Control Change (CC) list: Bank Select. Actually, there are two Bank Select messages: Most Significant Byte (MSB) and Least Significant Byte (LSB). To select a patch in a modern synthesizer via MIDI from a controller or computer, you first specify the bank by sending the appropriate Bank Select messages. Once the bank has been selected, you send a Program Change to select the desired patch within that bank.

Bank Select MSB is defined as CC 0. Like all CC messages, its value ranges from 0 to 127. Bank Select LSB is CC 32; its value also ranges from 0 to 127. Used together, they can address 128 x 128 = 16,384 different banks. Each bank consists of up to 128 patches, so when using Bank Select and Program Change together, you can address a total of 16,384 x 128 = 2,097,152 separate patches, which should be more than sufficient (at least, for a little while!).

As mentioned in Chapter 6, the first 32 CC messages (and a few others) include an MSB and LSB, but most products only use the MSB. For example, most products only use the MSB of MIDI Volume (CC 7), although there is a Volume LSB (CC 39). As a result, most manufacturers assume that only the MSB will be used for Control Changes.

However, Bank Select is not a normal Control Change. The MIDI spec states that "the transmitter must transmit the MSB and LSB as a pair, and the Program Change must be sent immediately after the Bank Select pair." Nevertheless, many manufacturers use only the MSB or LSB to select banks. This accommodates 128 banks, or a total of 16,384 patches, which is still sufficient for most applications, but it gives rise to much confusion.

The spec also states that the receiving synth must wait to change patches until it receives a Program Change; Bank Select alone should not change the patch. The receiver must remember the Bank Select message in preparation for the following Program Change to ensure that if you send Bank Select and Program Change messages to multiple devices, they will change their patches simultaneously.

In addition to single patches, most synthesizers also include banks of multitimbral combinations that each contain several patches, which provide layers and splits as well as multitrack sequence setups. Some synths also include separate banks of drum kits and/or sound effects (such as door slams, car engines, and screams). Bank Select can often be used to call up these banks as well.

In some cases, the same Bank Select value is used to select a given bank of patches and a bank of combinations, which means you must enter the desired mode (Program, Combination, etc.) from the front panel and then send Bank Select and Program Change messages. In other cases, different Bank Select values are used for these banks so you can send them regardless of the mode selected on the front panel.

Once you have sent a Bank Select message, you normally don't need to send it again unless you want to change banks. You can simply send Program Changes to select different items within the current bank. If you are programming a sequencer to send Bank Select and Program Change messages, include a few clock ticks between each message to give the receiving synth time to digest it.

Depending on how your controller, sequencer, and sound module specify MIDI codes, you might need to convert between decimal and hexadecimal to determine the correct Bank Select value. Unfortunately, most manuals are woefully inconsistent in this regard. Certain calculators, such as the Casio fx-115D, perform this conversion; I recommend getting one for this reason alone. (For more on hexadecimal, see "Using SysEx Hex" later in this chapter.) For now, I'll stick with decimal numbers.

If you have a relatively recent keyboard synth, selecting patches from the front panel normally sends the appropriate Bank Select and Program Change to the instrument's MIDI Out. (This capability can often be enabled and disabled.) The exact nature of the transmitted Bank Select message usually corresponds to how the instrument responds to incoming Bank Select changes. Each manufacturer implements Bank Select differently, so let's take a look at several examples.

Alesis

The Alesis QS-series keyboard synths include four preset ROM banks and one user RAM bank onboard, and an optional memory card can hold up to eight more banks. (The QS7 and QS8 provide two card slots, and each card can hold up to eight banks.) Each bank includes 128 Programs and 100 Mixes (multitimbral combinations), and Program Change selects either Programs or Mixes, depending on the instrument's current mode.

The QS series uses Bank Select MSB (CC 0) to select a bank via MIDI (see table, "Alesis, Ensoniq, and Kawai Bank Select Messages"). In the QS6, values above 12 "wrap around"; for example, a value of 13 selects the onboard User bank, a value of 14 selects

Preset bank 1, etc. In the QS7 and QS8, only two banks in the second card are available for remote selection. These banks use MSB values of 13 and 14, and values of 15 or higher wrap around.

E-mu

E-mu makes many sound modules and samplers that include more than 128 patches. For example, the Orbit and Proteus FX modules include four banks of 128 programs (called Presets) each. Banks 0 and 1 are in user RAM, and banks 2 and 3 are ROM-based. The Morpheus and UltraProteus include three onboard banks and two additional banks on an optional memory card. In these modules, bank 0 consists of Presets in RAM, bank 1 includes Presets in ROM, and bank 2 stores multitimbral constructs, called Hyperpresets, in RAM. Hyperpresets are collections of up to sixteen layered and split Presets per MIDI channel. Bank 3 stores Presets on a memory card, and bank 4 stores Hyperpresets on the card.

The engineers at E-mu decided to follow the MIDI spec to the letter, so all E-mu products use Bank Select MSB and LSB. An MSB value of 0 is followed by an LSB value from 0 to 4 to select the corresponding bank. If the device receives an LSB without an MSB, it assumes the value of the last received MSB. As a result, it is possible to send just the LSB after an initial MSB with value 0. However, E-mu doesn't guarantee the unit's behavior if you don't follow the MIDI spec completely. If you send a Bank Select value higher than the device can accommodate, it assumes the highest possible value.

Ensoniq

The Ensoniq KT76 and KT88 keyboard synths include one ROM bank and one RAM bank, and an optional memory card holds two more RAM banks. Each bank consists of 80 patches (called Sounds) and twenty drum kits (called Drum Sounds). Bank Select LSB (CC 32) is used to select these banks (see table, "Alesis, Ensoniq, and Kawai Bank Select Messages"). As in most synths, when you select a Sound with a Program Change, its associated effect is called up, as well.

In Multi (sequencer) mode, Bank Select LSB is used to select a bank from which to get a Sound for a sequencer track. In this case, the effect associated with the selected Sound is installed as the new sequence effect. You can select a Sound in Multi mode without its effect by using the Bank Select messages for Sound mode.

The KT series also includes a GM bank, but you must enter GM mode by pressing a front-panel button or by sending a GM On SysEx message. Once the KT is in GM mode, any MSB value from 0 to 126 selects the GM bank, and the LSB is ignored. An MSB value of 127 selects a variation of the GM Program Change map that corresponds to the patch map found in the Roland MT-32, a popular multitimbral sound module that was introduced before General MIDI was adopted. To exit GM mode, you must press a front-panel button or send a GM Off SysEx message.

Kawai

The Kawai K5000W includes two separate sound engines: PCM sample playback and additive synthesis. The onboard memory includes three banks of programs and one bank of multitimbral combinations. Bank A includes 128 additive programs in RAM, and bank B stores 128 PCM programs (including twelve drum kits). Of these programs, 47 are user-programmable (including one drum kit); the others are in ROM. Bank G is a GM bank in ROM, and bank C has 64 multitimbral combinations, which are in RAM.

The K5000W uses Bank Select MSB only (see table, "Alesis, Ensoniq, and Kawai Bank Select Messages"). As you can see in the table, an MSB value of 99 selects the RAM locations 103 to 116 in bank B. Other RAM locations in this bank are selected with MSB values from 1 to 9 depending on the exact memory location you want. The ROM locations in bank B are also accessed by sending different MSB values, depending on the location. This allows the programs and banks to conform to the Roland GS standard for Bank Select and Program Change messages.

Korg

The synths from Korg can be organized into three main families. The first family includes the 0-series modules (03R/W and 05R/W), X series (X3, etc.), and the N series (N364, etc.). These synths all have a GM bank in ROM. The 0 series also has two user RAM banks, called A and B. The X series includes one or more user RAM banks (depending on the specific model) in addition to the GM bank. The N series offers A and B RAM banks as well as C, D, and GM ROM banks. Banks A through D include 100 Programs and 100 multitimbral Combis each, and the GM bank offers the normal 128 Programs.

Both MSB and LSB are used to select a bank. However, this doesn't work quite as you might expect (see table, "Korg, Roland, and Technics Bank Select Messages"). In addition, you can use Bank Select to disable any Multi (multitimbral) track; an MSB value of 58 followed by an LSB value of 0 followed by any Program Change disables the track on that channel. Send any other Bank Select and Program Change messages to turn the track back on.

The second family of Korg synths includes various versions of the Trinity. The basic Trinity includes two banks, A and B, both of which are RAM banks.

Two more user banks, C and D, come with the flash ROM option (officially known as PBS-TRI). The Solo Synth option, which adds a Prophecy synth to the sound engine, includes its own S bank. In the Trinity, each bank includes 128 Programs and 128 Combis; the S bank provides an additional 64 Programs (128 with the PBS-TRI option). The Trinity uses both MSB and LSB to select banks.

The third family of Korg instruments includes the i-series instruments, which provide four banks, each with 64 Programs plus eight drum kits. As in other Korg instruments, the banks are labeled A, B, C, and D. However, the Programs are numbered to indicate bank and program, i.e., 11 to 18, 21 to 28, and so on to 88. Banks A, B, and C are in ROM, whereas bank D is in RAM. Both MSB and LSB are used to select banks in the i series.

Kurzweil

The Kurzweil K2000 and K2500 offer perhaps the greatest number of onboard memory locations in any synth. Ten banks (called the 0s, 100s, 200s, and so on up to the 900s) each include 100 Programs, 100 multitimbral Setups, and 20 Quick Access (QA) banks. (The 0s bank includes 75 QA banks.) QA banks each include up to 10 Programs and/or Setups from any main bank. The 0s and 100s main banks are in ROM; if you have either or both of the expansion boards installed, each one replaces one of the RAM banks with ROM Programs, Setups, and QA banks. Even so, this leaves hundreds of memory locations for user sounds.

These instruments also provide an extremely flexible means of calling up Programs, Setups, and QA banks remotely, including several Kurzweil-specific methods that address the older K1200/K1000 and QA banks. Extended Program Change mode supports normal Bank Select procedures, and you can configure the synth to respond to either MSB or LSB alone or both MSB and LSB together.

Bank Select values from 0 to 9 select the corresponding bank as you would expect, and values from 10 to 127 are ignored. However, Kurzweil provides an alternative to using Bank Select; you can also use Program Change messages to change banks because each bank holds 100 items, not 128. In this approach, Program Changes 100 to 109 select the corresponding bank; for example, if you send a Program Change of 100, the 0s bank is selected. Program Changes 110 to 127 are ignored.

Roland

The Roland Sound Canvas has become one of the most popular GM sound modules on the market. Like its predecessors, the SC-88 implements Roland's GS superset of General MIDI (see Chapter 7) and provides a total of 654 programs (Patches) and 24 drum kits. The basic 128 GM sounds are called Capital Tones, and they are located in bank 0. Most of the Capital Tones include several variations in different banks.

The Sound Canvas uses MSB to select banks. The specific value to use depends on the desired Capital Tone and variation; each variation uses a different Bank Select MSB in conjunction with the Program Change of the corresponding Capital Tone. For example, the "Tubular Bell" Capital Tone corresponds to Program Change 15. To call up this Patch, send an MSB value of 0 followed by a Program Change value of 15. If you send an MSB value of 8 followed by a Program Change value of 15, you get "Church Bell," which is a variation of "Tubular Bell." If you send an MSB value of 9 followed by a Program Change value of 15, you get "Carillon."

The JV-1080 synth module provides four ROM banks (including one GM bank) and one user RAM bank onboard. Each bank includes 128 Patches and two drum kits. In addition, the user RAM bank and two of the ROM banks each include 32 multitimbral Performances. You can also install up to four expansion boards, each offering two ROM banks of up to 128 Patches; some of these boards also include a few

drum kits. Finally, you can insert one RAM card and one ROM card. The RAM card duplicates the onboard user RAM bank (128 Patches, 32 Performances, two drum kits), and the available ROM cards include new samples and up to 63 Patches each.

This synth uses both MSB and LSB to select banks (see table, "Korg, Roland, and Technics Bank Select Messages"). If the instrument is in Performance mode (which is activated by pressing a front-panel button or sending SysEx), one channel is reserved for selecting banks and specific Performances via MIDI; the other channels can be used to select Patches within a Performance. In Patch mode, any of the sixteen channels can be used to select Patches.

Technics

Technics' first professional synth is the SX-WSA1, which includes two ROM banks and two user RAM banks, each with 128 patches (called Sounds). (An editable GM bank is derived from Sounds in the other banks.) Optional expansion boards each hold a bank of 128 additional Sounds. In addition, one of the ROM banks and one of the RAM banks each include 128 multitimbral Combis. There is one bank of sixteen drum kits in ROM, and the RAM banks include two drum kits each. All Sounds, Combis, and drum kits can be remapped to different Program Change numbers in one of three Remap banks.

The WSA1 uses both MSB and LSB to select banks (see table, "Korg, Roland, and Technics Bank Select Messages"). Unfortunately, the manual provides the composite Bank Select number for each bank. For example, the Bank Select value for the User 2 bank is given as 144, which translates to MSB and LSB values of 1 and 16, respectively.

Yamaha

Yamaha's MU80 is another entrant in the high-end GM sound-module sweepstakes. The company's superset of GM is called XG, which includes many enhancements to the GM architecture (see Chapter 7). The MU80 includes 729 patches (called Voices), nine drum kits, and two banks of sound effects.

Bank 0 is the standard GM sound set. Yamaha calls this the Capital bank, which is surprisingly similar to Roland's nomenclature. The MU80's other banks include variations of the basic sounds, which also resemble the architecture of the Sound Canvas. Unlike the Sound Canvas' banks, though, these banks are organized by the character of the variations they contain (bright, slow attack, resonant, single-element, etc.).

The MU80 can also operate in TG300B mode, which is identical to the B mode from the company's earlier TG300 sound module. The TG300's primary (A) mode evolved into XG, while the module's secondary (B) mode was more or less compatible with Roland's GS standard. The MU80's TG300B mode retains this GS compatibility, offering eight drum kits and two sound-effects banks. In C/M mode, the MU80 emulates the Roland CM-32 computer-card sound module, which was essentially compatible with the MT-32. This mode provides a single bank of 128 Voices and one drum kit.

A separate sound effects (SFX) bank holds 49 special effects, such as a door slam, car engine, scream, and explosion. This bank is intended for game developers and audio post-production. Finally, there are 64 multitimbral Performances in ROM and 128 user (Internal) Performances in RAM.

The MU80 uses both MSB and LSB for selecting banks. In XG mode, the normal Voice banks are selected by sending an MSB value of 0 followed by an LSB value that corresponds to the desired bank and a Program Change to select the Voice. Drum kits are selected by sending an MSB of 126 or 127 followed by a Program Change.

One interesting feature of the MU80 is its set of two audio inputs, which are called A/D inputs because they digitize the analog input signals, send them through the effects, and mix them with the module's internal sounds. These inputs are assigned to MIDI channels, and MIDI messages can be used to control various aspects of their operation. In particular, Bank Select can be used to configure the A/D inputs for various signal levels (see table, "Yamaha MU80 A/D Bank Select Messages"). Once the input level is selected, Program Change messages select different preset effects that are applied to the signal.

In TG300B (GS) mode, the functions of MSB and LSB are reversed. The LSB value is 0, and the MSB selects the bank. The TG300B drum kits do not use Bank Select; drums are always on channel 10 in the GS standard, so a Program Change is sufficient to select different drum kits. An MSB value of 64 selects the separate SFX bank. (TG 300B mode has no Voice bank with an MSB of 64.)

To select Performances, an MSB value of 1 followed by an LSB value of 0 selects the Preset (ROM) bank, and an MSB value of 2 and LSB value of 0 selects the Internal (RAM) bank of Performances.

As you can see, using Bank Select is not as straightforward as it could be. Unfortunately, manufacturers implement this important message in slightly different ways, making it difficult to manage patches in a complex system. Nevertheless, with a little knowledge, you can use Bank Select to call up virtually any sound in any synth in your studio from a computer or controller, which sure beats selecting banks and patches manually from the front panels of the different instruments.

KORG, ROLAND, AND TECHNICS BANK SELECT MESSAGES

Korg 0/X/N Series

MSB Value	LSB Value	Selected Bank
0	0	A
0	1	B
0	2	C
0	3	D
56	0	GM
62	0	GM Drums

Korg Trinity

MSB Value	LSB Value	Selected Bank
0	0	A
0	1	B
0	2	C
0	3	D
0	4	S

Korg i Series

MSB Value	LSB Value	Selected Bank
0	0	A/B (A11–B88)
0	1	C/D (C11–D88)
0	2	Drum

Roland JV-1080

MSB Value	LSB Value	Selected Bank
80	0	User
81	0	Preset A
81	1	Preset B
81	2	Preset C
81	3	Preset D (GM)
82	0	RAM Card
83	0	ROM Card
84	0	Expansion A (1–128)
84	1	Expansion A (129–256)
84	2	Expansion B (1–128)
84	3	Expansion B (129–256)
84	4	Expansion C (1–128)
84	5	Expansion C (129–256)
84	6	Expansion D (1–128)
84	7	Expansion D (129–256)

Technics SX-WSA1

MSB Value	LSB Value	Selected Bank
0	0	ROM 1
0	16	ROM 2
1	0	User 1
1	16	User 2
2	0	Ext (Expansion Board)
3	16	Remap 1
3	32	Remap 2
3	48	Remap 3
4	0	Drum (ROM)
5	0	Drum (User 1)
5	16	Drum (User 2)

YAMAHA MU80 A/D BANK SELECT MESSAGES		
MSB Value	LSB Value	Selected Input Level
0	0	Mic
0	1	Instrument (Guitar)
0	2	Line (Keyboard)
0	3	Stereo (line-level inputs panned hard right and left)

MIDI PROCESSING

Let's say you want to jam with a friend on two MIDI instruments and simultaneously record both parts into a sequencer. You plan to use a "Y" cord to combine the MIDI messages from the two instruments. Unfortunately, it's not that simple. Mixing MIDI messages is a tricky process requiring a specialized device dedicated to the task.

The type of device required, a MIDI merger, is one example of a MIDI processor. Similar in concept to an audio signal processor, a MIDI processor takes incoming MIDI messages, affects them in some way, and sends them out to their next destination. This is useful in a variety of situations, so it pays to know something about MIDI processing if you use MIDI in any way.

Most MIDI processors resemble audio multi-effects processors in that they can perform several tasks at once. You can accomplish most processing functions described here with a single unit. However, each unit is slightly different in design and implementation, so have a clear idea of what you want a MIDI processor to do before you buy one. In addition, several available software programs turn a computer into a MIDI processor.

In Fig. 9-1, several MIDI devices and a computer are connected to a MIDI processor with four MIDI Ins and four MIDI Outs. Other processors range from those with one MIDI In and four MIDI Outs (e.g., Yamaha MEP4) to those with fifteen MIDI Ins and fifteen MIDI Outs (e.g., Opcode Studio 5). Some processors also can be connected directly to a computer's serial port, providing a multiport MIDI interface in addition to their processing capabilities. Units in this category include the Studio 5 and Mark of the Unicorn's MIDI Time Piece.

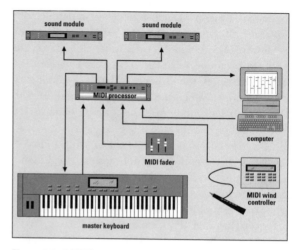

Figure 9-1. A MIDI processor is used to connect a master keyboard, wind controller, MIDI fader unit, computer, and two sound modules.

The Urge to Merge

As mentioned earlier, the solution to the problem described at the beginning of this section is a device called a "merger" (see Fig. 9-2). Mergers are often single-purpose devices, although most multiprocessing units include merging capabilities. A merger has two or more MIDI In jacks from which it receives multiple streams of MIDI messages. These messages are combined, or merged, into one stream of messages that is then sent to a MIDI Out jack.

Figure 9-2. The MIDI Solutions Quadra Merge accepts up to four streams of MIDI data and merges them to one MIDI Out.

This process requires some sophisticated computer power to ensure that each message remains intact. A merger must keep track of message types and values and merge different messages without breaking them up. Otherwise, the device that receives the messages from the merger might apply an incorrect value or become confused if the message isn't as expected.

Typically, MIDI processors also perform the opposite function, splitting. In this process, MIDI messages are sent to more than one device at a time, which obviously requires more than one MIDI Out. For example, this lets you send a MIDI stream from the master keyboard to one or more of the sound modules and the computer for sequencing.

If a processor can send the data from any MIDI In to any MIDI Out, it provides the routing capabilities of a MIDI patch bay. In conjunction with merging and splitting, this lets you send any MIDI signal to any device in the studio. Of course, beware of sending a MIDI signal from a device back to itself. This results in a MIDI feedback loop, which causes stuck notes and other weird problems, unless the device's local or echo function has been disabled (see Chapter 7).

Cold Filtered Natural Draft

Another important MIDI processing function is filtering, in which certain incoming messages are prevented from leaving the processor. You can filter all messages on a specific channel, specific types of messages on all channels, or specific types of messages on specific channels. In Fig. 9-1, for example, you might want to filter the MIDI Clock messages coming from the computer because there is no other equipment that must be synchronized (see Chapter 7).

Filtering primarily is used to prevent unnecessary messages from clogging up the MIDI datastream. For example, the wind controller in Fig. 9-1 sends Aftertouch messages in response to changing breath pressure, but the sound module it's controlling doesn't respond to Aftertouch. The MIDI processor should be used to remove Aftertouch messages from the channel on which the wind controller is communicating with the sound module.

Another form of filtering is called limiting. Unlike the audio effect of the same name (see Chapter 20), MIDI limiting restricts the range of values that make it through the processor. This can apply to note numbers as well as Velocity and CC values. For example, if a sound module produces a bassoon-like sound, it might sound unsatisfactory if played far outside the normal pitch range of a bassoon. Limiting the note numbers from the master keyboard or wind controller to those within the appropriate range ensures that the module always sounds reasonable.

Some people record MIDI Volume messages into the sequencer to automate the mixing of virtual tracks. Unfortunately, this uses a lot of computer memory. If you want to conserve memory while using this technique, consider thinning the datastream from the source of the MIDI Volume messages.

For example, the MIDI fader unit in Fig. 9-1 sends Volume messages to the computer, which records them in the sequence. By thinning the MIDI stream from the fader unit, some of the Volume messages are removed from the stream. The processor might remove only odd values, which cuts the number of messages in half. This conserves sequencer memory but can result in audible steps between values, so thinning should be used with care.

The Opcode Studio 5 is a multiport MIDI interface and processor.

MIDI processors are often used to simulate an audio delay. Incoming MIDI messages are held in the processor's memory for a user-specified period of time, after which they are sent on their way. This is used primarily with Note On and Off messages to create a delay effect. If you use this process to generate several delayed copies of the original notes, the polyphony of the receiving sound module will be reduced because it must play the same note several times.

Mapping the Universe

Most MIDI processors can change incoming MIDI messages in various ways, a process known as mapping. A common type of mapping is channelization, in which messages coming in on one channel are sent out on a different channel. This is particularly useful if your keyboard or other master controller is older and only can send on one channel. You can also use channelization to send a sequenced part from the computer to a different instrument without changing the channels on the instruments themselves.

Another important mapping function is called bias or offset. This function adds a constant value to note numbers, Velocities, or CC values. For example, adding an offset value of seven to all note numbers will transpose all notes up a perfect fifth (seven half steps). Offset values can raise or lower the overall level of Velocities or controller values, which is helpful if these messages are generally too low or high.

Velocity and controller values also can be scaled, which multiplies each value by a user-specified number. For example, the original Yamaha DX7 sends Velocity values only up to about 95. Multiplying each Velocity value by about 1.25 will "widen" the range of Velocity values sent to any sound module.

Scaling can also be used to reduce the range of values. For example, a wind controller might reach the maximum Aftertouch value before you reach maximum breath pressure. In this case, multiply the Aftertouch values by 0.5 or 0.75 to accommodate the range of your breath pressure.

As discussed in Chapter 6, most MIDI messages range in value from 0 to 127. Some MIDI processors provide a reverse function, which converts a high value to a low value and vice versa. For example, by reversing the note numbers of incoming Note On and Off messages, you can play an ascending scale on the keyboard and hear the receiving sound module play a descending scale. This function also can be applied to Velocity and any controller message. The "mid-point" about which the values are reversed is usually 64: a value of 63 becomes 65, a value of 107 becomes 20, and so on.

One of the most useful mapping functions is conversion. In this process, a MIDI message is converted into a different MIDI message. For example, the wind controller in Fig. 9-1 sends Aftertouch in response to changing breath pressure, but the receiving sound module only responds to MIDI Volume. The MIDI processor can take the incoming Aftertouch messages and convert them into Volume messages. You even can send both types of messages —Aftertouch *and* Volume—from the MIDI processor, but this often clogs the MIDI stream with lots of messages. It also can cause the receiving unit to audibly slow its response. If you want to send both types of messages, consider thinning the stream.

Getting It Together

As mentioned earlier, most MIDI processors perform several tasks at once. Among many other applications, this lets you add sophisticated master controller functions to instruments that lack them. For example, the master keyboard in Fig. 9-1 can transmit MIDI messages on only one channel across the entire keyboard. Using the limiting and channelization functions of the MIDI processor, notes from the lower and upper halves of the keyboard can be sent on different channels. Not only that, notes with different Velocity values can be sent on different channels as well. This is known as Velocity switching.

As you can see, a MIDI processor is a highly useful addition to any MIDI studio. If you have a computer, you might consider a processor that acts as a MIDI interface as well. With processing, routing, and interface capabilities, MIDI processors offer considerable power and enhanced functionality. If you use MIDI, a processor just might become an indispensable part of your setup.

MIDI MACHINE CONTROL

MIDI is an important cornerstone of electronic music. It lets musicians integrate and control synthesizers, samplers, computers, effects, and mixers in a coordinated system. And it doesn't stop there. The

designers of MIDI knew they couldn't predict all potential applications at the outset, so they included the ability to add new types of messages as applications arose—a feature that renders MIDI virtually immune from complete obsolescence.

Among the sets of messages that have been added to the MIDI spec since its initial publication is MIDI Machine Control (MMC). These messages are used to control transport-based devices, such as audio tape recorders (ATRs), videotape recorders (VTRs), and hard-disk recorders (HDRs). MMC also incorporates MIDI Time Code (MTC) to synchronize these devices with sequencers and other time-based MIDI products. (Watch out; this part of MIDI is real alphabet soup.)

MMC uses Universal System Exclusive (SysEx) format to represent its messages. As discussed in Chapter 6, SysEx is the part of MIDI normally used to represent product-specific information, such as synthesis parameters. However, it can also be used to represent new types of messages intended for many different devices, just as the basic MIDI messages can. To this end, the MIDI Manufacturers Association (MMA) established a standard format for two types of Universal SysEx messages: Real Time and Non Real Time.

With MMC, Real Time Universal SysEx is used because the controlled devices operate in real time. Aside from the Universal SysEx overhead bytes, no MMC message can be more than 48 bytes long. If more than 48 bytes are required, multiple messages must be sent; this is called segmentation. If the messages are short, more than one can be sent in a single SysEx packet.

In Control

Typically, there is one master device, called the controller, and one or more controlled devices in an MMC system. (The spec doesn't forbid using multiple controllers, but this isn't recommended.) The controller is usually a computer running MMC software, but it could be a dedicated device, such as the JLCooper CuePoint (see Fig. 9-3), BB3 MMC Transport Controller, or control software for the company's MCS Media Control Station and CS-1 and CS-102 Control Stations.

The controller issues commands, such as Play, Stop, and Fast Forward, to one or more controlled devices, which perform the requested action. They might send a response message back to the controller, as well. If there are two or more controlled devices in the system, their responses should be merged, preferably within the controller, using multiple MIDI In ports. You could use an external merger, which should work most of the time. However, this type of system could choke if the MIDI bandwidth is maxed out, so be careful.

Figure 9-3. The JLCooper CuePoint provides a universal MMC controller for many transport-based devices, including most digital multitrack tape decks.

The connection between the controller and a controlled device can be configured as an open or closed loop (see Fig. 9-4). In an open loop, the controller's MIDI Out is connected to the controlled device's MIDI In, but not the other way around. In a closed loop, the controlled device's MIDI Out is connected to the controller's MIDI In, which lets it send responses back to the controller.

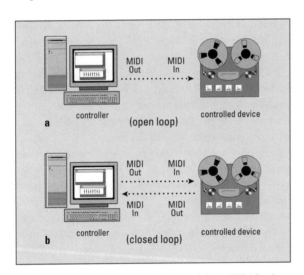

Figure 9-4. In an open-loop configuration (a), the MIDI Out from the controller is connected to the MIDI In of the controlled device, but not vice versa. A closed-loop configuration (b) lets the controlled device send responses back to the controller.

A closed-loop connection is also important for handshaking between devices. For example, each device stores received messages in a memory buffer until it can perform the requested action. If the buffer becomes full before the action is complete, the device sends a Wait command to the sender, which stops the transmission until it receives a Resume command. All MMC devices should expect a closed loop by default. If the controller doesn't receive the expected response from a controlled device, it should automatically switch to open-loop status.

Commanding Presence

As mentioned earlier, MMC commands are sent from the controller to one or more controlled devices. Each device is assigned a unique ID number that identifies the device for which a command is intended and from which a command or response is sent. Devices can also be assigned a group ID number, which lets the controller send one command to all devices with a common group ID. In addition, the controller can send a message to all devices in the system by using a special "all call" ID number.

There are several types of MMC commands; perhaps the most common of which are the control commands, which directly affect the operation of a controlled device's transport. Most control commands are also known as Motion Control States (MCS). Currently defined MCS commands include Play, Stop, Pause, Fast Forward, Rewind, Search, Shuttle, Step, and Eject.

The purpose of many of these commands is self-evident, but a few are not. For example, Search tells the device to move in the specified direction at the specified speed while producing audio or picture for monitoring, and Shuttle does the same thing without audible or visual monitoring. Step tells the transport to move a specified distance forward or backward with monitoring.

Additional MCS commands include Deferred Play, Variable Play, and Deferred Variable Play. The Deferred versions are used when the controlled device is in the process of locating to a specified point, after which the device drops into Play mode. The Variable versions let you specify the speed and direction of the transport as it plays.

Another type of control command is known as a Motion Control Process (MCP). This type of command causes the controlled device to implement its own commands to achieve the desired result. For example, the Locate MCP command moves the transport to a specified time-code value, which involves several MCS commands.

The remaining control commands relate to the record function in a controlled device. These commands include Record Strobe (i.e., engage record mode for the enabled tracks), Variable Record Strobe, Record Exit, and Record Pause.

A number of commands determine the flow of information from one device to another. These I/O commands include Read, Write, and Update, which apply to information within a controlled device (more in a moment). Communications commands include the aforementioned Wait and Resume, which can be sent by any device in the system, and Group, which assigns a Group ID to a device.

Finally, two commands provide some automated activity. The Event command tells a controlled device to execute any specified MMC command at a specified time-code value. The Procedure command defines a sequence of commands and tells the controlled device to execute that sequence.

It's About Time

Obviously, synchronization is an important issue when controlling transport-based devices. MMC uses two forms of MIDI Time Code to cue these devices to the desired location: full form and short form. Full-form MTC uses five bytes to represent hours, minutes, seconds, frames, and subframes (1/100 of a frame). The subframes can be replaced by status information, such as whether the incoming time code is "real" or is simply timing information from a tape deck's tachometer pulses during a fast wind.

Short-form MTC sends an initial value in hours, minutes, seconds, frames, and subframes, but thereafter sends only frames and subframes, which uses only two bytes per message. (Hours, minutes, and seconds are sent only when they change.) This conserves bandwidth in the MIDI datastream. In either case, System Common MTC Quarter Frame messages are sent four times per frame when the system is actually running to keep the devices synchronized (see Chapter 6).

There are a number of commands that relate specifically to time code. For example, the Sync commands include Assign System Master, which specifies the system's time-code source, and the Chase command, which is an MCP command that tells the controlled device to locate its transport to the current time-code value and lock to it.

Fields of Info

Most of the responses from a controlled device consist of data from the device's memory. This data is stored in memory locations called Information Fields. For example, the type of SMPTE time code (i.e., frame rate and drop/non-drop type) used by a device is stored in an Information Field called Selected Time Code. The controller accesses the data in any Information Field with a Read command. This command returns data that reflects the current condition of the device, not necessarily the data that was most recently written to the Information Field by the controller.

Data in an Information Field is updated with a Write or Update command. For example, each track in a device is record-enabled by writing to its Track Record Ready Information Field. This Information Field is used in conjunction with another section of the device's memory called the Track Bitmap. The tracks within a device are identified as active or inactive in the Track Bitmap, which consists of one bit for each track. Only an active track can be record-enabled. A Track Bitmap can support up to 317 tracks before message segmentation is required.

Responses and Information Fields are organized into several categories, just as the commands are. The Control responses include those that reflect the state of the transport, such as Stop Mode, Fast Mode, Play Speed Reference, Fixed Speed, and Step Length (which is used by the Step command). The Record/Playback Control responses include Record Mode, Record Status, Track Record Status, Track Record Ready, and Track Mute.

In addition, a number of Information Fields are related to monitoring. For example, Global Monitor determines whether the input signal for all active tracks is monitored. This monitor signal can be synchronous with any new material being recorded, but in the case of audio tape recorders, the quality of the monitor signal is not very high because the same head used for recording is also used for playback. The monitor signal can also be placed in Repro mode, which uses separate heads for playback, so the sound quality is better. However, a Repro monitor signal will not be in sync with new material being recorded.

Time-code synchronization Information Fields include Chase Mode and Selected Master Code. If you specify an offset (a starting time-code value other than 00:00:00:00.00), two Information Fields let the system compare the Requested Offset with the Actual Offset. If the device strays from the incoming time code, this is recorded in the Lock Deviation field. An MTC Input field is constantly updated with the most recent MTC value.

There are a number of commands that perform mathematical calculations on time-code values. These commands include Add, Subtract, Move, and Drop Frame Adjust. The results of these calculations are then stored in up to eight General Purpose (GP) registers within each controlled device. The GP registers are also used to store locate points. This makes it easy to identify important sections of the recording and to move to them.

Applications

As mentioned earlier, MMC is used to integrate several types of equipment in the studio. Typically, a computer running sequencer and/or hard-disk recording software is the controller in an MMC system that includes a multitrack ATR (such as an Alesis ADAT or TASCAM DA-88/38), 2-track ATR (such as a

DAT), stand-alone HDR, and/or VTR. If you start the computer at a particular measure, the controlled devices locate to the corresponding time-code value and play along. You can also arm and disarm tracks at will and automate punching in and out.

Ideally, you want bidirectional MIDI communication between the controller and each controlled device to accommodate commands, responses, and handshaking (see Fig. 9-5). However, most VTRs don't include MIDI ports; instead, professional models are controlled through another standard, bidirectional interface called Sony 9-pin. In addition, DAT decks don't typically include a MIDI interface, but a few (such as some from Fostex) include a Sony 9-pin interface. For these devices, you need an MMC-to-9-pin converter, such as the JLCooper MMC9.

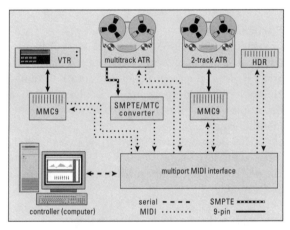

Figure 9-5. In an MMC system, some devices might need an MMC-to-9-pin converter, such as the JLCooper MMC9. If none of the devices generates time code internally, you might need to stripe SMPTE on the multitrack ATR and use it as the master sync source via the SMPTE-to-MTC converter.

If one of the devices in the system generates MTC (such as the sequencer software or HDR), it can be used as the master source of time code. If not, you might need to stripe SMPTE time code on one track of the multitrack ATR and use a SMPTE-to-MTC converter to synchronize the sequencer and other devices to the multitrack (see Fig. 9-5). Modular digital multitracks such as an ADATs or DA-88/38s can be equipped with a sync option that reads and generates SMPTE and MTC. Both units also require a hardware option to utilize MMC.

MIDI Machine Control demonstrates the power and flexibility of MIDI by allowing musicians to control more equipment with a single, consistent scheme. No matter what types of devices you prefer to use in your studio, they can probably be controlled via MIDI, which makes life a whole lot easier for recordists everywhere.

Your high-school math teachers were right. You really should have paid attention to everything they taught you, because one day it would have real-world relevance to your life. Like it or not, that day has arrived. If you really want to take the best advantage of all your electronic-music gear, you need to know some math. This is particularly true if you want to dive into the daunting but powerful world of MIDI System Exclusive, or SysEx.

System Exclusive messages represent the specific parameters of each instrument. Unlike all other MIDI messages, they are different from one device to another. (There are a couple of exceptions to this: Universal System Exclusive messages are defined for all devices to represent things such as MIDI Machine Control and the Sample Dump Standard.) With SysEx, you can do all sorts of things, such as requesting parameter values and bulk dumps, remotely controlling parameter values in synths and signal processors in real time, and programming custom applications in programs such as Opcode's *MAX*. Before you can use it, however, you need to understand the hexadecimal number system.

Hexadecimal Notation

Most computers use groups of eight binary digits, or bits, to represent data and instructions in a code; these 8-bit groups are called bytes. MIDI devices are nothing more than dedicated computers that use bytes to represent messages. Each byte can have one of 256 different values; the lowest value is 00000000 = 0, while the highest value is 11111111 = 255. Each value represents a different message.

Unfortunately, humans find binary bytes cumbersome to work with, so a more compact number system called hexadecimal, or hex, is used to represent bytes. The derivation of the name is straightforward: "Hexa" (6) plus "decimal" (10) indicates that this system uses sixteen digits. As a result, the hex system can represent any byte with just two digits.

The hex system uses the same digits as the familiar decimal system, 0 through 9, for its first ten digits. The other six digits are the first six letters of the alphabet. Therefore, the digits of the hex system are 0 through 9, followed by A through F. This lets us write any 8-bit byte as a 2-digit hex number (see table, "Running the Numbers").

The numbers 0 through 9 are equal in appearance and value in the decimal and hex systems. However, some of the numbers above 9 might look the same, but they are not equal. For example, 10 in hex is equal to 16 in decimal. For this reason, hex numbers are written with a "$" before the number or "H" after the number. (The latter form is more common in MIDI.) For example, $10 = 16 or 10H = 16.

System Exclusive

As mentioned earlier, most SysEx messages do not represent performance gestures and other musical information common to all devices. Instead, SysEx messages represent the parameters for sound generation and modification, samples, sequences, bulk-data dumps, and settings for effects processors. For example, editor/librarians use SysEx to communicate with devices in a system (see Chapter 10).

Unlike all other MIDI messages, System Exclusive messages can be any length because they represent individual parameters and bulk dumps in different instruments. So how do devices know when a SysEx message is finished? The last byte is always the same: it's called EOX (End Of eXclusive). This is actually one of the System Common messages, but it's used to end all SysEx messages.

The exact format of a SysEx message varies from one instrument and manufacturer to another, but they all begin with the hexadecimal number F0H, which indicates the start of a SysEx message. This is followed by an ID number that identifies the manufacturer of the device; each manufacturer is assigned a unique ID number by the MIDI Manufacturers Association (MMA) or the Japanese MIDI Standards Committee (JMSC). Some manufacturer IDs are one byte long, but more recent IDs are three bytes long to accommodate the growing number of manufacturers.

The next byte in most cases is the basic channel to which the device is set. The basic channel is sometimes replaced by a device ID, which is also set in the device itself. This allows several identical devices to be addressed separately. The next two bytes are often a product or model ID, which identifies the specific product model, and a message type, which specifies the type of message it is.

The specific data bytes follow these initial header bytes; the data can be of any length, but some devices limit it to 256 bytes or another fixed amount. The last byte is always F7H, which represents the end-of-exclusive message. By the way, the format of these first few bytes sometimes varies between devices, but the preceding example is a good guide to get you started.

Using SysEx Hex

Understanding hexadecimal notation and the general format of SysEx messages is vital to using this part of MIDI successfully. Another crucial step is the ability to read the SysEx implementation chart at the back of most owner's manuals. This chart usually covers several pages in very small type, unlike the MIDI implementation chart (see Chapter 6). The SysEx codes for all parameters in the device are listed here.

Some instruments require bidirectional connections to send or receive SysEx messages; in other words, you must connect both MIDI Out and MIDI In to the appropriate ports on the other device. This is not true for all MIDI devices, so check the owner's manual to be sure.

As discussed earlier, bidirectional connections allow handshaking between devices. This lets the devices establish an active communications link before any data is sent. It also allows the receiving device to send a message requesting a SysEx bulk dump from the transmitting device. In addition, the receiving device can send an acknowledgment to the transmitting device after each packet of data is received.

For Example

Consider the Roland Sound Canvas. Most of its programmable parameters are available remotely via SysEx or from the front panel in Micro Edit mode. However, this mode presents parameters in hex in the display, so the following discussion is applicable in either case.

The Sound Canvas's SysEx messages include three main sections: Header, Body, and EOX. The Header is virtually identical for most Sound Canvas SysEx messages:

F0H Start SysEx

41H Roland ID

dev Device ID (The possible numbers range from 00H to 1FH, specified by front-panel controls.)

mdl Model ID (This number is 42H if the instrument is in GS mode, 45H if it's in native Sound Canvas mode.)

cmd Command ID (The value is 11H if the message is a request for data, 12H if it is sending data.)

You can have up to 32 Sound Canvases in a system with Device ID numbers ranging from 0 to 31 (00H to 1FH). The Model ID depends on whether the unit is in GS mode or native Sound Canvas mode. There are two basic types of SysEx messages: requests for data and data to be sent. These are indicated by the Command ID.

If the message is a request for data, the Body of the message includes three bytes that specify the internal address of the parameter. Following that are three bytes that specify the number of data bytes requested. If the message is new data for a parameter, the address is followed by the new data (up to 256 bytes).

The last byte in the Body is called the checksum, which is not found in the SysEx messages of most other manufacturers. The checksum provides error correction in the following manner: the message is valid if the sum of the address bytes, data bytes, and checksum byte is a multiple of 80H (or 10000000 in binary). To calculate the checksum, simply add the address bytes and data bytes and subtract the result from 80H. I strongly recommend you use a calculator that can deal with hex, such as the Casio fx-115d. Performing hex arithmetic in your head or by longhand is a pain in the butt.

Let's look at a specific example. Suppose you have a Sound Canvas set to Device ID 1 (00H) and GS mode (Model ID 42H). The device is bidirectionally connected to a computer running a sequencer that lets you type and send individual SysEx messages; the program also displays SysEx messages sent by the Sound Canvas. (This can also be accomplished with a hardware sequencer, such as the Roland MC-50.) For the sake of this example, let's say you want to find out what MIDI channel is assigned to Part 1, then turn that Part off altogether.

The first step is to send a request for the required data. The address of the Receive Channel for Part 1 is 40H 11H 02H (the address for Part 2 would be 40H 12H 02H, and so on). The Receive Channel is specified with one byte, so we want to see only the single byte at the specified address. To calculate the checksum, start by adding all the address bytes and number of bytes requested.

$$40H + 11H + 02H + 01H = 54H$$

This is the number you subtract from 80H to calculate the checksum.

$$80H - 54H = 2CH$$

So the checksum byte is 2CH.

The entire message you type looks like this:

F0H	Start SysEx
41H	Roland ID
00H	Device ID
42H	Model ID
11H	Request Data
40H	Address of Receive Channel for Part 1
11H	Address of Receive Channel for Part 1
02H	Address of Receive Channel for Part 1
00H	Number of Data Bytes Requested (specified in three bytes)
00H	Number of Data Bytes Requested (specified in three bytes)
01H	Number of Data Bytes Requested (specified in three bytes)
2CH	Checksum
F7H	EOX

The response should look like this:

F0H	Start SysEx
41H	Roland ID
00H	Device ID
42H	Model ID
12H	Send Data (from Sound Canvas to sequencer)
40H	Address of Receive Channel for Part 1
11H	Address of Receive Channel for Part 1
02H	Address of Receive Channel for Part 1
00H	Receive Channel (00H = channel 1)
2DH	Checksum
F7H	EOX

To turn Part 1 off altogether, send a value of 10H to the same address. First, add the address bytes and data bytes.

$$40H + 11H + 02H + 10H = 63H$$

Then, subtract this value from 80H to find the checksum.

$$80H - 63H = 1DH$$

The entire message looks like this:

F0H	Start SysEx
41H	Roland ID
00H	Device ID
42H	Model ID
12H	Send Data
40H	Address of Receive Channel for Part 1
11H	Address of Receive Channel for Part 1
02H	Address of Receive Channel for Part 1
10H	Data Byte
1DH	Checksum
F7H	EOX

Admittedly, this hex stuff takes some practice. In particular, the Roland checksum is an additional pain that doesn't affect most other manufacturers. Nevertheless, learning SysEx hex is worth the trouble if you enjoy exploring beneath the surface of your synths.

RUNNING THE NUMBERS		
Decimal	**Binary Byte**	**Hexadecimal**
0	00000000	00H
1	00000001	01H
2	00000010	02H
10	00001010	0AH
15	00001111	0FH
16	00010000	10H
28	00011100	1CH
31	00011111	1FH
32	00100000	20H
63	00111111	3FH
64	01000000	40H
127	01111111	7FH
128	10000000	80H
240	11110000	F0H
247	11110111	F7H
253	11111101	FDH
255	11111111	FFH

Computers

Chapter 10: Computer Applications
Hard-Disk Recording
Editor/Librarians
Notation
Music Education

Chapter 11: SCSI

Computer Applications

Most people believe MIDI was developed exclusively to connect and remotely control synthesizers from different manufacturers. But there was another incentive: developers wanted to use personal computers to make music, and they designed MIDI to accomplish this. Shortly thereafter, music software was created, and low-cost computers became music collaborators.

Today, creative developers have produced an enormous variety of software to facilitate various musical activities, such as sequencing, audio recording, music printing, sound editing and organization, and education. These programs have made personal computers an invaluable assistant in any personal electronic music studio.

Basics

There are two major types of computers, or platforms, commonly used by musicians in the U.S.: Apple Macintosh and Windows-based PCs. Atari and Commodore Amiga computers used to be popular among musicians, but they aren't sold in the U.S. anymore. (Atari computers are still popular in Europe.) The Windows platform is by far the most common among amateurs and hobbyists, but the Mac still dominates among professional musicians and engineers.

Connecting a computer to a MIDI system requires a MIDI interface. The Atari computers include a MIDI interface as standard equipment, but the other platforms require a separate, optional interface. An interface can take the form of an external box that connects to one of the computer's serial or parallel ports, or a circuit board installed in an expansion slot. Many sound cards also include a MIDI interface. In any case, the interface includes one or more MIDI In and Out jacks, which allow MIDI data to be sent back and forth between the computer and connected MIDI devices.

More sophisticated interfaces (often called multiport interfaces) include many Ins and Outs, which lets you connect each device in your studio to its own, dedicated ports. In addition, these high-end interfaces often provide a variety of MIDI processing functions (see Chapter 9). With the right software, you can direct different streams of MIDI messages to different devices independently and process those messages in many different ways.

As computers have become more powerful, they have acquired the ability to run more than one music application (e.g., a MIDI sequencer and editor/librarian) simultaneously. As this capability was being developed, it raised the issue of sharing information (particularly MIDI data) between these programs and managing their access to the MIDI interface. On the Macintosh, this was first addressed by Apple's MIDI Manager system software, which lets you connect the "output" of one program to the "input" of another in an onscreen "patch bay."

Shortly after MIDI Manager was introduced, Opcode Systems released its own music-management system software called OMS (which originally stood for Opcode MIDI System and now means Open Music System). Mark of the Unicorn has also developed its own system software with a similar purpose called FreeMIDI.

Both of these software packages integrate various music applications by managing the flow of MIDI data between the applications and the MIDI interface(s). In addition, they keep track of the devices that are connected to the interface(s), which lets you select devices from within any compatible application based on their names rather than having to remember which port they're connected to. Both are available for other software developers to use, and various programs are now compatible with OMS or FreeMIDI.

As of this writing, Windows is somewhat behind the Mac in this regard. A system function called MIDI Mapper is included in Windows 3.1 and 95 that lets you remap channels on the way out of the interface, but it provides little if any support for system-wide interapplication communication between sequencers, editor/librarians, and so on. OMS is available for Windows, and Opcode's Windows software requires it, but no other software uses it on that platform. Windows NT has not supported MIDI until now, although a few software companies have written custom MIDI drivers; however, NT is about to get a set of MIDI drivers from some of the interface manufacturers.

One of the most common computer-music applications is sequencing, which is covered in Chapter 7. Other major applications are discussed in detail in this chapter.

HARD-DISK RECORDING

Ultimately, most electronic musicians want to record their music so it can be played and enjoyed (and hopefully bought!) by others. Most of us are familiar with analog tape, such as ¼-inch reel-to-reel or cassette, which has been widely used for many years (see Chapter 14). These days, however, more and more musicians are recording their material digitally, which is fundamentally different from analog recording. (For the basics of digital audio, see Chapter 5.)

Digital audio signals can be recorded on tape, hard disk, removable media (e.g., tape, MiniDisc, CD-R, and CD-RW), or computer memory (RAM or ROM). For long musical parts (e.g., vocals, acoustic guitar parts, entire tunes), removable media (including tape) and hard disk are preferred because they can hold much more data than RAM or ROM, and they provide semipermanent storage.

Decisions, Decisions

Once you decide to digitally record your tracks, you must then decide whether to record to tape or hard disk. Modular digital multitracks, or MDMs, offer the advantage of inexpensive media, while hard-disk recording lets you easily edit your tracks.

If you decide to use a hard-disk recorder (HDR), you must choose between a computer-based or modular system. A computer-based HDR (which is also called a digital audio workstation or DAW) requires a computer and includes a software package (see Fig. 10-1) and perhaps a hardware interface to get audio into and out of the computer. These systems offer a large graphic display (the computer monitor) and, in some cases, integration with MIDI sequencing. Effects are sometimes incorporated into the basic software and often can be added in the form of DSP plug-ins (more on this in a moment). Of course, computers are relatively expensive, especially those with enough horsepower to handle hard-disk recording. Desktop computers are not easily portable, but modern laptops can often perform hard-disk recording, as well.

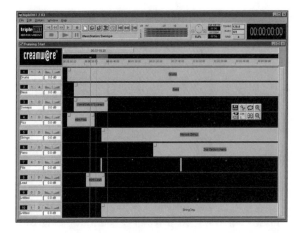

Figure 10-1. CreamWare's tripleDAT HDR system for the Windows platform lets you place blocks of audio data in different tracks.

A modular hard-disk recorder (M-HDR) is a self-contained unit with built-in hard disk, mixer, and, in many cases, effects (see Fig. 10-2). Its "brain" is nothing more than a computer dedicated to hard-disk recording. In most cases, you can combine several M-HDRs as need requires and budget allows, and you can sometimes control multiple M-HDRs from a single control panel. This is similar in principle to MDM tape decks.

Figure 10-2. The E-mu Darwin is an M-HDR with internal mixer and optional effects. The mixer is controlled with an external MIDI fader box or computer software.

M-HDRs are dedicated devices with familiar, tape deck–style controls. In addition, they are quite portable. However, they offer far fewer editing features than are available in most computer-based DAWs. M-HDRs have a relatively small display, which makes even basic editing more difficult than with a DAW. In addition, they require external synchronization to integrate with a MIDI sequencer. On the up side, M-HDRs are much more stable—crashes are far more common with computer-based systems—and because they have fewer in-depth editing features, they are generally easier to master. In addition, editing software for M-HDRs is starting to appear that essentially makes the M-HDR part of a digital audio workstation. This gives you the best of both worlds because the M-HDR can also operate autonomously.

In either case, hard-disk recorders are very useful in several applications. For example, they can be used to record individual tracks and mixdowns of entire tunes. In addition, they can perform various premastering and mastering chores. (For more on these procedures, see Chapter 22.) You can also use an HDR to backup and archive your material.

Storage Capacity

Digital audio that is recorded at a sampling rate of 44.1 kHz with a resolution of sixteen bits requires about 88 KB per second per track or 5.3 MB per minute per track. As a result, a 3-minute song with eight tracks consumes 127 MB of space. I recommend that you use a hard drive with a capacity of at least 1 GB for digital audio data.

Some HDR systems use data compression to reduce the storage requirements. Common forms of compression include µLaw, Macintosh Audio Compression/Expansion (MACE), and Adaptive Differential Pulse Code Modulation (ADPCM). Some types of compression, including most of the types currently in use in audio systems, can degrade the sound quality. As discussed in Chapter 5, lossless compression does nothing to the sound quality, but it yields the least amount of storage savings. Lossy compression actually removes some of the data, which can degrade the sound quality, but it yields greater savings, typically from 4:1 to 6:1 or more.

Other Important Criteria

HDRs can use several types of hard-disk media (which I'll cover shortly). However, they must all meet certain minimum criteria to be practical for this application. The most important of these criteria are average access time and throughput.

Access time (also called seek time) is the time it takes the drive to find a piece of data anywhere on the disk. Of course, if the disk drive's read/write head is near the location of the desired data, it takes less time than if the head is far away from the data. As a result, the average access time is calculated and used as a benchmark.

Throughput (also called data transfer rate) is the amount of data that can be sent to and from the disk per second. You can record many tracks on most hard-disk systems, up to the capacity of the disk. However, you can only play a limited number of tracks simultaneously, depending in part on the processing speed of the computer and the average access time and throughput of the disk.

If you're shopping for a hard-disk drive to use for digital audio recording, you might think it's as easy as finding a drive that meets certain seek-time

and throughput specs. As a general rule, any hard disk used for digital audio recording must have an average seek time of 12 milliseconds (ms) or less and a sustained throughput of 3 to 4 MB per second (MB/s) or more. However, it's actually a bit more complicated than that. For one thing, the minimum acceptable specs depend on the number of tracks the system must deal with simultaneously; an 8-track HDR requires a faster hard disk than a 2-track system.

In addition, many hard drives perform a routine called thermal recalibration, which compensates for slight changes in the size of the disk platter due to temperature variations. If this occurs during recording, you might miss several milliseconds of data. You can sometimes turn this function off or tell the drive to perform it only when it is not writing or reading data. Fortunately, many modern hard drives now use other means of compensation for temperature changes.

Finally, the type of connection between the computer's central processing unit (CPU) and the hard disk affects how much data can be transferred to and from the disk in a given amount of time. Some of the more common types of connections include SCSI, IDE, and ATA. In addition, each type of connection includes at least two variations, each with its own maximum throughput. (See Chapter 11 for more on SCSI.)

Fortunately, you don't typically need to worry about these issues. All you need to look for is an "A/V capable" drive, which should meet all minimum requirements for recording digital audio. In fact, most modern hard drives are A/V capable. Some computer-based DAWs, such as SADiE Inc.'s SADiE 3, supply a turnkey system, complete with suitable hard drive, while others, such as the various systems from Digidesign, provide a list of drives that have been tested for compatibility.

Types of Media

There are several types of hard-disk media, and most are available in external boxes or as internal units for computers or M-HDRs. The traditional type of hard disk is called a fixed disk, which is permanently sealed within an enclosure (see Fig. 10-3).

Figure 10-3. The Seagate Medalist 2132 is a 3.5-inch fixed disk with 2.1 GB capacity and 12.5 ms average seek time, and it uses the Fast ATA-2 bus to connect with the host CPU.

Removable cartridges behave much like floppy disks, but they hold much more data. Most of the older removable-cartridge drives are not fast enough for hard-disk recording, but recent advances in removable technology have enabled a few such products to be used for this purpose. Examples include the Iomega Jaz (1 GB), SyQuest SyJet (1.4 GB), and SY270 (270 MB). Akai uses magneto-optical (MO) removable media in their 8-track DD1500 M-HDR. This requires a custom controller chip and some sophisticated buffering of the data because MO technology is otherwise too slow for hard-disk recording.

One of the most important advantages of removable media is the fact that you can easily store the audio for each project on a separate cartridge. This makes it easy to keep track of your data and lets you take the cartridge to other studios. Removable media are also great for backing up your data (more on this in a moment).

MiniDisc is a relatively new type of removable MO cartridge that is being used in low-cost M-HDRs from Yamaha, TASCAM, and Sony (see Fig. 10-4). These units resemble the ministudios of the past, except that they use MiniDisc cartridges instead of cassette tapes. They can record and play up to four tracks of audio, and the storage capacity of a cartridge is 140 MB. These units use lossy 5:1 compression to record up to 37 minutes of audio per track. (You can also record in stereo for a total time of 74 minutes per track or in mono for a total time of 148 minutes.) According to the manufacturers, if you want to record four tracks, you must use MD Data cartridges, but for stereo recording, standard MD Audio cartridges work fine.

Figure 10-4. The Sony MDM-4X is one of a new breed of MiniDisc-based M-HDRs.

As you probably know, compact disc (CD) is a purely optical medium that holds approximately 650 MB of data, which translates to over 70 minutes of uncompressed, 44.1 kHz, 16-bit, stereo audio. Until recently, most of us could only read (play) the material that the manufacturer put on a CD. However, it is now possible for many home-studio owners to buy a CD recorder and "burn" their own CDs. This format, called CD-Recordable, or CD-R, requires a special type of blank CD.

In addition, CD-R can only be used once; you can't erase and re-record. As a result, CD-R is a write-once-read-many (WORM) medium. It is well suited for backups and archiving and has become a popular medium for premastering. It also is great when you only need small runs of music CDs for demos and promotions. A newer format called CD-Rewritable (CD-RW) lets you erase and re-record many times. Both of these formats are relatively slow compared to fixed disks, so they are generally used for stereo rather than multitrack files.

Recording and Playback

Basically, recording on an HDR is similar to using a traditional analog tape deck. Most HDRs provide tape-style transport controls, such as Play, Record, Rewind, Fast Forward, and Pause. Unlike tape decks, however, HDRs take virtually no time at all to jump from any point in the music to any other point thanks to random access. This means that the hard disk can find any piece of data in roughly the same time as any other data. By contrast, tape is linear; it must be shuttled to find a particular spot in the music. You can also punch in and out, and this does not necessarily replace the material in the punch section.

Most HDRs let you record lots of tracks, and you can typically play between two and eight tracks simultaneously from a single unit. Some systems (such as Digidesign's Pro Tools III) allow expansion to sixteen tracks and more. Even though a given HDR might be an 8-track device, it can typically hold many more tracks of data. These are sometimes called virtual tracks, which let you record many takes of each part and select the best one for playback. (Unfortunately, this term is also used to describe sequenced MIDI tracks, which can lead to some confusion.) MiniDisc recorders, by the way, do not allow virtual tracks.

In most cases, random access, nondestructive punches, and virtual tracks are possible thanks to the use of pointers, which are internal indicators the computer uses to identify and manipulate different sections of the audio data. For example, let's say you've recorded a guitar solo, and you punch into the middle of the solo to correct some mistakes. On tape, this would destroy the original material in the punch section.

With nondestructive editing on an HDR, however, the new material is stored on a different part of the disk, leaving the old material untouched. When the solo is played back, the computer uses pointers to jump to the new material and back to the old material at the correct moments. This lets you use either version of the punched section.

Pointers are also used to select the virtual tracks you want to play; you can even assemble material from several tracks into one composite track without destroying the original data. The user doesn't work with pointers directly. Instead, you tell the HDR which parts of which tracks you want to use by creating a playlist (sometimes called an edit decision list, or EDL), which is a list of the audio sections you want to play back in a certain order.

Many studio operators need to sync an HDR with a MIDI sequencer and/or tape deck. This is not an issue if you are using a digital audio sequencer that integrates hard-disk recording and sequencing. If you are using separate programs to sequence and record to hard disk, internal synchronization often works well but not always. There are different degrees of sync: some systems just trigger the audio files and MIDI files and hope they stay together, and other systems repeatedly check the synchronization and adjust the playback as required. Obviously, the more often the system checks its synchronization, the tighter the sync is likely to be.

Most M-HDRs include some form of synchronization capability, such as MIDI Time Code (MTC) or SMPTE (see Chapter 7). In some cases, these devices can only be the master time code source, which means that other devices in your system must sync to the HDR. In other cases, the HDR can be master or slave. If you are using an analog tape deck in conjunction with an HDR, the tape deck must be the master, so your HDR should be able to sync to it.

Editing and Mixing

One of the biggest advantages of HDRs is their editing capability. Typical editing functions let you cut, copy, and paste sections of digital audio. When you copy and paste a section of digital audio in a nondestructive system, the data is not actually copied and pasted. Instead, pointers are used to play the data at any moment you want during the song. This lets you record a short riff and repeat it as many times as you want without using up valuable storage space. Similarly, when you cut a piece of data, the data is not actually erased from the disk, only the pointer to that data. You can also merge the data in several tracks to one track so they all play back together.

Other common editing functions include fade ins, fade outs, and crossfades between different sections of data. Normalization adjusts the amplitude of the material so the highest peaks correspond to the system's highest allowable level to maximize the signal-to-noise ratio. You can also reverse a section so it plays from back to front.

In many cases, these operations are nondestructive. If you edit a piece of data, and you don't like what you did, you can undo it, and the original material returns unchanged. A few operations might be destructive, but the HDR will typically warn you of this before it proceeds with the operation.

Most HDRs include various effects-processing operations that can be applied to any section of the data. These include reverb, delay, chorusing, flanging, compression/limiting, and EQ (see Part 5). In many cases, the effects can be applied in real time as the data is playing back. This is much like sending the audio through an outboard effects processor.

In other cases, the computer must take some time to process the data with the desired effect. In this case, you must wait for the computer to finish its processing before you can play the material. This is sometimes called offline processing, which is often destructive, but the computer typically warns you before it proceeds. Computer-based HDR software often accepts ancillary programs called plug-ins, which let you add various forms of signal processing to the system.

In the end, you will probably want to mix your tracks and record them onto a stereo master tape. Most HDRs include their own internal mixer. In computer-based HDRs, the mixer appears on the screen. The faders and other controls can be manipulated with the mouse, but this is inefficient and sometimes impractical. It's much better to use a MIDI fader box or other dedicated mixing surface, such as JLCooper's FaderMaster or CS-10 or Peavey's PC 1600. Mixer manipulations can usually be stored and recalled during playback, which provides automated mixing.

Some M-HDRs, such as Roland's VS-880, include a physical mixing surface, which makes it easy to mix. Other M-HDRs, such as E-mu's Darwin, have an internal mixer with no physical controls. In this case, the mixer is controlled from a MIDI fader box or computer software. Because the internal mixer and effects are usually digital (i.e., the signals never leave the digital domain), there is none of the degradation of signal quality that so often accompanies conversions from analog to digital and back again.

Care and Feeding

Despite their popularity, hard disks are finicky creatures; they crash and corrupt data. As a result, it's critical to back up your data regularly (preferably after each and every session). Removable cartridges provide the most flexible solutions; if your primary storage crashes, the cartridge can be used immediately. CD-R is even better for long-term storage because it takes far longer to deteriorate than magnetic media does. You can also use a data DAT deck, but in this case you must restore the data to a hard disk before you can use it. Many modern computers and some M-HDRs include a SCSI port, which lets you connect an external device, such as a removable-media drive or data DAT deck. (Some PCs require an add-on SCSI card.)

A few systems let you back up to an audio DAT deck or MDM, but this also requires that you restore the data, and it's a bit of a kludge. For example, the Fostex DMT-8 has no SCSI port, but it backs up two tracks at a time to audio DAT via the S/PDIF digital audio outputs. The Digidesign HDR systems can also back up to audio DAT using a program called *DATa*. This program backs up the playlist information followed by the actual audio data, all of which is sent to the DAT deck from the digital audio outputs on the interface hardware.

As you record and edit material, it is stored in different places on the disk. If data already exists on the disk and the system is unable to write an entire file in one contiguous area, the data must be stored in pieces that are reassembled by the computer upon demand. Eventually, the data is so fragmented—spread out—that the computer can no longer find it efficiently. This also occurs when you do a lot of destructive edits, resulting in data being added and deleted. If the data becomes fragmented enough—and this can happen surprisingly quickly—disk access is slowed, and eventually crashes can occur.

As a result, the disk should be defragmented or optimized every so often, depending on how much you use the system. (In the Macintosh world, defragmenting puts each file in a contiguous space; optimizing not only defragments each file but reorganizes the entire disk so that data files are stored contiguously, applications are stored contiguously, and so on. In the Windows world, no such distinction is made: defragmenting includes optimizing.) This is easy on a computer-based system; simply run a disk-maintenance program and defragment the disk. Of course, make sure to back up the disk before performing the defragmentation. Most M-HDRs defragment automatically or provide a method to initiate the process manually.

If you opt for a computer-based HDR, I recommend that you dedicate a separate hard disk to your digital audio data. Of course, you can record onto your primary hard disk, which also holds your operating system, applications, and other data files. But dedicating a hard disk to digital audio makes it easier and safer to defragment and back up the disk on a regular basis.

EDITOR/LIBRARIANS

In the early days of electronic music, synthesizers had no memory for storing programs. You created a program by connecting various modules with patch cords and setting controls. Today, synthesizers and other electronic-music devices, such as effects processors, have memory to store hundreds of programs, which makes it easy to have lots of sounds on hand but difficult to organize and keep track of them.

You can edit these programs on the device's front panel, but a small display and nested layers of parameter pages can make this less than intuitive. Computers can help alleviate these problems with a type of software called an editor/librarian (or ed/lib for short). The editor portion of this software helps you create and edit synth and effects programs on the computer's large screen, and the librarian portion organizes and stores these programs and transfers them to and from each compatible device in your system.

Most ed/libs are universal, which means they work with many different MIDI devices. Some universal ed/libs include librarian modules but not editor modules for certain devices. In some cases, you can custom-configure the software by selecting only the editor and librarian modules that pertain to the devices in your studio.

Interestingly, there aren't all that many editor/librarians on the market as of this writing. The most common are Emagic *SoundSurfer* (lib only; Mac, Windows) and *SoundDiver* (ed/lib; Mac, Windows), Mark of the Unicorn *Unisyn* (ed/lib; Mac, Windows), Opcode *Galaxy* (lib only; Mac) and *Galaxy Plus Editors* (ed/lib; Mac), Sound Quest *Midi Quest* (ed/lib; Mac, Windows, Amiga, Atari), and Terzoid *NoiZe* (ed/lib; Windows). Sound Quest also offers a variety of individual editors for different devices on Windows, Mac, Atari, and Amiga platforms, and the Terzoid editors are available individually for Windows computers.

Foundation

Ed/libs use System Exclusive (SysEx) messages to communicate with the devices in your system. Each device creates sound and stores programs in its own unique way. SysEx was designed to allow manufacturers to encode all that is unique about each device, unlike the rest of MIDI, which provides a common language for all devices (see Chapter 9).

Some devices require a bidirectional MIDI connection to the computer for SysEx handshaking; these devices must send and receive acknowledgment messages for each chunk of SysEx. Other devices need only one-way connections. In either case, it's best to establish bidirectional connections for all devices in your system with a multiport MIDI interface or patch bay. This way, each device can send and receive SysEx from the ed/lib as needed without having to repatch MIDI cables.

It is often possible to integrate an ed/lib with other MIDI applications, such as a sequencer, under a common music-software management system. For example, *Galaxy* and *Vision* can be integrated under Opcode's Open Music System (OMS), and *Unisyn* and *Performer* can be integrated under MOTU's FreeMIDI. This lets the sequencer display lists of patch names rather than numbers, which is much more convenient.

The OMS Name Manager also allows some non-Opcode, OMS-compatible sequencers, such as Steinberg's *Cubase,* to access the names of programs stored in *Galaxy*. Similarly, *NoiZe* can send patch names to Twelve Tone Systems' *Cakewalk,* and you can edit a patch while the sequencer plays in the background, which lets you hear your edits in a musical context.

Emagic *Logic* and *SoundDiver* are integrated with a function called AutoLink at the program level; there are no system extensions to deal with. Like a system extension, AutoLink lets the ed/lib and sequencer share program names. In addition, you can record SysEx from *SoundDiver* into *Logic* and play it back from *Logic* to *SoundDiver,* which moves *SoundDiver*'s onscreen controls.

Editor

Editing synth and effects programs on a computer offers several important advantages (see Fig. 10-5). For one thing, the computer's large screen displays much more information at once than any display on music hardware. In addition, you can edit envelopes graphically, which is much more intuitive than tweaking numbers. In a computer-based editor, it's easy to

cut or copy and paste parameters from one program to another.

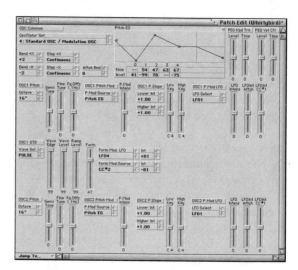

Figure 10-5. This is the *Unisyn* editor for the Korg Prophesy. Well-organized onscreen sliders and graphic envelopes make editing a relative breeze. (Courtesy Mark of the Unicorn)

In the early days of computer-based editors, each instrument required a separate, dedicated editor program. Now, most editors include modules for many devices. As new devices are introduced, new editor modules can be added to the main program. In some cases, the user can create custom modules for instruments that are not otherwise supported by the editor. However, this means you must learn the ed/lib's programming language.

When you tweak a parameter on the computer's screen, the editor sends the corresponding SysEx message to the synth, which behaves as if its internal parameter had been changed from the front panel. You can then play the synth and hear the effect of the changes you make in the editor in real time.

In addition, there are generally several ways to change the value of parameters. For example, you can type in a parameter value or drag the mouse to scroll through values. Envelopes can be changed by dragging graphic breakpoints with the mouse. MIDI note numbers, Velocity values, and Control Change values can often be entered by manipulating the appropriate item on your MIDI controller.

Librarian

Most librarians let you store programs in at least two different types of files: banks and libraries (see Fig. 10-6). Banks correspond exactly with the banks in each device, which are organized differently. Some might have banks of 8, 16, 32, 64, 100, or 128 programs. In addition, most modern synths include banks of different types of programs, such as single sounds, multitimbral programs, effects, etc. As a result, the librarian banks for each device must correspond with that device's bank structure.

Figure 10-6. This screen from *Galaxy* includes a Roland JV-1080 library, a bank of Performances, and a Bundle of different types of data. The keyboard at the bottom of the screen lets you audition selected sounds, and the transport controls let you play MIDI Files, record a sequence, or control *Vision* to hear selected sounds in a musical context. (Courtesy Opcode)

The advantage of this approach is that each bank can be received from and sent to the device all at once, which lets you back up and restore the contents of the device in case it crashes. In addition, the computer can store many more banks than the device's memory can hold. You can also assemble custom banks by cutting and pasting programs from one to another. This lets you easily configure the instrument with the sounds you need for a particular project. In most cases, you can even swap programs between locations in the same bank or different banks, which is great if you want to keep both programs and there are no free spaces.

Libraries typically store any number of patches (limited only by the computer's available RAM memory) in one large file. However, these patches must be transferred between the device and the computer one at a time. In general, libraries are used as a main repository of programs, which are then copied from the library and pasted into banks. For example, you might store all your bass patches in one library, all your string patches in another library, and so on. You can then assemble banks of basses and strings or banks with different sounds that are used in a particular live set or studio session.

Most ed/libs also offer a third type of file, which stores different types of banks. *Galaxy* calls this a Bundle, which can include banks of different types of files, even for different devices in your system. You can specify which banks to include in a Bundle, letting you combine banks for a specific device or project, or you can include all banks for all devices in your system.

When you send a Bundle from *Galaxy,* each

bank is sent to the appropriate instrument. Bundles can even keep track of which single and effects programs are used in multitimbral programs; in this case, the multi program is called the "parent" and the associated single and effects programs are called "children." When you move a multi program to a different location, its child programs retain their association. Conversely, a Bundle keeps track of where you move child programs and retains their connection with the parent program.

In *Unisyn,* this type of file is called a Performance. As in *Galaxy,* you can select what types of data to include in a Performance. In *Midi Quest,* this type of file is called a Group, and in *NoiZe,* it's called a Project. In all cases, the parent/child relationship between programs is maintained.

SoundDiver is organized a bit differently than the others. For one thing, it saves only libraries, not banks or Bundle-like files. However, its libraries are much more flexible than those in most other editor/librarians. For example, a library can include any number of different types of programs for multiple devices, and these programs can be sent to the appropriate memory locations of each device at once.

A function called Memory Manager mirrors the memory architecture of each device, which lets you save individual banks as separate libraries. In addition, AutoLink allows *SoundDiver* to save a library of programs used in a *Logic* sequence, which can be automatically sent to the devices in the system when you open the sequence in *Logic.* As in the other ed/libs, parent/child relationships between programs in a library are maintained.

Icing on the Cake

After you have amassed thousands of programs in a librarian, it is critical to be able to locate the program you want, and most ed/libs include several database functions to help in this regard. Perhaps most important, they let you associate keywords with each program. For example, you might assign the keyword "bass" to all your bass programs.

In most cases, you can enter several keywords for each program. If you have a bunch of bass programs, you might want to distinguish between them with additional keywords such as fretless, slap, acoustic, etc. This lets you quickly and easily search for all fretless bass sounds in the library. Most ed/libs can also identify and delete duplicate programs, which helps avoid redundancy and free up space for other programs.

Once you find the types of sounds you want, you can easily audition them to select the best sound for any particular application (see Fig. 10-6). When you select any program in the ed/lib, it is sent to a temporary memory area in the instrument called the edit buffer. Some ed/libs, such as *Midi Quest* and *Sound-Diver,* even include a simple sequencer or MIDI File player to audition programs in a musical context from within the software.

One of the most interesting aspects of ed/libs is their ability to generate new programs automatically. There are typically two ways to do this. Random generation sets any selected parameters to random values, which can often be constrained to user-specified limits. Program blending combines the parameter values from two or more programs to create a new program. Some ed/libs can generate an entire bank of programs in these ways. Many of these programs are pretty lame, but sometimes you find a few that are really good. These winners can be used directly or can serve as the starting point for your own tweaking.

As you can see, editor/librarians are useful pieces of software for any electronic musician. They help keep your synth, effects, and other programs organized, and they make editing a breeze. Just make sure that your devices are supported by the software before you buy; once you do, you can really start cleaning up your act.

What's in a Name?

Throughout my discussion of editor/librarians, I use the term "program" to refer to specific sounds, effects, and other sets of data that are created and stored within various MIDI devices. However, different manufacturers of MIDI devices and ed/libs use different terms for these entities. For example, a single sound on a synth might be called a patch, voice, or tone, which can become quite confusing.

In addition, most manufacturers have their own names for different types of programs or patches. For example, a multitimbral combination of sounds might be called a multi, combi, setup, or performance. Other types of entities include drum kits, effects, sequences, and global or system settings. (For more on this issue, see "Tower of Techno-Babel" in Chapter 23.)

In MOTU's *Unisyn,* different types of data (e.g., patches, combis, effects, etc.) are called Modules. I prefer to use the term "program" when referring to a generic sound entity, which might be a synth patch, drum kit, multitimbral combination, effects program, or some other type of data. In all cases, the data must be "programmed," which is why I prefer this term for generic purposes.

It's the dream of every musician in the computer age: instant, flawless transcriptions of live performances and an end to tedious copying, transposing, and arranging with pen and paper. After all, word processors have changed the face of writing with words; why not apply this idea to music notation?

Of course, many software companies have been working hard to do just that. Spawned by the inherent graphic orientation of the Macintosh and MIDI's representation of musical performance gestures, music notation software has come a long way since its inception. There are titles for all major platforms, and their capabilities are far more advanced than earlier attempts. However, the dream has yet to be fully realized.

Background

Let's face it: we're asking the computer to perform a daunting task. The written language of music is extremely dense and 2-dimensional, unlike the written language of words. In addition, the relationship between written music and its performance depends on convention and interpretation. For example, eighth notes in swing jazz are written as equal in length, but they are played long-short-long-short. Not only that, humans are notoriously inaccurate by computer standards; in effect, we want them to transcribe what we mean, not what we actually play!

Nevertheless, notation software can help musicians in many ways. These programs do not resemble word processors as much as page-layout software; their strengths lie in the manipulation of musical symbols for printing. With one of these programs and some time, you can generate lead sheets, ensemble scores, and parts. You can also rearrange existing music for different instruments, key signatures, and so on.

One important element is the inevitable trade-off between ease of use and power. It seems that the more powerful and feature-laden a notation program is, the harder it is to use. This is partly due to the nature of the process; music notation is not a trivial pursuit. Some companies offer simpler, scaled-down versions of their more powerful products for those who don't need the more sophisticated features; Coda's *Finale* and *MusicProse* (Mac, PC) are examples of a powerful program and its simpler sibling.

Input

The first step in using any notation software is getting musical data into the program. In addition to a symbol palette from which you select and place notes, rests, etc., virtually all notation programs include a sequencer of some sort. This feature lets you enter notes in real time or step time from a MIDI instrument. However, the sequencers in most notation software are designed to get MIDI data into the program; they normally don't have the full capabilities of dedicated sequencer programs.

Another common method of data entry is to import a Standard MIDI File (SMF) from another sequencer (see Chapter 7). Simply save the file in SMF format within the sequencer and open it in the notation program. This method lets you tweak the data before it gets to the notation software, which can result in a more accurate initial transcription.

The accuracy of initial transcription varies widely from one program to the next, but it's safe to say that no program gets it perfect on the first try. In fact, no program gets it perfect without some help. For example, enharmonic "spellings" (e.g., F# or G♭) often need to be fixed, and it's difficult to determine whether short eighth notes should be notated as eighth notes with staccato marks or sixteenth notes with rests between them (see Fig. 10-7).

Figure 10-7. If you play four short eighth notes in a row, do you intend it to be sixteenth notes with rests or staccato eighth notes?

Manipulation

Once the raw data is input, it must be massaged before it is printed. The first step is to set up the score. Depending on the instrumentation, you can typically combine different types of staves. For example, a piano solo is notated on a grand, or piano, staff. A lead sheet or accompanied solo might include a grand staff and a single staff, while an ensemble score includes several staves, one for each instrument or group of instruments.

Most programs offer at least two ways to view the score. A scroll view displays the score as if it were on a continuous horizontal roll of paper. The page view displays the score as it appears on individual sheets of paper.

The initial clefs, key signature, and time signature are all specified at the beginning of the score. Some programs allow different key signatures for each part and/or odd key signatures like those in Balkan music (e.g., F# and B♭). Other programs also allow complex time signatures such as 2+¾. Most programs let you insert clefs, key signatures, and time signatures at any point in the score, as well.

The next symbols to deal with are the notes themselves. MIDI represents each pitch with a unique number, so the transcription of pitch is generally quite accurate (with the possible exception of enharmonic spelling). More problems arise with respect to rhythm. Even slight inaccuracies can bring unexpected results.

The nature of transcription requires that the displayed notes be quantized; each note must be assigned a certain standard rhythmic value. Each program has a rhythmic resolution, which determines the shortest note that can be represented in the score. Most programs stop at 128th notes, which is fine for virtually all applications; Coda's *Finale* goes up to 4,096th notes!

Alternate noteheads are important for percussion and spoken-word parts. These noteheads often consist of a diamond and/or "x." Diagonal slashes are used in comping chord parts for keyboards, guitar, and bass. Grace notes are also available in some programs; these appear in a smaller-than-normal size and represent very short, ornamental notes.

Consecutive eighth, sixteenth, and shorter notes are usually beamed in groups of one or two beats. In some programs, these notes are initially transcribed with individual flags, after which you select the appropriate groups and apply a beaming function; others do this automatically. Several programs allow cross-staff beaming, which lets you connect notes across staves, an important feature for piano music.

Rests are sometimes inserted automatically, or you might have to insert them manually after the initial transcription. If they are inserted automatically, you will almost certainly have to adjust them as you tweak the notes in the score.

The next step is the addition of any lyrics. Most programs let you type in lyrics directly, but with some programs it's usually better to type them into a word processor, save them as a text or ASCII file, and import them into the notation program. Unlike with normal writing, many programs require that all multi-syllable words be completely hyphenated. This is how lyrics are associated with music; one syllable per note. Some programs automatically attach syllables to notes, while others require you to place them manually. Either way, lyrics can affect the placement of notes, so they should be added before any other symbols (see Fig. 10-8).

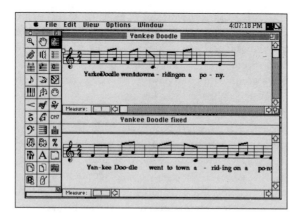

Figure 10-8. Lyrics affect the spacing of notes on the screen and printout.

After the notes, rests, and lyrics, other symbols can be added. These symbols include dynamics and articulations, such as tenuto and staccato. Chord symbols are usually in the form of text and/or guitar fretboard graphics, depending on the program. All of the standard symbols are usually included in a special music font, such as Adobe's Sonata. Some programs also provide a custom symbol editor that lets you create your own symbols.

Among the last steps is the placement of slurs and ties. While ties are usually included in the initial transcription, they often require some tweaking. On the other hand, slurs must be placed manually. This is usually accomplished by marking the start and end points of each slur on the screen; some programs let you specify the "high" point of the arc as well.

Parts

Many programs automatically extract instrumental parts from the score and create separate part files. Some programs even "concatenate" several measures of rest into a single multi-measure rest symbol with the number of measures over the symbol. A few programs can even extract monophonic parts from chords played on a keyboard.

Some instruments require transposed parts, so many programs transpose individual parts according to your specifications. Some, such as Mark of the Unicorn's *Composer's Mosaic* (Mac), can transpose the parts while leaving the score at concert pitch. If you use a lot of chord symbols, make sure the program you select transposes them along with the rest of the music.

Unfortunately, some programs wreak havoc with a carefully formatted part or score in the process of transposition. This process sometimes yields incorrect enharmonic names and might wipe out all beaming.

Output

Once the score and parts are saved in the appropriate format, it's time to print. If you have access to a phototypesetter and the program supports PostScript printing, the output will look gorgeous; these machines have a resolution of 1,250 to 2,500 dots per inch (dpi), which is fully adequate for professional publication. Laser printers normally have a resolution of 300 or 600 dpi, which results in fine-looking parts and scores (see Fig. 10-9). Many inkjet printers have 300 or 600 dpi resolution and look almost as good as laser printers if high-quality paper is used. If you print on a dot-matrix printer, photocopying the output will darken the symbols.

Figure 10-9. Laser printers produce fine-looking output at 300 dpi. (Courtesy Robert Wilkinson)

Some symbols, such as slurs, are problematic for most programs. Many people use notation software to print notes, rests, and other easy symbols, after which they add slurs and other difficult symbols to the printed output by hand. This process is often easier than trying to position slurs within the program.

Most programs provide some form of MIDI playback capability in addition to printed output, allowing you to audition the music before printing. Several integrated sequencing and notation programs, such as *Musicator* from Musicator A/S, provide separate quantizing features for the display/printout and MIDI playback. This option lets you optimize the data for printing without quantizing the MIDI sequence itself, which retains the human feel of the performance. A few programs assign appropriate MIDI messages to symbols such as dynamics and accents, which are

Anatomy of a Home Studio

reflected in the MIDI playback.

Some day, you will be able to scan a piece of sheet music into a computer and compile the image into meaningful musical data. Some day, artificial intelligence, desktop supercomputers, and fuzzy logic will provide near-perfect transcriptions with virtually no human intervention. But today, computers running the current generation of notation software can ease the burden of transcription and copying, which is a blessing for anyone who works with musical notation.

MUSIC EDUCATION

Some argue that computers and MIDI have dealt a fatal blow to traditional music skills. Sequencers don't require music to be written down, so musicians needn't learn how to read or write music notation. In addition, a mediocre musician can tweak performances on the computer until they are better than the musician's actual performance ability. This, of course, is nonsense; if you approach music with such an attitude, you are likely to end up with bad music. Computers are wonderful tools, but for the most part, musicianship is required to use them to create good music.

Furthermore, these critics overlook the fact that computers and MIDI can help keep traditional music skills alive. Music-education software on a personal computer offers users the opportunity to learn about virtually any area of music, regardless of their musical background.

Music-education software has several advantages. For example, there are plenty of titles appropriate for all ages and experience levels. Classroom music teachers can use cost-effective computers to supplement their regular instruction, which might be suffering from the budget cuts affecting many school music programs.

Students can proceed at their own pace without the embarrassment of performing in front of a teacher or class before they're ready. In addition, it can be difficult to motivate children to take lessons and practice. However, kids respond well to computers and digital keyboards; these are familiar musical tools used by many of their favorite groups. Technology also makes practicing more fun. As a result, children are motivated to spend more time learning.

Equipment Requirements

As you might imagine, music-education software requires a computer. Most programs are written for the Macintosh and/or DOS or Windows. A few developers have catalogs for the Apple IIe and IIGS, thanks to their significant penetration into schools.

Most programs have MIDI capabilities, which means they can use a MIDI keyboard to play musical examples, exercises, and accompaniments. Of course, you must have a MIDI interface for your computer to take advantage of these capabilities.

In general, the PC programs use a sound card, such as the Creative Labs Sound Blaster, for audio and synth sounds. Macintosh programs do not require a sound card: some require an external sound module for synth sounds, but many can use the computer's internal sound circuitry, which can provide both audio and synth sounds.

Students interact with the programs in several ways. Of course, the computer keyboard is essential, and most programs rely heavily on a mouse or other pointing device. If the program has MIDI capabilities, it's important to have a MIDI keyboard for playing exercises. Some programs let you play notes with the mouse on an onscreen musical keyboard or guitar fretboard, or directly from the computer keyboard, but these techniques are far less effective than playing on a musical keyboard, and it does nothing to develop instrumental skill. If a program is aimed at developing the ability to sing or play an acoustic instrument, a microphone input is essential. (Most modern Macs include an integral microphone input.)

In this age of multimedia, more and more programs are being published on CD-ROM. This allows the developer to combine CD audio, MIDI files, enhanced graphics, and software code in an easily distributed form. Naturally, this type of software requires a CD-ROM drive.

Instructional Formats

Most computer-aided instruction (CAI) software is interactive in nature, allowing users to customize the learning process. The material usually is presented in one of several formats, which are often combined within one program. The lesson format presents information in a series of screens organized into conceptual groups. Users can often navigate their way through these lessons in any order they choose, but most software recommends a particular sequence for maximum effectiveness, especially the first time through the material.

The drill-and-practice format presents a series of interactive exercises designed to reinforce the material in a lesson, which might have been presented by the program or in a book. Users respond to the exercises on a MIDI keyboard or the computer keyboard and mouse.

The game format provides another way to practice skills such as note and chord recognition in a fun and engaging manner. Most software incorporates several of these activities in one program or a coordinated series of programs.

The various formats usually accommodate different skill levels. As users become more proficient at a particular skill, the level of difficulty is automatically or manually increased. For example, once a student is able to easily recognize the difference between major and minor chords, augmented and diminished chords can be added to the exercises. Another option is decreasing the time limit or increasing the length of an exercise. This allows teachers or students to select the appropriate material and tailor the exercises to concentrate on specific skills that need work.

The opposite scenario must also be considered. If a student starts with an exercise that is too difficult for them, the skill level should be automatically or manually reduced.

Many programs keep track of a student's progress over time; some even keep track of several students separately, which is handy for families and teachers. The ability to monitor a student's progress is invaluable to the learning process. If multiple students are tracked, access to those records should be restricted with a password.

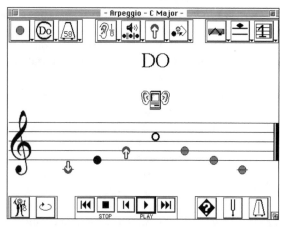

In this example from Opcode's Claire, the student sang the first note too high (the arrow indicates the student must sing a lower pitch), the second note just right, and the third note too low. The program is waiting for the student to sing the fourth note.

What to Look For

There are several essential attributes to look for in music-education software. The material must be factually accurate, and the program must provide appropriate responses that are positive and nonjudgmental. The skill required to operate the program must be consistent with the skill level of the material being taught. Onscreen instructions must be clear, concise, and complete, and the objectives must be readily apparent.

Technically, the software must be free of bugs, and the use of color and graphics must be appropriate

and clear. Audio and instructional pacing must be under user control, except when they are an integral part of the teaching strategy. Expected student responses must be consistent, and unanticipated responses must be handled smoothly without disrupting the program. The operation and display screens must correspond to the documentation, which must also include system requirements, installation procedures, and instructions for use.

Beyond these minimum requirements, there are several desirable attributes to look for. For example, it's nice to have multiple levels of difficulty that are automatically selected according to the skill demonstrated by the student. These levels should also be manually selectable. The program's responses to student errors should be helpful in guiding them to the correct answers. The student should also remain in control of the program and actively involved in the learning process.

Other desirable attributes include a way to select specific parts of the program and the ability to bypass instructions at will. The student should be able to correct a response before the software evaluates it, and help screens should be available from any part of the program. Students should be able to exit the program from any point and return to that point directly from the beginning of the program, without losing track of their progress.

The documentation should include a description of educational objectives, skills to be taught, and prerequisite skills. Other desirable information includes expected time to complete the program, representative screen shots, and a tutorial if the program is complicated.

Some music-education software products shine as examples of excellence. These programs use innovative approaches and foster creativity in students. Alternate methods of presentation provide cyclic reinforcement of concepts. Truly excellent programs present material not easily provided by other methods or engage the student in experiences not readily duplicated in the real world.

Areas of Study

Different CAI packages address various areas of music education. For example, basic concepts include musical symbols, melody, rhythm, harmony, timbre, texture, and form. Advanced study of these topics is called music theory.

Another important area is musicianship, which refers to a wide variety of skills. Among the most important is ear training, in which students learn to recognize scales, chords, and harmonic progressions as well as rhythmic patterns. Sight reading is another musicianship skill that involves the immediate recognition of notes on a staff and the ability to sing or play them.

Most people who are interested in learning music want to play an instrument, and many programs can help, particularly if you want to practice keyboard skills. Most of these programs also provide instruction in different aspects of musicianship, as well.

Once you have some basic performance chops, nothing is more fun than jamming with a full ensemble. However, it's difficult to assemble a group of musicians whenever you want to play, to say nothing of fitting them in your living room. Fortunately, there's a convenient alternative: automatic accompaniment software.

Auto-accompaniment software provides a computer-generated backup band, complete with drums, bass, and rhythm guitar or keyboard parts as well as horns and other background instruments. All you have to do is input the tempo, style, and chords of the song you want to play, and the computer does the rest. If your keyboard isn't multitimbral, you will need a multitimbral sound module, such as the Roland Sound Canvas.

One of the best-known auto-accompaniment programs is PG Music's *Band-in-a-Box*. *BIAB* generates a five-part backup arrangement with drums, bass, piano, guitar, and strings. The program comes with many different musical styles, and you can buy additional libraries of styles or create your own. Not only can you input the chords to any song you wish, you can buy libraries of popular songs that are ready to play. A basic sequencer lets you record melodies, as well. New versions of the program even create lead parts, which you can study.

Another excellent auto-accompaniment program is Soundtrek's *The Jammer*. This software generates its own drums, bass, and rhythm parts in a wide variety of styles, and it can also create its own chord progressions and melodies if you're out of ideas. The program includes a rudimentary sequencer to record your own performances.

Coda has developed a unique system that helps students practice virtually any instrument. Called Vivace Practice Studio (see Fig. 10-10), this system includes a multitimbral synth, microphone input, and software for the Mac and Windows. The software includes orchestral and piano-reduction accompaniments to much of the major solo literature for most common instruments. As you play the solo part into the microphone, the accompaniment follows your tempo, even if you slow down or speed up unpredictably during the piece. The repertoire is extensive and growing all the time, and it includes selections for every skill level.

Figure 10-10. Coda's Vivace Practice Studio lets music students practice any instrument with a full orchestral or combo accompaniment that follows their tempo in real time.

Lesson Over

Many people have an inherent interest in music that might have been stifled in boring music-appreciation classes or frightening private lessons. With the help of a MIDI keyboard and your computer, you can rekindle that interest by learning just what you want to learn at your own pace. Thanks to modern technology, music can take its rightful place in the hearts, minds, and hands of everyone who dreams of a harmonious world.

CHAPTER 11

SCSI

s electronic music matures, computers become ever more integral to the creative process. These machines offer many advantages, but they also pose some unique problems. Among these problems is the need to store and transfer large amounts of data, particularly digital audio files. Of course, fixed and removable hard disks, CD-ROMs, and data DAT recorders have enormous storage capacities, but this data isn't much good if it can't be quickly accessed and transferred from one device to another.

That's where the Small Computer System Interface (SCSI, pronounced "scuzzy") comes in. In the last ten years, SCSI has become one of the standard means of transferring data between computers and high-volume peripherals, such as storage devices and scanners. It is also commonly used to transfer audio data to and from samplers and hard-disk recorders (HDRs).

Although SCSI has been a boon for many applications, it can behave somewhat strangely. In particular, many people experience mysterious problems when they try to connect several SCSI devices together. At times, it seems as if only black magic will solve certain problems. However, there is almost always a more rational solution to these problems if you understand how SCSI works.

On the Bus
SCSI is a parallel interface or bus; it sends several bits simultaneously on separate wires within the SCSI cable. In addition, SCSI devices are connected in a daisy-chain configuration (see Fig. 11-1). As a result, most SCSI devices include two SCSI connectors on the back panel, which allows them to be placed anywhere in the chain. It is not possible to split or merge SCSI signals with a "Y" adapter, and ring and star configurations are not allowed. There can be no more than eight devices in a single SCSI chain, and all SCSI connections should be made with all devices powered off.

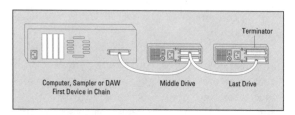

Figure 11-1. SCSI devices must be connected in a daisy chain, and the devices at each end should be terminated. (Courtesy Glyph Technologies)

There are several flavors of SCSI, which we'll get to shortly. These varieties differ in several important respects. For example, the data-path width determines the number of bits that are sent simultaneously, each on its own wire within the cable.

Another important characteristic is the rate at which data is sent along the cable. There are actually two data rates to keep in mind: the maximum data rate, which can usually be maintained only for short bursts of data, and the average data rate, which is much lower than the maximum rate. The average data rate is determined by a number of factors, including the specific characteristics of the devices in the chain (e.g., seek time, latency, throughput, and bit density) and the controlling computer, which is called the initiator in SCSI-speak.

The maximum cumulative length of all cables connecting SCSI devices in a single chain (including any cables that reside within a computer or sampler) depends on the type of SCSI you are using; in general, the faster the data rate, the shorter the cables must be. In addition, 25-conductor cables (which were popularized by Apple for the Macintosh and are also used on virtually all samplers) don't include many of the ground wires found in standard 50-conductor SCSI cables, which decreases the maximum cable length.

There are four common types of connectors found on SCSI devices and cables. As mentioned earlier, Apple decided on a 25-conductor cable for the Macintosh, which uses a DB25 connector. (Power-Books use a smaller 25-pin connector.) A DB25 connector is also used on most samplers and modular

116

hard-disk recorders because it is smaller than the standard Centronics 50-pin connector (see Fig. 11-2) that is commonly found on computer storage peripherals and PC printer cables.

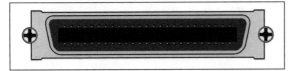

Figure 11-2. One of the standard SCSI connectors is the Centronics 50-pin. (Courtesy Glyph Technologies)

A high-density 50-pin connector (which is sometimes called a micro DB50) is used with the faster forms of SCSI, and forms of SCSI with a data path wider than eight bits use a micro DB68 high-density connector. Fortunately, it is normally possible to use an adapter to join one type of connector with another.

Most forms of SCSI are single-ended; i.e., voltage values of +5V and 0V relative to a common ground reference represent digital zeros and ones on each wire in the cable. The faster varieties of SCSI sometimes use a differential bus in which zeros and ones are represented by voltage differences between two twisted pairs of wires for each bitstream. This is similar to balanced mic cables, and it allows much longer cable lengths. However, it is relatively rare and is found only in very high-end SCSI systems.

SCSI Zoo
Over the last few years, several varieties of SCSI have been developed (see table, "SCSI Zoo"). Normally, devices that implement older forms of SCSI should work with devices that implement newer forms of SCSI, but this is not always the case; the SCSI implementation in some older devices is not close enough to the spec to work with the newer ones. Except as noted, all forms of SCSI use a single-ended bus.

The original version, which is sometimes called SCSI-1, was finalized in 1986. It has a maximum data rate of 5 megabytes per second (MBps), an average data rate of 2 MBps, and a data-path width of 8 bits. The maximum cable length is three meters. SCSI-2 is an extension of the original SCSI command set that doubles the maximum cable length but offers no increase in data rate or data-path width. In fact, there is little difference between the two, and they are essentially interchangeable.

Fast SCSI increases the maximum data rate to 10 MBps, but on average, anything over 5 MBps is considered excellent. Ultra SCSI (also called Fast-20) increases the maximum data rate to 20 MBps, and Ultra2 SCSI (also called Fast-40) increases the maxi-

mum data rate to 40 MBps. Unlike the slower forms of SCSI, which are single-ended, Ultra2 uses a low-voltage differential (LVD) bus to extend the cable length. An even faster form of SCSI, called Ultra3 or Fast-80, is under development and should achieve a maximum data rate of 80 MBps using an LVD bus.

Fast, Ultra, and Ultra2 are all types of SCSI-2 that are said to be narrow, which denotes an 8-bit data path. All three types are also available in wide versions, which use a 16-bit data path to increase the effective data rate. If a SCSI bus is capable of supporting data paths from 16 to 32 bits wide on a single cable, it is sometimes called SCSI-3. SCSI-2 can also support these data-path widths, but it requires two cables to do so. Most devices with wide forms of SCSI are high-end fixed-disk drives. In addition, wide SCSI does no good if you don't have a wide controller in your computer. Finally, wide SCSI is very expensive and not used much in the music industry.

It is possible to mix devices that implement different forms of SCSI in the same chain, but there are a few caveats. For example, the slowest device should be the last one in the chain. In addition, don't put a wide device between the initiator and a narrow device; in this case, the wide device reverts to the narrow bandwidth. Glyph Technologies, manufacturers of SCSI products for media applications, recommends you not combine wide and narrow devices in the same chain.

Many Macintosh models provide a single SCSI bus for both internal and external devices. However, some newer models provide two separate buses: one for internal devices and another for external devices. In this case, the internal bus is often Fast SCSI, and the external bus is regular SCSI. As a result, it's better to use an internal, A/V-capable, Fast SCSI drive for hard-disk recording in such a computer. (One exception to this is Digidesign's Pro Tools system. The higher-end versions of Pro Tools require the use of a Digidesign Disk I/O card, which provides a SCSI connection to an external hard disk.)

Device ID
All SCSI devices in a chain must be assigned their own, unique ID number from 0 to 7. No two devices in a chain can have the same ID number; if they do, chaos will reign. However, ID numbers need not correspond to the location of the devices in the chain.

The higher the ID number, the higher the priority of that device. For example, if two devices try to access the SCSI bus at the same time, the device with the higher ID number gets to go first. ID number 7 is usually reserved for the initiator, which would normally be the computer; in a music system, a sampler or modular HDR might be the initiator. All other hard disks, CD-ROMs, scanners, and all other SCSI devices (including devices installed within the computer) are assigned unique ID numbers from 0 to 6; ID 0 is normally the boot disk. In newer Macintosh computers, the internal CD-ROM is normally assigned to ID 3, which can cause problems if you unwittingly assign ID 3 to an external device on the same SCSI chain.

External devices typically include a small switch that lets you set the ID number for that device. In older (and internal) devices, this might be a circuit-board jumper or DIP switch. Samplers typically let you set their device ID in software, but some devices (for example, Macintosh computers) have a fixed ID number that can't be changed by the user.

A new protocol called SCSI Connect Auto-Magically (SCAM) is under development as of this writing and promises to automatically set the ID numbers of all of the SCAM-compliant devices in a chain. This will help users set up SCSI chains with less hassle.

Termination

To minimize noise and ensure a clean signal in a SCSI chain, the devices at both ends of the chain must include a terminator. This is a source of much confusion for many people, but it's actually quite simple: a chain of SCSI devices must have an impedance-matching terminator circuit at each end of the chain and nowhere else. This includes the SCSI controller within the initiator (computer, sampler, etc.) and any internal devices (hard drives, CD-ROMs, and so on), which many people forget.

If this rule is not followed (i.e., if one or both of the devices at the ends of the chain are not terminated and/or devices in the middle of the chain are terminated), several mysterious problems can crop up. Proper termination assures a clean signal, which greatly increases the reliability of the SCSI bus.

Many SCSI devices include internal termination, which often consists of one, two, or three "resistor packs" called single in-line packages (SIPs). These are typically yellow, blue, or black blobs of plastic with several pins in a straight line, and they are located on a circuit board within the device. They are sometimes soldered in place, but more often they can be removed or installed as necessary.

These SIPs must be removed if the device is not at the end the chain, and they must be installed if it is at the end. Unfortunately, this normally involves opening the case and fiddling with the internal circuit board. If you remove the SIPs, store them carefully so you can reinstall them if you reconfigure your SCSI chain. Don't lose them because finding exact replacements can be difficult. Some devices include a termination on/off switch or circuit-board jumper,

and many modern devices automatically detect whether they need to be terminated and set themselves accordingly.

Another termination option is an external terminator, which looks like a SCSI connector with no cable (see Fig. 11-3). An external terminator is attached to either one of the SCSI connectors on the device at the end of the chain. Many people remove all internal SIP terminators and use external terminators as needed. This makes it relatively easy to reconfigure your SCSI bus (i.e., add or remove devices).

Figure 11-3. This is a micro DB50 external terminator, which is commonly used with the faster forms of SCSI. (Courtesy APS Technologies)

One type of external terminator is called a pass-through terminator, which includes a male SCSI connector on one end and a female connector on the other end. It can be connected to an external device just like a normal external terminator, and its extra female connector duplicates the device's own connector.

But why would you terminate a device (call it device A) with a pass-through terminator (assuming it's the last device in the chain) and then connect another device (call it device B) to the terminator's duplicate connector? In this case, device A would no longer be the last one in the chain, and it shouldn't be terminated. In an ideal world, you wouldn't do this; you would simply remove the terminator from device A, connect device B to device A, and place the terminator on device B.

However, this is not an ideal world. Occasionally, the SCSI bus must be "tuned," which means that you might occasionally need to add termination where it shouldn't normally go. Adding a pass-through terminator to the middle of a SCSI chain can sometimes solve a mysterious problem that doesn't respond to other solutions. If you try this, however, proceed with caution; you can easily create more problems than you fix.

SIPs and external terminators provide passive termination, which consists of a simple resistor circuit. An active terminator (see Fig. 11-4) includes additional circuitry to adjust the termination resistance to varying voltages. Active termination is superior to passive termination, and it can solve many problems with unreliable SCSI devices. It's particularly important for fast and/or long SCSI chains. However, active termination is more expensive than the passive variety. (Some people use the word "active" to refer to automatic, passive termination instead of termination that uses active circuitry, which can lead to some confusion.)

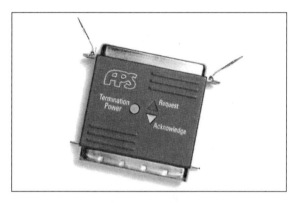

Figure 11-4. The APS SCSI Sentry II is a pass-through active terminator that adjusts the termination resistance to varying voltages. Active termination can solve many problems with unreliable SCSI devices, especially in long SCSI chains. (Courtesy APS Technologies)

Terminators need some power to operate properly, so many SCSI devices supply terminator power to the SCSI bus. If you have terminated a SCSI chain properly but there is no terminator power, you can still encounter problems. Make sure that at least one device in the chain (preferably the initiator) supplies terminator power. SCSI-1 devices are not required to supply terminator power, but SCSI-2 requires it from the initiator, so this is not much of an issue these days. In addition, other SCSI-2 devices are allowed (but not required) to supply terminator power.

If terminator power from one device fails, the entire bus could become nonfunctional. On the other hand, if several devices are supplying terminator power, the bus might remain functional. This is one reason that all devices in the chain should be turned on, even if you are not using them. (In general, you should power up all SCSI devices before booting the initiator.) Some external terminators include an LED that indicates the presence of terminator power on the SCSI bus.

Terminating Computers

If you think the preceding discussion of termination was hairy, the issues surrounding the termination of a SCSI bus within a computer are downright furry. A few Intel-based PCs include a SCSI port, but most require an optional controller card to use external SCSI devices. In addition, most PCs don't use SCSI for their internal storage devices; they use an IDE or PCI bus instead.

On the other hand, most Macintoshes use a SCSI bus for both internal and external devices. Unfortunately, termination is handled in various ways, depending on the specific model. For example, models that predate the Quadra 800 (e.g., the Mac SE/30) include passive termination on the internal hard drive but not on the motherboard. There is only one terminator in the internal SCSI chain, but this chain is very short, and the bus operates at a relatively slow speed, so it actually works with only one terminator. If you connect one or more external devices to the SCSI port, the last one *must* be terminated or you will certainly have problems.

Apple added automatic, passive termination to the Quadra 800's motherboard, which detects the presence of all SCSI devices and enables or disables its termination accordingly. The internal hard drive is permanently terminated and remains at one end of the chain.

The Power Mac 8100 added a separate Fast SCSI bus for internal hard drives while retaining the standard bus for external devices. The new internal bus is permanently terminated on the motherboard, which also provides automatic termination for the external bus. Interestingly, the internal CD-ROM is connected to the *external* bus (officially called the "Internal/External" bus) rather than the faster internal bus. If the internal CD-ROM is the only device on this bus, it should be terminated (which is done at the factory); if there are external devices connected to this bus, only the last one should be terminated.

The Power Mac 7500, 8500, and 9500 models use a similar SCSI design, but the internal CD-ROM is connected to the faster internal bus along with the internal hard drives. In addition, the internal bus is now controlled by a custom chip called Macintosh Enhanced SCSI Hardware (MESH). High-end Power Macs will continue to use MESH for the internal bus, which will probably be implemented for the external bus, as well.

SCSI Helpers

Several companies make helpful devices that extend the capabilities of SCSI. For example, SCSI repeaters amplify, clean, and resend the SCSI signal, allowing longer cable lengths. Among other applications, this lets you isolate a noisy computer in a closet or even in another room while your removable hard-disk drives remain in the music studio.

SCSI switchers let you add or remove devices (or entire chains of devices) from a SCSI bus while the power is on without physically connecting or disconnecting any SCSI cables. You should always use an electronic switcher rather than a mechanical switch, and the switcher should terminate the branches that are not active. In addition, a switcher should poll the active SCSI bus and not switch until there is no activity on the bus.

Music Systems

It's possible to have more than one initiator on a single SCSI bus (e.g., computer and sampler), but this doesn't always work as expected. For the most reliable operation, use a SCSI switcher to select the desired initiator. A simpler option is to place the initiators at opposite ends of the SCSI chain, but this is a hit-or-miss proposition; the initiators might or might not share the same bus nicely, depending on their individual SCSI implementations.

Most SCSI-capable samplers have only one SCSI connector, which means that they must be at the end of the chain. Two notable exceptions are the Kurzweil K2000R and K2500, which include two SCSI connectors. All current K2500s include active termination with a switch on the back panel, which makes it easy to configure the unit for any SCSI setup. However, the first production units used passive termination and did not have a switch, which means you must fiddle around with the SIPs on the internal hard drive (if installed) and the K2500 SCSI controller to properly terminate the system. In this case, it's best to have a qualified technician do the dirty work.

When using SCSI with a hard-disk recording system, the higher the average data rate, the more tracks you can record and play simultaneously. In general, you need an average data rate of at least 5 MBps for eight tracks of digital audio. Of course, the performance of any HDR system also depends on the characteristics of the drive itself (see Chapter 10).

EM Editor Steve Oppenheimer has established a complex SCSI system that illustrates some of the points I've discussed (see Fig. 11-5). His Power Computing PowerWave 604/132 computer provides two separate SCSI buses: internal (Fast SCSI) and external (normal SCSI). The internal bus includes the computer itself and a Quantum internal hard drive, Iomega Zip removable drive, and Toshiba CD-ROM drive.

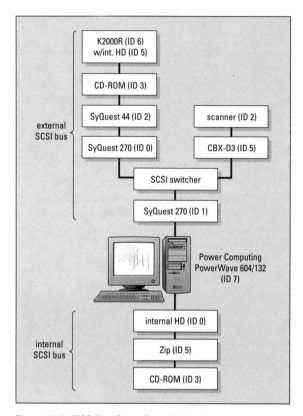

Figure 11-5. *EM* Editor Steve Oppenheimer has created a complex SCSI system in his studio.

The first external device is a SyQuest 270 MB removable drive followed by a Glyph GSS-210S 2-position SCSI switch/extender. One branch of the switcher includes a Yamaha CBX-D3 digital audio recorder and an HP ScanJet IIcx scanner, terminated by an APS SCSI Sentry active terminator (see Fig. 11-4). The other branch includes another SyQuest 270, a SyQuest 44 MB removable drive, an Apple CD300e CD-ROM drive, and a Kurzweil K2000R with its own internal hard drive.

This setup offers several advantages. For example, the same ID number can be assigned to one device in each branch of the chain after the SCSI switch and within the computer. (The only exception is the computer's ID number, because the computer is a part of both the internal and external chains.) In addition, the branch that includes the K2000R can operate independently from the rest of the system. If the switcher is set to the branch that includes the CBX-D3 and scanner, the K2000R can still access the removable and CD-ROM drives because the switcher automatically terminates the unused branch.

SCSI ZOO				
Type	Data Path Width (bits)	Max. Data Rate (MBps)	Average Data Rate (MBps)	Max. Total Cable Length (meters)
Original (SCSI-1)	8	5	2	3
SCSI-2	8	5	2	6
Fast	8	10	6	3
Ultra (Fast-20)	8	20	8	1.5
Ultra2 (Fast-40)	8	40	10	3
Fast Wide	16	20	10	3
Ultra Wide	16	40	12	1.5
Ultra2 Wide	16	80	14	3

Troubleshooting

As mentioned earlier, SCSI problems can seem like black magic at times, but these problems can normally be traced to more rational sources. The most common sources of trouble are poor-quality cables—use only high-quality, shielded, twisted-pair cables—and a cumulative cable length that is too long. For example, when Oppenheimer added the second SyQuest 270 drive to the K2000R branch in his setup, that branch became unreliable. He determined that even with the repeater included in the Glyph GSS-210S SCSI switch/extender, he had exceeded the maximum cable length when he added the new device. Replacing some of the cables with shorter ones solved the problem. In general, use the shortest cables you can in any SCSI system.

The new Glyph 2U rack enclosure can hold a 3-1 SCSI switcher in the left half, which lets three initiators (such as samplers) share the CD-ROM drive (or any other device) in the right half. (Courtesy Glyph Technologies)

Other sources of trouble include incorrect termination, incorrect driver software, and two or more devices with the same ID number. Problems can also arise if a device implements SCSI incorrectly or includes a poor-quality power supply and/or enclosure, in which case there's not much you can do except replace the device. IRQ conflicts with other devices sharing the same memory space in Windows can also cause problems.

Occasionally, you might encounter a problem that does not respond to any reasonable treatment. In this case, try swapping the physical order of devices in

the chain. In addition, check to see if there is a conflict between the software drivers in your system. As mentioned earlier, try inserting a pass-through terminator at various points in the chain. If all else fails, it might be a good idea to pray to the SCSI gods while lighting incense before stone idols under a full moon!

SCSI is an important standard for all electronic musicians who use computers, samplers, and/or modular hard-disk recorders. The ability to quickly transfer large amounts of data is essential for modern music making. Once you understand SCSI, you can use it to streamline your studio and get the data where you want it in short order.

Part

4

In the Studio

Chapter 12: Audio Connections
Analog Connections
Digital Connections

Chapter 13: Input Devices
Microphones
Direct Boxes

Chapter 14: Tape Decks

Chapter 15: Signal Routing
Mixers
Patch Bays

Chapter 16: Output Devices
Power Amplifiers
Monitors

CHAPTER 12

Audio Connections

Audio connections form the circulatory system of any recording studio; cables and connectors carry the audio signals from one device to another, each of which processes the signal before sending it on to the next device. It seems obvious that all audio connections are made from the output of one device to the input of another.

However, you can't simply connect *any* output to *any* input. For one thing, audio signals can be conveyed in analog or digital form, which are mutually incompatible without A/D and D/A converters (see Chapter 5). Within the analog domain, different devices exhibit different input and output impedances, produce and/or accept analog audio signals at different levels, and use different connectors. Similarly, digital devices produce and/or accept digital audio signals in several different formats that use different types of connectors.

ANALOG CONNECTIONS

As you might guess, analog audio connections are much older and more well established than their digital counterparts. Nevertheless, you should be aware of several different types of these connections.

All analog inputs and outputs are designed to handle signals in a certain range of levels (see Chapter 4). Many audio problems arise from mismatched levels between devices. (Problems also arise from mismatched impedances; see Chapters 3 and 13). If a high-level output is connected to a low-level input, the result can be a garbled and grungy sound that bears little resemblance to the original signal; this is called distortion. (This problem can often be solved by simply lowering the input level.) If a low-level output is connected to a high-level input, the resulting sound is generally quite noisy and extremely low in volume.

On the Line

As mentioned in Chapter 4, analog audio signals are sent along cables at different levels. There are four ranges of levels common to all studios: line level, mic level, instrument level, and speaker level.

Line-level signals are produced by synths and accepted by power amplifiers. In addition, they are produced *and* accepted by mixers, recorders, and signal processors. Unfortunately, "line level" means slightly different things in consumer or semipro equipment and professional gear. Semipro line level is -10 dBV (often called simply "-10"), and professional line level is +4 dBu (often called "+4").

Most consumer and semipro gear accepts and produces signals at a lower voltage than fully professional equipment, and it operates with higher impedance (typically in the range of 10 kΩ and above). The nominal level of this lower voltage is 0.316V, which is equivalent to -10 dBV. This typically corresponds to 0 on the level meters of consumer and semipro tape decks, mixers, signal processors, and other such equipment.

Professional audio equipment produces and accepts signals at a higher nominal voltage of 1.228V. This corresponds to +4 dBm into an impedance of 600 Ω, which is normally considered to be a low impedance. This is equivalent to +4 dBu in equipment that exhibits a high impedance, so you sometimes see the nominal level expressed in dBu. This typically corresponds to 0 on the level meters of fully professional tape decks, mixing consoles, and other audio equipment.

Some modern audio equipment, such as mixers and DAT machines, can be switched to operate at -10 or +4 levels. It's very important to make sure that all the equipment in your studio is operating at the same level to ensure a good signal-to-noise ratio.

Balancing Act

Semipro (i.e., -10) line-level signals are often carried in unbalanced cables that include two electrical conductors; one of the conductors is a braided or solid metal shield that surrounds a central wire (see Chapter 3). At both ends of the cable is a 2-conductor, ¼-inch phone plug (see Fig. 12-1). This type of plug is sometimes called a TS (Tip-Sleeve) plug; the tip of the plug is connected to the central ("hot") wire and the sleeve is connected to the shield. Another common type of unbalanced connector is called a phono or RCA plug, which is often used with consumer stereo gear (see Fig. 12-2). Both types of plugs are inserted into corresponding jacks on various pieces of equipment; simple adapters that change one type of connector to the other are readily available at Radio Shack and other electronics-parts stores.

Figure 12-1. A ¼-inch TS phone plug (left) has two conductors: tip and sleeve. It's used on -10 dBV unbalanced line-level and guitar cables. A ¼-inch TRS phone plug (center), has three conductors: tip, ring, and sleeve. It's used on balanced-line cables or console send/return inserts. 3-conductor XLR connectors (right) are used on +4 dBu line-level and balanced-mic cables. (Courtesy Switchcraft)

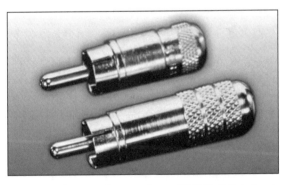

Figure 12-2. Some semi-pro analog and S/PDIF digital signals use RCA connectors with unbalanced cables. (Courtesy Switchcraft)

Professional (i.e., +4) line-level signals are normally carried over balanced cables with three conductors: two central wires surrounded by a shield. The two central conductors both carry the audio signal, but they are 180° out of phase with each other. When the signals reach a balanced input, one of them is flipped 180° in phase and added to the other

signal, which reinforces it. However, any noise that was induced along the way is in phase on both conductors. When one signal is phase-reversed, the noise cancels itself out. This provides greater protection from induced electrical noise than an unbalanced cable, especially over long cable runs (see Chapter 3).

Balanced cables can use two types of connectors: XLR and ¼-inch TRS (Tip-Ring-Sleeve) phone plugs, which look just like stereo headphone plugs (see Fig. 12-1). In a TRS plug, the "hot" and "cold" central conductors are connected to the tip and ring, and the shield is connected to the sleeve. Plugging an unbalanced TS plug (e.g., from a synth) into a balanced TRS input (e.g., on a pro mixer) is usually fine; the extra conductor at the input simply connects to the sleeve of the unbalanced TS plug, which usually causes no trouble.

Plugging a balanced line output (e.g., from a pro tape deck) into an unbalanced line input (e.g., on a semipro mixer) often results in a low level because only one of the two signals is received; the phase-reversal process does not occur. This also negates any immunity from induced noise offered by balanced cables.

Some manufacturers include both types of line connections on their gear, especially mixers, so be sure to use the appropriate connector for each piece of equipment. There are also several interface boxes that translate between the two types of line levels.

Microphones and Guitars

Most mics use a 3-conductor balanced cable and XLR connectors. The output from a microphone is said to be at mic level, which is about -40 to -30 dBV. Many mixers include both mic and line inputs to accommodate both types of signals. The mic input is accompanied by an internal mic preamp, sometimes called a mic pre, which amplifies the mic-level signal up to line level so it can be mixed with other line-level signals.

If you want to connect a microphone to a line input, you normally need to use a separate, outboard mic preamp. These are usually better quality than the internal mic preamps of most mixers, but they can be expensive. Make sure the line output of the preamp matches the mixer line input (-10 or +4).

Electric guitars use the same kind of cables and ¼-inch TS connectors as synths and other -10 gear, so it should be possible to plug them directly into a mixer's -10 line input, right? Not necessarily. If you try this connection, the result could be increased noise and distortion. The signal from a guitar pickup is said to be at instrument level, which is approximately 0 dBV. In addition, the output of a guitar needs to "see" a very high input impedance in order for you to hear its complete harmonic spectrum (see Chapters 3 and 13).

The output from the guitar should first be connected to the input of a guitar amp with a line output, which can then be connected to a line input on a mixer. You can also connect the output from a guitar to the input of a preamp or multi-effects processor that includes an instrument-level, high-impedance input. These devices convert the signal to line level before sending it to a mixer line input. Another option is connecting the guitar's output to the input of a direct-injection (DI) box, which converts the unbalanced, high-impedance, instrument-level signal to a balanced, low-impedance, mic-level signal and sends it to a mixer's mic input (see Chapter 13).

Power to the Speakers

Once the signals are mixed and processed through the mixer, and perhaps recorded on tape, you'll want to listen to the music over speakers or headphones. Virtually all mixers include a headphone output, which requires no additional connections. However, the signal from a mixer's main output is at line level, which must be amplified before it reaches the speakers.

This is the job of a power amplifier (see Chapter 16), which includes line-level inputs and speaker-level outputs. (Speaker level depends on the power from the amplifier and the impedance of the speaker. For example, if the amp generates 500 watts and the speaker's impedance is 8 Ω, the signal level from the amp's output is +36 dBV.) Some amps include balanced and unbalanced inputs; use the balanced inputs, if possible. Mixers intended for live-sound applications sometimes include an internal power amp, which makes these connections unnecessary. However, it's better to use a separate power amp in the studio, because it can be treated separately if something goes wrong.

The connection between the power amp's outputs and the speakers' inputs is made with speaker cable, which is typically unbalanced and unshielded. It carries a very high-level signal, so it must be quite hefty, as well; 12-gauge or better is usually recommended. (Interestingly, lower gauge numbers translate to thicker, heavier wire.) Speaker cables usually have no connector on either end; they terminate in bare wires that are screwed down to terminals on the amp and speaker. Sometimes, speaker cables are terminated with spade lugs or banana plugs, which make the connections easier to establish.

Keep the speaker cables as short as possible. Because they are unbalanced and unshielded, they can pick up induced noise, although the high signal level reduces this risk. Place the power amp as close as possible to the speakers, and run long, balanced cables to it from the mixer's main outputs.

DIGITAL CONNECTIONS

As you probably know by now, digital audio offers several distinct advantages over the analog variety. For example, there is no generational loss when making copies, and it's relatively easy to edit digital audio with a computer. (See Chapter 5 for more on the basic concepts of digital audio.)

As a result, many engineers want to keep audio signals in the digital domain as it passes from one device to another. However, connecting a digital audio output to a corresponding input is not always as straightforward as performing the same task with analog signals.

Digital audio signals can be passed from one device to another in any of several formats. These formats define such potential variables as electrical characteristics, physical connectors, how the digital audio is encoded, the rate at which data is transferred, the bit resolution and sample rate, and extra housekeeping and error-detection information. Unfortunately, different formats are generally incompatible, although it is possible to convert from one to another in many cases.

With electrically conductive cables, digital audio signals are transmitted as a series of quickly alternating voltages, which represent the 0s and 1s of the signal. With fiber-optic cables, the bits are represented by pulses of light from a laser or photo-diode. In addition, two or more separate channels of audio information are often sent along the same cable; this is called a serial interface. In some cases, each channel of audio is sent along its own wire; this is known as a parallel interface.

Timing Is Everything

Digital audio signals are extremely sensitive to timing. Each word of data must arrive at its destination at precisely the correct moment. (A word of data includes sixteen or more bits and represents one measurement of the instantaneous amplitude of the audio signal at a particular moment in time. The entire signal is represented by many data words, typically 44,100 or 48,000 per second.) If the timing is off, even by a microsecond, the final sound will be distorted when the words are converted into an analog audio signal. A timing inaccuracy in a digital signal is often called jitter.

The timing of each word is determined by a clock signal. The most common type of clock signal is called a word clock. This word-clock signal jumps between two values at a frequency equal to the sample rate of the digital audio data. For example, if the sample rate is 44.1 kHz, the word clock oscillates at 44.1 kHz. Each cycle of the word-clock signal corresponds to one word of digital audio data, which is why it's called a word clock.

All digital audio devices have their own internal clock, which regulates the timing of their own signals. If you want to transfer digital audio from one device to another, their clocks must be synchronized. This is similar in principle to synchronizing performers using a metronome or click track. It is not the same as SMPTE or other forms of time code, which are not nearly accurate enough for this task.

There are two ways to synchronize the clocks in several devices. If you are sending digital audio from a single device, the easiest approach is called self clocking (see Fig. 12-3 [a]). The sender's clock signal is embedded within the digital audio data itself, and the receiver syncs its clock to this signal.

On the other hand, if you want to send data from several sources simultaneously, perhaps through a digital mixer, you must use a technique called master clocking (see Fig. 12-3[b]). In this process, one device's clock signal is sent from its dedicated word-clock output to a dedicated word-clock input on all other devices in the system over a separate cable, which typically terminates with a BNC connector (see Fig. 12-4). This is similar to the house sync found in most video-production facilities, in which a dummy video signal is generated by a master source and distributed throughout the facility to synchronize the video equipment.

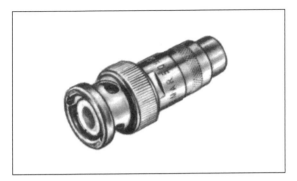

Figure 12-4. Most word-clock cables use BNC connectors. (Courtesy Switchcraft)

AES/EBU

In 1981, the Audio Engineering Society (AES) and the European Broadcasting Union (EBU) began working on a standard format for stereo digital audio signals. This resulted in a format commonly called AES/EBU. (Its official name is AES3-1985, which identifies when it was finished.) It was also sanctioned by the Electronic Industries Association of Japan (EIAJ), which called it CP-340 Type I.

According to the standard, AES/EBU uses balanced cables with XLR connectors (see Fig. 12-5). It was originally designed as a self-clocking system, but a later addendum to the specification provides for master clocking.

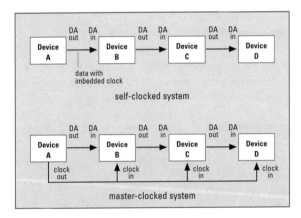

Figure 12-3. In a self-clocked system (top), the word-clock signal from the sender is embedded in the digital audio datastream and used by the receiver(s) to sync their clocks. In a master-clocked system (bottom), the word-clock signal from the master device is sent to all other devices in the system on a separate cable.

Figure 12-5. AES/EBU digital audio uses XLR connectors with balanced cables. (Courtesy Switchcraft)

Two channels of digital audio data are multiplexed on a single conductor within the cable. This means that one word of data from channel 1 is followed by one word from channel 2, which is followed by one word from channel 1, and so on. The resolution of the audio data words can be up to 24 bits, but most digital audio currently uses sixteen bits. This provides for future enhancements in digital audio resolution.

The data is transmitted at a bit rate that is 64 times the digital audio's sample rate. For example, if the sample rate is 48 kHz, the AES/EBU data transmission rate is over three million bits (three megabits) per second (3 Mbps). This makes it possible to send two channels of 24-bit audio plus the extra housekeeping and error-detection bits and play the resulting stereo signal in real time.

S/PDIF

Many engineers who worked on AES/EBU worked for Sony or Philips at the same time. Both companies wanted to develop a standard for transmitting digital audio between consumer devices, such as CD players and DAT machines. (At that time, DAT was thought to be the next major consumer recording medium.)

As a result, the Sony/Philips Digital Interface Format (S/PDIF) is almost identical to AES/EBU. The primary physical difference is the type of cable and connector used for this format. S/PDIF uses unbalanced, coaxial ("coax") cable and RCA connectors, which are much less expensive than balanced cables and XLR connectors. Other differences include the way digital audio data and the auxiliary information is encoded. This format was also sanctioned by the EIAJ and called CP-340 Type II.

In addition to its electrical version, S/PDIF can also be implemented with fiber-optic cable made of plastic or glass and a connector called Toslink. This interface is found on several devices, including many consumer audio products and the Kurzweil K2000 and K2500 sampling inputs. Optical interfaces avoid all problems associated with electrical connections, such as cable capacitance and grounding issues. The Fostex COP-1 converts between optical and coax S/PDIF.

It is possible to convert AES/EBU into S/PDIF and vice versa. This normally requires a format converter, such as the Digital Domain FCN-1. Some digital audio devices, such as the Lexicon Model 300 digital reverb, include an internal format converter, which lets them deal with digital audio in either format. Some manufacturers implement software-switchable AES/EBU and S/PDIF interfacing on a single connector, which can be XLR, RCA, or even a nonstandard connector such as ¼-inch. In such cases, you might need an adapter.

Some manufacturers have implemented AES/EBU or S/PDIF only partially or even incorrectly. As a result, some gear can't deal with a converted format or even the same format from another device. If one device implements a subset of the spec and another device implements a different subset, they might not work well together. This is one of the primary pitfalls of digital audio interfacing.

Another potential problem area is cabling. In particular, avoid using analog audio cables for digital audio connections (i.e., balanced mic cables with XLR connectors for AES/EBU or unbalanced line cables with RCA connectors for S/PDIF). Both digital audio standards require a specific impedance in the cables they use, and analog cables do not typically exhibit this impedance, which can increase jitter. In addition, the bandwidth of analog audio signals is in the kilohertz range, while digital audio bandwidths are in the megahertz range. As a result, be sure to use digital audio cables, which are designed with these specs in mind.

The length of the cables should be as short as possible and never longer than five meters. Long cables can result in more jitter, and many people report that shorter cables produce a warmer, smoother, and more detailed sound.

Multichannel Formats

When Alesis introduced the ADAT modular digital multitrack (MDM) tape recorder in 1992, they had a huge hit on their hands (and they threw a great party at the NAMM show that year!). The ADAT records eight tracks of digital audio on S-VHS videocassettes. Among its features is an optical, self-clocking digital audio interface called ADAT Optical, which is commonly referred to as the "ADAT Lightpipe" (see Fig. 12-6).

Figure 12-6. The Alesis ADAT uses a proprietary optical interface called ADAT Optical.

The ADAT Optical interface is serial, multiplexing eight channels of digital audio on a single fiber-optic cable with a proprietary connector. It can accommodate a resolution of 24 bits, even though the ADAT currently records 16-bit audio. Thanks to forward-thinking designers, this interface will avoid obsolescence and remain useful for future products with higher resolution. The data-transmission rate is 256 times the sample rate, which is four times the data rate of AES/EBU and S/PDIF. This makes sense, because an ADAT Optical cable carries four times as much data (eight channels instead of two).

Among the growing number of products that include an ADAT Optical interface is the Alesis Quadra-Synth line, which sends audio from the synthesizer directly to an ADAT without leaving the digital domain. Other products with an ADAT Optical interface include the ADAT clones from Fostex, and it is an option for the Yamaha 02R digital mixer and dedicated hard-disk recorders such as E-mu's Darwin and Roland's DM-800. Several computer audio cards, such as Korg SoundLink DRS 1212 I/O, support the ADAT Optical interface, as well. This makes it possible to simultaneously transfer eight tracks of digital audio back and forth between a computer and any other device that has this interface. The Alesis AI-1 converts any two consecutive channels of data between ADAT Optical and AES/EBU or S/PDIF.

Shortly after the ADAT was introduced, TASCAM answered the 8-track MDM challenge with the DA-88. The multichannel digital audio interface used on the DA-88 (and its siblings, the DA-38 and DA-98) is called TEAC Digital Interface Format (TDIF). This master-clocked format carries eight channels of digital audio on an electrical cable with 25-pin D-sub connectors, which are used on many computers. Each wire in the cable carries two multiplexed channels, which closely resembles AES/EBU. The entire cable can handle eight channels to and from any compatible device; in other words, TDIF is bidirectional. (ADAT Optical is unidirectional.) The maximum resolution is 24 bits, although the DA-88 records with 16-bit resolution. In addition, the data rate is the same as AES/EBU, i.e., 64 times the sample rate.

Like ADAT Optical, TDIF is a standard or optional feature on a variety of products, including the Yamaha 02R digital mixer. The TASCAM IF-88AE converts all eight digital audio channels into AES/EBU on XLR connectors and any two consecutive channels to S/PDIF on RCA connectors.

There are several other multichannel digital audio interfaces that are used mainly on high-end professional equipment. The second-generation of the Sony Digital Interface Format (SDIF2) was the first multichannel format, developed in 1981. This master-clocked, parallel format can accommodate up to 24 channels of 20-bit digital audio.

One year later, Mitsubishi introduced its Melco (Mitsubishi Electric Company) multichannel interface, which is also known as ProDigi after the recording format used by Mitsubishi and Otari digital audio tape recorders. This parallel, master-clocked system carries up to 32 channels of 16-bit digital audio. There are three versions of Melco/ProDigi, called Dub-A, Dub-B, and Dub-C.

Yamaha introduced its Y2 proprietary digital interface in 1988 as a method of cascading (chaining) two or more DMP7 digital mixers. Later the company expanded Y2's applications to include several other Yamaha digital audio products. Y2 is a parallel, master-clocked format that carries one channel of 24-bit digital audio per line. Its flexible architecture can be configured to carry almost any number of channels; a cable with 25-pin D-sub connectors can carry eight channels of digital audio bidirectionally.

The Multichannel Audio Digital Interface (MADI) is essentially a multichannel version of AES/EBU developed in 1991 by Sony, SSL, Neve, and Mitsubishi for high-end digital mixers and multitrack recorders. MADI multiplexes up to 56 channels of AES/EBU digital audio onto a single coax cable with BNC connectors. This master-clocked system operates at a fixed data rate of 100 Mbps.

Clearly, sending digital audio signals from one device to another is not trivial. However, a little knowledge goes a long way toward making a successful connection. Of course, experience is the best teacher, so try making a few digital audio connections of your own. You'll probably find that the benefits of staying in the digital domain far outweigh any difficulties.

CHAPTER 13

Input Devices

At the beginning of any signal path is a sound source. This can be a synthesizer, microphone, recorder, or electric guitar. As mentioned in Chapter 12, synths typically use line-level outputs, and Chapter 2 describes how they work. Similarly, recorders generally use line-level outputs for playback; hard-disk recorders are discussed in Chapter 10 and tape recorders are described in Chapter 14. That leaves microphones and electric guitars, which are the subjects of this chapter.

MICROPHONES

The job of a microphone is simple. It converts an acoustic sound into an electrical signal that corresponds to the original waveform as closely as possible. This signal can then be processed, mixed with other audio signals, and recorded.

As discussed in Chapter 1, acoustic sounds occur when something physically vibrates at a frequency between 20 Hz and 20 kHz in air or another medium. This creates small regions of high and low pressure around the vibrating source. As the molecules in these regions move in response to the changing pressure, they jostle nearby molecules, causing the regions of high and low pressure to expand outward.

Once these regions of changing pressure reach a microphone, they impinge on a flexible diaphragm within the mic, causing it to vibrate in response. This physical vibration is then converted into an electrical signal, which is sent to a mixer, signal processor, or other device. The difference between types of mics is the specific manner in which this conversion is performed.

Physical Attributes

Before we take a look at the different types of mics, let's examine some concepts that are common to all. As mentioned earlier, all mics include a diaphragm, which is usually mounted in something called a capsule. The capsule is then mounted in an outer case, along with any support electronics. Some cases can be hand-held or stand-mounted for stage use, while others must be mounted on a stand. Stand-mounted mics

sometimes include a shock mount, which isolates the mic from unwanted vibrations in the stand itself.

In most cases, the capsule is located behind a screen of some sort, which allows the acoustic sound to enter while protecting the diaphragm from physical damage. This screen often includes a layer of foam to reduce wind noise and vocal "pops," although an external pop screen is usually more effective in the latter application.

Once the acoustic sound has been converted to an electrical signal, it is conveyed to another device along a cable. Some inexpensive mics include a permanent cable that terminates in a 2-conductor, ¼-inch or ⅛-inch phone plug. The cable includes one central conductor that carries the audio signal surrounded by another conductor (called the shield) that connects to ground. However, this type of cable is susceptible to induced hum and other environmental noise. As a result, most professional and semi-pro mics use a 3-conductor XLR connector at the end of a balanced cable (see Chapter 12).

Frequency Response

The frequency range within which a mic accurately translates the sound-pressure level (SPL) of acoustic sounds into electrical signal levels is called its frequency response, which is measured in decibels (dB) over a range of frequencies. But what does "accurately" mean here? For a given sound-pressure level, the output signal level typically varies by no more than ±3 dB from its nominal level. This is normally depicted in a graph of frequency vs. output level (see Fig. 13-1). A mic with a flat frequency response generates the same audio signal level for a sound of any frequency within the specified range at a given sound pressure level.

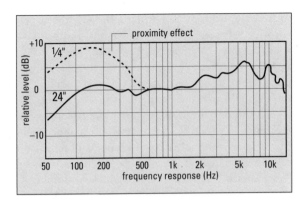

Figure 13-1. The frequency response of a microphone is depicted in a graph of frequency vs. relative output level. If the sound source is close to most directional mics, the proximity effect boosts the low end. Also notice the presence peak between 2 and 10 kHz.

However, most mics do not exhibit a flat frequency response, partly because it's very expensive to make such a mic and partly because an uneven frequency response can be of some benefit. For example, many vocal mics boost the upper frequencies; this is called a presence peak (see Fig. 13-1), and it helps improve the intelligibility of words. However, a presence peak can exaggerate a shrill upper vocal range.

At the low end, the frequency response of a vocal mic often falls off below 100 Hz. Because the human voice can't produce frequencies that low, there is no reason to make a mic that reproduces them accurately. Instrument mics generally fall off below 50 Hz. However, the low-end response of many mics can be greatly enhanced by moving the sound source close to the mic. This bass boost is called the proximity effect (see Fig. 13-1), and it helps radio announcers achieve their characteristically deep sound. However, moving too close to the mic increases breath noises and vocal "pops."

Pickup Patterns

All mics exhibit a pickup pattern, which determines how the mic responds to sounds at different frequencies coming from different directions. An omnidirectional mic responds more or less equally to sounds coming from any direction. This pickup pattern is particularly well suited for ambient mics, which are used to pick up the "sound" of the room in which an acoustic source is radiating.

In most cases, omnidirectional mics are not used in live performance, because they pick up sounds from all directions, which can lead to feedback. However, omni mics are generally less susceptible to wind and breath noise, and they tend to have a relatively flat frequency response with no pronounced peaks, which can actually help to avoid feedback. Omni mics

also tend to have excellent low-frequency response, and they do not exhibit the proximity effect.

If a mic does not respond equally to sounds from any direction, it is called a directional mic. There are several types of directional mics, most of which respond best to sounds coming from directly in front of the mic's capsule. (The main exception is the mid-side, or MS mic, which contains two capsules. MS mics pick up sounds from both sides as well as the front.) Sounds that strike the mic at its most sensitive spot are called on-axis; sounds from any other direction are said to be off-axis. Directional mics are prone to the proximity effect, and their frequency response is normally less flat than omni designs.

The pickup pattern of any mic can be depicted in a polar graph (see Fig. 13-2). In this type of graph, the mic's axis is defined as 0° (usually located at the top of the graph), and the outer circle defines a flat frequency response. The smaller, inner circles represent a drop in frequency response. The curve within this graph indicates how the mic responds to sounds from different directions. The polar pattern of an omnidirectional mic forms a circle. Keep in mind that although polar patterns are conventionally graphed in two dimensions from a bird's-eye view, the mic's actual pickup pattern is 3-D.

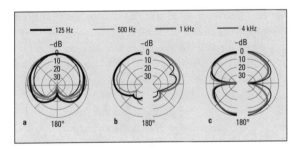

Figure 13-2. Various pickup patterns: (a) cardioid, (b) supercardioid, (c) figure-eight. Notice that the patterns are slightly different at different frequencies. In b and c, the left half shows the curves for 125 and 500 Hz, while the right half shows the curves for 1 and 4 kHz.

The most popular type of directional mic is the cardioid (see Fig. 13-2 [a]). Its polar pattern resembles an inverted heart, hence the name. The mic is most responsive to on-axis sounds, while off-axis sounds are attenuated; sounds from 180° off-axis are almost completely rejected. In addition, notice that the polar pattern changes slightly at different frequencies. These extra curves give you a rough idea of a mic's frequency response and pickup pattern in one graph.

A supercardioid mic is often used in live performance because it rejects more sound from the sides than a cardioid design (see Fig. 13-2 [b]). However, it does have some response to sounds coming from 180°, as indicated by the small rear pickup lobe. Another variation of this design, called the hypercardioid, is even more directional.

Some mics exhibit a bidirectional or figure-eight pickup pattern (see Fig. 13-2 [c]), so called for obvious reasons. These mics are most sensitive to sounds from the front and rear, while rejecting sounds from the sides. This works well for miking two sources (e.g., two toms in a drum kit or two singers facing each other) with one mic.

Dynamic Range and More

Not only must mics reproduce different frequencies coming from different directions, they must also contend with sounds at different levels. If the sound reaching a mic is above a certain amplitude, the signal from the mic becomes distorted, and the diaphragm might even be damaged. This upper amplitude limit is called the dynamic range, and it's measured in dB SPL. The dynamic range of most mics is typically between 100 and 120 dB SPL; some go up to 130 dB SPL or more. (Note that dynamic range is defined differently for a mic than for a mixer or signal processor; see Chapter 4.)

At a given source level, different mics produce an audio signal at different levels. The relationship between the input level and the output level is called the sensitivity of the mic; the higher the output level at a given input level, the more sensitive the mic.

Sensitivity is usually measured with a 1 kHz tone at one or two levels: 74 dB SPL (the level of the average speaking voice at a distance of three feet) and 94 dB SPL (which corresponds to a loud speaking voice at a distance of one foot). The output level is expressed in dBV (decibels referenced to 1 volt RMS) or dBm (decibels referenced to 1 milliwatt). For example, a mic's sensitivity might be specified as an output level of -47 dBV at 94 dB SPL. Many mics also include a pad switch, which lowers the overall output level by 10 or 20 dB. This is useful if the sound source is particularly loud.

Microphones also exhibit another important electrical characteristic: impedance. This is the mic's resistance to the flow of electrical current, which changes as a function of frequency. Most professional and semipro mics are low-impedance (typically between 150 Ω and 250 Ω, but sometimes as low as 50 Ω; also called low-Z), while most inexpensive mics are high-impedance (usually above 20 kΩ; also called high-Z).

Low-Z mics are less susceptible to extraneous electrostatic noise in the cable, such as that caused by fluorescent lights or motors, but they are more likely to pick up hum from electromagnetic interference,

such as that from AC power lines. Because they operate with relatively high current levels and use balanced cables, low-impedance mics can drive cables that are hundreds of feet long. High-Z mics, especially those using unbalanced lines, are limited to cable lengths of no more than about twenty feet.

It's important to match a mic's impedance with the input to which it is connected. To connect one type of mic to the other type of input, you must typically use a matching transformer (discussed in more detail later in this chapter). In a pinch, you can connect a low-Z mic directly to a high-Z input, but you will lose too much level if you connect a high-Z mic to a low-Z input.

Dynamic Mics

There are many types of microphones that use different methods to convert an acoustic sound into an electrical signal. Of these types, three are most common today: dynamic, condenser, and boundary.

In most dynamic mics, the diaphragm is attached to a coil of wire, called the voice coil, which is free to move near a permanent magnet (see Fig. 13-3). As the diaphragm vibrates in response to an acoustic sound, the voice coil moves back and forth within the magnetic field. This induces an oscillating electric current in the wire, which corresponds to the original sound's waveform. This design is also known as a moving-coil mic. Common moving-coil dynamic mics include the AKG Tri-Power series, Audix OM-3xb and OM-5, beyerdynamic M 88 and TG-X series, Sennheiser 421, and the ever-popular Shure SM57 and SM58.

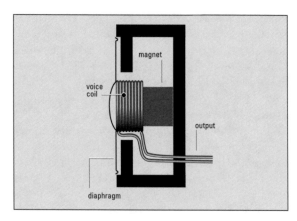

Figure 13-3. In a moving-coil dynamic mic, the diaphragm is attached to a coil of wire that vibrates within a magnetic field. This induces an electrical signal in the wire that corresponds to the incoming acoustic waveform.

Moving-coil dynamic mics are often housed in a hand-held case. They are also quite rugged and able to withstand rough treatment and high SPL levels. As a result, they are great for miking drums, electric guitar cabinets, and vocals. Most dynamic mics use a cardioid, supercardioid, or hypercardioid pickup pattern to reject onstage ambient noise. Good dynamic mics have an excellent frequency response, but the diaphragm/voice coil assembly is relatively heavy, so these mics are somewhat less sensitive to fast transients.

A variation of the moving-coil design is called the ribbon mic. Instead of a diaphragm and voice coil, this type of mic uses a thin ribbon of metal suspended in a permanent magnetic field. As the ribbon vibrates in response to an acoustic sound, an electric current is generated in the metal.

Although they're not made much these days, ribbon mics have excellent transient response, and they are famous for their warm sound. However, they are extremely fragile and delicate; you can destroy the ribbon by coughing into the mic! Their output level also is generally lower than moving-coil designs.

Condenser Mics

In a condenser mic, the diaphragm is a very thin sheet of Mylar coated with gold or other conductive material and suspended over a parallel, conductive surface called the back plate (see Fig. 13-4). This forms an electrical capacitor, which is sometimes called a condenser, hence the name. A static voltage of 9 to 48 VDC is applied across this capacitor. As the diaphragm vibrates in response to incoming acoustic sounds, the voltage varies slightly as the diaphragm moves closer and farther away from the back plate, generating a tiny signal. This signal must be amplified with an internal preamp before it is sent to the mic's output. Popular condenser mics include the AKG C414, Audio-Technica 4033 and 4050/CM5, beyerdynamic MC 834, and the Neumann TLM 193.

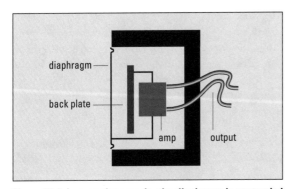

Figure 13-4. In a condenser mic, the diaphragm is suspended over a parallel back plate, forming a capacitor. As the diaphragm vibrates, the voltage across the capacitor varies, producing an electrical signal, which must be amplified by an internal preamp.

The static voltage across the condenser element and the power required to operate the internal preamp are typically supplied by a battery and/or the input of the device (e.g., a preamp) to which the mic is connected. The voltage from the device's input is called phantom power, because it is sent along the same cable that carries the signal from the mic to the input; there is no separate power cable. This doesn't interfere with the audio signal, because the phantom power is a fixed voltage, while the audio signal changes over time.

A variation of this approach is called an electret condenser. In this type of mic, the diaphragm or back plate is made of a material (such as Teflon) that retains a permanent electric charge, which removes the need for an external power supply. (The internal preamp still needs power, though, which is normally supplied by a battery.) In most cases these days, the back plate retains the charge so the diaphragm can be made of Mylar instead of Teflon, which is less sensitive to acoustic vibrations. This design is called a back-electret condenser.

Condenser mics can exhibit different pickup patterns. In fact, many condensers offer several switchable patterns, which is very handy. Condenser mics have excellent transient response because the mass of the diaphragm is very low. They are most often used in the studio for vocals, acoustic instruments, and just about everything else. However, they are more delicate than dynamics, so they are not used as much in live performance.

Boundary Mics

Another variation of the condenser approach is the boundary mic. In this design, a small electret capsule is mounted in the center of a flat, metal plate, which forms a sonic boundary, hence the name. Incoming sound waves are reflected from the plate and reach the capsule at virtually the same instant as the direct sound waves. This reinforces the acoustic signal at the diaphragm.

Crown's version of the boundary mic, called a Pressure Zone Microphone (PZM), has become the most common form of boundary mic in the United States (see Fig. 13-5). Unlike other boundary designs, in which the capsule faces away from the plate, a PZM capsule is suspended above the plate by a very small distance and faces downward, toward the plate. The gap between the plate and capsule is the pressure zone, where the direct and reflected sound waves meet and add coherently to stimulate the diaphragm.

Figure 13-5. The Sound Grabber is one of Crown's PZM microphones. The electret capsule is suspended over the plate facing downward.

In most boundary mics, the electret capsule is omnidirectional. However, the plate effectively blocks any sound coming from the side opposite the capsule, so the practical pickup pattern is hemispherical. These mics are often mounted on a large board or wall for picking up room ambience. They also work well on instruments with a large sound radiation pattern, such as vibes or woodwinds. A few boundary mics have a cardioid pattern, in which case the capsule axis is parallel to the plate, rather than perpendicular. These mics are often used on stage floors for actors.

Unless you record and perform instrumental music on synthesizers exclusively, you need at least one microphone in your tool box. However, mics can be very expensive. I recommend that you invest in at least one high-quality condenser for recording purposes and one or more dynamics for recording and live performance.

Keep in mind that each mic has its own unique "sound," so experiment with different models until you find the right one for each instrument or voice. Once you've found the right mics for your applications, the world of acoustic sound awaits your pleasure.

DIRECT BOXES

When I first started playing around with electronic music equipment as a kid, I tried connecting the output of an electric guitar directly into a line input on a mixer. I thought I didn't need a guitar amp because the mixer, power amp, and monitor speakers would do its job instead. However, it didn't quite work out that way. When I played the guitar, it sounded completely dead and very low in volume. "How can I correct this?" I wondered.

Although I didn't know it at the time, I had two relatively simple options. If I really wanted to use the mixer's line-level input, I could have plugged the guitar into an instrument preamp. But a simpler and

cheaper alternative would have been to use a direct-injection box (also called a DI or direct box). This device converts an unbalanced, line- or instrument-level, high-impedance signal (e.g., from an electric or electronic musical instrument) to a balanced, mic-level, low-impedance signal that can be connected directly to a microphone input on a mixer or mic pre-amp (see Fig. 13-6).

The output from a DI box can be sent over long cables with much better noise rejection than is possible with a high-impedance, unbalanced signal from a guitar or synth. However, this is not the only application for direct boxes; we'll discuss more uses shortly.

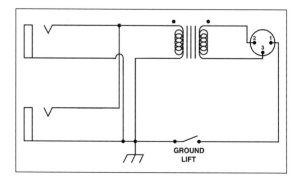

Figure 13-6. The Whirlwind IMP2 DI box is about as simple as it gets. The two ¼-inch input jacks are connected to the primary of a 10:1 step-down transformer, and the secondary is connected to an XLR jack. Notice the ground-lift switch. The unused input can be used as a "thru" jack. (Courtesy Whirlwind)

For more on impedance, see Chapter 3. For more on levels, see Chapter 4. For more on balanced and unbalanced audio connections, see Chapter 12.

Transformers

The basic component of most DI boxes is a step-down transformer. All transformers consist of two or more long, thin wires that wind many times around a metal core. The ends of each coil of wire protrude from the windings; one pair of ends is the input and the other pair is the output of the transformer. The input coil is called the primary, and the output coil is called the secondary.

When you send an electrical signal through the primary coil, it creates a corresponding magnetic field around the coil. This field induces an analogous signal in the secondary coil, which appears at the output leads. If the primary has more windings than the secondary, it is called a step-down transformer because the signal level and impedance are lower at the output than they are at the input.

If the secondary has more windings than the primary, it is called a step-up transformer because the signal level and impedance are higher at the output;

however, the *power* does not increase with respect to the input. Step-up transformers are used at the input stage of mic preamps and adapters to connect a microphone to a line-level or guitar-amp input (more in a moment). If the primary and secondary coils have the same number of windings, it is called a 1:1 transformer, which is used in noise-reducing, signal-isolation boxes (see Chapter 3).

In general, the primary and secondary coils are wound around the core concentrically (e.g., the secondary coil is wound first, and the primary coil is wound around it). In addition, the primary and secondary coils are often separated by copper foil called a Faraday shield, which helps reject radio-frequency interference (RFI) between the coils. As the number of turns in the coils increases (i.e., the length of the wire increases), the transformer exhibits greater level-handling capability and lower distortion, but it also has less high-frequency response. The primaries of step-down transformers used in DI boxes typically include thousands of turns.

The relationship between the input and output signals is determined by the ratio of the number of turns in the primary and secondary coils. The change in signal level is directly proportional to the turns ratio. For example, if the turns ratio of a step-down transformer is 10:1 (i.e., the primary has ten times as many windings as the secondary), the signal level drops by a factor of 10; if the signal level into this transformer is -10 dBV (a typical guitar or line level), the output level is -30 dBV (a typical mic level).

The change in impedance is proportional to the *square* of the turns ratio. For example, if the turns ratio of a transformer is 10:1, the change in impedance is a factor of 100. However, a transformer has no intrinsic impedance of its own; instead, the impedances of the devices connected to a transformer determine its impedances. Specifically, the output impedance of the source device (e.g., guitar) is modified by the square of the turns ratio to calculate the output impedance of the transformer, and the input (load) impedance of the destination device (e.g., mic preamp) is modified by the square of the turns ratio to calculate the input impedance of the transformer.

For example, the typical input impedance of a mic preamp is 3 kΩ. If the input to this preamp is connected to the output of a 10:1 step-down transformer, the transformer's input impedance becomes 300 kΩ. If you were to connect the same transformer to a mic preamp with an input impedance of 1.5 kΩ, the input impedance of the transformer would be 150 kΩ.

Most audio transformers have a metal core that is constructed from thin, E-shaped laminations. This core provides a magnetic path to couple the primary and secondary coils (i.e., it facilitates the transfer of magnetic energy between coils). Without this core, the transformer would have no low-frequency response below about 10 kHz.

In high-quality audio transformers, the core material is an 80-percent nickel alloy (commonly called Mu-Metal), which provides the best low-frequency response and lowest possible distortion. Lower-cost transformers use a 50-percent nickel alloy, and steel is used in the cheapest transformers. Steel is also used in high-power transformers, such as guitar-amp output transformers, because of its higher level-handling characteristics.

For Example

To illustrate these concepts, let's examine the Jensen JT-DB-E, which is a 12:1 step-down transformer used in many DI boxes. It has a low-frequency response that is 3 dB down at 0.6 Hz and a high-frequency response that is 3 dB down at 100 kHz (see Fig. 13-7). (Frequency response is often specified with 3 dB down points, which are the frequencies at which the device's response is 3 dB below the nominal level.)

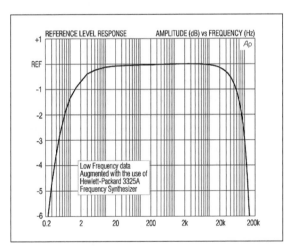

Figure 13-7. The frequency response of the Jensen JT-DB-E transformer is 3 dB down at 0.6 Hz and 100 kHz and very flat in the range of 20 Hz to 20 kHz. (Courtesy Jensen Transformers)

Why do you need a frequency response from 0.6 Hz to 100 kHz? For one thing, this means the transformer is basically transparent (i.e., it exhibits a very flat frequency response) in the audio range. It also assures a flat phase response (i.e., the phase relationship between different frequencies remains constant) in the audio range (see Fig. 13-8).

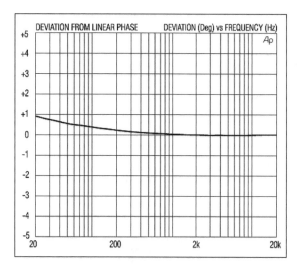

Figure 13-8. The phase response of the Jensen JT-DB-E transformer is very flat in the range of 20 Hz to 20 kHz, deviating only 1° in the low end. (Courtesy Jensen Transformers)

Phase response affects the fidelity of the output waveform and the relative delay of different harmonics (which is also known as time alignment). Poor phase response results in a lack of localization, clarity, and imaging. Maintaining a flat phase response from 20 Hz to 20 kHz requires a flat frequency response between 0.8 Hz and 50 kHz at least and higher if possible. A high-frequency response up to 100 kHz is fine for audio requirements; 200 kHz is state of the art.

The JT-DB-E's typical input impedance is 200 to 400 kΩ, depending on the mic preamp's input impedance. This is fine for a synth, but it might seem a bit low for guitar. However, if the DI box's input impedance is in this range, it helps roll off the excessive brightness that often occurs when a guitar is connected directly to a mixer through the DI box. The transformer's output impedance depends on the source device, but its typical value is 150 Ω, which is ideal for a mic-preamp input.

Other Components

Some high-end DI boxes, such as the Whirlwind Hot Box, have no transformer at all. Instead, they use active electronics for level and impedance matching. (Active electronics include semiconductor components, such as integrated circuits, whereas transformers are a type of passive component, as are resistors and capacitors.) The Hot Box has an input impedance of 10 MΩ, which improves the frequency response at both ends of the spectrum.

In addition to a transformer or active electronics, many DI boxes include a ground-lift switch (see Fig. 13-6), which helps eliminate ground loops in certain equipment (see Chapter 3). There is a wide variety of good and bad techniques for designing and

manufacturing audio equipment, and ground-lift switches help compensate for bad designs.

As mentioned earlier, if you run a guitar directly into a mixer through a DI box, it can tend to sound very bright. As a result, DI boxes often include a switchable lowpass filter that simulates the rolloff of a guitar amp/speaker combination. The speakers in a guitar cabinet don't have much response above 3 to 5 kHz, so this filter normally rolls off above this frequency range.

Some DI boxes, such as the Whirlwind Director, include an attenuator that lets you connect the speaker output from a guitar amp to the mic input on a mixer. This lets you include the compression and distortion components of the amplifier in the signal that goes to the mixer.

The Jensen Iso-Max stereo DI box uses two JT-DB-E 12:1 step-down transformers, which are the round, metal objects in this open view.

Applications

DI boxes are helpful in several ways beyond letting you connect a guitar to a mixer's mic input. For example, many home-studio owners have lots of synths, which eat up the line inputs on their mixer. However, the mixer might have plenty of mic inputs available. Using DI, you can bring the signals from extra synths into the mixer via the open mic inputs.

Perhaps the most common application for DI boxes is to connect equipment with high-impedance outputs (such as synths) to a mixer's low-impedance inputs via long cables (e.g., snakes or studio tie lines). Cables that must run a considerable distance should always be balanced and low impedance to minimize signal loss, induced noise, and grounding problems.

If you were to run a long cable (say, 100 feet) from a guitar to an amp, it would completely load the guitar; you'd lose high-frequency response and, as with a synth, add noise. However, if you connect the guitar to a nearby DI box with a short instrument cable, you can then run a 100-foot mic cable to a mic preamp near the guitar amp. The output of the mic preamp is then connected to the input of the amp.

Instead of using a mic preamp in this situation, you could use a less-expensive matching transformer, which is typically a 1:10 step-up transformer that is used to connect a low-impedance mic to a high-impedance input, such as a guitar amp. This transformer is normally housed in a barrel-type case with a female XLR connector on one end and a $\frac{1}{4}$-inch, unbalanced plug on the other end.

Such a transformer works optimally if it "sees" a few hundred $k\Omega$ as a load, which means a typical 10 $k\Omega$ line input does not provide enough input impedance, but a 1 $M\Omega$ guitar-amp input is fine. Using the "square of the turns ratio" rule in reverse (remember, this is a step-*up* transformer), a 10 $k\Omega$ load on the transformer's output would present a 100 Ω input impedance to the mic-level signal from the DI box, which is far too low. However, a 1 $M\Omega$ load would present a 10 $k\Omega$ input impedance to the signal from the DI box, which is sufficient.

Unfortunately, most matching transformers are not very high fidelity. Because the transformer must fit within a barrel-type housing, it isn't large enough to produce good low-frequency response. These transformers also exhibit lots of phase distortion in the lower midrange and bass ranges. They're okay in noncritical applications, but you wouldn't want to use them in the studio.

DI boxes are one of the unsung heroes of electronic music. They can help improve your sound in many ways, but many people don't understand how they work or how to use them. Hopefully, you can now appreciate the important role that DI boxes play onstage and in the studio and begin to use them in your setup.

CHAPTER 14

Tape Decks

Most musicians are familiar with tape decks, which have been used to record and play music and other audio for many years. However, few musicians understand the basic workings of these devices. All tape decks fall into one of two categories: stereo (2-track) and multitrack. In addition, both types of decks are available in two forms: analog and digital.

Despite these differences, all tape decks use the same basic principle to record and play audio signals. A length of plastic tape coated with a magnetically sensitive material is unwound from a supply reel, drawn past tape heads (discussed shortly) at a constant speed, and wound onto a takeup reel. During recording, the record head encodes a representation of the incoming audio signal in the tape's magnetic material. During playback, the repro head reproduces an audio signal from the magnetically encoded information on the tape.

As discussed in Chapter 12, studio tape decks accept and produce signals at line level. (Tape decks intended for field recording typically accept a mic-level signal and include an internal mic preamp.) Professional decks use a line level of +4 dBu, and semipro and consumer decks use -10 dBV; some machines provide switchable operation. In addition to analog line-level inputs and outputs, digital decks typically have digital inputs and outputs, which can include AES/EBU, S/PDIF, ADAT Optical, and/or TDIF.

Both types of line level correspond to 0 on the deck's VU (volume unit) meters. Analog decks let you record slightly above 0 VU with no objectionable distortion, but digital decks start clipping the signal above this level (see Chapter 5). Some digital decks set the 0 VU point a few decibels below clipping so you can record above 0 VU like an analog deck.

Heads Up

Most high-quality analog tape decks include three heads: erase, record, and repro (short for reproduction; also called "play"). All three types use the same basic construction. A permanent magnet is constructed with a gap, and a coil of wire is wound around it (see Fig. 14-1).

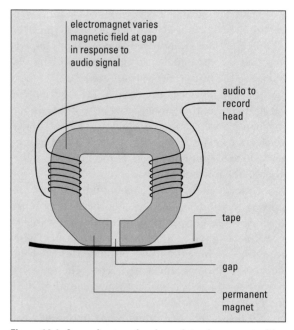

Figure 14-1. An analog tape head consists of a magnet with a gap wrapped in a coil of wire.

During recording, the tape is drawn past the record head's gap as the input signal flows through the coil of wire. The current in the wire alters the magnetic field in the gap in direct correspondence to the input signal. This fluctuating magnetic field aligns the magnetically sensitive particles (which are sometimes called "domains") on the tape in direct correspondence to the input signal (see Fig. 14-2). Before the tape reaches the record head, it passes by the erase head, which produces a steady, high-frequency magnetic field (in the 100 kHz range) that randomizes the orientation of the magnetic particles, providing a clean slate on which to record your audio.

During playback, the tape is drawn past the repro head. The changing orientation of the magnetic particles on the tape alters the magnetic field in the head's gap, which induces a corresponding current in the coil of wire around the head. This current is then amplified and sent to the rest of the sound system.

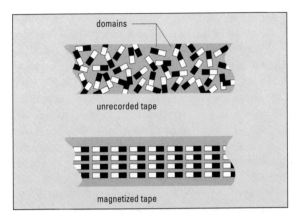

domains

unrecorded tape

magnetized tape

Figure 14-2. Initially, the magnetic particles, or domains, of recording tape are randomly oriented. After recording, they are aligned to correspond to the input signal.

These heads are arranged in a particular order (see Fig. 14-3). As the tape is drawn past the heads, it first encounters the erase head, which erases anything that might have been there previously. (That is, if the deck's record function has been engaged. More in a moment.) Next, it passes the record head, which aligns the particles to correspond with the input signal (that is, if the deck's record function has been engaged; more in a moment). Finally, it passes the repro head, which senses the alignment of the magnetic particles and produces a corresponding electrical signal.

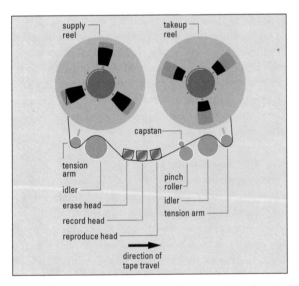

supply reel

takeup reel

capstan

tension arm
idler
erase head
record head
reproduce head

pinch roller
idler
tension arm

direction of tape travel

Figure 14-3. In a typical open-loop tape transport, the tape encounters the erase head first, then the record head, and finally the repro head.

Some analog tape decks include only two heads: erase and record/repro. Older 2-head decks normally produce a lower-quality result, but head technology has improved to the point that this is no longer true

of modern 2-head designs.

The record head in 3-head decks normally includes low-fidelity repro capabilities for multitrack overdubbing (see Chapter 22). If you record one musical part, then rewind the tape and listen to the recorded part while recording a new part along with it, the two parts will be out of sync if you listen to the repro head, which is located a certain distance from the record head. The tape takes a certain amount of time to move from the record head to the repro head. As a result, you must listen to the previously recorded signal from the record head so that what you record is in sync with the previous material on the tape.

Track Speed Record

All modern tape decks record and play at least two channels of audio. In analog decks, the tape is divided lengthwise into two or more tracks (see Fig. 14-4). There is an erase, record, and repro head for each track arrayed across the width of the tape.

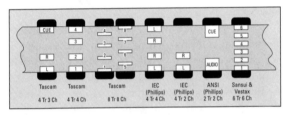

Figure 14-4. Analog tape can be divided into various track configurations. From left to right, the cassette configurations depicted here are TASCAM 2-track plus cue, TASCAM 4-track, TASCAM 8-track, quarter-track stereo, half-track stereo, ANSI/Philips mono plus cue, Sansui/Vestax 6-track.

There are two types of stereo analog tape decks: half track and quarter track. Half-track decks divide the tape into two tracks. A few half-track decks divide the tape into three tracks; the extra track is usually located in the center of the tape and is used to record time code for synchronization (see Chapter 7).

Quarter-track decks divide the tape into four tracks. This lets you record a stereo signal on one side of the tape, then turn the tape over and record another stereo signal on the other side. In both cases, the two audio signals are recorded simultaneously as a stereo pair; you normally can't record one channel and then the other.

Most multitracks divide the tape into 4, 8, 16, 24, or 32 tracks. The erase, record, and repro heads can be activated independently for each track, letting you record on one track, then record on another track while listening to the first track. This is like having several independent, mono tape decks within a single machine (see Fig. 14-5).

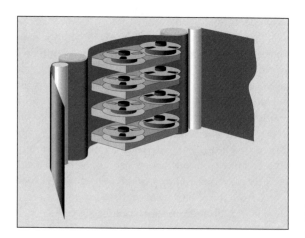

Figure 14-5. Multitrack tape decks behave as if there were several independent, mono tape decks within one machine.

Three main factors determine the quality of the audio recorded on an analog tape deck: gap width, track width, and tape speed. The overall frequency response of the machine depends on gap width; the smaller the better.

The wider the tracks, the higher the signal-to-noise ratio; wider tracks provide more "real estate" on which to record a signal. As a result, a ¼-inch, 8-track analog deck will have a similar S/N as a ½-inch, 16-track. In addition, narrower tracks are more prone to dropouts, in which the signal is momentary lost because the magnetic particles in a short section of the tape are not well aligned.

Another problem associated with track width is crosstalk. This occurs when the magnetic field of the particles on one track influence the alignment of the particles on an adjacent track. As a result, you can often hear a faint duplicate of one track while listening to the track next to it, especially if you solo the track you are listening to. Wider tracks are less prone to crosstalk because it constitutes a lower percentage of the signal on each track, so it is more effectively masked by the intended signal.

The faster the tape is drawn past the heads, the more magnetic particles are affected in a given amount of time, which improves the high-frequency response. Tape speed is measured in inches per second (ips). Of course, the faster the tape speed, the less record time you have on a tape of a given length. Some decks offer variable tape speed, which adjusts the pitch of playback as well as the speed. There should be a switch that turns variable speed on or off, so you can return to the precise nominal speed if necessary.

Loop the Loop
Analog tape decks come in two varieties: open reel and cassette. As the name implies, open-reel decks use open reels of tape. In most home studios, these reels are seven or ten inches in diameter. Of course, cassette decks use standard audio tape cassettes.

Open-reel decks use a mechanism called an open-loop transport to move the tape (see Fig. 14-3). The tape unwinds from the supply reel on the left and wraps around a tension arm, which maintains a constant tension in the tape. The tension arm includes a roller that passively spins as the tape moves past it, and the center of this roller can move perpendicular to the direction of tape travel to keep the tension constant.

Next, it passes by a roller, or idler, which also spins as the tape goes by. Then, the tape passes across the heads, which erase and record or play the audio signal. In open-reel decks, the heads are stationary. After leaving the heads, the tape passes between the capstan and pinch roller. The capstan rotates at a constant speed, and the pinch roller presses against it, thus pulling the tape from the supply reel at a constant rate. After passing by another idler and tension arm, the tape is wound onto the takeup reel.

It is the capstan motor that moves the tape; the reel motors pull gently in opposite directions to maintain tension in the tape (with the help of the tension arms). Common open-reel tape speeds are 3 ¾, 7½, and 15 ips; professional decks go up to 30 ips. Of course, the tape also can be shuttled at high speed from one reel to the other; this is sometimes called fast winding. Rewinding shuttles the tape from the take-up reel to the supply reel, and fast forwarding shuttles the tape in the opposite direction.

In either case, the appropriate reel motor takes over from the capstan motor. The pinch roller moves away from the capstan and the tape moves between them without making contact. In some tape decks, a tape lifter pulls the tape away from the heads during fast winding to prevent unnecessary wear to the tape and heads.

Merrily We Analog
Stereo open-reel decks can be half-track (with or without a center time-code track) or quarter track and use tape that is ¼ or ½ inch in width. Multitrack open-reel decks use tape that is ¼ to 2 inches wide; the more tracks, the wider the tape must be. Eight-track machines typically use ¼- or ½-inch tape; 16-track normally decks use ½- to 1-inch tape; and 24- and 32-track decks use 2-inch tape.

Cassette decks use the same basic type of open-loop transport as open-reel decks, but there are a few differences. For example, the heads move into place against the tape during recording and playing, so there is no need for tape lifters or tension arms. In addition, the idlers are built into the cassette casing, not the deck itself, and the standard speed is 1⅞ ips, although some cassette multitracks increase this to 3¾ ips for improved fidelity.

Cassettes are identified by the total length of record time they provide; for example, a C90 cassette offers 90 minutes of total record time (45 minutes per side) at 1⅞ ips. In addition, the tape is only ⅛-inch wide. Standard cassettes are used for both stereo and multitrack recording.

Stereo cassette decks are almost universally quarter-track. Most multitrack cassette recorders are integrated with a small mixer; TASCAM calls this type of product a Ministudio or Portastudio, and Fostex calls it a Multitracker. These decks typically offer four tracks in one direction; you can't turn the tape over in this case. A few offer six tracks, and some TASCAM and Yamaha cassette decks provide eight tracks.

Many analog tape decks (particularly cassette and ¼-inch, 8-track decks) include some form of noise reduction. The most popular are dbx and Dolby B, C, and S (see Chapter 21). Sync tones and time code (see Chapter 7) do not work well if they are recorded with dbx noise reduction, so some decks let you defeat noise reduction on an outside track while applying it to the other tracks. In addition, cassette decks typically boost the high frequencies during recording (which is called pre-emphasis) and cut these frequencies during playback (de-emphasis) to improve the S/N ratio.

Recording tape is made with different materials (see sidebar, "Tape Formulations"). As a result, analog tape decks should be calibrated (or electronically aligned), to optimize their operation with a particular type of tape. Professional decks include user-accessible calibration controls, and commercial studios calibrate their decks to match the type of tape brought in by the client. Semipro and consumer decks often require partial disassembly to access the calibration controls.

One of the most important calibration parameters is called "bias." Many analog decks take the high-frequency signal that is applied to the erase head and mix it with the incoming signal to be recorded. This bias signal provides a "backdrop" that brings the input signal into the best dynamic range for the particular type of tape you are using. Cassette tapes are especially sensitive to biasing, so some professional cassette decks include a control that adjusts the level of the bias signal.

Unfortunately, the word "bias" is also used to mean something different with analog cassettes. In this case, it refers to the pre-emphasis/de-emphasis curve used by the cassette deck. "Normal bias" represents a less drastic de-emphasis curve than "high bias." Many cassette decks automatically select the appropriate EQ setting when you insert a tape, but some let you select the setting manually.

In addition to calibration, complete deck maintenance includes physically aligning the record and playback heads with the tape to ensure proper performance. This procedure requires training, test gear, and experience, so don't try it at home unless you are absolutely sure you know what you're doing.

Rotating Heads

Not long ago, digital tape decks were the exclusive purview of fully commercial studios. Now, however, they are available to just about any home studio at very reasonable prices. Digital decks come in three basic varieties: open reel, DAT, and modular digital multitrack (MDM). (A few years ago, Philips introduced a fourth variety of digital tape, Digital Compact Cassette, which used the cassette format and could even play regular analog cassettes. Although its technology was good, DCC never caught on with the public.) Open-reel digital machines are very expensive and used only in commercial facilities; DATs and MDMs are becoming quite common in personal studios, so these are the formats I will discuss here.

The fundamental principle used to record and play audio is the same as it is for analog decks: Tape coated with magnetically sensitive particles is drawn past magnetic heads, which align and sense the orientation of the particles. However, the particles are aligned in only two ways, which represent 0 and 1; when an audio signal enters the deck's analog input, it is converted into a digital signal (see Chapter 5), which is nothing more than a string of 0s and 1s. (The particles on an analog tape can be aligned in many different ways to correspond to the rising and falling analog waveform.) In addition, the digital data is stored in packets, rather than in a continuous stream, as with analog tape.

DAT and MDM decks use a different type of head mechanism that was first developed for VCRs. This is called a rotating head because it rotates as the transport pulls the tape past it. In addition, its rotational direction is oriented at an angle to the direction of tape travel (see Fig. 14-6). As a result, the actual tracks on the tape are diagonal to the length of the tape. If you were to curl the tape into a long, lengthwise tube, the diagonal tracks would form a helix (a cylindrical spiral), so this mechanism is called a "helical recording system."

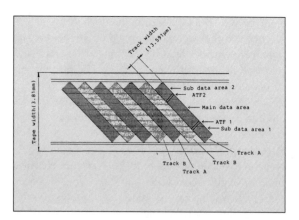

Figure 14-6. A helical recording system is used in DATs and MDMs. The heads rotate at an angle to the direction of tape travel. (Courtesy Fostex)

In most helical recording systems, the actual head gaps are located on the surface of a rotating cylinder, and there is no separate erase head; the record head overwrites any previously recorded information. In 2-head designs (e.g., DAT decks), the record and repro heads (which are often called write and read heads in this case) are generally located 180° apart (see Fig. 14-7); in 4-head designs (e.g., ADAT), there are two write heads 180° apart and two read heads at right angles to the line connecting the write heads.

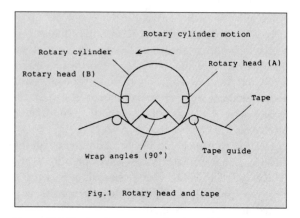

Figure 14-7. The heads on a rotary head are 180° apart, and the tape is wrapped partly around the head assembly. (Courtesy Fostex)

Because the heads rotate, they cannot write or read a continuous stream of data on the tape. As a result, the incoming data is stored in a temporary RAM buffer until the write head is in the proper position to record the data on the tape. Similarly, data from the read head is stored in the buffer and sent to the DAC at the correct time. This also allows the system time to perform various error-correction chores.

Interestingly, track width and tape speed don't

necessarily have any effect on audio quality (although track width does affect tracking accuracy by allowing a margin for error when the heads drift out of alignment). What matters is the manner in which the analog signal is converted into digital and stored on the tape in addition to the type of error correction used. Digital decks do not need to be calibrated for different types of tape, but they do need periodic adjustments, such as transport, tape-path, and back-tension alignment.

That Darn DAT

DAT is strictly a stereo medium; virtually all DAT decks record both channels at once. It is "half-track" in the sense that you can record in one direction only; you can't turn the tape over and record on the other side. In addition, the tape is not divided into lengthwise tracks because DAT machines use a helical recording system. Like analog cassettes, DAT tapes are enclosed within a plastic shell, and they are identified by the amount of recording time they offer (e.g., a D60 DAT offers 60 minutes of continuous record time).

DAT decks are available in professional and consumer versions (although consumer models are quickly fading away). Consumer models typically can record *analog* signals only at 48 kHz, which must be sample-rate converted to 44.1 kHz if the material is intended for CD distribution. (Consumer DATs can record and play *digital* audio at 44.1 kHz.) Both varieties currently record with 16-bit resolution.

Consumer decks also include the Serial Copy Management System (SCMS, pronounced "scums"), which prevents digital copies beyond the second generation; i.e., you can make a copy of the original recording, but you can't make a copy of the copy. This was mandated for consumer DAT decks to fight piracy. Professional DAT decks can record analog audio at 44.1 or 48 kHz, and in some cases 96 kHz, and they have no SCMS or offer defeatable SCMS.

Because the track width is so narrow, there are bound to be dropouts, so an extensive error-correction system is used. In this system, multiple copies of the data are interleaved, or stored in non-sequential packets; if a dropout occurs in a packet, the deck can reconstruct the data using one of the redundant copies.

In addition to the digital audio data itself, DAT decks record a variety of ancillary, or subcode, data in the helical scan. Embedding subcode data in the helical scan is part of a system called Auto Track Finding (ATF), which helps steer the heads to the correct helical track.

The subcode data includes Start IDs (which number the beginnings of selections on the tape) and timing information, such as elapsed and remaining time for the entire tape and each selection. This lets you quickly cue the tape to the desired location and display cumulative or selection-specific elapsed and remaining time. Subcode data can even be added or changed after the audio has been recorded, which lets you renumber the selections on tape.

MDM Madness

Modular digital multitracks (MDMs) have brought digital multitrack tape recording to the masses in a big way. As of this writing, all MDMs can record eight tracks of digital audio; most record at sampling rates of 44.1 or 48 kHz, with 16-bit resolution.

The first MDM was the Alesis ADAT, which was soon followed by the TASCAM DA-88. Since then, several manufacturers have produced compatible MDMs under license from Alesis or TASCAM; ADAT-compatible MDMs are made by Fostex and Panasonic, and DA-88-compatible MDMs are made by Sony. In addition, Alesis and TASCAM have updated their original MDMs: Alesis now offers the ADAT XT and Meridian (which records at 20-bit resolution but still plays ADAT tapes), and the TASCAM line now includes the DA-88, DA-38, and DA-98.

The ADAT uses a modified VHS transport and standard S-VHS videocassettes. The tape speed is 3¾ ips, which provides 40 minutes of record time on a T-120 videocassette. TASCAM selected the Hi-8 (8 mm) format for the DA-88 and its siblings. In this case, the tape speed is only slightly faster than a standard Hi-8 videotape transport, so you get about 108 minutes of record time on a "120-minute" tape. In both cases, the tape must be formatted (like a computer disk); this can be done as you are recording, but it is generally better to format an entire tape before using it.

Formatting on an ADAT encodes information such as the selected sample rate and timing on a separate, linear control track. The TASCAM DA series uses ATF and encodes this information in the subcode data as part of the helical scan, much like a DAT deck.

As discussed in Chapter 7, it is possible to synchronize a MIDI sequencer to a tape deck by striping SMPTE time code or a sync tone on one track. Most MDMs also provide optional or built-in hardware that generates SMPTE time code without having to stripe it on a track. In either case, the tape deck is the master and the sequencer syncs to it.

Many newer tape decks can also respond to MIDI Machine Control (MMC) messages (see Chapter 9). However, the tape is still the master sync source in this case; the sequencer is a glorified remote control, but it still syncs to the tape. The ADAT has no MIDI In, so it can't respond to MMC directly, but synchronizers such as the JLCooper DataSync can convert incoming MMC commands

into ADAT codes and send them to the ADAT's 9-pin sync connector. This type of device can also be used to generate SMPTE, MTC, and MIDI Clock from the ADAT's sync signal.

Although current MDMs are limited to eight tracks, you can combine several units to increase the number of tracks. (This is why they are called modular digital multitracks; they are multitrack modules that can be combined into larger systems.) At the most basic level, all you need to do is connect the sync output of one deck to the sync input on another deck and designate one deck as the master and the other deck as the slave. When you operate the transport controls on the master, the slave responds, as well. (The sync connector is a 9-pin D-sub on the ADAT and a 15-pin D-sub on the DA-series MDMs. In addition to proprietary sync signals, it also carries word clock for the digital audio; see Chapter 5.)

Location, Location, Location

All tape decks include some sort of tape counter, which indicates the passage of tape through the machine. In older and less-expensive decks, this counter is a meaningless 3- or 4-digit number. In more sophisticated decks, the counter indicates the passage of time in minutes and seconds. DAT and MDM counters can also indicate elapsed and remaining time on the tape thanks to the subcode data (or control track in the ADAT).

Each point on the tape can be identified by the value of the counter as that point passes the heads. On analog decks, this works best if you rewind the tape to the beginning (i.e., so that all the tape in wound onto the supply reel) and reset the counter to zero. Some decks can read time code from the tape and set their counter accordingly.

Some tape decks let you store one or more counter values and shuttle to them automatically at the touch of a button. This is great for locating different sections of a song or different songs on the tape. Most decks also have a Return to Zero (RTZ) button that shuttles the tape to the point at which the counter reads zero.

To achieve even greater control over the tape, you can use an autolocator. This external device can store many tape locations in its memory and shuttle the tape between them. Alesis makes two autolocators for the ADAT series: the LRC (Little Remote Control) is included with each ADAT and provides limited control for one machine, and the BRC (Big Remote Control) provides expanded control for one or more synchronized machines. The TASCAM equivalent is the RC-848.

Several manufacturers make autolocators for a variety of tape decks. For example, JLCooper Electronics makes the CuePoint, which can be used with MDMs, M-HDRs, or any device that responds to MIDI Machine Control (see Chapter 9). You can also install an optional ADAT card that connects directly with the ADAT 9-pin sync interface, and it can generate SMPTE and MIDI Time Code from the ADAT sync codes.

Fruit Punch

All types of multitracks let you punch in and out. In this process, you engage the record function for one or more tracks as the tape is playing. This lets you replace a section of the track with new material. For example, suppose you flubbed one phrase in an otherwise brilliant track. Rewind the tape to a point before the flub and start playing. When you get to a point just before the flub, hit the Record button and record the phrase again; this is called punching in. After the new phrase is finished, disengage the record function to retain the previously recorded material; this is called punching out.

Normally, it's best if there is a section of silence before the flubbed phrase begins and after it ends. The shorter these silent sections are, the "tighter" the punch (i.e., the more accurately you must engage and disengage the record function to avoid erasing the material you want to keep). In addition, some older multitracks leave a short gap of silence after punching out. Newer machines provide "gapless" punching, which allows much tighter punches.

If your hands are full (e.g., with an instrument), many multitracks let you punch in and out with a footswitch connected to a special connector on the back panel. Many newer machines also provide an auto-punch feature that lets you program punch-in and -out times from the tape counter; this can also be done with most autolocators.

Tape Storage

Because recording tape is a magnetic medium, it should be kept away from all magnetic sources, including speakers, power amps, and refrigerator magnets. Exposure to magnetic fields can disrupt the orientation of the magnetic particles and mess up your recordings. In addition, make sure to store your tapes in a cool, dry place; heat and/or moisture can also destroy the recorded signal.

At the end of the day, you can wind the tape onto the supply reel or the take-up reel for storage. Storing it on the supply reel is called "heads out" and makes it ready to use immediately, but you normally rewind the tape onto the supply reel at high speed, which stores the tape in a tightly wound condition in which the layers of tape are pressed against each other. This can lead to print-through, a process in which the magnetic field from the particles on one

layer of tape affects the particles on adjacent layers, producing a "ghost" signal on the adjacent layers.

As a result, it's better to wind the tape onto the takeup reel at normal playing speed, which stores the tape in a loosely wound condition and reduces any chance of print-through; this is called "tails out." When you want to use that tape, you must rewind it to the correct location, which poses no print-through problem for short periods of time.

Maintenance

Over time, all tape heads become dirty from dust and bits of material that wear off of the tape and stick to the heads; the capstan and pinch roller get dirty for the same reasons. This can lead to dropouts and other problems, so it is critical to clean the heads and capstan/pinch roller regularly.

The basic procedure is the same for all analog tape decks. Wipe the critical components with a cotton swab dipped in an appropriate cleaning fluid. Pure (100%) alcohol is the fluid of choice for metal parts, such as the heads, because it cleans well and completely evaporates. However, alcohol can cause rubber parts, such as the pinch roller, to dry out and crack; special cleaning solutions, such as Intraclean, have been developed to safely clean rubber and metal parts.

In most analog tape decks, the heads are recessed but accessible. Dip a cotton swab into an appropriate cleaning fluid and wipe the front and side surfaces of the heads. Next, clean the tape guides, tension arms, and idlers. Then, clean the pinch roller (remember, don't use alcohol); keep scrubbing until all brown residue is removed. Finally, clean the capstan

As discussed earlier, DAT and MDM decks use rotating-head transports. You can get special "cleaning tapes" that look just like normal recording tape, but the "tape" is actually a head-cleaning material. You simply insert the cleaning tape and hit Play. However, you should use a particular tape only once for five to ten seconds and not rewind it; rewinding and using the tape again can redeposit dirt on the heads. Unfortunately, these cleaning tapes are not generally adequate for machines that see heavy studio use, but unless you are a video technician, do not attempt to manually clean rotating heads yourself; let a professional do this.

Any metal parts along the tape path can become magnetized over time, which can wreak havoc with the recorded material. As a result, you should demagnetize these components periodically. This requires a demagnetizer, which is available at most electronic supply stores. This device produces a randomized magnetic field that erases any organized magnetism in a nearby metal object.

Before you begin, make sure the deck's power is off; the magnetic field generated by the demagnetizer can damage the deck's internal circuitry if it's brought near an active erase or record head. In addition, make sure there are no recorded tapes or other magnetic media (such as floppy disks) anywhere near the demagnetizer.

Turn on the demagnetizer while holding it about an arm's length away from the deck, then slowly bring the tip toward the right idler. Working right to left, slowly pass the demagnetizer over each metal part of the transport mechanism. (You can reverse the procedure if you're left handed.) When you're done, slowly draw the demagnetizer away from the deck before turning it off; if you turn it off too close to the deck, it could redeposit magnetic debris back onto the deck.

Tape Formulations

The materials and construction of recording tape vary for different formats (analog open reel, cassette, DAT, S-VHS, Hi-8), but the basic principles are the same. Recording tape of any type consists of a polyester base film coated with a magnetic material on one side and an inert back coat on the other side (see diagram right). The back coat is a carbon-based material that helps the tape wind and unwind without slipping, reduces print-through, and minimizes static-electricity buildup. Digital tape also includes a top coat over the magnetic coat to produce an extremely smooth surface.

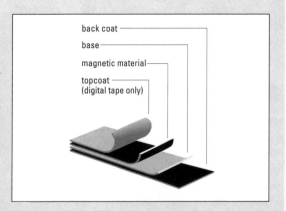

Recording tape includes at least three layers (four for digital tape).

The magnetic coat actually includes several ingredients. The magnetic particles themselves are typically some form of iron oxide; tapes that use iron oxide are known as ferric, which means iron. Chrome tapes originally used particles of chromium dioxide, but this term now refers to any magnetic material that exhibits certain criteria; these days, it usually means iron oxide with cobalt. Metal tapes use particles of pure iron or an alloy of iron and nickel or cobalt.

The magnetic particles are mixed with a binder that adheres to the base film, a dispersive agent that keeps the particles evenly distributed, and other materials designed to lubricate and combat problems such as static-electricity buildup and chemical breakdown. Taken together, the magnetic coat is called the tape formulation.

All types of magnetic particles exhibit some resistance to being aligned by an external magnetic field (such as from an erase or record head); this resistance is called coercivity, and it's measured in units of oersteds after Danish physicist and chemist Hans Christian Oersted. The coercivity value determines the magnetic field strength required to align the particles effectively. Once the particles are aligned, you want them to stay aligned; the degree to which the particles remain aligned is called retentivity.

If you apply a strong enough magnetic field, virtually all the particles will be firmly aligned; this is called saturation. Applying an even stronger field forces the particles out of alignment, which results in distortion. This saturation distortion builds up slowly as the strength of the magnetic field is increased. Tape manufacturers typically measure the level of the distortion's third harmonic (known as third harmonic distortion, or THD, not to be confused with total harmonic distortion, which is also abbreviated THD) in relation to the total output. Values above 3% are considered unacceptable. The level at which this occurs with a 1 kHz test tone is said to be the tape's maximum output level (MOL).

In cassettes, the type of magnetic particles used and the EQ setting (which is unfortunately called the bias of the tape, even though it has nothing to do with the high-frequency bias signal) are identified by a Type designation. Type I cassettes are ferric with a "normal bias" of 120 µs, and Type II cassettes use a chrome formulation and "high bias" of 70 µs. Type IV tapes use metal particles and high bias. (Type III tapes use a ferrichrome formulation, but this type of cassette is now obsolete.) DAT, S-VHS, and Hi-8 tapes use a metal-particle formulation.

CHAPTER 15

Signal Routing

Input devices, signal processors, recorders, and output devices occupy the periphery of a recording studio. At its heart is a mixer, which routes all audio signals to and from the other devices. Its assistant in this effort is the patch bay, which is discussed in the second section of this chapter.

MIXERS

Mixers are the central hub of activity in any studio, accepting many different signals at once and sending them anywhere you want. The path each signal follows through a mixer is somewhat circuitous, with many options and forks in the road. But unlike the protagonist in Robert Frost's poem, these signals can (and often do) take all roads simultaneously. In the end, all these signals are combined (hence the name "mixer"), so we can hear them from a pair of speakers or headphones.

Channel Inputs

The mixer signal path starts at the channel inputs. The outputs from microphones, preamps, guitar amps, DI boxes, and synthesizers are connected to these inputs. Each channel includes several controls, arranged vertically, that determine the specific signal path and levels at various points. The exact configuration of these controls varies from one mixer to another, but they usually follow a similar overall pattern. Fig. 15-1 illustrates a simple, generic channel, while Fig. 15-2 provides a road map through this channel and the rest of the mixer.

Starting at the top of Fig. 15-1, the first control is the mic/line switch. This switch selects the appropriate input connector. (Mics are typically connected to a balanced XLR jack, while synths and guitars are connected to ¼-inch jacks. Both types of inputs are present on many mixers.) The mic/line switch also determines whether the channel's internal mic preamp is engaged or bypassed. Some mixers also include a phantom-power switch near the top of each input, which sends 48 VDC to charge a condenser microphone (see Chapter 13). Many mixers only have a global phantom-power switch, which sends phantom

power to all or none of the mics.

The next control is called the trim or gain pot, which adjusts the gain of the input signal. This is important because different sound sources output signals at different levels; the trim pot helps even out the playing field.

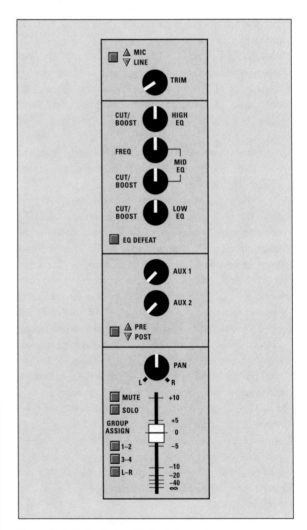

Figure 15-1. A simple hypothetical channel

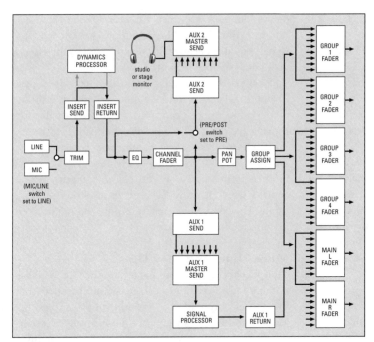

Figure 15-2. The signal path through one channel in a mixer is somewhat complex. The boxes with extra arrows are fed from all channel inputs; these are the aux send, group, and main buses.

The trim pot feeds directly to the insert point, a ¼-inch, 3-conductor, TRS (tip-ring-sleeve) connector that lets you detour the input signal out of the mixer, through an external device (such as an outboard equalizer or dynamics processor), and back into the channel before it proceeds further. If you don't connect anything to the insert point, the signal continues unaltered to the rest of the channel. Note that some mixers have separate insert send and return jacks, instead of a single TRS connector. In some mixers, the insert point is located *after* the EQ, aux sends, and channel fader (described shortly).

The next landmark in the primary signal path is the equalization (EQ) section. These controls let you tweak the tone of the input signal by raising (boosting) or lowering (cutting) the amplitude of certain frequency bands. At the very least, most mixers include high and low shelving EQ, which cuts or boosts the frequencies above or below a certain threshold, respectively. For example, the high EQ usually cuts or boosts the frequencies above 10 kHz, while the low EQ acts on frequencies below 100 Hz. (These frequency thresholds vary between mixers.)

Many mixers also include at least one mid-band EQ, which cuts or boosts the frequencies within a certain band in the middle of the entire frequency range. The mid-band EQ often includes a frequency control, which lets you specify the center of the affected band; this is called a sweepable mid, because you can sweep

through different center frequencies. A sweepable mid-band EQ is great for zeroing in on specific frequencies. However, the width of the band usually is fixed in less expensive mixers. In many mixers, the EQ section also includes an EQ defeat switch, which lets the signal pass through without being affected by the EQ settings.

Next on our tour are the aux send controls, which I'll discuss in a moment. The channel fader is perhaps the most recognizable control on any mixer; it invites curious fingers to move it up and down just to see how it feels. This fader is the final arbiter of the signal level in the channel before the signal proceeds to the master section (which we'll get to shortly).

Each channel can be silenced by pressing the mute button or isolated by pressing the solo button (which mutes all the other channels). It's a good idea to mute all unused channels during mixdown to reduce the inevitable noise that accumulates as more channels are added. In most inexpensive mixers, the solo button bypasses the pan pot, placing the signal in the center of the stereo field. However, some mixers include a feature called solo in place, which retains the pan position of the soloed channel. The solo button is sometimes called PFL (prefader listen), because it sends the signal to the outputs before it is attenuated by the channel fader.

Aux Buses

Immediately after the insert return at the top of the channel, the signal path splits (see Fig. 15-2). One path proceeds through the rest of the channel, while the other is mixed with the corresponding split signals from the other channels. This mixed signal, called an auxiliary, or aux, signal, is then sent out of the mixer to an external device, such as a multi-effects processor. The signal path by which the aux signal is sent to an external device is called an aux-send bus, because it combines signals from different channels and takes them to the same place (a particular output connector), much like a school bus takes different students to the same school.

If the split occurs before the channel fader, the aux bus is called a prefader aux send. Sometimes the prefader aux send splits from the primary signal path before the EQ section as well; in other words, it is prefader, pre-EQ. In some configurations, the split occurs before the fader, but after the EQ, so the bus is referred to as prefader, post-EQ. Like all buses, a prefader aux send is shared by all channels.

After the signal passes through the channel

fader, it is often split once again (see Fig. 15-2). One path continues through the remaining channel controls, while the other path is routed to another aux-send bus and out of the mixer to an external device. Because this path splits after the EQ and channel fader, it is called a postfader aux send. (The EQ usually precedes the channel fader, so a postfader send is also post-EQ.) Like the prefader aux send, such a bus is shared by all channels.

Most mixers have at least one aux-send bus, and some have as many as six or more. Each channel includes a separate level control for each aux send, which lets you control the level of the channel's signal on the aux-send buses. In essence, this provides a "mixer within a mixer." The more aux-send buses a mixer has, the more external signal processors can be independently applied to the channel's signals.

Now we can return to the aux section of our hypothetical channel (see Fig. 15-1). The individual level of each input signal on the aux 1 bus (which is a postfader aux send) is controlled by the aux 1 knob, while the level of the signal on the aux 2 bus is controlled by the aux 2 knob. The aux 2 bus can be switched to operate as a prefader or postfader bus from each channel. This lets you send some input signals to the aux 2 bus before the EQ and fader while sending other input signals to the bus after the EQ and fader.

A prefader aux send is often used to route the input signals to a studio or stage monitor system. The aux level knobs in each channel let you establish a mix for performers that is completely independent from the main mix. If they want to hear more of themselves than the main mix should have, you can simply adjust the appropriate aux-send control, without affecting the final mix. In this application, the corresponding aux return is not used, so the return can be used to bring a different signal into the mixer, if necessary.

You can also send signals to an effects device on a prefader aux send. For example, suppose you want to apply reverb to a signal, and you want to hear only the processed sound, not the dry sound. This produces a haunting, ghost-like quality. First, set the wet/dry control on the reverb to 100% wet (see Chapter 17). Then, send the signal to the reverb on the prefader aux send and pull the channel fader all the way down or disengage the postfader signal from the main L/R bus with the group-assign button, if one is included. This way, none of the dry signal reaches the main L/R bus. You can also produce an interesting effect by lowering the channel fader slowly; the dry signal fades while the wet signal remains.

Postfader aux sends are typically used to send one or more signals to effects devices, such as reverbs, delays, flangers, etc. (see Chapter 17). In this case, however, the channel fader affects the wet and dry signals equally, because the signal is sent to the effects unit after passing through the fader.

Once the signals from the aux buses pass through the effects devices, they are returned to the mixer at the aux return inputs. In most cases, the aux returns are mixed directly with the main L/R buses, but some mixers let you route these returns to any group bus, as well (more on these buses in a moment). You can also use channel inputs as aux returns, which lets you EQ and reroute the returning signal. However, this takes up inputs you might need for instruments or mics.

More Than One Way Out

The primary signal from each channel (i.e., the signal that wasn't split onto the aux-send buses) reaches the master output section via the pan pot and group-assign buttons. The group-assign buttons let you specify where the signal is sent after it leaves the channel. The possible destinations include the main left/right (L/R) bus and several group buses (sometimes called subgroups).

Notice that the group-assign buttons in Fig. 15-1 are labeled in pairs: 1-2, 3-4, and L-R. (Our hypothetical mixer has four group buses and two main buses.) Once you select a pair of buses with a button, the pan pot controls the relative balance of the signal between them. If you want a signal to go only to the group 1 bus, press the 1-2 group-select button and turn the pan pot all the way to the left. If you want a signal to go only to the group 4 bus, press the 3-4 group-select button and turn the pan pot all the way to the right. You can send each input signal to any or all of these buses, including the main L/R output.

Some mixers include direct outs for each channel, which send the channel's signal out of the mixer without mixing it with anything else. Normally, these direct outs are post-EQ and postfader. This is very useful if the mixer doesn't have group buses; you can send each channel to a multitrack recorder from the direct outs. Even if the mixer has group buses, there might be more recorder tracks than groups, so direct outs come in very handy. If a mixer doesn't have direct outs, the insert sends can be used in the same way, assuming they are postfader. (See the "Patch Bays" section of this chapter for more on this technique.)

Master Module

Once a signal passes through its channel input, it is routed to one or more group and/or main buses, as described earlier. The master controls for these buses are located in the master module (see Fig. 15-3), which typically resides to the right of the channel controls. At the top of the master module, meters indicate the overall signal level in each group and main bus. The overall level of each bus is controlled by the faders at the bottom of the master module. Often, each group bus can also be muted or soloed.

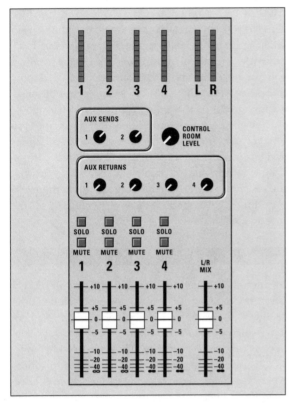

Figure 15-3. The master module includes level meters, master aux-send and aux-return controls, a control-room level control, solo and mute buttons for each group, and faders for each group and the main L/R output.

The master module also includes the master aux-send and aux-return controls. The master aux-send controls determine the overall level of each aux-send bus. The aux-return controls determine the level of the processed signal returning from wherever they were sent on the aux-send buses. In Fig. 15-3, notice that there are two master aux sends and four aux returns. In many mixers, the aux returns are stereo, because many effects units produce a stereo output from a mono input.

Each aux send, group, and main bus has a corresponding output jack on the mixer. As we've already seen, the aux-send outputs are usually connected to the input of a monitor system or effects device. The group jacks are usually connected to the inputs of a multitrack recorder. This lets you route any group of input signals to any recorder track. As mentioned earlier, the direct outs are sometimes connected to the multitrack inputs instead of the group

outputs. (By the way, the groups and main L/R buses often include insert points so you can externally process their mixed signals.)

For example, suppose you are miking an acoustic drum kit with several mics placed around the kit. After you refine the relative mix between individual drums with the channel-input faders, you can control the overall level of the kit with a single group fader. If you want the drums in stereo, pan each mic as desired with the channel-input pan pots and control the overall level with two group faders. This submix (or premix) is then recorded on two tracks.

The main L/R buses often include two output jacks each. One pair of outputs is connected to the stereo mixdown tape deck, which is usually a DAT recorder these days. In many mixers, the output from the mixdown deck is connected to an extra pair of inputs on the mixer with a switch that lets you listen to the main mix or the stereo tape deck.

The other main outputs are connected to the power amp and speakers in the control room (see Chapter 16). The control-room level knob adjusts the overall level of the entire mix as it is played back on this sound system without affecting the level of the signal going to tape.

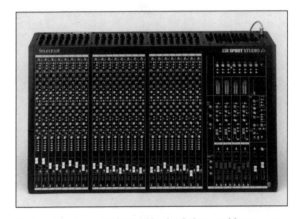

At first glance, the plethora of knobs, faders, and buttons on a typical mixer can seem like a road map to confusion. However, if you patiently trace the signal path, all will be revealed.

Tape Inputs

Once you have all your microphones, guitars, and synths connected to the channel inputs, how can you hear the tracks you've already recorded on the multitrack? How do you connect the outputs from the multitrack to the channel inputs on the mixer without unplugging and reconnecting zillions of cables every time you want to hear the recorded tracks? How do you mix the recorded tracks with any sequenced virtual tracks onto a stereo master tape?

Many mixers solve this problem by providing extra inputs for multitrack recorders called tape returns (which can also be used for the outputs from a multitrack hard-disk recorder, but the name was firmly established before such devices were available). In many mixers, these tape returns are included with each channel input. This is called an in-line design, in which there are actually two signal paths through each channel: one for the primary input (called the channel path) and the other for one track from the multitrack (called the monitor path because it lets you monitor the recorded tracks). If you have fewer recorded tracks than tape-return inputs, you can use the extra inputs for line-level instruments or effects returns. Some mixers include dedicated tape returns that look like separate channel inputs. This is called a split design, and the tape returns are generally located to the right of the master module.

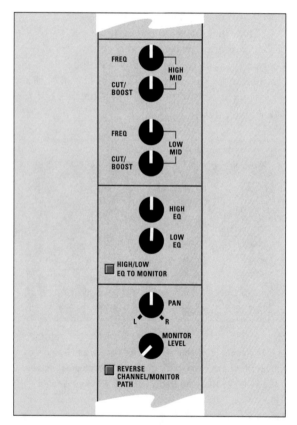

Figure 15-4. An in-line mixer includes two signal paths through each channel. The EQ section is split between the primary input (channel path) and the tape return (monitor path), but you can assign the channel EQ to the monitor path if you wish. The monitor path also includes its own pan pot and level control. You can even reverse the channel and monitor paths.

In Fig. 15-4, the two sweepable midbands affect the monitor path, while the high and low bands affect the channel path. A switch lets you assign the high and low bands to the monitor path if you need

more tonal control over the recorded track. In addition, the monitor path includes its own, independent pan pot and level controls. However, the monitor path is usually hard-wired to the main L/R buses; you can't send its signal to any of the group buses.

You can also reverse the channel and monitor paths in the hypothetical mixer depicted in Fig. 15-4. This lets you control the recorded signals with the main fader and other primary controls. Because most modern synths include their own effects, EQ, and panning, you can mix them with MIDI Volume and use the monitor path to send them directly to the main L/R buses during mixdown. This is very handy in a MIDI studio.

A mixer is the Union Station of any sound system; it routes incoming signals to various destinations and lets you control these signals in many ways. Hopefully, you now have a basic understanding of what mixers do and how signals flow through them. So head on over to your mixer and see what kind of traffic cop you can be.

PATCH BAYS

Anyone who operates even a moderately sophisticated home studio knows the joys of crawling around behind the gear to rewire the connections. Unless you have designed your studio so you can reach the rear connectors easily, this process quickly becomes a big hassle.

Fortunately, there is a simple solution: audio patch bays. These devices let you easily change connections from their front panels, instead of slithering around behind your racks. Of course, it takes some planning to make the most of a patch bay, and you must establish the rear-panel connections when you first install it. But once that is done, you rarely need to get your clothes dirty clambering around behind the gear.

Basic Description

Most patch bays are 1U rack-mount boxes with two horizontal rows of connector jacks on the front and back; each rear jack is connected directly to the corresponding front jack. Typically, there are 16 to 24 jacks in each row. The front and back panels are known as jackfields, and each jack is called a patch point. A few patch bays have jacks only on the front panel; they usually have punch blocks (which make a connection with bare wires) for the rear-panel cables, but in some cases you must solder the connections on the back. This type of patch bay is more common in commercial studios.

The type of jacks on the front and back panels of a patch bay varies according to the equipment found in the studio. RCA jacks are most often used for consumer and semipro equipment, while ¼-inch, 2-conductor jacks are used for devices such as synthesizers. However, it is better to use ¼-inch, 3-conductor, TRS (tip-ring-sleeve) jacks so you can connect either 2- or 3-conductor cables without problems. Most commercial studios use patch bays with TT jacks (Tiny Telephone, also called bantam), which are smaller than other types of jacks, allowing up to 48 jacks in each horizontal row.

To use a patch bay, you connect the inputs and outputs of your equipment to the rear-panel jacks. Thereafter, to route the output from one device to the input of another, you simply connect a short patch cord to the appropriate jacks on the front panel.

Internal Connections

In many cases, the jacks in each vertical pair on the rear panel are internally connected; this is called a normaled connection (see Fig. 15-5 [a]). Any signal appearing at one jack passes directly to the other one. This configuration lets you connect your equipment to the rear jacks in such a way that the normal connections between devices are maintained without using front-panel patch cords (hence the term "normaled").

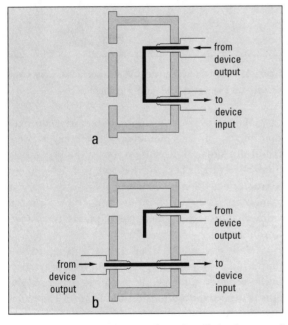

Figure 15-5. In a normaled configuration, if the front-panel jacks are unused, the rear-panel jacks are internally connected (a). If the lower front-panel jack is connected to anything, the normal connection is broken (b).

For example, you might connect the outputs from a multitrack recorder to one rear-panel row of jacks and the tape-return inputs on the mixer to the corresponding jacks in the other row. The recorded tracks are then connected to the mixer's tape returns without requiring front-panel patch cords. However, be careful not to connect two inputs or outputs to the same vertical pair of normaled jacks, which would

route an output to an output or an input to an input. Many engineers use a simple convention to avoid this problem: the upper jacks are connected to outputs, and the lower jacks are connected to inputs, or vice versa. This is not always convenient (or even possible), but it helps organize the system and prevent connection mistakes.

In older, fully normaled patch bays, the default connection between the upper and lower jacks is broken if you plug a cable into either front-panel jack of the vertical pair. For example, if you want to send different signals (say, from some extra synthesizers) to the mixer's tape returns, you can connect the desired outputs to the tape-return jacks on the front panel of the patch bay. This breaks the normaled connection (i.e., disconnects the multitrack outputs from the tape returns) and sends the new signals to the tape returns.

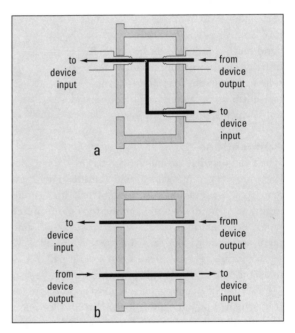

Figure 15-6. A half-normaled configuration splits the incoming rear-panel signal to both the rear- and front-panel outputs (a). In a denormaled configuration, the upper and lower jacks are not internally connected (b).

These days, however, most patch bays are half-normaled. In this configuration, the rear-panel input is routed (normaled) directly to the corresponding rear-panel output, just like in a fully normaled patch bay. Plugging into the lower front jack breaks the normaled connection (see Fig. 15-5 [b]). However, if you connect something to the upper front-panel jack only, the signal is sent to *both* destinations (see Fig. 15-6 [a]). This provides a mult, or signal splitter, which can be useful in a number of situations. For example, you could use a mult to send the same signal to two outboard processors or two mixer channels for separate equalization. Another possibility is to split a mixer group output and simultaneously route it to a tape deck and a sampler, so you don't have to repatch for different applications.

Sometimes, you don't want the upper and lower jacks to be internally connected at all. This configuration is called non-normaled or denormaled (see Fig. 15-6 [b]). This lets you use both upper and lower jacks as inputs or outputs, but it also requires that you make all desired connections with patch cords on the front panel.

Many patch bays let you configure the internal normaling for each vertical pair of jacks. In some cases (e.g., patch bays made by Re an for dbx, Conquest, and others), you simply reverse a circuit card in the patch bay to normal or denormal a particular vertical pair. In other products, you must make or break solder connections to establish normal, half-normal, or non-normal connections, which is pretty inconvenient.

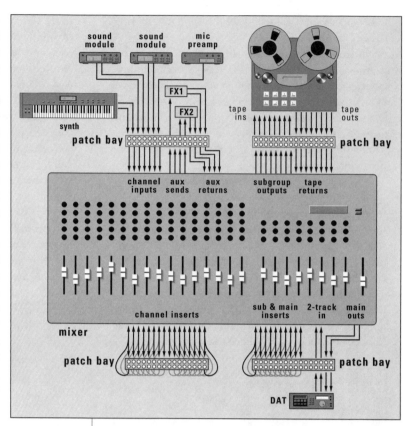

Figure 15-7. In this hypothetical studio setup, all inputs and outputs are connected to normaled patch bays.

Applications

When you decide to install a patch bay in your studio, there are a few things you should consider. First, how many patch points do you need? These include all inputs and outputs to and from the mixer, multitrack tape deck, mixdown deck, signal processors, samplers, and/or hard-disk recording system, as well as all synth outputs. Typically, you need several patch bays to accommodate all these inputs and outputs.

What type of connectors are most appropriate for your system? I recommend ¼-inch, TRS jacks for maximum flexibility. In this case, however, you will need adapters for RCA-equipped gear. In addition, if you connect a 2-conductor cable to any TRS patch point, the ring is shorted to ground, and that particular signal path is 2-conductor thereafter. This won't typically cause a problem, but you should be aware of it.

Make a chart of all patch-bay connections. This can take the form of a graphic diagram (see Fig. 15-7) or a table that lists all patch points along with their normaling status and rear-panel connections. You might also keep a blank table handy to document front-panel patches. In addition, it is critical to label all front and rear patch points and rear-panel cables. This makes it easy to establish new front-panel connections at a glance and reconfigure the rear-panel connections, if necessary.

Many people have more outboard gear than their mixers can accommodate. A patch bay is essential in this situation because it moves the inputs and outputs from the back of the rack to a convenient location near the mixer, making them easy to access as needed. The "extra" inputs and outputs can be connected to denormaled patch points for added flexibility.

Many engineers normal their effects inputs and outputs to the mixer's aux sends and returns, respectively. However, some people prefer to denormal the effects inputs and outputs on the front of the patch bay. This lets you configure the effects in any way (e.g., in a chain) and assign them to any aux send and return, which is especially useful when you have more outboard processors than you have aux buses.

If your mixer's input channels don't include direct outs (e.g., the Mackie CR-1604), a patch bay can adapt the channel insert points for this purpose. When wiring the insert points to the patch bay, you simply normal the insert sends to their corresponding returns. (If your mixer's insert points use a TRS jack for each send/return pair, you'll need a "Y" cable to separate the send and return.) If you don't plug anything into the front-panel jacks, each channel's signal passes from the send to the return, just as if nothing had been plugged into the channel insert. You can still use the individual send and return jacks as you normally would, but the insert send can also be used as a direct out. Generally, the insert send/return pairs on the patch bay are half-normaled, so you can mult the sends to other inputs (e.g., a multitrack or sampler) without disrupting the signal flow through the mixer. Some engineers make such connections on the front of the patch bay and leave them semi-permanently patched.

If you perform live or travel to other recording studios, you might have a portable rack with the gear you need for these applications. If so, consider installing a patch bay in the rack. This lets you easily access the inputs and outputs of the rack gear in any situation. To create a totally integrated live-performance system, you can rack-mount a line mixer and normal everything in the rack to it. When you bring the rack to a studio, just plug in the studio snakes to break the normals and send the signals directly to the mixing station.

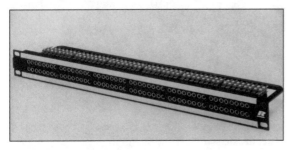

This 48-point patch bay by Re an uses ¼-inch TRS jacks. Each set of front and rear patch points is on a reversible card. To change from half-normaled to denormaled, you simply remove, reverse, and replace the card.

To maintain clean rear-panel connections, you should usually install the patch bay in the back of the rack. The most common exception is when the rack will be located at the sound-reinforcement mixing station, and you anticipate that the engineer may need to repatch on the fly. In this case, the patch bay is front-mounted for convenient access.

Patch bays can make your life in the studio much easier. Once you make the initial connections on the rear panel, reconfiguring those connections on the front panel is a snap. In addition, you can add new gear to your rig with a minimum of fuss and muss. Patch bays are the unsung heroes of the studio, so get out from behind your gear and give them a try.

CHAPTER 16

Output Devices

Once your music has passed through the various devices in your studio, you probably will want to hear it. Of course, you can simply plug a set of headphones into the appropriate jack on your mixer, but this doesn't let you share the music with others. In addition, monitoring on headphones can become very tiresome very quickly.

As a result, most engineers monitor on one or more pairs of speakers. In order to drive the speakers properly, the line-level output from the mixer must be amplified, which is the job of a power amplifier.

POWER AMPLIFIERS

As its name implies, a power amplifier is intended to boost the power of a signal. Typically, a power amp accepts a line-level signal and increases its voltage and/or current without changing the shape of the input waveform. The amplified signal is sent to a speaker, which converts the signal into acoustic sound waves (discussed later in this chapter).

Power amps are used in three primary applications: studio monitoring, sound reinforcement, and instrument amps (e.g., guitar and bass). The general principles of all power amps are essentially the same. For the purposes of this book, we'll focus on studio amps, which typically amplify two channels from a mixer's main output and send them to speakers.

Power Supply

Unlike most studio gear, a power amp draws some serious current from the AC outlet. This current is converted to DC by the power supply. (Virtually all electronic devices include a power supply that converts AC voltage to DC in order to operate their internal components.) The first step in this process is performed by a power transformer, which increases or decreases the incoming AC voltage (see Chapter 3), depending on how much power the amp is meant to deliver. The AC voltage from the transformer is converted into a DC voltage by a set of diodes and several large capacitors.

One common type of power-amp transformer is

called toroidal because it looks like a doughnut (a shape known as a toroid in mathematical circles; see Fig. 16-1). This shape is important because the magnetic field of a toroidal transformer is more confined to the core, reducing leakage into the audio circuitry.

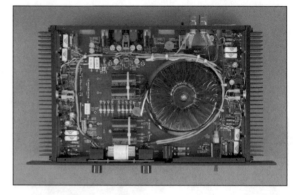

Figure 16-1. The BGW 200 power amp includes a huge toroidal power transformer. (Courtesy BGW)

The DC voltage from the power supply is symmetrically arranged around the ground point (0V). For example, the output from the power supply might be ±50 VDC. These positive and negative voltages are called the power-supply rails, which are used to operate the amp's internal circuitry. In particular, they provide power to a set of output transistors, which perform the actual amplification. (In early power amps, the job of the output transistors was performed by tubes, and some people still think tubes sound better than transistors. However, transistors are more durable and reliable.)

The output transistors amplify the input signal by drawing power from the capacitors in direct proportion to the input signal's voltage as it varies over time. As the capacitors discharge in this process, they are replenished by the transformer. The electrical capacity of these capacitors and the speed with which they are replenished are critical factors in the quality of the amp.

Most power amps use either bipolar or MOSFET (Metal Oxide Semiconductor Field Effect Transistor) output transistors. Bipolar transistors generally have a higher current capacity, which is especially important in a power amp. However, their impedance decreases as they get hotter, letting more current through, which heats them up even more, letting even more current through, and so on. This is called thermal runaway, which can quickly damage the transistors. As a result, most amps with bipolar transistors include thermal-protection circuitry.

MOSFETs are popular because they exhibit a very high input impedance. However, they exhibit significant gate capacitance, which can make their high-frequency performance unstable. This can be circumvented with good design, but it can be tricky. On the plus side, MOSFETs do not suffer from thermal runaway.

You often hear power amps labeled as Class A, B, or AB. In a Class A power amp, the output transistors handle both the positive and negative swings of the waveform. In Class B designs, one set of transistors handles the positive swings and another set handles the negative swings. This also applies to Class AB amps, but there is some overlap as the signal changes polarity; when the signal is near 0V, both sets of transistors are conducting.

The power-supply rails determine the maximum amplitude that the amp can produce. For example, if the rails are at +50V and -50V, the amp can produce signals of nearly 100 volts peak-to-peak. If the amp tries to produce a signal that exceeds this limit, the tops and bottoms of the waveform are cut off; this is called clipping (see Fig. 16-2). Interestingly, the resulting distortion applies much higher average power to the speaker and generates severe high-frequency components that can be very damaging to tweeters. As a result, many amps include a clipping or current limiter to minimize this problem.

Some amp designs use multiple power-supply rails (see Fig. 16-2). When the peaks of the output signal are small to moderate, the low-voltage rails are used; most musical material falls within this range most of the time. When the output peaks are large (as in momentary, loud transients), the high-voltage rails are used.

This is more efficient than single-rail designs, and it provides extra headroom when necessary (more in a moment). In addition, it can lower the AC current draw and cooling requirements by up to 40 percent. If the same set of output transistors is used with both sets of rails, this is called a Class H design; if different transistors are used with the different rails, it is called a Class G design.

Another way to improve the efficiency of a power amp is to use a switching power supply (also known as a high-frequency power supply). Long used in computers and other devices, a switching power

supply converts the incoming 60 Hz AC power to a much higher frequency, often over 100 kHz. This improves the performance of the transformer (the behavior of which is frequency dependent), allowing smaller, lighter transformers to be used.

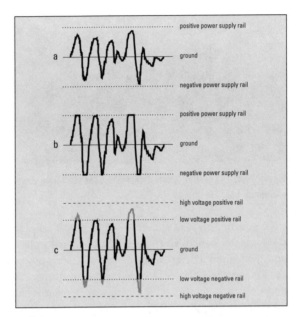

Figure 16-2. As long as the voltage swings in the output voltage don't exceed the power-supply rails, the shape of the waveform is preserved (a). If the voltage exceeds the rails, the peaks are clipped (b). In a multi-rail design, the amp switches to higher-voltage rails as needed (c).

Many people believe this type of power supply results in a more open sound with a clearer high end, but that it also inherently compromises bass performance. Others contend that this problem is related to design implementation and undersized supplies. Correct design provides better voltage regulation, which results in improved low-frequency performance over 60 Hz power supplies. However, switching power supplies use more components and require more space. In general, they are more beneficial in high-power amps.

Let's Get Physical

One of the most apparent physical characteristics of most power amps is the heat they generate. This occurs because power amps are very inefficient; typically, less than half the power from the wall is converted into a signal for the speaker. The rest of the incoming power turns into heat within the amp.

As a result, most amps use a variety of heat-management techniques. Perhaps the most obvious one is a heat sink, which includes large metal fins that dissipate heat by radiating it from large surface areas (see Fig. 16-3). Some amps include fans, which might remain on continuously or kick in when the temperature rises above a certain threshold, but these can be distracting in a quiet studio environment. Thermal-overload protection circuitry shuts the amp down if the temperature rises too high.

Figure 16-3. The Hafler P3000 dissipates heat via large, cast-aluminum heat sinks.

Another physical characteristic of power amps is their weight, which is primarily due to transformers and heat sinks. The greater the amp's power output, the greater the heat and the heavier the transformers and heat sinks tend to be (at least, with conventional 60 Hz power supplies).

Most power amps have very few controls and indicators. The most common controls are a power switch and gain knobs, but many amps don't even include these. Some amps include an LED that indicates the presence of AC power, and they may have additional LEDs that indicate if the outputs are clipping (discussed shortly). A few amps include level meters, but these are pretty useless; most dangerous transient peaks happen much more rapidly than the meter can indicate. However, meters can warn you if you are approaching clipping.

Of course, all power amps include input and output connectors. The inputs are typically balanced XLR or ¼-inch TRS jacks. The outputs are often 5-way binding posts, which let you connect speaker cables terminated with banana plugs or bare wires. In some cases, the outputs are simple barrier strips, which accept only bare wire.

Output Power
Output power is the most commonly used (and abused) amplifier spec. The actual power output from an amp depends on the impedance of the speaker to which it is connected as well as the frequency range in which the power is measured and total harmonic distortion (THD; discussed shortly). As a result, power specs are normally stated with respect to a specific impedance, frequency range, and THD. For example, a power amp might be specified as producing 200 watts per channel (W/ch.) into 8 Ω

over a frequency range of 20 Hz to 20 kHz with a THD of 0.1%.

If the speaker impedance is lower, some amps can produce more power; for example, the same amp might theoretically produce 400 W/ch. into 4 Ω. (In practice, cutting the speaker impedance in half does not quite double the output power because of the impedances within the amp itself.) Of course, this can't go on forever; as you decrease the speaker impedance, it tries to draw more and more current from the amp. At some point, the power supply can't supply any more current, and the signal starts clipping. Many amps include current-limiting protection circuitry to prevent this.

These power measurements are normally conducted in one of two ways, as specified by the Federal Trade Commission (FTC) and Electronic Industries Association (EIA). In the FTC measurement process, the stated power output must be achieved with both channels driven over the stated frequency range (usually 20 Hz to 20 kHz) at no more than the stated THD (generally 0.1%). An EIA power rating is stated for a single channel at a single midband frequency (typically 1 kHz) with 1% THD. This yields power ratings that are 10 to 20 percent higher than FTC measurements.

In general, an FTC rating tells you much more about the amp's actual performance. However, it is rare to see an FTC rating for a 2 Ω load, which is near the point at which current-limiting protection circuitry kicks in. The EIA measurement can reliably deal with a 2 Ω load, so it's best to see an FTC rating for 8 Ω and 4 Ω and an EIA rating for 2 Ω.

There are two other power specs that must be considered: continuous and peak power. Continuous power is the maximum power level the amp can maintain over long periods of time, and peak power is the maximum amount of power the amp can deliver for a short time (typically less than half a second). The difference between an amp's continuous and peak power capabilities is called dynamic headroom. If an amp's continuous power rating is 100 watts and its dynamic headroom is 3 dB, it can provide short bursts of up to 200 watts. (As discussed in Chapter 4, doubling the power increases the level by 3 dB.)

One of the most common questions that most studio owners ask themselves is, "How much power do I need?" The answer is generally, "The more the merrier!" It's better to have too much power than not enough. You might think that too much power can damage the speakers, but this is rarely the case (at least, if you're fairly responsible). You can always turn down the input to a powerful amp, which leaves lots of headroom. In addition, this causes the amp to operate in its linear range, which results in less noise and a cleaner signal. An underpowered amp can be driven into clipping more easily, and it doesn't have much headroom because it's operating in its extreme range.

The next question is, "How loud can the sound be from a given amp?" This depends on the amp's power output and the sensitivity of your speakers (discussed later in this chapter). At a given speaker sensitivity, the peak power output must increase by a factor of ten to increase the peak sound-pressure level by 10 dB. For example, suppose you have speakers with a sensitivity of 90 dB SPL at 1 watt at 1 meter (90 dB SPL @ 1W/1m). You only need one watt of power to achieve a peak of 90 dB SPL at that distance. To achieve a peak level of 100 dB SPL, you need 10 watts, and 100 watts will get you 110 dB SPL.

As mentioned earlier, however, most music peaks only occasionally; a typical ratio of peak-to-average levels is 6:1. To sustain an average sound-pressure level of 90 dB SPL with the ability to handle peaks cleanly would require about 500 watts. However, an average sustained level of 90 dB SPL is simply too loud, and an amp with reasonable dynamic headroom can handle short, high peaks, so most home studios can do quite well with less power.

Spec Wars

In addition to continuous and peak power ratings, there are several other specs that help you evaluate the performance of power amps. As in other audio equipment, frequency response is the range of frequencies that the amp can pass with relatively little alteration from the input to the output (except for amplification, of course). The minimum requirement for an amp's frequency response is 20 Hz to 20 kHz, ±1 dB, which is usually specified at a nominal power level (typically 1W).

Some power amps publish frequency-response specs that far exceed this minimum (e.g., 0 Hz to 40 kHz). If the amp actually produces a 0 Hz (i.e., DC) signal (often called a DC offset), this can damage the speakers, so most amps include a protection circuit to prevent a DC offset from getting to the speaker. A high-frequency response above 20 kHz is generally not a problem; in fact, a very high response means that the high end of the human hearing range (20 kHz) will be reproduced with less distortion because it is in the amp's linear operating range, not at the extreme high end of the range. However, if the frequency response extends too high, the amp might not be protected from radio-frequency interference (RFI).

A related spec is power bandwidth, which is the range of frequencies the amp can reproduce at full power. If an amp can reproduce frequencies outside the range of human hearing at full power, it should have no trouble with frequencies within that range. As a result, the power bandwidth typically extends beyond the human-hearing range. However, a very broad power bandwidth can reduce the stability and reliability of an amp.

There are two types of distortion common to all power amps, which should be as low as possible. Total harmonic distortion (THD) is the presence of extraneous frequencies that are multiples of the input frequencies. THD is normally expressed as a percentage of the total output. Some manufacturers measure THD at a single frequency, while others measure it across the entire audible range. A THD of 0.1% or less is adequate, and values less than 0.01% are excellent.

Intermodulation (IM) distortion consists of the sum and difference frequencies of the two input signals to a stereo amp, and it is also expressed as a percentage of the total output. IM distortion is generally considered to be more objectionable than THD because its frequency components are not multiples of the input frequencies. The standard means of measuring IM distortion was developed by the Society of Motion Picture and Television Engineers (SMPTE), so this spec is often indicated as IM (SMPTE). IM values tend to be lower than THD values; anything below 0.1% is fine.

As discussed in Chapter 4, signal-to-noise ratio (S/N) is the difference in decibels between the nominal signal level and the noise floor of the equipment. In power amps, S/N is the ratio of the maximum output power to the residual noise level (typically measured with the inputs shorted out, which produces slightly better results). In addition, S/N is sometimes measured across the full audio bandwidth and sometimes measured with A weighting (see Chapter 4), which takes into account the ear's increased sensitivity to mid-range frequencies. In general, a S/N over 100 dB (20 Hz to 20 kHz) is fine for a quiet room.

Slew rate is an amp's ability to reproduce a quickly changing voltage in the input signal. (The rate at which the voltage changes in a signal is called the rise time.) Slew rate is measured in volts/microsecond; i.e., if the input signal jumps instantaneously from zero to maximum, how quickly does the output rise? The higher the slew rate, the "faster" the amp, which translates into broader power bandwidth and better reproduction of high frequencies and fast transients as well as any waveform with a fast rise time. Values above 10 or 20 volts/microsecond are generally fine, but if the slew rate is too high, it could indicate a susceptibility to high-frequency or RF instability.

Damping factor is the ratio of the load (speaker) impedance to the amp's output impedance. As mentioned in Chapter 3, the input impedance of an analog audio connection should be at least ten times the output impedance. In the case of a power amp, the input impedance of a speaker should be at least 200 times the output impedance of the amp. If the speaker has an input impedance of 8 Ω, the output impedance of the amp should be no more than 0.04 Ω. The higher this ratio (i.e., the lower the output impedance), the better the amp can overcome the inertia of the speaker's moving voice coil and control its motion, resulting in less speaker distortion. Values of 200 and above are fine.

However, the amp's damping factor might be relatively insignificant compared to the overall system damping, which is determined largely by the impedance of the speaker wire (from the amp to the speaker and within the speaker itself), passive crossovers (especially lowpass filters that include inductors with yards of wire in series with the speaker), and connectors (¼-inch connectors are notoriously poor in this regard). As a result, the overall system damping factor might be 30 or 40, even when using amps with damping factors in the thousands.

To improve this situation, use large-gauge speaker wire (at least 12 to 14 gauge) that is as short as possible, and employ low-impedance connectors, such binding posts or Neutrik Speakons. In addition, active crossovers increase the system damping quite a bit; in this case, it's a good idea to use biamping or triamping to power each speaker driver independently (discussed later in this chapter). This is the single best way to improve the bass performance of the system. Finally, use 8 Ω speakers; reducing the speaker impedance by 50% cuts the system damping factor in half.

As mentioned earlier, many power amps include protection against thermal overload, DC offset, and clipping. In addition, some amps offer protection against loud transients when you turn the amp on or off, input overload, AC short circuits, RFI, and subsonic and ultrasonic frequencies that waste amplifier power.

Although specs are important indicators of a power amp's performance, they don't tell the whole story. In fact, some amps have relatively poor specs but sound fabulous, while other amps have spectacular specs and sound lousy. Ultimately, you must let your ears be the final judge when selecting a power amp.

MONITORS

Ironically, the devices at the extreme ends of the signal chain—microphones and speakers—utilize the same technology. Both are examples of transducers, which convert one type of signal into another. Of course, microphones convert acoustic sound waves into electrical signals, and speakers convert electrical signals into acoustic sound waves.

In most studio monitor speakers, this conversion process is essentially identical to the technology in moving-coil dynamic microphones, but in reverse. An audio signal passes through a coil of wire, called the voice coil, which is suspended in a permanent magnetic field. As the current fluctuates in the wire, it generates an oscillating magnetic field that alternately pushes and pulls against the permanent magnet, which causes the voice coil to vibrate.

The voice coil is attached to a diaphragm, which vibrates with the coil (see Fig. 16-4). As the diaphragm vibrates, it jostles nearby air molecules, creating acoustic sound waves that eventually reach our ears. The combination of voice coil, magnet, and diaphragm is called a driver.

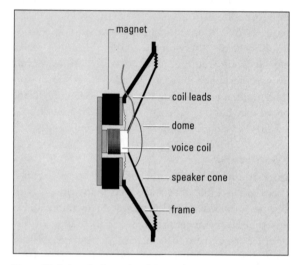

Figure 16-4. A typical speaker driver includes a voice coil, permanent magnet, and diaphragm, which can be a cone or dome.

There are four basic applications for speakers: home entertainment, car stereos, sound reinforcement, and studio reference; speakers used in the studio are called monitors. Studio monitors can be divided into two types: main and near-field or compact. If you've ever been in a commercial recording studio, you've probably seen a pair of gigantic speakers mounted in the wall of the control room; these are the main monitors. In addition, you might have noticed one or more pairs of smaller speakers sitting on or near the mixer console; these are near-field reference monitors. Most home and small project studios don't have room for large main monitors, so engineers in these facilities rely exclusively on compact reference monitors to hear the results of their work.

Purpose
Commercial studios started using small reference monitors to check the mix as it would sound on a car stereo or boom box. The first commonly used compact reference monitor was a small cube speaker

from Auratone. As car and portable sound systems got better, engineers needed better near-field reference monitors, so many recording engineers adopted the Yamaha NS-10M, a bookshelf speaker originally intended for home use. This speaker soon became the *de facto* standard for compact reference monitors and is now found in a large number of commercial studios. Of course, there are many other popular options for small reference monitors.

By commonly accepted definition, near-field reference monitors are placed close to the engineer's ears, typically at a distance of about one meter. In this position, most of the sound you hear comes directly from the speaker itself, rather than reflections from the walls, ceiling, and other objects in the room. This minimizes the effect of the room on what you hear.

However, the monitor must be far enough away that the sounds from the individual drivers "fuse" into an apparent point source. If you are too close to the monitor, you can distinguish the sound from each driver separately. (This is usually not a problem in coaxial designs; more on this shortly.)

Many home-studio owners mistakenly think they can use home-stereo speakers as studio monitors, but these two types of speakers are designed with different goals in mind. Home speakers are intended to make recordings sound as good as possible, masking any problems that might appear. Many home speakers emphasize the high and low frequencies with the familiar "smile" EQ curve (see Chapter 19). This might sound good, but it isn't accurate. Using home speakers as studio monitors also tends to cause ear fatigue, because the midrange is often de-emphasized, which causes you to strain to hear it. Finally, home speakers are designed to be used in the far field, where most of the sound you hear is reflected.

On the other hand, near-field reference monitors should reveal any flaws in the recording so you can fix them before your music is released. They must be as accurate as possible, adding nothing to the sound that isn't in the original signal.

Drivers

Compact reference monitors consist of one or more drivers mounted in a box, or enclosure (more in a moment). The two main types of drivers used in these monitors are cones and domes. Cone diaphragms are used in drivers called woofers to reproduce the lower frequencies. Midrange drivers use smaller cones to reproduce the middle of the sonic spectrum. Cones are often made from a material such as treated paper, polypropylene, or Kevlar.

Cones are impractical for high-frequency drivers, called tweeters, because the voice coil is too small to handle a reasonable power level from the

amplifier. As a result, most tweeters use a small dome as the diaphragm, which allows the voice coil to be much larger. Domes also exhibit a wide dispersion pattern and fast transient response. Most domes are made from metal, such as titanium or aluminum, although some people think metal domes sound harsh. For this reason, Alesis uses stiffened-silk dome tweeters in the Monitor One and Monitor Two.

Most near-field reference monitors include two drivers: a woofer and a tweeter. This is called a 2-way design. A few models, such as the Alesis Monitor Two, are 3-way designs with three drivers: woofer, midrange, and tweeter. Some monitors include multiple drivers for one or more of the frequency ranges, but they are still called 2-way or 3-way designs. In any case, the drivers must be placed as close together as possible so that the sound from each one fuses into a coherent point source at the proper distance from the speaker.

Monitors with separate drivers are said to use a discrete design. Typically, the drivers are mounted next to each other on the front face of the enclosure. This works well as long as you remain in the sweet spot, where the sound from the drivers becomes coherent. This location depends on the dispersion pattern and might not be directly in front of the monitor (which is called on axis). But if you move away from the sweet spot, particularly along the imaginary line that connects the centers of the drivers, the sound can change dramatically.

Some companies, most notably Tannoy and UREI, employ a coaxial design in some of their monitors. In this approach, the tweeter is mounted at the apex of the woofer (see Fig. 16-5). This is more expensive than discrete designs, but it is naturally coherent, making an excellent point source from just about any distance. In addition, there are fewer anomalies as you move away from the sweet spot.

Figure 16-5. The Tannoy System 800 uses a coaxial design, which Tannoy calls Dual Concentric, and a front port.

Enclosure

Compact reference monitors should be as small as practical for the driver complement. This lets you take them from one studio to another, providing a reliable, familiar sound no matter where you work. However, small enclosures do not support low frequencies well. The lowest practical frequency in most small monitors is typically around 60 Hz. In addition, the edges and corners of the enclosure are usually rounded to improve the high-frequency response and dispersion of sound.

Most near-field reference monitors include one or two extra holes in the enclosure; this is called a vented or ported design (see Fig. 16-5). In this design (which is sometimes called bass reflex), the port "tunes" the enclosure to resonate at a frequency below the woofer's natural rolloff. As the frequency drops below this rolloff, the woofer generates less acoustic energy. However, the enclosure starts to resonate at these frequencies, which acts like an equalization boost. This amplifies the woofer's signal and extends the low-frequency response of the monitor well below a similarly sized but completely sealed enclosure. (Sealed enclosures are sometimes referred to as infinite baffle or acoustic suspension designs.)

Some designers place the port in the front face of the enclosure, while others locate the port in the rear face. Rear-ported designs can cause problems if mounted too close to a wall, which tends to emphasize low frequencies in any monitor, especially rear-ported models. On the other hand, rear ports allow smaller front faces. Also, the front face can become weakened if it has too many holes, increasing the possibility of unwanted mechanical vibrations. Some ported monitors come with a port plug, which reduces the low-frequency response and might be useful if you mount the monitor near a wall or corner.

It is well known that the sound waves from the drivers are slightly delayed with respect to the electrical input signal (we're talking microseconds) and that the sound from the woofer is delayed more than the sound from the tweeter. One major factor in this discrepancy is the distance from your ear to the voice coils of the woofer and tweeter, where the sound actually originates. A tweeter voice coil is less than an inch from the dome, while a woofer voice coil is several inches from the edge of the cone. If the woofer and tweeter are mounted in the same flat face of an enclosure, the tweeter's voice coil is closer to your ear than the woofer's voice coil. This causes the high frequencies to arrive slightly ahead of the low frequencies, which can diminish detail and blur the overall sound.

Another important factor in the delay discrepancy is the crossover, an electronic circuit that splits the incoming signal into separate frequency bands and directs each band to the appropriate driver (discussed shortly). Crossovers tend to delay the low frequencies more than the highs, which compounds the problem.

There are two ways to correct this situation. Some designers physically recess the tweeter with respect to the woofer so the voice coils are in the same plane (see Fig. 16-6); examples include the JBL 4200 series and several models from KRK. In some coaxial designs, the problem is eliminated by mounting the tweeter at the apex of the woofer cone. Other manufacturers mount the drivers in the same plane and use electronics to correct the time discrepancy by slightly delaying the tweeter with respect to the woofer. Still others use both techniques.

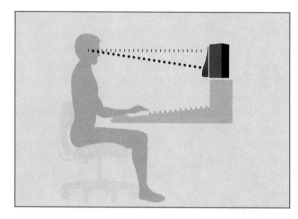

Figure 16-6. The JBL 4200 series of near-field reference monitors recess the tweeter with respect to the woofer so high and low frequencies arrive at your ears simultaneously.

Electronics

As mentioned earlier, the crossover splits the incoming signal into bands, which are then sent to the appropriate driver. Most inexpensive monitors include a passive crossover, which splits the signal from a power amp with a simple lowpass and highpass filter. More sophisticated systems often include an active crossover, which splits a line-level signal before it gets to the power amp. In this case, each driver requires its own amp; this is called biamping in a 2-way monitor or triamping in a 3-way design.

Because active crossovers are normally located before the power amps in the signal chain, most monitors with active crossovers also include internal power amps. These are called powered monitors, and they provide a greater degree of consistency when you take them from one studio to another. In addition, there is no crosstalk between amplifier channels and no risk of overtaxing the amp's power supply, and the internal wiring is much shorter than with an unpowered monitor and external power amplifier. Powered monitors offer the added advantage that the amps and electronics are specifically designed to match the drivers and enclosure.

Other aspects of a monitor's electronics, such as equalization and time correction, can also be passive or active. In fact, there are different degrees of active operation. For example, a monitor might have an active time-correction circuit and a passive crossover. Active systems are more "tweakable" than passive designs, but they add more electronic components to the signal path, which tends to increase noise and distortion.

Speakers are rated as to the amount of power they can handle from the amp. Like power amps, most speakers include a continuous and peak power rating. Make sure your amp and speakers have similar power ratings. You might think it's safer to use an underpowered amp than one that is overpowered. However, underpowered amps are more likely to be driven beyond their rated output, which results in clipping and generates distortion that could damage the drivers. It's much better to use an overpowered amp, as long as you exercise caution. Such an amp can easily supply enough continuous power with minimum distortion, and it has plenty of power in reserve (which is called headroom) for quick transient peaks.

Another important speaker spec is impedance, which is measured in ohms. As discussed in Chapter 3, this is the electrical resistance the speaker presents to the current from the amp. The higher the speaker's impedance, the less current it draws from the amp. As the impedance drops, the amp must work harder to supply the current drawn by the speaker. In addition, the power output of an amp drops when it's connected to high-impedance speakers. For example, a particular power amp might deliver 100W to an 8 Ω speaker or 200W to a 4 Ω speaker.

Many speakers have an impedance of 8 Ω, while others have an impedance of 6 Ω, 4 Ω, or even 2 Ω. Most amplifiers can handle speakers with different impedances, but if the impedance drops too low, the amp could be damaged, so you should make sure that the impedance levels of your amp and speakers match.

Performance

Unlike many home-entertainment speakers, reference monitors must reproduce as many audible frequencies as possible without emphasis or attenuation. The frequency response of a monitor is the range of frequencies it can reproduce at a given amplitude, usually within ±3 dB of a nominal level. The frequency response should be as flat as possible, and it should fall off evenly as you move away and/or off axis from the monitor. Among other things, frequency response can be greatly affected by the room in which the monitor is used.

The efficiency with which a monitor converts an audio signal into an acoustic sound wave is called its sensitivity or efficiency. This specification relates the output sound pressure level (in dB SPL) with an input signal of one watt measured at a distance of one meter. Most near-field reference monitors are rated at 88 to 93 dB SPL (1W/1m).

You often hear the words soundstage and imaging applied to speakers of all types. Soundstage refers to the imaginary stage between the two speakers (which includes width and depth), and imaging refers to how well the speakers can localize individual instruments in the soundstage. (Note that some people use soundstage to mean the front-to-back placement of instruments and imaging to mean the left-to-right placement, while others use either term synonymously to mean left-to-right placement.)

Good imaging depends on coherent sound from the drivers at the proper distance. Uniform dispersion of sound from the monitor is also critical, particularly in the horizontal direction. As you work at the mixer, you tend to move horizontally to reach controls, but you rarely move vertically. As you move between the monitors, the tonal balance should remain consistent.

Evaluation

If you're in the market for a pair of near-field reference monitors, here are a few tips to help you shop. Bring along a couple of familiar CDs with wide dynamic range and well-recorded vocals and/or instrumental passages; solo piano tracks are also useful. Listen to the monitors in the near field (about one meter), not from across the room. Move around the monitor to see how it performs off-axis.

Try to find a monitor that accurately reproduces what's on the CD, not one that makes it sound as good as possible. The midrange reproduction might be the most important, because this is the range of the vocals and many solo instruments. The tonal balance should remain consistent at different volume levels, and a sound mixed to the center should be well defined directly in the center of the stereo field.

Placement

Once you have selected your monitors, it's time to place them in your studio. An excellent starting point is to form an equilateral triangle with the two monitors and your head in the normal listening position (see Fig. 16-7). The distance from each monitor to your head should be approximately one meter. You can increase the distance between the monitors, if necessary.

To allow more flexibility, try to mount the monitors on separate stands, not directly on the console or meter bridge of the mixer. Make sure the stands are solid and secure the monitors by using rubber feet or other nonslip measures. Small, lightweight speakers can actually crawl around when reproducing loud, low-frequency material if they are not secured in some way.

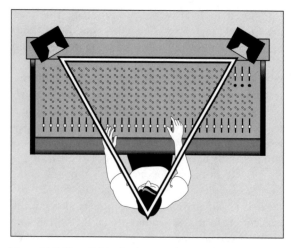

Figure 16-7. Near-field reference monitors are typically placed to form an equilateral triangle with the engineer's head.

Angle the monitors inward toward your head and adjust their height so the tweeters are at the same level as your ears. Adjust the angle of the monitors to maximize the width of the sweet spot at the listening position.

Try to keep the monitors at least two to three feet from any wall or corner, particularly if they are rear-ported. (Alesis designers claim that anything over six inches is okay.) If they are too close, the bass response will be emphasized. You might want to use port plugs to reduce the bass response if you must place the monitors near a wall or corner. Also, place the monitors far from any reflecting surface, which eliminates any external influence on the speaker's frequency response. (This is called placement in the free field.)

Another important technique is minimizing reflections in the room, which can introduce phase and amplitude distortions and confuse the soundstage. The biggest culprits are walls, windows, and mirrors. In addition, parallel surfaces (opposite walls, ceilings, and exposed hardwood floors) can lead to standing waves, which greatly affect the frequency response you hear. If possible, install acoustic treatment to minimize these problems.

Keep the cable runs from the amplifier to the monitors as short as possible to prevent induced noise and signal loss. Use fairly large speaker cable, at least 10 or 12 gauge. If you place a speaker near a video monitor, the image might become distorted due to the strong magnetic field from the speaker. Some speakers are magnetically shielded, which prevents this video distortion. In any case, don't put magnetic storage media, such as floppy disks and recording tape, near a speaker; this can spell disaster.

Finally, try not to mix at extremely high levels. This reduces the amount of time you can spend in front of your monitors, thus reducing your chances of getting an accurate mix; it also can permanently damage your hearing (see Chapter 4). With the proper caution and application, your near-field reference monitors will provide years of useful service, helping you create the best possible sound for your music.

Part

5

Effects

Chapter 17: Basic Effects
Reverb
Delay
Pitch Shifting

Chapter 18: Modulation Effects

Chapter 19: Equalization
Spectral Enhancers

Chapter 20: Dynamics Processors

Chapter 21: Other Effects
Noise Reduction
3-D Processing

Basic Effects

Among the most common effects available to electronic musicians are reverb, delay, and pitch shifting. In addition, the modulation effects of flanging and chorusing are based on delay and pitch shifting, respectively. As a result, this chapter presents the basics of these three fundamental effects and how to use them in the studio.

Although the chapters in this part of the book primarily address outboard, hardware effects processors, I should mention that there is an alternative: software plug-ins. If you work with a computer-based hard-disk recorder, these plug-ins can be added to the primary software to perform a wide variety of effects chores, including reverb, delay, pitch shifting, flanging, chorusing, EQ, spectral enhancement, dynamics processing, noise reduction, 3-D processing, and much more. Nevertheless, the fundamental principles are the same as they are for hardware processors.

Connections and Levels

The basic types of effects processors discussed in this chapter are connected to a mixer in the same ways, which I'll discuss here in general terms. In many cases, the processor is connected to a mixer's aux send and aux return (see Fig. 17-1). However, a processor is sometimes connected in line; the instrument's output (e.g., from a synth or electric guitar) is connected to the processor's input, and the processor's output is connected to one of the mixer's channel inputs or directly to an amplifier input.

An audio cable carries the signal to the input of the effects device, which processes the signal according to its parameter settings. Once the signal leaves the processor's output, it is carried to the aux returns or channel inputs, which have their own level controls. (Less-expensive processors accept a mono signal and produce a simulated stereo signal, which is sent to a pair of aux returns or channel inputs.) The signal from the processor is then mixed with the unaffected signals in the mixer and sent to the final output.

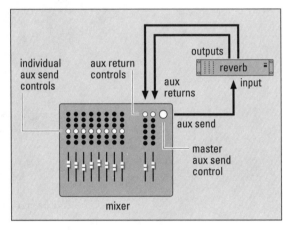

Figure 17-1. A reverb unit is connected to a mixer via the mixer's aux sends and returns.

Once the processor is connected to the mixer, it's time to set some levels. Most processors include an input control, which determines the level of the input signal, and an output control, which determines the level of the output signal.

Virtually all effects processors split the input signal from the mixer's aux send, processing one copy while passing the other copy with no processing. The balance or wet/dry control determines the relative balance between the affected ("wet") and unaffected ("dry") signals. These two signals are then mixed within the unit. The wet/dry control is especially useful when the effects processor is connected in line between an instrument and the mixer or amplifier.

When the effects processor is connected to the mixer's aux send/return loop, it is generally advisable to keep the wet/dry control at 100 percent wet (no dry signal gets through at all) and control the balance between the affected and unaffected signal with the mixer's aux-send and aux-return controls. If you want one of the mixer's inputs to be more heavily processed, turn up its individual aux-send control. If you want all the signals in the mixer to sound more processed, turn up the master aux-send control or master aux-return control.

At one time or another, you've probably walked down a large hallway with a polished marble floor and stone walls. Each step you take is followed by an echo that seems to hang in the air for awhile. The echo is not a clear repeat of each footfall, but a smear of sound that dies away slowly.

That lingering sound is called reverberation, or reverb, and it is a vital part of virtually every sound you hear. Your brain uses it to determine the size, shape, and other characteristics of the space in which the sound was produced. It occurs naturally almost everywhere, and it is artificially simulated in the recording studio. In fact, reverb is probably the most common signal-processing effect of them all.

Acoustic Origins

Almost all enclosed and semi-enclosed spaces exhibit some reverberation. The process starts with a sound wave that emanates in a more or less spherical pattern from a sound source and expands toward any listeners in the room, as well as nearby surfaces: walls, ceilings, windows, furniture, etc. (Speakers don't necessarily radiate sound in a spherical pattern; the radiation pattern depends on the design of the speaker.)

Once the sound wave reaches a surface, it is reflected back into the room (see Fig. 17-2), where it is reflected again and again by various surfaces. These multiple reflections also reach the listener. However, the initial sound waves almost always reach the listener first because the path between the source sound and listener is shorter than the path taken by any of the reflections.

Each reflection is generally lower in amplitude than the preceding one, because the sound wave loses some energy each time it is reflected. Most materials absorb some of the sound wave's energy and reflect the rest. As a result, the reverberation dies away over time.

Normally, you can't hear these reflections individually because they happen in such quick succession. Most rooms are no more than a few dozen feet long in any direction, and sound travels at about 1,130 feet per second in air. Therefore, the sound waves are reflected many times per second in every direction (up/down, right/left, front/back). Our brain tends to smear all these rapid reflections into a continuous sound, which we call reverberation. This sound has a haunting, ringing quality that lingers for some period of time after the original sound stops.

Figure 17-2. Theoretically, sound waves emanate from a performer in a roughly spherical pattern toward the listeners, walls, and ceiling. They generally reach the listeners first, after which they reflect from the walls and ceiling. The reflections reach the listener a few milliseconds after the direct sound.

Several factors contribute to the specific reverberation of a particular space. For example, the larger the space, the longer it takes sound waves to reach the walls and reflect back to your ears. Heavy drapes and thick-pile carpeting absorb much more sound than marble walls and hardwood floors. In addition, people tend to absorb a fair amount of sound energy (unless they're wearing suits of armor), so an empty room has different reverb characteristics than the same space when it's crowded with people.

The phenomenon of reverb can be distilled into several distinct parts. The most obvious component is the time it takes the reverberation to become inaudible. This decay time depends primarily on the reflective properties of the room—as determined by the texture of the walls, ceiling, floor, and furnishings—and the amplitude of the original sound. Also, high frequencies tend to fade away more quickly than low frequencies. In very large spaces, such as enclosed stadiums, there could be a perceptible delay between the original sound and the onset of reverberation.

Reverb Parameters

One problem with acoustic reverberation is that you can't easily control it. The physical size of the space limits what you can do, so studio recordings normally rely on artificial reverb. For maximum flexibility and creativity in signal processing, acoustic musicians are often recorded in a relatively "dead" (that is, nonreverberant) environment, and their signal is passed through a reverb unit that digitally simulates various acoustic environments. Electronic sound sources also benefit from passing through a reverb unit.

Many modern reverb units are actually multi-effects processors that perform reverb, modulation effects, and several other signal processing chores, which I'll discuss later in this part of the book. Many synthesizers also include onboard multi-effects processors that apply reverb in addition to other effects.

To program a reverb unit effectively, you need to know the basic parameters you will encounter. The most fundamental parameter is reverb type. Most units offer several types of reverb, generally based on different acoustic environments. As you might expect, a room reverb simulates a small to medium-sized room, while a hall reverb simulates a large room or auditorium. Some units offer a stadium or cathedral reverb, as well. Select the reverb type that best suits the acoustic space you wish to simulate.

Many reverb units also include several digital simulations of early types of reverb processing. In the early days of recording, engineers sent a recorded signal to a speaker in a small, tile-lined chamber. A microphone placed in the chamber picked up the sound from the speaker along with the subsequent reflections inside the chamber. Reverb chambers are prized for their lush, blossoming quality and were a major component of the classic Phil Spector sound in the early 1960s.

Spring reverbs employ a physical spring with a microphone transducer attached to one end and a speaker transducer attached to the other end. The signal passes through the spring to create a reverb effect. Spring reverbs tend to produce a boingy, chattery timbre with accentuated high end. Plate reverbs use a metal plate instead of a spring, with pickups placed at various locations on the plate. Plate reverbs typically produce a sharp timbre that greatly enhances the punch of drum and percussion tracks.

Many units also offer several reverb types that have little to do with acoustic reverb. These types are generally known as nonlinear reverb. For example, a reverse reverb starts from silence and grows to maximum level, after which it cuts off abruptly, which is opposite from the way natural reverb works. A gated reverb starts normally but suddenly is cut off after a user-definable gate time. Gated reverb is often applied to the snare drum in pop and rock music.

Once you have selected the basic reverb type, there are several parameters you can play with. The first and most obvious parameter is reverb or decay time. This parameter determines how long the reverb effect remains audible, and it lets you control the apparent size and reflectivity of the simulated acoustical space. For example, a room reverb might have a decay time of one or two seconds, whereas a hall reverb might last three to five seconds. A cathedral reverb might last as long as eight to ten seconds.

If the environment is highly reflective, the reverb time is longer.

Sometimes, you can actually discern the first few reflections separately before the reverberation starts to smear together, particularly in large acoustical spaces (see Fig. 17-3). These early reflections have a strong influence on how you perceive reverb in a large space. In a digital reverb unit, the time between the original sound and the very first reflection is controlled by the predelay parameter. As the predelay time gets longer, the apparent size of the space increases and your apparent location within the space gets closer to the "center" of the room. Predelay is generally no more than 500 milliseconds and typically in the 10 to 50 ms range.

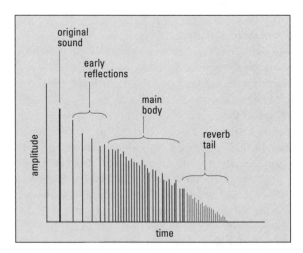

Figure 17-3. The original sound is immediately followed by a few early reflections, after which the main body of reverb decays to silence.

Another parameter that relates to early reflections is called—reasonably enough—early reflections (in some units, it's called density). This parameter controls the time between the first few reflections, which is generally just a few milliseconds. This might seem insignificant, but it determines the "opacity," or density, of the reverb sound during the first few moments. Like reverb time, density helps simulate different room sizes; higher density values simulate larger spaces, because it takes longer for the early reflections to reach your ears in a large space.

The diffusion parameter controls the separation of the reflections within the main body of the reverb sound, which determines its "thickness." Reducing the diffusion value produces a thinner sound because the reflections are more widely spaced in time. This parameter lets you determine the complexity of the simulated acoustical space. Keep in mind that many reflective surfaces in a room result in a thicker, denser reverb.

One of the characteristics of acoustic reverberation is that high frequencies typically die away faster than low frequencies. As a result, many reverb units include a high-frequency damping parameter, which lets you control the decay rate of high frequencies separately from the main reverb decay. Some reverb units even include a low-frequency damping parameter. Both of these parameters provide additional control over the apparent size and reflective characteristics of the simulated acoustical space. For example, softer surfaces cause high frequencies to decay more rapidly, while smaller rooms cause low frequencies to decay more rapidly.

Applications

As mentioned earlier, one of the primary applications of artificial reverb is to simulate an acoustical space within which your recorded ensemble "performs." To accomplish this, send the entire mix through the same reverb unit programmed to re-create the type of space you wish to simulate.

You can also apply different reverbs to individual instruments for special effects. In many pop drum mixes, for example, the snare is heavily processed (often with a gated and/or reverse reverb), while the kick drum is relatively dry. This approach lends an air of drama to the snare backbeat without washing the kick drum in confusing reflections that would diminish its cohesiveness with the bass. Many guitar players like to apply liberal amounts of reverb to enhance their solo sounds.

Another interesting application is playing in a highly reverberant environment à la Paul Horn's *Inside the Taj Mahal*. Use a hall or cathedral reverb type with a long decay time and high aux-send and aux-return levels.

In many synthesizers with onboard multi-effects units, the effects are an integral part of each patch. Unfortunately, most of these kinds of synths can produce only one combination of effects at a time. If the synthesizer is multitimbral, all parts are passed through the same effects. If you're not careful, this overall effect will be the one assigned to the last patch you called up, which might or might not serve the other parts well. Instead, you should set the synth's effect mode to "master," which lets you select the effects you want for all the parts from that synth. (Fortunately, some synths now include several separate effects processors; some effects are global and others are applied as "insert" effects to individual patches.)

Reverb is inescapable. You hear it everywhere, and rightly so. Almost all music sounds better with reverb, which is why church choirs generally sound better than one would expect from the singing skills of their members. Your music will sound better with

reverb, too. All you need to do is experiment a bit with a digital reverb unit to discover just how much better.

DELAY

DELAY

If you ever travel through the Swiss Alps, you might hear the haunting call of an alphorn. You might also hear an echo that exactly duplicates the initial phrase a few seconds later. This echo occurs because the sound from the 12-foot-long, bugle-like instrument is reflected from nearby mountains. Of course, the nearest mountain is typically thousands of feet away, so it takes several seconds for the sound to get from the alphorn to the mountain and back to the alphorn player.

This classic "Alps echo" is probably the best acoustical example of delay. Like reverb, delay is produced by reflected sound waves. Unlike reverb, however, these reflections are separate and distinct.

In both cases, it's nearly impossible to control the acoustical phenomenon with any precision, so the effect is simulated digitally to process recordings and live performances. As we'll see, digital delay has many interesting applications.

Single Delay

The simplest type of delay is called a single delay (see Fig. 17-4). As in a digital reverb unit, an audio signal is sent into a digital delay unit, which splits the signal into two copies. One copy is sent directly to the output with no modification; this is the dry signal. The other copy, the wet signal, is digitized in much the same way as a sampler captures audio data.

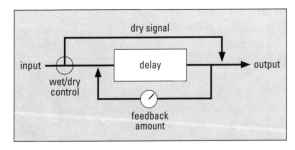

Figure 17-4. In a simple, single delay, the input signal is split into two copies; one proceeds directly to the output, and the other is delayed by a certain amount of time before it is mixed with the original signal. The delayed signal can also be split into two copies, one of which is fed back into the delay's input to be delayed again.

The delay unit then stores the sample in RAM for a user-specified period of time (called delay time, explained shortly), after which the signal is converted back into analog, mixed with the undelayed dry signal, and sent to the unit's output. (Early delay units used analog circuitry to delay the signal, which is still used in some current models.) In more expensive units, the dry signal is also digitized and mixed with the wet signal in the digital domain before being converted back into analog. The user can set the percentage of the wet/dry mix to produce effects that are subtle (the delayed signal is barely audible behind the original dry signal) or aggressive (the delayed signal appears at the same or greater volume than the dry signal), and everything in between.

The fundamental parameter in any delay is the delay time, which determines how long the delayed signal is held in memory before it is sent to the output. Depending on how much memory a unit has, the delay time can range from one millisecond to several seconds. The amount of available memory determines the maximum delay time, but most delay units can delay up to at least one second.

Another primary characteristic of most delays is called regeneration or feedback. In this process, the wet signal is split into two copies: one copy is sent to the output, and the other copy is sent back to the delay's input, where it is delayed again (along with any new signal that enters the delay). This causes the signal to repeat over and over at intervals determined by the delay-time settings.

The amount of feedback—how many times the original signal repeats before fading away—is controlled by a feedback parameter. Inexpensive delay units, such as guitar-oriented stomp boxes, usually have a solitary feedback knob. The more you turn the knob, the more repeats you get. (If you leave the knob in the "off" position, you only get one repeat.)

Multitap Delay

Most modern delay units offer the ability to apply several different delays to the input signal. In early analog units, the delayed signal was accessed, or tapped, producing multiple echoes. Digital delays work in much the same way. For example, if the delay time is one second and you tap the signal at the midpoint and at the end, you hear the signal delayed by a half-second and by one second.

Such a device is called a multitap delay (see Fig. 17-5), and you can specify where to place the taps with respect to the overall delay time. For example, let's say that in a 4-tap delay, you specify delay times of 250 ms, 500 ms, 750 ms, and 1 second. This would send the signal out four times after the original, once every quarter-second.

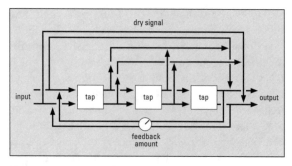

Figure 17-5. In a multitap delay, the delayed signal is accessed, or tapped, two or more times. In this example, the signal has been tapped in three places, so you hear at least three distinct echoes. This delay also has a regeneration feature, which causes the signal to repeat over and over at intervals determined by the delay-time settings.

Most multitap delays include a stereo output. In addition to individual delay-time and output-level controls, each tap has a pan control that determines where the delayed signal is placed in the stereo field. This stereo facility lets you produce effects such as ping-pong delay, in which the repeating signal bounces back and forth between the right and left channels. A simple ping-pong delay requires two taps. A more complex ping-pong delay bounces between right, left, and center; this type requires at least three taps.

Some delay units have a stereo input as well as a stereo output. In many cases, each input can be delayed independently with its own multitap delay, which lets you produce some extremely complex effects.

Most studio-oriented, multi-effects processors, such as DigiTech's TSR-24, include powerful delay algorithms that can be "chained" to reverbs and other effects.

Applications

There are many potential applications of delay. For example, you can "fake" a stereo signal by sending a mono signal through a single delay set between 30 and 50 ms with no feedback. This setting effectively clones the original signal. Pan the dry signal hard left and the delayed signal hard right, and *voilá:* faux stereo! If you don't hard-pan the signals, the stereo image collapses, and the original signal sounds as if it was doubled.

Many vocalists enjoy using a slapback delay of 75 ms or so, with no feedback. Slapback delay, or echo, was characteristic of the vocal sounds of early Jerry Lee Lewis and Elvis Presley recordings. Some contemporary artists, such as Bono of U2, use a more distinct echo of anywhere between 150 to 500 ms to produce an ethereal, lingering effect. The feedback control is set to repeat the signal a few times before fading away, and the delay time is often synchronized to the tempo of the song.

To sync delay time to a song tempo, simply divide the tempo in beats per minute (bpm) by 60 to get the number of beats per second. For example, 120 bpm = 2 bps. Then, divide 1,000 by the number of beats per second to calculate the number of milliseconds per beat. In this example, each beat takes up 500 ms, or half a second. If the beats are quarter notes, then eighth notes occupy 250 ms, eighth-note triplets occupy 166.67 ms, and sixteenth notes take 125 ms.

These calculations might seem a bit daunting to mathophobes. Fortunately, there are a several ways to avoid the horrors of relearning simple division. For one thing, you can probably find a small computer program that performs delay-time calculations, such as *Studio-Pal* for the Macintosh. If you own a delay unit with MIDI sync, it's even easier. These devices can synchronize their delay time to incoming MIDI Clock messages, which keeps the delay synchronized even if the tempo changes. Some delay processors, such as the Lexicon JamMan, offer a Tap Tempo feature; you tap the tempo on a front-panel button or footswitch, and the unit automatically calculates the delay time.

With a multitap delay synchronized to the tempo of your song, you can create some wild rhythmic effects by playing nothing more complicated than whole notes, half notes, or quarter notes. Suppose you have a 3-tap delay, and the song tempo is 120 bpm. Set the first tap to 125 ms, the second to 250 ms, and the third to 375 ms. As you play quarter notes, you'll hear sixteenth notes coming from the delay.

You can also set different delay times for each tap. If you want a dotted eighth-sixteenth pattern after each quarter note, set the first tap to 375 ms, the second tap to 500 ms, and the third to 875 ms. You can also set different output levels for each tap, which lets you establish an accent pattern.

I once saw a percussionist use delay to "overdub" sounds in concert. He performed an extended solo with a wide variety of percussion instruments routed through a delay set to about ten seconds with a medium feedback level. When he played a series of short sounds on different instruments, the delay repeated the sounds over the next ten seconds as he added new sounds. The delay processor turned the solitary performer into a virtual percussion orchestra. It was a remarkable, wonderful effect.

Delay is one of the most diverse and flexible effects in a musician's rack. You hear it applied to vocals and electric guitar solos in just about every pop song on the radio. So give it a try on your next recording project; you'll be glad you did glad you did glad you did glad you did....

PITCH SHIFTING

Pitch shifters are among the most useful and least understood signal processors in the electronic musician's arsenal. These devices take an input signal and shift its pitch up or down, in real time, by a user-specified amount. Accomplishing this with any degree of success requires some heavy-duty digital signal processing.

Basically, there is only one parameter to master: the amount by which the pitch is shifted. This is usually specified in terms of a musical interval, such as a major third, perfect fifth, octave, etc. You can also shift the pitch of the input signal by very small amounts, which are specified in cents. (One hundred cents equal a semitone or half-step.)

These days, most pitch shifters are found within multi-effects units. In the recording studio, they are connected to the mixer's aux send and return loop in the same manner as other effects, such as reverb and delay. In this case, you would typically set the wet/dry mix to 100% wet and control the balance between the original and pitch-shifted signals with the aux send and return level controls on the mixer. Alternatively, you can dedicate the pitch shifter to one instrument by patching it into one of the mixer's channel insert points and controlling the wet/dry mix from the processor.

You can also connect the output of a guitar or synth directly to the input of a pitch shifter and connect its output to the input of another effects device, a P.A. mixer, or an amplifier. In this application, you control the wet/dry mix from the effects processor.

Detuning

Very small pitch shifts are collectively known as detuning. If you mix a piano sound at its normal pitch with the same sound detuned a few cents up or down, it resembles a honky-tonk piano. (The original honky-tonk pianos sounded that way because they weren't tuned very often; honky-tonk establishments had other priorities.) This technique is often used to "thicken" individual drum sounds, as well.

As I mentioned in the section on delay, you can thicken an individual track by delaying it 30 to 50 ms and mixing it with the unprocessed signal for a doubled effect. If you add a bit of detuning to the equation, the effect is even more pronounced. You can also simulate a stereo image by panning the unprocessed signal to one side of the stereo sound field and panning a slightly delayed signal to the other side. If you include a little pitch shifting, the results can be quite satisfying. Try one of these techniques on a bass part to fatten it up.

Bruce Springsteen, among others, often uses a modified version of this technique on his lead vocals. The vocal track is split; one signal remains unprocessed and is panned to the center, and the other signal is sent through two pitch shifters. One is set to shift upward by a few cents, the other shifts down by the same amount. The output from one shifter is panned hard right, and the other is panned hard left. (There are a number of devices that incorporate several pitch shifters and stereo audio outputs in one unit. In this case, the output of each shifter is panned hard right or left within the unit.)

You might think that the same effect can be achieved by making copies of samples and delaying and detuning them. This is indeed a similar process, but the final result is noticeably different. All pitch shifters have an inherent, inconsistent processing delay because of the time it takes to identify the pitch of the input signal and shift it up or down. In general, low frequencies take longer to identify because they take longer to complete a full waveform cycle, resulting in a longer processing delay. This delay makes a qualitative difference in the final sound, which some people describe as "spread out."

Some engineers perform a neat trick with detuning and reverb. They send the 100 percent wet sound from a reverb unit into a pitch shifter set to detune a few cents flat. The output of the shifter is then sent to the aux return on the mixer. This is said to give the sound a more "poignant" quality. You can also detune upward for a more "excited" quality.

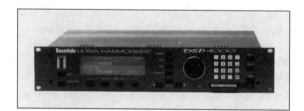

The Eventide DSP4000 is the latest incarnation of their powerful multi-effects processor, which includes some of the most sophisticated pitch shifting available.

Pitch Correction

Another important application of detuning is pitch correction. If a singer or instrumentalist is consistently sharp or flat, it's relatively easy to run the signal through a pitch shifter to correct the problem. But what if only a few notes are out of tune? This is particularly irksome if the performance is otherwise great.

The traditional, and somewhat painful approach is to first bounce the offending track to an empty track, then send the original track through a pitch shifter set to correct the pitch of one bum note, and punch that one note into the bounced track. Repeat the process for each bad note, setting the pitch shifter accordingly each time. This is tricky and tedious, but it gets the job done. It helps a great deal if you can automate the punch in and punch out using MIDI messages from a sequencer (see Chapter 7), which depends on the tape deck and sequencer you use.

If the pitch shifter responds to MIDI, it might be possible to correct the pitch of a performance by manipulating the pitch wheel on a synth or master keyboard. Make sure that MIDI Pitch Bend messages are assigned to control the amount of pitch shift. As you listen to the track, simply ride the wheel up or down to correct any notes that are out of tune. You can also automate this process by recording these movements into a sequencer that's synchronized to the audio recorder. Once the Pitch Bend data is recorded in the sequencer, you can tweak it to achieve a perfect take.

If you have enough dough, you can buy an intelligent pitch shifter, which includes the Eventide Harmonizer brand of effects processors (such as the H3000, H3500, and H4000), DigiTech's Vocalist line, and Lexicon's PCM 80 with pitch-shifting card. These devices can actually "quantize" the pitch of all incoming notes to the nearest pitches within a specified scale. This automatically corrects the pitch of all notes in a performance, which is a lot easier than the note-by-note process described previously.

Intelligent pitch-correction works well if there are only a few bad notes; set the shifter to correct only those notes, leaving other notes untouched. However, if most of the notes need correction, the end result can sound pretty artificial. This is more problematic for lead tracks than background parts.

The BOSS PS-3 Digital Pitch Shifter/Delay stomp box produces some wild effects for guitarists and keyboardists.

The latest and greatest approach to pitch correction is to use software plug-ins with a DAW (see Chapter 10). For example, several pitch-shifter plug-ins are available for such digital audio editing programs as Sonic Foundry's *Sound Forge* for Windows (which supports the Microsoft DirectX plug-in format) and Digidesign's *Pro Tools* for Macintosh (which supports the company's TDM and AudioSuite formats). These plug-ins generally let you correct pitch problems precisely, and in many cases you can automate the process.

Transposition

Pitch shifting by intervals larger than a semitone is called transposition. Octave doubling is one of the most common forms of parallel transposition. Most people double a part an octave below the original pitch, which sounds less artificial than shifting an octave higher. In fact, the ear is much more sensitive to artifacts in signals that are up-shifted, so it's a good idea to keep large upward shifts to a minimum (unless you like a helium-inspired chipmunk effect). This is another situation in which pitch-shifting software offers an advantage. Many pitch-shifting programs can preserve the formants of the original signal during transposition, thus avoiding the chipmunk effect.

Most pitch shifters can also produce parallel lines at intervals other than the octave. For example, trumpeter Jon Hassell often uses a pitch shifter to double his melodies a perfect fourth below the original pitch. He also uses a unit with several shifters to produce parallel chords, which is a wonderful effect. Some multishifters also let you specify a different set of transpositions for all twelve chromatic notes.

At the next level of sophistication, intelligent pitch shifters can do much more than automatically correct out-of-tune performances. In most cases, they can also transpose intelligently. To use such a device, you specify a key and the type of intervals you want, and the shifter transposes each input note appropriately for that key.

For example, suppose you specify the key of C major and the intervals of a third up and a fourth down. If you play a C, the shifter produces an E (a major third above) and a G (a perfect fourth below); if you play a B, the shifter produces a D (a minor third above) and an F (an augmented fourth below). Both chords are diatonic to the key of C major.

Intelligent pitch shifters let you do some remarkable things. For example, you can create an entire vocal harmony part in real time with a single singer. A horn player can become a horn section with appropriate chord voicings on each note. (No horn section has absolutely perfect timing, however. If your pitch shifter has multiple outputs or internal delay lines, you can make the horn-section effect more realistic by adding slightly different, very short delays to each note.) Even if the musician hits a note slightly sharp of flat, the harmonies remain in tune, thanks to pitch quantization.

DigiTech's The Vocalist is an intelligent pitch shifter designed specifically for vocals.

Some intelligent shifters also let you specify the intervals on the fly from a MIDI keyboard. As each note in the audio track enters the shifter, you can play a chord on the keyboard, which tells the shifter what intervals to produce. The actual notes you play on the keyboard are not used; only the intervals between them. This lets you create any chords you want in real time, even different chords for the same input note at different times.

Combining transposing pitch shifters and delays can be lots of fun. Most multi-effects processors include both types of signal processing, as do some stomp boxes, such as the BOSS PS-3. Sending a delayed signal into a pitch shifter can create some great arpeggiation or "stairstep" effects if there is a feedback path from the output of the pitch shifter to the input of the delay.

For example, if you specify a delay time of a few hundred milliseconds and a shift interval of a minor third upward with some feedback, you get an upwardly arpeggiating diminished chord that fades out over time. You could also try this with a shift interval of a perfect fourth or fifth upward for soothing quartal or quintal arpeggios. In multi-shifter units, you can specify simultaneous upward and downward shifts for an even wilder effect.

Clearly, pitch shifters are powerful creative tools for studio recording or live performance. However, they require some experimentation to get the most out of them. So find the pitch shifter in your multi-effects box and get to know its capabilities. A wonderful world of sonic manipulation awaits.

CHAPTER 18

Modulation Effects

Basic effects such as reverb, delay, and pitch shifting are essential tools for most recording and performing musicians. These basic effects can be enhanced to produce new modulation effects that change over time according to your specifications.

This change occurs when the effects processor's parameters are automatically or manually varied, or modulated. For automatic modulation, you typically use a low-frequency oscillator (LFO) or envelope generator (EG) to control the value of the selected parameter over time. In addition, you can manually modulate an effects parameter with a MIDI controller or footpedal.

Standard Bearers

One of the most common modulation effects is flanging, in which the input signal is split into two copies. One copy is delayed by continually varying amounts of time, then mixed with the other, unprocessed copy.

The name "flanging" comes from the early days of recording, when effects were primitive and engineers had to be very resourceful. Copies of the same program material were played on two tape decks simultaneously. The engineer applied varying pressure with a finger on the outer edge, or flange, of one of the tape reels. This delayed the signal with respect to the other machine by different amounts, depending on the finger pressure on the flange. The end result was a cool "swooshing" effect as the two signals were mixed together.

These days, the same thing is accomplished by modulating the delay time with an LFO (see Fig. 18-1). The delay times are very short—typically from 1 to 15 ms—so you don't hear individual delays. Instead, you hear the changing phase relationship between the delayed and dry signals when they are mixed together. In some flangers, you can also manually control the delay time with a mod wheel or other MIDI continuous controller. Flanging is great for swirly background pads; a low LFO rate and depth produces a subtle movement, while a faster rate and/or greater depth is more obvious.

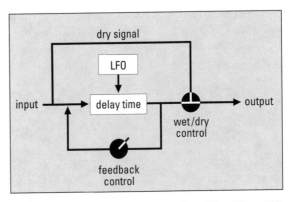

Figure 18-1. In a flanger, the delay time is modulated by an LFO, and the result is mixed with the dry signal.

Another common modulation effect is chorusing, which is a form of modulated pitch shifting (see Fig. 18-2). Once again, the amount of pitch shift is very small—only a few cents—and the detuned signal is mixed with the dry signal. As the amount of pitch shift changes, the two signals go in and out of tune with each other, which produces a different kind of swooshing effect than flanging.

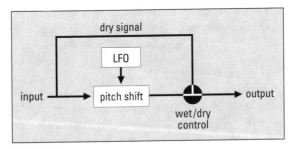

Figure 18-2. In a chorus, the amount of pitch shift is modulated with an LFO, and the result is mixed with the dry signal.

The term "chorusing" comes from the fact that each unison voice in a choir or chorus varies slightly in pitch with respect to the other voices singing the same part. Used judiciously, this effect can make a solo instrument sound like a group. Guitarists also like to use more pronounced chorusing with a very slow LFO for a thick, dense sound.

One of my favorite modulation effects is phase

shifting. The relative phase of a waveform describes how its cycle relates to another waveform or an arbitrary starting point. For example, imagine a sine wave that begins at a level of zero and rises before reaching its peak (see Fig. 18-3 [a]). Now imagine a second sine wave of the same frequency and amplitude that starts at the same time but begins at its peak level and heads downward (see Fig. 18-3 [b]). These two sine waves are said to be 90° out of phase. If a third waveform starts at a level of zero and heads downward (see Fig. 18-3 [c]), it is said to be 180° out of phase with the original waveform. A fourth waveform that starts at the bottom of its cycle and heads upward (see Fig. 18-3 [d]) is said to be 270° out of phase with respect to the original waveform.

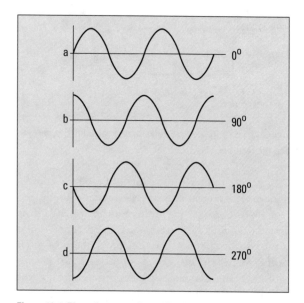

Figure 18-3. These four waveforms illustrate different phase relationships. If waveform a is arbitrarily defined as 0°, then b is 90° out of phase with respect to a. Following the same logic, c is 180° out of phase with respect to a, and d is 270° out of phase.

As in flangers and choruses, a phase shifter splits the input signal into two copies. The dry copy proceeds directly to the output and is mixed with the processed signal, which goes through a series of allpass filters. This seems like an oxymoron: these filters let all frequencies through without any attenuation. However, like most filters, they shift the phase of each harmonic component of the signal by different amounts, depending on the frequency of each component. These filters are then modulated with an LFO or other modulation source to change their frequency-dependent phase-shifting patterns.

When the processed signal is combined with the dry signal, you hear another type of swooshing effect as the two signals go in and out of phase with each other. It is best to use phase shifting sparingly because

of its unique, characteristic sound; once you've heard it, you can recognize it instantly. I like to apply it to background pads or certain lead sounds, such as clarinet, flute, and brass.

Down to Basics

You can also modulate different aspects of a signal without mixing the result with the dry (unprocessed) signal. For example, if you modulate the pitch of a signal with an LFO set to a frequency of 4 to 7 Hz and a low amplitude (depth), you get vibrato. In a synth or sampler, this is normally accomplished by applying an LFO to the oscillator within a patch. However, you can also add vibrato to any acoustic sound by sending it through a modulated pitch shifter.

If possible, try setting the LFO in the modulated pitch shifter to oscillate in the audible frequency range (above 20 Hz) at maximum depth. This produces a wild and crazy sound with lots of extra spectral components that are different for each note you play. This is the basis for frequency modulation (FM) synthesis, made famous in the Yamaha DX7 and its offspring. Although you typically don't have the same degree of control over the FM process in a modulated pitch shifter, experimentation can yield interesting results.

You can also modulate a pitch shifter to simulate the Doppler effect. You've probably heard an ambulance or fire truck speeding past you with its siren blasting. As it passes you, the siren appears to drop in pitch; this is called a Doppler shift. The physics of this phenomenon are too involved to explain here. However, you can simulate it by applying an EG or manual modulator to a pitch shifter. To make it even more realistic, pan the sound from hard right to hard left (or vice versa) as the pitch shifts. (The greater the speed of the passing vehicle, the greater the drop in pitch; a Doppler shift of a tritone corresponds to a speed of 137 mph.)

Modulating the cutoff frequency of a lowpass filter produces an effect with an onomatopoeic name (the name sounds like the thing it identifies): wahwah. This effect is particularly popular with guitar players, mostly thanks to Jimi Hendrix. There are many makes and models of wah-wah footpedals that accept a signal from an instrument and produce a filtered output. You simply move the pedal to sweep through the internal filter's cutoff frequencies. Many multi-effects units also include an auto-wah setting, which automatically modulates the cutoff frequency with an LFO.

Remember the old tremolo guitar amps? These classics included an amplifier that could be modulated with an LFO, which produces a tremolo effect. In some older styles of pop music, the frequency of the LFO is relatively high (in the 5 to 10 Hz range). If you have a tremolo effect unit with an LFO that can oscillate in the audible range, you can produce some interesting timbres, as well. This form of amplitude modulation is similar to FM, except that the amplitude of the input signal is modulated instead of the frequency.

Another old technology has become popular again, thanks to digital simulation. Leslie rotary speakers were used by virtually every rock organist and many guitarists in the 1960s and '70s. These devices consist of a woofer and horn tweeter mounted on a rotating spindle within a wooden cabinet. As the two speakers rotate, they create a unique vibrato effect. Typically, there are two rates of rotation: slow (1 or 2 Hz) and fast (about 10 Hz). The musician changes the speed of rotation with a switch, and the transition from one speed to the other takes a few seconds as the spinning speakers overcome inertia to rotate faster or slower.

These days, many multi-effects units include a rotary-speaker simulator. This simulation is not trivial; it must take into account the acoustic characteristics of the cabinet and the cyclic Doppler shifts as the speakers move toward and away from the listener during rotation. One of the most important parameters is the time it takes to accelerate or decelerate from one speed to the other; this can make the difference between a convincing simulation and a cheap imitation. In many cases, the speed of the high-frequency and low-frequency speakers can be controlled independently, as well.

MIDI Modulation

Most multi-effects units now include the ability to modulate various parameters with MIDI Control Change (CC) and other messages, although the degree of MIDI control varies widely between effects processors. If well implemented, this capability lets you do some interesting things. For example, try modulating the reverb time and/or early reflections parameters in a reverb to change the apparent size of the "room" over time. A manual modulator, such as a mod wheel or footpedal, lets you change the size of the room slowly during the course of a song, or quickly for added emphasis at the climax of the tune.

If you have a MIDI-controllable flanger or chorus, you can typically control the rate and depth of the LFO with CC or Pressure messages. These messages are also useful for controlling the wet/dry mix of a MIDI-controlled effects unit.

If you don't have a flanger or chorus device, you can create these effects with a delay or pitch shifter that responds to MIDI. Simply set the wet/dry mix to include both signals and modulate the delay time or

pitch-shift amount with a message such as Modulation or Pressure. To maintain the effect, you must continue to manipulate the controller.

To automate the effect, as in a genuine flanger or chorus, you need to send a stream of Modulation or Pressure messages that repeatedly fluctuate up and down. Unfortunately, I know of no products on the market that produce such a "MIDI LFO." It is possible to kludge something together for this purpose with a MIDI arpeggiator and a MIDI processor such as the Yamaha MEP4, but it is not at all straightforward. Perhaps a manufacturer will add this useful capability to a future product.

Modulation effects are among the many spices in the musician's kitchen. As such, they can add a wonderful flavor to most tunes. However, I tend to use them sparingly; after all, a diet of nothing but spices gets old fast. Add a dash of flanging here, a pinch of chorus there, and you'll be surprised at how much it helps your music sound rich and full of life.

CHAPTER 19

Equalization

ost musical sounds include four distinct attributes: pitch, volume, timbre, and duration. As we've seen in Chapters 17 and 18, pitch shifters and chorus devices affect pitch. An equalizer is a type of device that affects timbre.

Equalizers got their name during the early days of telephone communication. The pioneers of telephony discovered that different frequencies within the signal carried over telephone cables were attenuated by different amounts over long distances. Special amplifiers were designed to selectively boost the strength of the various frequency bands back to their original (input) levels, which made the spectrum at the output equal to the spectrum at the input.

These days, equalizers not only boost (amplify) certain frequencies, they also cut (attenuate) selected frequencies in the input signal by combining a set of filters and amplifiers into a single device. This lets you alter the harmonic content, or timbre, of the signal as well as reduce feedback and acoustic anomalies.

The Right Connections

As discussed in Chapter 15, most mixers include some form of EQ in each input channel, which is used to affect the timbre of the signal in each channel independently. However, you can also use an external equalizer for more precise control. In this case, the equalizer is connected to the mixer somewhat differently than most other effects.

Unlike many other effects units, which split the input signal into two copies and mix the processed and unprocessed versions, all of the signal is routed through an equalizer. Otherwise, a copy of the unprocessed signal would get through, which is exactly what we're trying to prevent. With an equalizer, you don't want to hear the original timbre at all.

As a result, an external equalizer is connected to the mixer's insert points, rather than the effects or aux send/return loops (see Fig. 19-1). This routes the entire signal out of the mixer through the equalizer and back into the mixer.

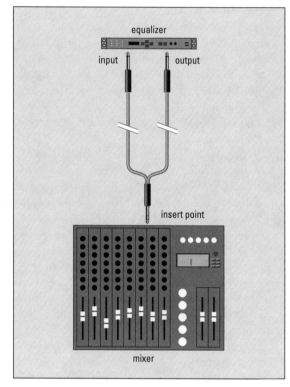

Figure 19-1. Outboard equalizers are connected to a mixer's insert point, which routes the entire signal out of the mixer, through the EQ, and back into the mixer.

This connection usually requires an insert or Y cable with one ¼-inch, TRS (tip-ring-sleeve), stereo plug at one end and two 2-conductor cables that terminate in standard, TS (tip-sleeve) ¼-inch plugs at the other end (see Fig. 19-2). The ring of the stereo plug is connected to the hot wire in one mono cable, which carries the signal from the mixer to the equalizer. The other mono cable returns the signal from the equalizer to the mixer via the stereo plug's tip. (This is reversed in some mixers; check your mixer's specs to be sure.)

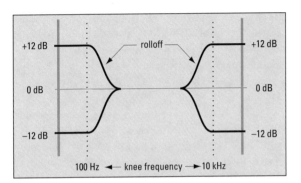

Figure 19-3. High-and low-shelving EQ boosts or cuts all frequencies above or below the knee frequency. The EQ has progressively less effect as frequencies get farther outside these boundaries.

The amount by which the high or low frequencies are boosted or cut is measured in decibels (dB). The decibels used in EQ settings indicate changes in the relative levels of the incoming signal and the processed (equalized) signal, so they are not referenced to a particular absolute value. In addition, EQ decibels are related to power rather than voltage, so a change of 3 dB halves or doubles the level of the electrical signal.

For example, a setting of 0 dB allows the corresponding frequencies to pass unaffected. A setting of -3 dB cuts the level of the affected frequencies in half, while a setting of +3 dB doubles their level. Most EQs have a boost/cut range of ±12 dB, which means the level of the corresponding frequencies can be boosted or cut by a factor of up to sixteen.

All frequencies below the bass knee or above the treble knee of a shelving EQ are affected equally by their respective settings. But what about the frequencies outside these boundaries? In Fig. 19-3, notice that the curves depicting the effect of the bass and treble controls taper down to 0 dB as you move farther from the knee. This indicates that frequencies are affected less and less by the EQ as they move farther from the knee boundary.

The slope of the curve outside the knee boundary is called the rolloff. When referring to EQs, you'll often hear specs such as "a rolloff of 6 dB per octave." This simply means that a frequency one octave away from the knee will be affected one quarter as much as a frequency that is within the knee boundary. If the rolloff is 12 dB/octave, a frequency one octave away from the knee will be affected one sixteenth as much as a frequency that is within the boundary.

Getting Graphic

Bass and treble controls are fine for broad tonal adjustments, but what if you need more specific control? One answer is a graphic EQ. This device divides

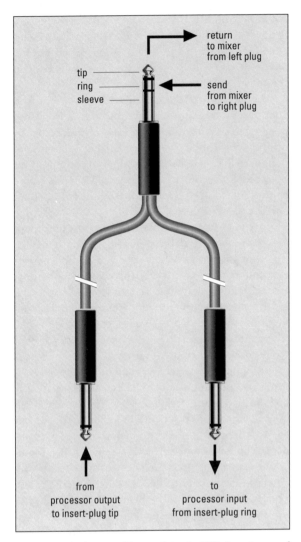

Figure 19-2. An insert cable consists of a TRS plug at one end and two 2-conductor, ¼-inch or XLR plugs at the other end. In most mixers, the TRS ring sends the signal to the processor, and the tip returns the signal to the mixer.

On the Shelf

Almost everyone has used an equalizer at one time or another. Virtually all stereo systems in cars and homes include bass and treble controls, which are a rudimentary form of EQ. (Most mixers also include these controls in each channel input; see Chapter 15.) This type of EQ is often called shelving EQ because the graph of frequency versus amount of boost/cut looks like a shelf (see Fig. 19-3). The bass control lets you boost or cut all frequencies below a preset threshold (called the knee or shelving frequency), which is usually 100 Hz. The treble control boosts or cuts all frequencies above its knee frequency, usually 10 kHz.

the entire frequency spectrum into several fixed bands. The controls include a set of sliders that let you boost or cut the frequencies in each band independently. The positions of the sliders form a graph of the EQ's frequency response, hence the name "graphic."

Each band is identified by its center frequency, and each can be boosted or cut by as much as 12 dB or more. The range of effect for each band forms a hump in the graph of frequency vs. boost/cut (see Fig. 19-4). The setting of each band is applied fully to the center frequency only; other frequencies are affected less and less by a particular band as they move farther away from the center frequency.

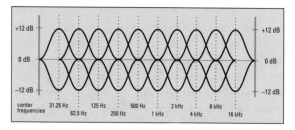

Figure 19-4. This graphic EQ divides the frequency spectrum into ten bands. Notice how the bands overlap.

As you can see in Fig. 19-4, however, the bands overlap. If you boost two neighboring bands, the frequencies between them are boosted, as well. In extreme cases, the frequencies between the bands can be affected more than the center frequencies. In addition, you can create an uneven frequency response called the ripple effect if you boost all bands to their maximum setting.

One important characteristic of graphic EQ bands is the bandwidth, which is defined as the range of frequencies that are affected within 3 dB of the band's setting. For example, if a band is set to boost by 12 dB, the bandwidth is the range of frequencies on either side of the center frequency that are boosted by at least 9 dB. The points on the frequency vs. boost/cut curve that correspond to the boundaries of the bandwidth are called the 3 dB down points.

The range of frequencies that define bandwidth can be expressed in two ways: the difference between the boundary frequencies or the ratio of these frequencies. Most people use the ratio, which is equivalent to expressing the bandwidth as a musical interval. If two bands have the same width, it can be expressed as the same interval. However, the difference between the boundary frequencies will be different for these bands.

For example, consider two bands, one centered at 150 Hz and the other at 1,500 Hz. Both bands have the same width. The 3 dB down points of the 150 Hz band

are at 100 and 200 Hz, while the 3 dB down points of the 1,500 Hz band are 1,000 and 2,000 Hz. Both bands have a bandwidth of one octave. As you can see, the difference between the boundary frequencies depends on the center frequency of the band.

As a result, electrical engineers came up with another way to express bandwidth in relative terms: quality factor, or Q. This expression is calculated by dividing the center frequency by the difference in boundary frequencies. Returning to the previous example, if the center frequency is 150 Hz and the bandwidth is 100 Hz, Q = 1.5; if the center is 1,500 Hz and the bandwidth is 1,000 Hz, Q = 1.5. In a graphic EQ, both the center frequency and bandwidth of each band are fixed, so each band's Q is also fixed.

You might think that the bandwidth remains constant regardless of the band's boost/cut setting, but this isn't quite true. At low settings, the bandwidth tends to be wider than it is at the maximum setting. As a result, companies such as Rane make "constant-Q" graphic EQs, which maintain a constant bandwidth at all boost/cut settings.

Graphic EQs are often found on mixers designed for live-sound applications. These mixers generally include two separate graphic EQs, one for each stereo output, and each EQ typically includes five to ten bands. These EQs are used to reduce feedback at certain frequencies and tailor the sound to the room. Outboard graphic EQs include ten to 31 bands; the latter variety is often called a ⅓-octave graphic EQ, which describes the width of each band.

Many people start by setting the sliders on a graphic EQ in the shape of a smile. This compensates for the fact that the human ear is less sensitive to high and low frequencies and more sensitive to the midrange, particularly in the 3 to 4 kHz region. As a result, it helps to boost the low and high frequencies and cut the midrange, particularly at low to moderate volumes. (At high volumes, the ear's frequency response flattens out, so this type of setting can actually hurt the sound quality.) The loudness control on many stereo systems activates a fixed version of this concept. Following this initial setting, it's important to adjust the EQ for any room resonances or speaker anomalies (discussed shortly).

Parametric Power

The most flexible type of equalizer is a parametric EQ (see Fig. 19-5). Unlike graphic models, the center frequency and bandwidth of each band in a parametric EQ are fully user-adjustable. Parametric EQs generally have fewer bands than graphic EQs because their primary purpose is to tailor a few precisely defined problem frequencies.

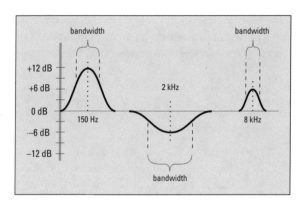

Figure 19-5. This parametric EQ is set to boost 150 Hz by 12 dB, with a moderate bandwidth; cut 2 kHz by -6 dB, with a wide bandwidth; and boost 8 kHz by 6 dB, with a narrow bandwidth.

A variation of parametric EQ is quasi-parametric EQ, which offers full control over center frequency and boost/cut level but only provides a few preset bandwidths from which to choose. More common is the semiparametric or sweepable EQ. In this case, the center frequency and boost/cut level are user-definable, but the bandwidth is fixed. Many mixers include one or more sweepable bands in each channel input (see Chapter 15).

Applications

Tonal correction is among the most common applications for EQ. If a sound or recorded track seems too bright, too boomy, or too dull, an EQ can help. The trick is to determine the offending frequency and the amount to cut or boost it. This takes some experimentation. If the track is too bright, the high frequencies should be cut; if the track is too boomy, the lower mid frequencies (in the 150 to 300 Hz range) should be cut.

In such cases, I set a sweepable band to boost by a relatively large amount (12 dB or more) and play the track while sweeping the frequency knob back and forth until I hear the offending frequency as loud as possible. Then, I play the track again while cutting the offending frequency to taste.

Another important application is tonal matching. For example, sometimes two singers' voices don't blend as well as you might wish. In addition, the same singer's voice can vary on different days, which can be a problem if you wish to combine recordings from separate sessions. These timbral mismatch problems can sometimes be addressed by applying EQ. Once again, the trick is to identify the frequencies that are different and boost or cut them to match. This requires a trained ear that can identify the specific frequencies within a complex timbre that are too loud or too soft.

This skill is not easily mastered, but there is

help. For example, KIQ Productions offers the *Golden Ears Audio Training Program* (available through Mix Bookshelf; [800] 233-9604). This program includes a workbook and four CDs with audio examples designed to train your ears to hear the effects of different signal processors, including EQ.

If you've used amplified sound, you have probably encountered feedback. All acoustical environments (rooms, auditoriums, etc.) and audio circuits exhibit resonances at specific frequencies. If these resonant frequencies are stimulated, you get feedback. EQ can be instrumental in reducing feedback by cutting the resonant frequencies that might be in the sound.

However, this also affects the timbre of the sound, so exercise care when reducing feedback with EQ. Parametric EQs are commonly used for this task, because you can dial in a specific frequency and use a narrow bandwidth to minimize the effect on other parts of the sound. The Sabine FBX-series Feedback Exterminators expand on this idea, identifying which frequencies are feeding back and automatically applying narrow-band (0.1-octave), dynamic EQ to reduce the offending frequencies.

Room resonances can color the sound of a P.A. or monitor system drastically. In addition, many speaker systems distort the timbre of the sound they reproduce. Graphic EQs are often used to correct these anomalies. Many engineers place a microphone in the room, play pink noise (which includes all frequencies at equal intensity in each octave) over the sound system, measure the frequency response at the mic position, and adjust a ⅓-octave graphic EQ to flatten the response. However, this might not fix the anomalies at other positions in the room.

In general, I recommend using EQ as little as possible, particularly boosting. It can be a big help in many situations, but boosting also increases the noise level. If a band of frequencies is too low, try cutting the frequencies around it first.

Any application of EQ (or any type of filter, for that matter) affects the phase of the signal. This might not matter in some applications, but it is critical in others. For example, if nearby frequencies are phase-shifted with respect to each other, they might cancel or reinforce each other, leading to unexpected tonal results. Physics dictates that frequency, amplitude, and phase are inexorably linked, so there's no way to avoid this phase shift entirely. Nevertheless, some intrepid design engineers try to reduce or compensate for it.

EQ is one of the most common signal processors in the entire electronic music arsenal. It has many uses and helps the sound engineer to tailor the timbre, reduce feedback, and tame room and speaker anomalies. Start with the bass and treble controls on your home or car stereo; many of these systems also include a graphic EQ, so play with their controls. If you have a mixer, try using the EQ on tape or CD tracks. Some synthesizers include a parametric EQ for onboard sounds, which is excellent territory to explore.

When people discuss signal processing, they're usually referring to effects such as reverb, delay, and flanging. But there is another, less well-known type of signal processing that can enhance audio signals dramatically. These processors are generically known as spectral enhancers.

The primary purpose of spectral enhancers is to add more "presence" to a sound. Sometimes, they are used to "brighten" a dull stereo mix or add a sense of transparency to a sonic environment. The process can also compensate for subtle—and sometimes not so subtle—losses in clarity when analog masters are duplicated onto cassette. In some instances, the sonic quality of older recordings (we're talking 1930s, '40s, and '50s) can be improved with spectral enhancers. However, the use of spectral enhancers is not limited to complete mixes. They can also process individual instruments or vocals to improve clarity and definition.

Basic Concepts

As discussed in Chapter 1, all sounds can be broken down into a set of simple sine waves of different frequencies, amplitudes, and phases. This set of sine waves is called the harmonic spectrum of the original sound. To work their magic, spectral enhancers alter the amplitude and relative phase of the various frequencies within the spectrum of the signal.

Conventional graphic and parametric equalizers alter the amplitude and phase of the frequency spectrum in a static fashion. For example, if you boost 1 kHz by 3 dB, any frequency components at or near 1 kHz are boosted by the same amount. However, spectral enhancers are generally dynamic; that is, they do their thing based on the amplitudes and frequencies in the spectrum of the input signal as it changes over time.

Most enhancers are based on a sidechain design (see Fig. 19-6) that splits the input signal into two copies; one goes to a summing amplifier and then to the output, while the other is diverted through the enhancement circuitry. (Most spectral enhancers have two channels so they can process stereo signals.) Then, the direct and processed signals are combined before being sent to the outputs. This internal mixing often increases the level of the output signal, particularly on short peaks such as snare cracks. Because

"surprise" hot levels can cause distortion on tape (or through a sound system), most enhancers are designed to maintain an even (1:1) input/output amplitude ratio.

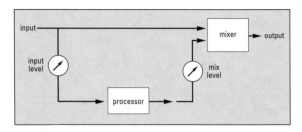

Figure 19-6. In a sidechain design, the input signal is split into two copies; one proceeds to a summing amp and then to the output, while the other is diverted through the processor. In the sidechain, an input level control determines how much of the signal is processed. The processed signal is then mixed with the original sound and sent to the output.

Harmonic Generation

There are three basic types of spectral enhancers. The first type employs harmonic generation or harmonic synthesis. This process generates harmonics not present in the input signal and adds them to the original sound. Traditionally, mid and high harmonics are added to brighten the sound.

As with most enhancement methods, harmonic synthesis splits the input signal into two copies, one of which is directed to the sidechain. The processed signal first passes through a level control and variable highpass filter, which allows frequencies above a user-specified threshold to pass through unaffected while frequencies under the threshold are attenuated. The signal then enters the harmonics generator, which creates harmonics at frequencies determined by the input spectrum. Finally, the processed and unprocessed signals are mixed and sent to the output.

The Aphex Aural Exciter, which was the first harmonic-synthesis processor, has undergone several evolutions. The current model is designated Type C^2. The Aural Exciter Type C^2 includes a second sidechain called "Big Bottom" (see Fig. 19-7). This sidechain, which is parallel to the Exciter circuitry, enhances bass frequencies by employing a lowpass filter to remove high harmonics from the input signal. The effect is more pronounced at low input levels and diminishes as the input level increases. Most importantly, the peak level of the signal is not increased by the process.

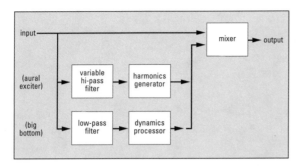

Figure 19-7. The Aphex Aural Exciter Type C² with Big Bottom includes two sidechains. The Exciter itself includes a high-pass filter and harmonics generator, while Big Bottom enhances the bass frequencies that make it through a lowpass filter.

Some spectral enhancers are designed expressly to give signals a bigger boom. The dbx 120XP Subharmonic Synthesizer and Furman PUNCH-10 both create a "subharmonic" one octave below the fundamental note of the input signal.

Dynamic EQ

The second type of enhancement is called dynamic EQ. In this process, the audio spectrum is divided into a number of bands, each of which is boosted or cut dynamically. In other words, as the spectral content of the input signal changes, the amount of boost or cut changes as well. This treatment can be used to affect the entire spectrum, rather than just highs or lows.

For example, the Dolby Model 740 Spectral Processor is a 2-channel dynamic EQ that divides the audio spectrum into three bands. It then boosts only the low-amplitude signals in each band (by as much as 20 dB) without affecting the high-amplitude signals or changing the overall dynamic range. As you might expect from Dolby, the Model 740 also includes a noise-reduction circuit on each channel (see Chapter 21).

Another spectral enhancer based on dynamic EQ is the Vitalizer from SPL. The Vitalizer analyzes the input signal for its spectral content and amplitude, then sends it through a sidechain of five filters that are interactively linked to each other; the action of each filter affects the others.

The 296 Spectral Enhancer from dbx's Project 1 signal-processing series also uses dynamic EQ. However, unlike some enhancers, the sidechain signal passes through a hiss reduction circuit *before* the EQ section. This signal routing is designed to prevent audible hiss (or other noises) from being enhanced along with the original sound.

Dynamic Phase Shifting

The remaining type of spectral enhancement is called dynamic phase-shifting. In this process, it is the phase of each harmonic—not the amplitude or frequency—that is shifted dynamically.

This approach is used by BBE in their Sonic Maximizer products. The Sonic Maximizers are based on the principle that any sound played by a loudspeaker is delayed—and therefore phase-shifted—by different amounts, depending on the frequencies present. As a rule, high frequencies are delayed more than low frequencies. The resulting distortion often makes sharp transients, such as drum hits, sound "mushy."

The Sonic Maximizer compensates by adding more delay time to the low frequencies of an input signal and less delay time to high frequencies. This action/reaction delay allows the different frequencies of the audio spectrum to reach your ears at the time nature (and acoustics) intended. After the dynamic phase-shifting is complete, the unit analyzes the spectrum of the input signal and applies dynamic EQ without inducing additional phase shifting. Unlike other enhancers, the Sonic Maximizer uses no sidechain; the entire signal is affected by the process.

Other products combine several types of enhancement. The Orban 290RX Adaptive Enhancement Processor's sidechain includes two types of processing: harmonic and spectral restoration. Harmonic restoration generates new harmonics down to 1 kHz, depending on the control setting. Spectral restoration is a form of dynamic EQ and phase shifting that is particularly useful for enhancing vocals without increasing sibilance. A noise-reduction circuit is located after the restoration section.

Applications

Enhancers are normally used in the recording studio during the final mix. Most mixdown effects are usually patched into the aux sends and returns to facilitate a user-determined balance between the wet and dry signals. But enhancers are often patched into a mixer's insert points so that the entire signal passes through the device. Patching into the insert points also ensures that the phase relationship between the original and processed signals is maintained.

In general, use as little enhancement as possible. Don't forget that the process enhances the intended sound *and* any noise present in the input signal. You might be clarifying a bad sound along with the good. Although several devices include noise reduction to minimize enhanced noise, it's always a good idea to use just enough effect to get the job done and no more.

Enhancing individual sounds can be very effective in helping certain instruments stand out in the mix. Vocals are a good place to start. Enhancement not only improves overall sound quality, but also intelligibility. However, be careful when enhancing overly sibilant voices; an enhanced high-frequency "s" sound often drowns out everything else.

Enhancers can also be patched into a mixer's stereo bus insert points to process an entire mix. But beware of employing enhancers during a marathon mix session. The impact of the effect diminishes as your ears become accustomed to it, which might lead you to wonder why you used the effect in the first place. Also, the high-end shimmer of dull master tapes can be revitalized by patching an enhancer between two mastering decks. One deck plays your original master, while the second records the processed signal from the enhancer. Hopefully, your mixes are good enough that they need little enhancement.

Used with care, a spectral enhancer can add a professional edge to home recordings. However, it's easy to overdo it; as the commercial says, "a little dab'll do ya." With the proper restraint, enhancers can become an indispensable tool in any studio's arsenal.

CHAPTER 20

Dynamics Processing

uppose you've just recorded a killer lead vocal on your new modular digital multitrack (MDM), the best you've ever sung. But when you listen back, you hear some ugly distortion in the loud passages. You were so caught up in the performance, you didn't notice that the level meter went above 0 dB. This inevitably results in clipping, a nasty form of digital distortion. How could you have avoided this tragedy?

The most common method is to use a compressor/limiter, which is a particular type of dynamics processor. Dynamics processors serve a multitude of purposes by altering the dynamic range of an audio signal in various ways.

Dynamic range is simply the difference, measured in decibels (dB), between the lowest and highest levels in a given signal or audio device. (The lowest level is generally equivalent to the noise floor; see Chapter 21.) The term can also be used to describe the maximum range of signal levels that a given audio device or recording medium can accommodate without distortion.

For example, Ampex 499 open-reel analog tape has a dynamic range of about 80 dB. Cassette tape has less dynamic range than high-quality, open-reel tape; Type II cassettes generally offer a dynamic range of about 60 to 70 dB.

Digital-audio systems that record with 16-bit resolution, such as the Alesis ADAT and TASCAM DA-88 MDMs, exhibit a theoretical dynamic range of 96 dB, although the practical range is more like 90 dB. This is much better than most audio recording media, but unlike analog tape, you must not exceed the upper limit by any amount, or you will hear the dreaded digital clipping.

Compression and Limiting

Compressors are probably the best-known dynamics processors. If the level of an input signal rises above a user-specified threshold, the compressor reduces the amount by which the signal's level can continue to rise. If the input signal stays below the threshold, it is not affected.

The ratio parameter determines the extent to which the level of a signal above the threshold is compressed. For example, if the ratio is 2:1, and the input signal is above the threshold, a 2 dB increase in the input level results in a 1 dB increase in the output level. If the ratio is 4:1, a 4 dB increase in the input level results in a 1 dB increase in the output level.

Other important compression parameters include input gain and output gain. The input-gain control is used to adjust the overall input level to compensate for a particularly strong or weak incoming signal without clipping the compressor's input circuitry. Output gain adjusts the final output level, which is especially important because it lets you compensate for the way a compressor attenuates signals. (In fact, this is sometimes called "makeup gain.") However, raising the output level also raises low-level signals, including noise. This can be corrected using a different type of dynamics processor, which I'll discuss shortly.

The operation of a compressor can be illustrated in a graph of input level versus output level. As you can see in Fig. 20-1, if the input level is below the threshold, it is equal to the output level; what goes in comes out unscathed. Above the threshold, the rate of increase in the output level is controlled according to the ratio. This is indicated graphically by the slope of the line above the threshold; the closer that line is to being horizontal, the greater the compression ratio.

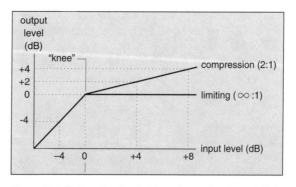

Figure 20-1. Below the threshold, an input signal at -4 dB is output at -4 dB. If the compression ratio is 2:1, a +4 dB input signal is output at +2 dB. If the limiter is set to a threshold of 0 dB and a ratio of ∞:1, all signals above the threshold are output at 0 dB, no matter what their input level.

The angle in the graph at the threshold point is called the knee. In some compressors, the knee is rounded rather than forming a sharp angle. This is called soft-knee compression. Soft-knee compression tends to smooth out the transition at the threshold setting, making it less noticeable when the compressor kicks in.

Some compressors offer attack and/or release parameters. Once the input signal rises above the threshold, the attack parameter determines how long it takes before the compressor starts attenuating. This might seem a bit strange. Why would anyone want to delay the compressor's operation? Sometimes, you want to pass high-level peak transients, such as drum hits and instrumental attacks, through the compressor to retain the bite or sizzle of the original sound. By setting the attack parameter to 100 ms or more, quick peaks get through before the compressor can process them.

As the level of the input signal drops below the threshold, the release parameter determines how long it takes for the compressor to stop working. Slower release times smooth out the signal and, in some applications, help increase sustain (discussed shortly).

When the ratio is high (10:1 and above), compression becomes limiting. This effectively prevents the output level from rising much beyond the threshold level. At a ratio of ∞:1, the limiter clamps a lid on the signal level, allowing it to rise no higher than the threshold (see Fig. 20-1). A compressor/limiter is a dynamics processor with a wide variety of compression ratios to accommodate both applications. Many compressor/limiters can even perform both tasks simultaneously.

The Right Connections
As with an equalizer, all of the signal is routed through a compressor/limiter. (By contrast, recall from Chapters 17 and 18 that the signal is split into two copies for reverbs, delays, pitch shifters, and modulation effects; one copy is processed and the other copy is left alone.) As a result, compressor/limiters are connected to the mixer's insert points, rather than the effects or aux send/return loops (see Fig. 19-1).

Sometimes, you need to process the signal from only one mixer channel, in which case you connect the compressor/limiter to that channel's insert point. If you want to process several signals from different input channels with the same device (e.g., if you have several mics on a horn section or choir), just route those channels to one of the mixer's subgroups and connect the processor to that subgroup's insert point.

Finally, many engineers compress the entire mix during mixdown. You need a stereo compressor for this job. Most stereo compressors include a switch that links the two channels to operate together; they can also be unlinked to operate independently. Simply connect the processor to the insert points for the mixer's main L/R buses using two insert cables. If the main buses lack inserts, connect the compressor inline directly after the mixer outputs and before the mastering deck inputs.

Applications
One of the primary applications of compression is smoothing a vocalist's performance dynamics. If a singer's mic technique or vocal control is less than optimal, a compressor can clean up the volume surges and fades. This can be a real gig-saver onstage and in the studio. When recording vocals to tape, I use relatively mild compression with a threshold of -10 dB and a ratio of about 3:1.

If you want to increase the impact and punch of virtually any recorded sound, try compressing it slightly. This is particularly true when recording to digital media, which lack analog tape's coloration and slight, natural compression.

A compressor is also useful for preventing unwanted or excessive tape saturation when you are pushing the limits of the recording medium's dynamic range. For example, if you are planning to release your music on cassette, compression is vital to accommodate its limited dynamic range.

If you're recording on a digital machine, where even the slightest amount of clipping is unacceptable, you might need to go beyond simple compression and limit the signal. Place the limiter between the signal source and the tape deck, and set the threshold to 0 dB and the ratio to ∞:1. (Note, however, that limiting can alter the sound's timbre; for instance, it can sap the life out of snare drums. Therefore, this is an emergency tactic. It is far better to avoid clipping by allowing sufficient headroom at the recorder inputs whenever possible.)

As mentioned earlier, compression is also commonly applied to an entire mix during mixdown. This produces a tighter, more professional sound, with more impact and kick. It is especially important for radio airplay because radio transmitters have a very narrow dynamic range. As a result, radio stations routinely compress the heck out of their signal.

Another application of compression is to artificially sustain each note. Guitar and bass players often use compressors for this purpose. To increase the sustain of a sound, set a relatively low threshold (-20 to -30 dB or lower), high ratio (5:1 to 10:1 or higher), very fast attack time, and slow release time. Adjust the input and output gain as high as possible without distortion in your system.

Under these conditions, the input level can vary over a wide range, while the output level remains relatively constant. For example, as a vibrating guitar string dies away, the instrument's level might fall by 10 dB or more. If the ratio is set to 10:1 or higher, the output from the compressor will fall by only 1 dB, which sustains the sound and makes it more punchy and even. This works very well on lead and rhythm guitar, as well as bass.

Limiting can also protect speakers and eardrums from being blown out by levels that are too hot. However, you must be especially careful how you set the limiter's threshold in sound-reinforcement applications. If the threshold is too high, you're unprotected; if it's too low, your amplifiers must work extremely hard, but you won't get enough sound.

Compressors and limiters are essential tools in the studio and onstage, offering a variety of useful functions. Using them properly requires a little practice, however, so it's a good idea to spend some time experimenting.

The Aphex Model 106 Easyrider compressor has four independent, mono channels that can be linked as stereo pairs. The Drive control sets both the compression ratio and the input gain. An unusual, 2-position Process switch controls the attack and release.

Expansive Gates

Imagine you are engineering for a singer who belts out a great take. After requesting a particularly loud headphone mix, however, the singer moves one cup of the headphones off the ear. When you solo the vocal track on playback, you can hear the drums almost as loud as the voice. The sound from the headphones bled into the vocal mic! Even worse, if you apply reverb to the vocal track, the drum sounds will also be affected, even when there is no active vocal part. What can you do?

If the singer is uncomfortable performing with both phones on, the answer lies in a specific type of dynamics processor called an expander.

Expanders are similar to compressors in that they attenuate certain incoming signals. However, they operate at opposite ends of the amplitude range. When the input signal's level falls *below* the user-specified threshold in an expander, it lowers the signal's level even more. (In a compressor, the input

signal is attenuated when its level rises *above* the threshold.) As you might surmise from its name, this type of processor expands the total dynamic range of the input signal by attenuating low-level signals.

An expander's parameters are much the same as those found on a compressor. The ratio parameter determines how much low-level signals are attenuated. For example, suppose you set the expansion ratio to 1:2. If the input signal is below the threshold and drops by 1 dB, the output from the expander drops by 2 dB. If the ratio is set to 1:4, a drop of 1 dB in the input signal results in a drop of 4 dB in the output. (Compression ratios are specified with the larger number first, e.g., 2:1, which is the opposite of expansion ratios.) If they are available, attack and release parameters also work in the same way as the corresponding parameters in a compressor.

The most common application of expanders is noise reduction. Let's refer back to the earlier example, in which the sound from the singer's headphones bled into the vocal mic. The unwanted sound is usually pretty low in level by the time it reaches the mic. If you set the threshold above the level of the headphone bleed, it will be attenuated to near inaudibility when no other signal is present.

This also helps when miking noisy guitar amps and recording vocalists who smack their lips or breathe loudly. When the intended signal is present, the expander lets the noise through, but the signal is generally louder than the noise, so the noise is masked.

Just as limiting is an extreme form of compression, gating is an extreme form of expansion. When the input-signal level falls below the threshold, the gate "closes" suddenly, shutting off all output. Gates are normally used to eliminate all noise when no intended signal is present. In most cases, however, I prefer to use an expander, which is not so abrupt; it's a kinder, gentler gate. What if the track includes a very soft passage? A gate might prevent some of the intended material from getting through at all. In addition, you can often hear the gate opening and closing. On the other hand, a gate is preferable with sharp, percussive sounds such as drums. An expander tends to soften the attack and reduce the punch of such sounds.

Aside from noise reduction, gates are used to create the gated snare sound made popular by Phil Collins. To achieve this sound, send a heavily reverbed snare through a gate with a relatively high threshold and fast release time. You can also use an expander and gate together to tame particularly loud headphone bleed.

Ducking Out

At the heart of all analog dynamics processors is a voltage-controlled amplifier (VCA), which doesn't actually *amplify* anything in these processors, but rather *attenuates* signals from their full amplitude by various amounts. A VCA actually has two inputs: primary and control. The amount by which it attenuates the primary signal is determined by the voltage (called the control voltage) at the control input. As this control voltage changes, so does the amount of attenuation.

In a simple dynamics processor, the input signal is split into two copies (see Fig. 20-2). One copy is fed directly into the VCA's primary input, while the other copy is fed into a level detector, which reads the amplitude of the input signal. This amplitude tells the level detector what voltage to send to the VCA's control input, which determines how much the primary signal is attenuated.

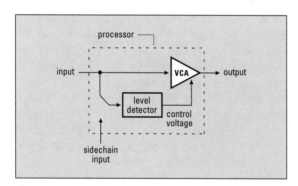

Figure 20-2. In a dynamics processor, the input is split into two copies. One copy proceeds to the VCA's primary input, while the other copy is sent through a level detector, which controls the attenuation of the VCA.

For example, if the input signal's amplitude is below the user-specified threshold in a compressor, the level detector typically sends no control voltage (0 volts) to the VCA, which causes it to pass the signal at unity gain (i.e., the level of the output signal equals the level of the input signal). However, as the input amplitude rises above the threshold, the level detector sends higher control voltages to the VCA, which attenuates the signal accordingly. Similarly, as the input level falls below the threshold in an expander, the level detector sends increasing control voltages to the VCA, which attenuates the signal further. The VCA attenuates the signal completely if the control voltage reaches its upper limit, which is usually 5 or 10 volts.

Many dynamics processors include a separate input called a sidechain, control, or key input (see Fig. 20-2). If nothing is connected to the sidechain, the processor behaves as previously described. However, if you connect an external signal source to the sidechain, the processor's input is disconnected from the level detector, which no longer directly controls the VCA. Instead, the amplitude of the external signal controls the attenuation by telling the level detector what control voltage to send to the VCA (see Fig. 20-3).

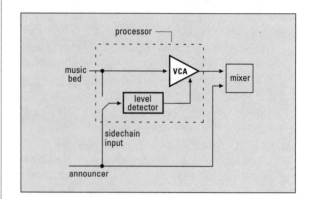

Figure 20-3. If an external signal is connected to the sidechain input, its level controls the VCA's attenuation of the primary signal. In this example, the music bed automatically lowers in volume whenever the announcer speaks.

One classic application of a compressor sidechain is called ducking. Often, you might want to lower the volume of the music in relation to a voice or lead instrument. For example, the background music in a public-address system should drop in volume during an announcement or page. If you are recording a commercial with a music bed and a voice-over announcer, you want the music bed to drop in volume when the announcer begins to talk about the product and return to the previous volume when the announcer is finished.

These situations are easily handled with a ducker. Simply connect the music to the compressor's primary input and the announcer to the sidechain input. Whenever the announcer speaks, the level detector sends a higher control voltage to the VCA, which attenuates the music. Set the threshold and ratio of the compressor to drop the music volume as desired. When the announcer stops speaking, the music automatically returns to its previous volume.

It's important to understand that none of the sidechain signal passes through the VCA to the output of the compressor. You must split the announcer's signal, sending one copy to the sidechain and the other copy to a mixer, where it is combined with the output from the compressor (see Fig. 20-3).

Don't Dis a De-Esser

Many compressors also include a sidechain output, which lets you send the input signal to an external device before returning it to the sidechain input. The most common application of this technique is frequency-dependent processing, such as de-essing. As you might know, some vocal sounds are louder than others. This is particularly true of the sibilant sounds "sss," "sh," and "tch." These sounds are laden with high-frequencies in the range of 2 to 10 kHz; when they appear in a vocal track, they can stick out like a sore thumb.

Of course, you can use an equalizer to cut these frequencies, but in this case, they are cut by the specified amount no matter how loud or soft they are. A better solution is to use a de-esser, which compresses the incoming signal only when the specified frequencies exceed the threshold. This is accomplished by sending the input signal from the sidechain output to an equalizer and returning the signal from the EQ to the sidechain input (see Fig. 20-4).

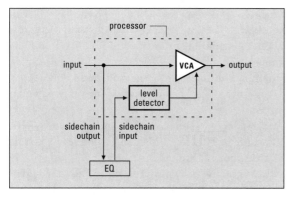

Figure 20-4. Patching an EQ into the sidechain loop lets certain frequencies control the VCA's attenuation. Commercial de-essers include a simple EQ within the processor.

Set the EQ to boost the offending frequencies and cut the other frequencies. Then, when the input signal includes excessive sibilants, the EQ boosts these frequencies even further before sending them to the level detector, which causes the VCA to attenuate the input signal only as long as these frequencies are present. The sound quality of the EQ doesn't matter, because none of its signal is ever heard; it's only used to control the attenuation of the VCA.

Most commercial de-essers include an internal, single-band EQ with a selectable frequency and threshold. These parameters are set according to the type of sound you want to reduce. For example, "sss" occurs around 6 to 8 kHz, while "sh" is somewhat louder and lower in frequency at about 2 to 3 kHz. In one recording project with a female singer, I set the de-esser at about 7 kHz with a threshold of -5 dB, which gently reduces the "sss" sounds without affecting the rest of the performance. You can also use a de-esser to reduce the plosive sounds of "p," "k," and "t" and control other sounds, such as a boomy bass or

guitar and ringing drums. If you use an external EQ, the compressor's attack time should be very fast to catch the beginning of the sound.

Another useful technique is frequency-dependent gating. When miking drums in the studio, you often hear the sound of the hi-hat bleeding into the snare mic. When the snare is silent and the hi-hat is played, you hear the hat clearly through the snare mic, complete with any reverb or other processing intended for the snare. (A similar problem arises with toms and crash or ride cymbals.) But if you simply remove the cymbal frequencies with EQ, you will probably color the intended drum sound unacceptably.

A common solution is to use a gate that opens when the drum is played and closes when the drum is silent, shutting out the cymbal. (When you play the drum, you'll still have cymbal bleed, but hopefully the drum will be loud enough to mask it.) To accomplish this, send the drum signal through a gate with a sidechain loop that is connected to an equalizer. Set the EQ to boost the drum frequencies and cut the cymbal frequencies. The gate opens when the loudest signal—which you've ensured will be the drum—reaches the threshold. If there is no drum sound, the gate closes.

Gate Closed

Most modern dynamics processors include a combination of functions in one device. A good all-around choice is a 2-channel, or dual, compressor/limiter/expander, in which the two channels can be linked to operate together as a stereo pair. This type of device is more expensive than a dedicated stereo unit, but it offers the most flexibility. If you want to process several tracks independently, there are 4-channel compressor/limiters that can also be linked into stereo pairs. Vocal processors often include a de-esser with standard compression, and multi-effects units sometimes include one or more types of dynamics processing.

CHAPTER 21

Other Effects

In addition to the effects discussed·in previous chapters, I'd like to present two more that are very important to most electronic musicians: noise reduction and 3-D processing. Noise reduction, especially Dolby and dbx, is commonly used in recording, but simulating a 3-D sound field is difficult to achieve successfully, so it is not as pervasive. Nevertheless, it can add a unique spice to recordings, and it is appearing on more and more professional projects.

NOISE REDUCTION

Anyone who has used electronic audio equipment knows that you always get a little something extra in addition to the intended sound: noise. In general terms, noise is any unwanted audio signal that makes its way into your recordings or live sound system. Knowing how it gets there and how to reduce it will help clean up your sound in a big way.

Noisy Concepts

There are many types of noise, which fall into two broad categories: tape noise and source noise. Tape noise is endemic to analog tape; digital tape does not suffer from this problem. Perhaps the best known type of tape noise is hiss, which arises from randomly oriented iron oxide particles on the tape. Even after a signal is recorded, a few particles are not aligned with the others to represent the signal. As a result, you hear tape hiss, which includes mostly higher frequencies.

The level of inherent noise in any audio device is called the noise floor, which is measured in decibels. Typical analog-tape noise-floor ratings are in the range of -45 to -65 dB with respect to the reference operating level, which corresponds to zero on the meters of most tape decks. The noise floor remains relatively constant, although it might seem to fluctuate if the program material has a wide dynamic range, which sometimes masks the noise and sometimes doesn't. The difference between the nominal signal level and the noise floor is called the signal-to-noise ratio (S/N). Other forms of tape noise include cross-talk and print-through. Crosstalk arises when the signal recorded on one track "bleeds" onto adjacent tracks. In this case, you can hear a faint copy of the offending track when you listen to an adjacent track.

Print-through occurs when tape is stored for long periods in a tightly wound condition. The magnetic field generated by the particles on each layer of tape affects the particles on adjacent layers. This sounds like a faint "pre-echo" of the material that is about to be played as the tape unwinds. This problem can be minimized by storing your tapes tails out or wound at normal speed onto the takeup reel.

Source noise includes such things as noisy guitar amps, effects, and synth patches, as well as 60 Hz hum, induced radio-frequency and electromagnetic interference (RFI and EMI), and ambient noise from a microphone. Although noise-reduction systems can help fight these problems, you should also take other appropriate actions. For example, 60 Hz hum probably indicates ground loops, which can be eliminated with proper grounding (see Chapter 3). RFI and EMI can be addressed with proper cable shielding and routing.

Double-Ended NR

Most people are familiar with Dolby and dbx noise reduction found on many cassette decks. Both of these systems are known as double-ended noise reduction, because they encode the signal as it is recorded and decode it during playback. The encoding stage compresses the signal, and the decoding stage expands the signal, so the term companding is applied to this process (see Chapter 20).

During the encoding process, the input signal is compressed by raising the level of soft sections (that is, when the input level falls below a certain threshold). In contrast, loud signals are reduced in level with normal compression. If the input to the encoder is above the threshold, it masks the noise, so no compression is applied. Note that compression is applied before the signal is recorded to tape, so it does not increase the level of tape hiss. However, any low-level source noise is boosted along with the program material.

During the decoding process, the taped signal is

expanded, lowering the soft sections. But decoding is applied to the *taped* signal, so both the program material and the hiss are reduced. The hiss is not compressed (boosted); it is expanded (attenuated). As a result, the difference in amplitude between the program and noise (i.e., the signal-to-noise ratio) is greater than it would be without companding.

For example, if the compression ratio is 2:1 and the expansion ratio is 1:2, the noise floor is lowered by a factor of 2. If the original noise floor is -45 dB, the expanded noise floor is -90 dB (see Fig. 21-1). No expansion is applied to high-level signals, which are assumed to mask any inherent noise. The noise floor "follows" the signal level, rising and falling with the level of the program material.

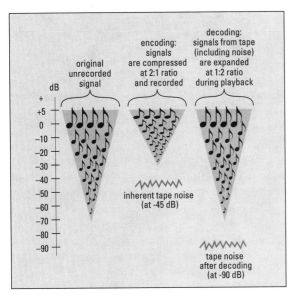

Figure 21-1. Compansion squeezes the dynamic range before recording so all the program material is well above the noise floor of the tape. The original dynamic range is restored during playback, and the tape noise is reduced at the same time.

Some companding systems also use another technique to further reduce tape hiss. During recording, the signal is slightly boosted in the high frequencies; this is called pre-emphasis. As with the primary compression, pre-emphasis is applied before recording, so it does not affect the level of tape noise. During playback, the same high-frequency range is cut by an equivalent amount in a process called de-emphasis. This brings the high end of the signal back to its original level and reduces the high-frequency tape hiss at the same time.

If you play an encoded recording without decoding, the results will vary depending on the system. Some systems, such as Dolby B and C, are designed to produce encoded signals that can be played without decoding. Others are simply intolera-

ble; with encoded dbx that hasn't been decoded, for example, you are likely to hear a lot of noise. In both cases, the dynamic range will usually sound "squashed"; pianissimo passages will sound mezzo-forte. If pre-emphasis is applied, the undecoded signal will sound very bright.

dbx and Dolby

One of the most popular forms of noise reduction in semipro multitrack recorders, dbx compresses low-level signals equally across the entire frequency spectrum. However, this can cause a new problem. If the input signal includes only a limited range of frequencies but it is above the threshold level, compansion is not applied. The signal masks part of the tape noise but not necessarily all of it. As a result, the noise level can appear to fluctuate with the signal level, producing a side effect called breathing or noise modulation. This is not a problem if most of your music encompasses a full range of frequencies and does not exhibit a wide dynamic range.

Another common problem with companding is gain mistracking, which occurs if your tape deck is not properly calibrated, causing an uneven frequency response. If tape-deck miscalibration lowers the response at certain frequencies and the decoder then lowers those frequencies further, an unpleasant pumping effect results.

There are two types of dbx noise reduction: Type I and Type II. Type I is designed for full-frequency formats, such as open-reel tape, whereas Type II is intended for limited-frequency formats, such as cassette. Both types reduce the noise floor by about 30 dB. For the most part, Type II dbx is incorporated into cassette decks, although both types are available in outboard units (see Fig. 21-2).

Figure 21-2. The dbx 140X provides two channels of dbx Type II noise reduction in a half-rack unit.

Dolby noise reduction also uses companding, but it isn't applied equally to all frequencies. Instead, it compands different frequency bands independently according to the level within each band. This reduces the effect of noise modulation dramatically by companding only the low-level frequencies. The idea is that the program material will mask the remaining noise. However, the noise floor is lowered less than with dbx.

Dolby A was the first successful, commercially available companding system, and it was used primarily in professional situations. It operates in four fixed frequency bands: below 80 Hz, 80 Hz to 3 kHz, 3 to 9 kHz, and above 9 kHz. Overall, Dolby A reduces the noise floor by about 10 dB below 9 kHz and by about 15 dB above 9 kHz.

In 1986, Dolby Labs introduced another professional compansion scheme called Spectral Recording (SR), which utilizes five fixed bands and five "sliding" bands. Some of the fixed bands operate in the same frequency range but over different level ranges. The five sliding bands automatically adjust their center frequencies according to the input signal, dropping the noise floor by about 25 dB.

In the consumer electronics market, Dolby B is used in millions of cassette decks. It reduces tape hiss by about 10 dB. It uses a single sliding band that starts at 500 Hz, and it achieves maximum noise reduction from 1,500 Hz to 20 kHz. Its successor, Dolby C, uses two sliding bands that start at about 125 Hz, and it provides maximum reduction from 375 Hz on up to lower the noise floor by about 20 dB. In both cases, the processing bands slide up and down to center on the most appropriate frequency.

Dolby S is a consumer version of SR that was designed specifically for cassettes. It uses three fixed bands and two sliding bands to lower the midrange and high-frequency noise floor by about 24 dB and the low-frequency floor by about 10 dB.

Dolby B and C are available in many consumer cassette decks and semipro recorders, and Dolby S is now being incorporated into cassette decks and semipro multitracks. Dolby A and SR are available in the form of stand-alone units or circuit cards that plug into certain professional multitrack recorders.

Single-Ended NR

Unlike companding systems, single-ended noise reduction requires no encoding or decoding; it processes the entire signal in one pass. As a result, single-ended systems reduce source noise. These units are generally applied to sound sources, such as microphones, guitars, and synths. They are also applied to the main L/R signal during mixdown, especially if compansion was not used during recording. In this case, tape noise is reduced because it behaves like source noise from the multitrack.

Virtually all single-ended systems use one of two techniques to reduce source noise: dynamic filtering or downward expansion. In dynamic filtering, a variable filter is applied during quiet passages; the center frequency of the filter depends on the frequency content of the program material. This works well with

noise that changes with the level of the signal, such as noisy synth patches. However, this process can produce pumping and breathing effects.

BBE's 362 NR (see Fig. 21-3) combines a dynamic-filter noise-reduction circuit and the company's Sonic Maximizer technology (see Chapter 19). Although dbx is well known for companding noise reduction, the company also makes a single-ended dynamic-filter unit, the 929, which is installed in a card cage with other devices in the 900 series.

Figure 21-3. The BBE 362 NR combines single-ended, dynamic-filter noise reduction with the company's Sonic Maximizer technology.

Downward expanders work like the decoding stage of a companding system, reducing the level of any signal that drops below the threshold (which presumably includes any low-level source noise). This is most effective with ambient noise and relatively constant noise, such as the buzz from a guitar amp. If the unit is not carefully configured, however, this can do some annoying things, like cutting off the reverb tail or other low-level, intended signals.

The Roland SN-550 (see Fig. 21-4) applies downward expansion to five frequency bands independently, each with its own parameter settings, which helps alleviate this problem. It also includes a hum-cancellation circuit that reduces 60 Hz hum and other induced noise from computer monitors, light dimmers, etc.

Figure 21-4. Roland's SN-550 applies downward expansion to five frequency bands independently and includes hum cancellation.

Some noise-reduction systems incorporate both techniques. Rocktron makes several such products. For example, the Hush Elite combines two bands of dynamic filtering with a downward expander for each stereo channel. The Pro Hush includes one band of dynamic filtering and one band of downward expansion for each stereo channel with programmable parameters and MIDI control; the Hush IICX offers one band of dynamic filtering and one band of downward expansion for each stereo channel. The company even makes a Hush Pedal for guitarists that includes one band of filtering and one band of expansion with two sets of controls.

Noise is a fact of life in any audio system. With careful planning, you can eliminate much of it, but there will always be some residual noise to deal with. Noise reduction can help wipe out any remaining gremlins and allow your music to shine through in all its pristine glory.

3-D PROCESSING

The holodecks in the 24th-century universe of *Star Trek* represent the ultimate simulation. Within the black-and-yellow confines of a relatively small room, the computer re-creates any environment you care to program. The boundaries of this environment can appear to extend far beyond the walls of the room via holographic projection.

Although holodecks are currently restricted to the realm of fiction, it is possible to experience some of their magic in the audio domain with the help of 3-D audio processors. These devices improve conventional stereo playback by extending the apparent soundstage (the area from which the sounds seem to come) beyond the physical location of the two speakers. Many of these processors can also affect each individual source of sound (instrument, voice, etc.) in the recording, making it appear to emanate from a specific point around the listener.

Natural Localization

Before we look at these processors, we must understand how humans determine the direction and distance from which a sound is coming; this is called localization. There are four basic aural cues that help the brain localize a sound source: amplitude, timing, timbre, and ambience.

The effect of amplitude on localization is easy to see. Sounds from nearby sources are louder than those from sources that are farther away. In addition, if a sound comes from the right, it is louder in the right ear. Timing is also straightforward: If a sound comes from the left, it reaches the left ear first. This delay can be as short as a few microseconds, which

amounts to a phase shift from one ear to the other.

The effect of timbre on localization is not so simple. For one thing, low frequencies travel farther than high frequencies. This is why elephants can communicate over great distances using subsonic vocalizations. As a result of this effect, distant sounds appear to be rolled off in the high end. In addition, as a sound reaches you, it is diffracted, reflected, and absorbed by your head and shoulders, which affects the timbre. As the sound enters your ears, it is affected by the acoustical properties of the pinnae (the large outer ear flaps) and the ear canal that leads to the ear drum. The exact timbral effect depends on the direction from which the sound comes.

Whenever a sound is made in a reverberant environment, you hear both direct and reflected sound waves. Assuming there are no intervening reflective surfaces, the closer you are to the source, the higher the proportion of direct sound to reflected sound you hear. The arrival times of the reflections depend on the position of the sound source, which provides additional localization cues.

Simulated Localization

Unfortunately, the recording and playback process distorts or removes many of these subtle localization cues. Microphones do not respond to sounds from different directions in the same way ears do; they have no head or pinna to affect the sound. In addition, stereo speakers do not reproduce the effect of localized sounds very well, especially outside the physical location of the speakers. You'd need many speakers arrayed around the listener to achieve this effect.

As a result, many companies have undertaken extensive research to determine exactly how we localize sound. They have then used this research to develop various ways to simulate localization by applying digital signal processing (DSP) to a stereo signal. The result is a number of products for the recording engineer and end user.

Although these products are commonly called 3-D audio processors, this is a bit of a misnomer. They can simulate an expanded soundstage from right to left rather effectively, but it is extremely difficult to simulate up-down placement with a single pair of speakers. Nevertheless, 3-D processors can be useful in a number of situations, including musical recordings, video and film soundtracks, multimedia, and computer games.

Most 3-D audio systems describe the position of a sound source in terms of distance, azimuth, and elevation. Azimuth is expressed in angular degrees around the listener's head. An azimuth of 0° is directly in front of the listener, whereas 180° is directly behind. It is very difficult to simulate a sound source behind the listener with stereo playback, so most two-speaker systems expand the soundstage to encompass an arc of 180° around the front of the listener.

As you might expect, elevation is expressed in degrees above the listener. An elevation of 0° is directly ahead of the listener, while 90° is directly overhead. In some cases, you can specify a sound source's static position or program a moving source's trajectory and speed. However, few 3-D processors can effectively simulate elevated sound sources with stereo playback.

Simulating amplitude cues is easy: simply make the sound louder in one channel. Timing cues are also relatively easy to simulate: delay each sound by different, minute amounts in each speaker. As mentioned earlier, this delay is so short that it is often accomplished by phase shifting.

Timbre cues are more difficult to simulate. Researchers have developed mathematical models of the timbral effect of the head, shoulders, and pinnae, which are called head-related transfer functions (HRTFs). These HRTFs are implemented with powerful DSP. Equalization also plays an important role, especially dynamic EQ, which changes according to the input signal.

All speaker-based systems suffer from the same problem: The sounds from the speakers are acoustically combined in the air between the speakers and the listener. In addition to hearing each speaker's sound in the appropriate ear (right speaker in the right ear, left speaker in the left ear), you also hear the right speaker's sound in the left ear and vice versa. This makes it even more difficult to simulate localization effectively.

One solution to this problem is to use headphones, which isolate the left and right channels from each other. An effective technique in this regard is called binaural recording. Tiny microphones are mounted in anatomically accurate ear models on a dummy head, which is placed in the vicinity of a sound source (e.g., in the audience at a concert). The signals from the mics are affected by the shape of the dummy head and pinnae as they are routed directly to the right and left tracks of a stereo recorder. Then, these tracks are played back on headphones without interacting in any way. The HRTF effects of the dummy head are captured automatically, providing a convincing soundstage. However, wearing headphones all the time is impractical, so the search for speaker-based 3-D audio continues.

Two-Speaker Systems

As mentioned earlier, most 3-D audio processors use standard stereo playback with two speakers. In addition, virtually all of these systems are single-ended,

which means they are applied only at one end of the recording/playback chain. Most are applied to a mixed stereo signal as it is mastered for duplication, but in some cases you can apply 3-D processing to several individual sounds as they are mixed. Finally, there are several systems that are applied to a conventional stereo signal during playback.

One of the major players in this field is Roland. The Roland Sound Space (RSS) system is one of the few that claims to simulate full spherical localization, including right-left, up-down, and front-back. Introduced in 1991, its first incarnation was an expensive processor available only to the top of the recording profession. Since then, it has been repackaged in a less-expensive, single-rackspace unit, the RSS-10 (see Fig. 21-5), with control software for Windows or the Macintosh. The RSS process is also available in several other Roland effects processors. The process is designed to be applied during mixdown and requires no decoding during playback.

Figure 21-5. Roland's RSS-10 system includes hardware and software to process stereo signals.

The RSS-10 accepts two input signals (left and right) and sends each one through two processors. The Binaural Processors apply the HRTF that corresponds to the desired position of the sound source. This includes amplitude, timing, and timbre adjustments. The Transaural Processors cancel the crosstalk signals (i.e., right speaker to left ear and vice versa). The effect is most pronounced if the listener is centered between the two speakers at the "sweet spot."

Hughes took a different approach when they developed the Sound Retrieval System (SRS) to enhance in-flight audio. They eventually offered a consumer-oriented box that enhanced the soundstage during playback of conventional stereo signals. Since then, a separate company called SRS Labs was started to develop the technology and license it to third-party manufacturers. (SRS is now found in TVs and other consumer-electronics products from Sony,

RCA, and Packard Bell.) Multimedia companies such as MediaVision, NuReality, and Genoa Systems license SRS for use in sound cards, games, and other products.

The basic idea behind SRS is to restore the localization cues that are lost in the recording and playback process. SRS separates the sum (L+R) and difference (L-R and R-L) components of the stereo signal and applies corrective transfer functions, called selective emphasis and de-emphasis, to each component. This restores the ambience that is otherwise masked by louder direct sounds. In addition, it widens the soundstage while localizing individual sounds. SRS can also synthesize a stereo signal from a mono input. The company claims there is no sweet spot, unlike many other systems.

Spatializer Audio Laboratories' Spatializer is a single-ended 3-D processor that can be used at either end of the audio chain (during recording or playback). The process affects the difference signals by boosting the frequencies that provide the most important spatial cues (300 to 3,000 Hz). The difference signals are also slightly delayed to produce a sense of spaciousness.

The Spatializer is available in several forms. The original unit accepts up to eight signals (expandable to 24), each of which can be placed and moved around in the expanded soundstage. The Digital Spatializer accepts a stereo input and produces a stereo output. There is also a chip that manufacturers can include in their products. Licensees include Matsushista (Panasonic), Sharp, Hitachi, AdLib, and Orchid.

QSound is a single-ended, 3-D process that is normally applied during the recording/mixing stage. QSound was first available only in the QSystem, an expensive unit that processes up to eight inputs using HRTFs derived from over a half-million listening tests. Many artists, such as Sting, Madonna, and Pink Floyd, have applied QSound to their recordings. In addition, several TV soundtracks, such as *Picket Fences, Wonder Years,* and *X-Files,* use the process. Multimedia and computer licensees include Atari, Sega, Analog Devices, IBM, and Intel.

QSound Labs now offers several products in addition to the QSystem. For example, QXpander is a stereo process based on the QSystem's algorithm. This stereo process is available in several forms, including a family of chips that should find their way into inexpensive hardware products. The company also offers several software plug-ins for the Microsoft DirectX and Digidesign TDM formats (see Fig. 21-6).

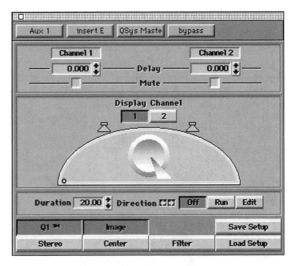

Figure 21-6. QSound's *QSys/TDM* plug-in lets you position a sound source within a 180° soundstage. In this example, the source is in the extreme left corner of the soundstage.

Crystal River Engineering also offers 3-D processing in both hardware and software products. Their approach is called AudioReality, which refers to an HRTF-based, real-time, immersive, 3-D audio rendering technology that localizes each sound independently as it is mixed. The company's first product was the Convolvotron, a PC-based system developed in conjunction with NASA/Ames Research Center for flight simulators and other virtual-reality applications. Since then, they have created the Acoustetron II stand-alone system, the Beachtron and Alphatron PC cards, and a Digidesign Pro Tools plug-in called *Protron* (see Fig. 21-7).

Multispeaker Systems

In the end, it's very difficult to coax clear localization out of two speakers. As a result, the film industry converged on multispeaker setups for commercial cinemas and, later, for home-theater systems. This approach doesn't require HRTFs or other complex sonic manipulations, but it is not single-ended. The signals destined for each speaker must be encoded during mastering and decoded during playback.

Dolby Laboratories is the most prominent name in this field. The Dolby Surround Pro Logic system is designed for soundtrack applications. The process encodes two extra channels—center and surround—in the main stereo program. Dolby doesn't sell the encoder; you must lease it when you mix.

However, the decoder is widely available in consumer receivers, TVs, and surround processors. This decoder extracts the center and surround signals and sends all four channels to the appropriate speakers: front left and right, center, and rear left and right. (Both rear speakers get the same surround signal, which is rolled off below 100 Hz and above 7 kHz.) If the program is played on a conventional stereo system, it sounds normal.

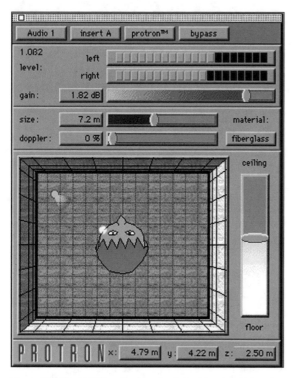

Figure 21-7. Crystal River Engineering's *Protron* plug-in lets you specify the position of a sound source in three dimensions.

The next generation of the company's multichannel audio is called Dolby Digital. In this scheme, all five speakers receive their own independent, full-bandwidth signal. There is also a separate, low-frequency effects (LFE) channel; as a result, this is sometimes called a 5.1-channel format. These audio channels are digital, not analog. However, the audio is compressed to reduce storage and transmission requirements, a process to which some purists object.

RSP is another company that offers a multi-speaker surround system. Called Circle Surround, this system is designed specifically for musical applications. The system includes an encoder (which you can buy), a controller with four joysticks, DOS-based control and automation software, and a decoder. Four separate inputs are encoded into a stereo signal, which is then decoded into as many as eight discrete, full-bandwidth channels. The company claims that Circle Surround is fully compatible with Dolby Pro Logic decoders. In addition, the decoder can synthesize center and surround channels from any conventional stereo signal.

Although holodecks are a supercool idea, they remain beyond our current technical capabilities. However, it is possible to simulate various aural expe-

riences from the comfort of your favorite chair with 3-D audio processors. These systems take one small step for their manufacturers and one giant leap beyond the aging stereo format without rendering it obsolete, offering a new dimension that should open a lot of ears to new possibilities.

Part 6

Tips, Tricks, and Tidbits

Chapter 22: Recording Technique
Tracking
Mixdown
Premastering

Chapter 23: Manufacturer Mumbo Jumbo
Alphanumeric Soup
Tower of TechnoBabel

Recording Technique

The process of recording an album or other body of musical work involves four distinct stages: tracking, mixing, premastering, and mastering. Each stage includes a number of steps. Tracking means recording the basic parts (rhythm section), vocals, lead instruments, sound effects, etc. Mixing is more than simply adjusting faders; you need to think about effects and other studio tools, such as EQ and compression. In addition, you must think about preparing your mixed tunes for mastering (which, as you might expect, is called premastering). Last, and certainly not least, comes mastering, the process of preparing the final tape that will be used to press CDs or other media for distribution.

Of these stages, you have control over the first three; mastering is typically done at a mastering house by a professional mastering engineer, especially if the end product is to be a professionally replicated CD. This chapter presents some basic tips and techniques to help in the tracking, mixing, and premastering stages. Throughout this chapter, I generally refer to multitrack tape decks (see Chapter 14), although the information applies to multitrack hard-disk recorders, as well (see Chapter 10).

TRACKING

Just about every musician dreams of being immortalized on tape. Luckily, you don't need a genie to make this wish come true. Live performers can simply plop two microphones in front of the stage and record a gig onto a cassette or DAT recorder. But while live recordings can capture the excitement of a performance, they also document audience noise, technical glitches, and musical mistakes.

More pristine recordings are usually produced in a studio environment. In the recording studio, audience noise is obviously not a problem (unless you troop around with an entourage of rowdies), and any technical or performance foul-ups can be corrected by re-recording the offending musical part. In addition, recording technology can turn a three-piece band into an entire orchestra. Each musician can double (or triple or quadruple) his or her performance, play different instruments, and add sonic colors and musical counterpoints that would be difficult or impossible to pull off in live performance. The technique that makes this all possible is called overdubbing.

During the overdubbing process, you can listen to one or more tracks of previously recorded material while recording a new part onto a fresh (unused) track. Obviously, the more tracks you have, the more musical parts you can overdub.

Let's say you record a guitar part onto one track of a multitrack deck. If you want to add a vocal, you can listen to your guitar performance through headphones while singing into a microphone to record, or overdub, the vocal on a separate track. The overdubbing process can be repeated to add as many musical parts as there are tracks to do so.

Overdubbing also lets you easily fix mistakes. If your band is recording a song and the bass player hits a wrong note, you don't have to make the whole band play the song over again. If you record each instrument onto its own track, the player can re-record the bass part at his or her leisure, without disturbing the other recorded performances. In essence, each track of the multitrack deck is a separate entity, and what is recorded or re-recorded on track one of an 8-track deck does not effect tracks two through eight.

First Things First

Before you succumb to the common malady of "overdub madness," you must first record a basic foundation tracks from which to build your masterpiece. There is no set rule regarding the order in which a musical project should be recorded. What works for some musicians doesn't always work for others. Typically, though, the rhythm section (drums, bass, rhythm guitar, and/or keyboard) or a click track is recorded first to provide a reference as you overdub other parts. These are called the basic tracks.

Once you have the basic tracks recorded, it's a good idea to overdub a scratch vocal (assuming your music has vocals). A scratch vocal is yet another reference for future overdubs that indicates the melody and (hopefully) where other instruments and vocals fit into the big picture.

After the scratch vocal is down, you can start filling in all the other instruments (strings, oboe, etc.) and background vocals. The final lead vocal is usually saved for the last overdub so the singer can listen to the entire arrangement. (Unless, of course, the singer nailed the performance on the scratch track, rendering futile any attempts at improvement.) Lead instruments, such as guitar and sax, are typically recorded during the final overdub stage for the same reasons.

Hearing the Past

Obviously, overdubbing requires listening to previously recorded tracks. In many situations, you can use headphones to hear (or monitor) what is already on tape. A major benefit of headphones is that they provide some sound isolation. For instance, if you monitor your tracks through your stereo speakers while recording a vocal, the previously recorded track will be picked up by the microphone along with your voice. Not only can this "re-recording" cause an uncomfortable feedback loop, but it can ruin the clarity of your vocal track. (Some professionals record without isolation for artistic or performance-enhancing reasons, but they usually have the technical chops to minimize potential audio problems.) If you are overdubbing instruments that are not miked, such as synths or a bass plugged directly into the mixer, you can use speakers without problems.

Keep in mind that the relative volume level of each recorded track is changeable. Your mixer should allow each track to be played back at volumes that might be louder or softer than the level set during actual recording. This balance of prerecorded tracks is called a monitor mix and makes overdubbing more comfortable because desired reference instruments (or vocals) can be adjusted until they are dominant.

Out of Tracks

Because most home studios are limited to four or eight tracks, you might think that you need to buy another multitrack deck to get all those wonderful ideas of yours on tape. Luckily, there are less-expensive ways to expand your tracking horizons.

Increasing the number of parts you can record involves bouncing. In this process, several recorded tracks are mixed together and re-recorded, or bounced, onto one or two empty tracks. For example, suppose you've recorded drums on track one, bass on track two, and a rhythm guitar on track three of your 4-track deck. To free up more tracks, you can take tracks one, two, and three; mix them together; and record them all onto track four (see Fig. 22-1). This process frees up tracks one, two, and three for additional parts. (Keep in mind that you might lose some audio quality after the bouncing process if you're using analog tape.)

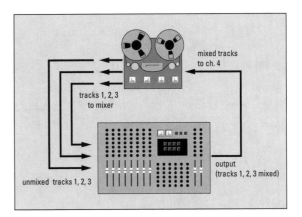

Figure 22-1. In this example of track bouncing, three recorded tracks are mixed and re-recorded onto track four, freeing the other three tracks for additional recording.

After bouncing these tracks, your rhythm track is now mono. (Remember, you bounced three tracks to one.) Also, because you've committed your rhythm tracks to a submix, it is essential that you're happy with the balance of guitar, bass, and drums. Once you erase the three original tracks to make room for more parts, the balance of your mono rhythm track cannot be changed. Ever.

A less-destructive technique for saving tape tracks involves MIDI sequencing. In this process, a computer or a keyboard's built-in MIDI sequencer records all the parts played by electronic instruments. Typically, keyboard sequencers provide eight or sixteen tracks, while software sequencers often offer hundreds of tracks. Because these sequencer tracks are not recorded onto tape, they are often called virtual tracks.

Combining virtual tracks with tape or hard-disk audio tracks requires synchronizing the sequencer to the multitrack so they can play together (see Fig. 22-2). A link between the two formats is established by recording a sync tone on one track of the tape deck. Recording a sync tone reduces your available tape tracks by one, but because you can now access many virtual tracks, the tradeoff is worth it. (For more detail about sequencing and tape synchronization, see Chapter 7.)

Overdubbing Tips

Keep several things in mind while overdubbing. First, record all tracks as "hot" as possible without causing unwanted distortion. The loudest musical passages should send your recording level meters just above the zero mark. (This might not apply to digital multitracks, which tend to distort at any level above zero.) Maximum recording levels can minimize hiss and other nonmusical noises on analog tape.

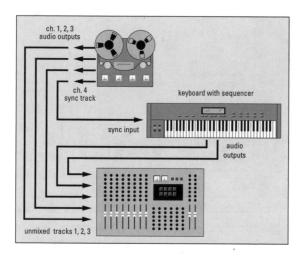

Figure 22-2. When synchronizing a sequencer to a multitrack tape deck, the sync tone on the last track is sent to the sync input of the sequencer (in this case, within an electronic keyboard). The sequencer then starts and stops along with the tape.

It's a good idea to avoid recording overdubs with effects such as reverb or delay, unless you're certain you want to live with the effect forever. (As with the rhythm-track submix, once the effect is recorded to tape, it's there to stay.) Decisions regarding effects are usually saved for the final mixdown, where several options can be auditioned without risking permanent commitment. Also, go easy on the EQ while overdubbing. If you "over-EQ" during the recording process, then decide to re-EQ at the final mixdown, you're risking additional noise. Get in the habit of recording a good sound "flat" (without EQ) by concentrating on mic placement or synth programming.

In addition, keep your bass and drum tracks well separated from the sync-tone track. If a loud instrumental track is recorded next to the sync track, the sequencer might not be able to read the sync tone because the instrumental sounds can bleed over and interfere with the sync track. It's best if you can leave a blank guard track between the sync track and other instrumental tracks, but this is often impossible. If you can't afford a guard track, musical pads and other sustained parts at a steady, moderate volume are the best "neighbors" for your sync tone.

While overdubbing is a great recording technique that adds flexibility to the recording process, it can also cause your music to lose the live-group feel. It's important to look at the big picture, the overall sound of your music. Remember that the overdubbed parts should work together to create seamless music.

If you're recording music in a multitrack environment, hearing the final result on a stereo system is the ultimate goal. As a result, all the parts must be mixed down into a stereo recording. This process is not as well-defined as overdubbing. How an artist or producer conceptualizes a "good" mix depends on the recording's musical style and the personal taste of the decision makers.

Get Ready

Before you start mixing your own material, play commercial recordings of similar music on your studio sound system. Try to get a feel for what professionals do with your type of music. Pay close attention to the relative level of each part, its position in the stereo field, the use of effects, and so on.

Now you must get your studio set up for the mixdown process (see Fig. 22-3). Connect the main stereo outputs from the mixer to the inputs on the stereo mastering deck (typically a cassette or DAT recorder). Set the input selectors on the mixer to "tape" so the channel faders now control the level of the tape tracks. Assign each track to the main stereo output; the pan pots control the apparent position of each track in the stereo field.

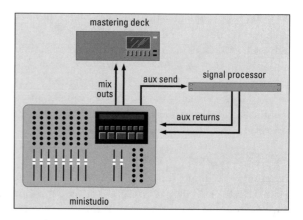

Figure 22-3. The mix outputs from a ministudio are connected to the inputs of a stereo mastering deck. The aux send is connected to the input of an external signal processor, and the outputs from the processor are connected to the aux returns on the ministudio.

Balance Your Image

One of the most important aspects of mixing is the volume, or level, of each instrument. You should be able to hear each instrument clearly in the final mix, although some parts are obviously louder than others. For example, the lead vocal is usually the most important part of a song, so it's usually the loudest element in the mix.

There are several general approaches to setting volume levels. For example, you can start with all faders fully down and raise the master output level to its zero mark. Then, bring the drums up to a level of about -10 VU on the meter and raise the monitor level until the drums are as loud as you like to hear them. Now bring in the bass and other rhythm instruments until they are balanced with the drums. Next come the background parts, followed by any instrumental solos and the lead vocal. Mix all parts relative to the drums.

Another approach begins by bringing the lead vocal to a level of -5 to 0 VU on the meter and raising the monitor level. Then bring in the rhythm instruments, followed by the background parts, and finally the solos. Mix everything relative to the lead vocal.

Another important factor is the position of each part in the stereo field. In commercially recorded tunes, the instruments appear to come from the right, left, or center in varying degrees. This right-left placement of each part adds variety and interest.

The pan pots for each channel on the mixer determine the placement of each track in the stereo field. The pan-pot settings are sometimes specified with a clock metaphor. For example, five o'clock indicates that the pan pot is hard right. A hard right position routes all the signal to the right side and the track is not audible in the left channel. (Obviously, hard left does the opposite.) A setting of one o'clock places the track just to the right of center, and twelve o'clock is dead center (effectively mono).

Here's a specific example in which the tune includes drums, bass, rhythm keyboard, rhythm guitar, background horns, background vocals, lead guitar solo, and lead vocal (see Fig. 22-4). The level of the rhythm section is relatively low, although it's loud enough to drive the track. The drums were recorded in stereo, so the two tracks are panned hard left and right to preserve the original stereo image. (If the drums must be recorded or bounced to mono, they are normally placed in the center along with the bass.) The rhythm keyboard is placed at the ten o'clock position, while the rhythm guitar is placed at two o'clock.

The background vocals and horns are more widely spaced at nine o'clock and three o'clock, respectively. Both parts appear intermittently, which heightens the dimensional effect of the wide spacing. The background vocals are mixed somewhat louder than the horns, because the words should be clearly audible. The guitar solo is just under the level of the lead vocal and placed near the center at eleven o'clock. The lead vocal is the loudest of all and placed at one o'clock.

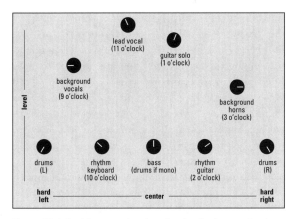

Figure 22-4. In this example of a mix, the rhythm section is at the lowest volume. The background horns and vocals are spaced relatively wide, and the guitar solo and lead vocal are close to the center.

It's important to rehearse the mix many times before you actually record it, especially if the levels of certain instruments change during the song. If this happens, mark the levels with a wax pencil or white tape along the fader's travel on the mixer so you can repeat the correct levels during each pass. In addition, try to mute any tape tracks during long periods of silence to reduce tape hiss. (This can be automated if you are using a MIDI sequencer and a mixer that responds to MIDI messages; see Chapters 7 and 9.) The input levels on the mastering deck should be set so the loudest section of the tune registers about 0 VU on the meters (slightly less if you're using a DAT; the levels should *never* go above 0 VU).

If you decide to fade out the ending of a song, take care to move the master fader downward slowly and smoothly. Slower tunes usually fade out more gradually than fast tunes. In any case, it's often musically pleasing to reach zero volume at the end of a phrase.

EQ and Effects

Each input channel on the mixer includes some EQ, which can range from simple controls for treble and bass to more sophisticated controls for high, high-mid, low-mid, and low frequencies. These controls let you tailor the tone quality of each track by cutting or boosting the selected frequency range. If one track sounds too dull, boost the high end. If another track sounds too tubby, cut the low end. In general, try to cut rather than boost, because boosting frequencies can also add noise.

Effects such as reverb, delay, chorusing, and flanging are generally added during mixdown. Most mixers and ministudios have at least one auxiliary or effects send/return. Typically, there is a master aux control for each aux send that determines the overall level of all signals routed to the processor. A master return control—which is the master volume level for the processed signals—helps determine the proportion of original and processed signals in the final mix.

If the mixer has only one aux send, all tracks selected for processing are sent to the same effect. However, each track can be processed more or less than other tracks according to the level of its individual aux send control. If the mixer has two or more sends, each track can be processed by any or all of the connected processors.

If you use a MIDI sequencer in conjunction with multitrack tape, you must synchronize the sequencer and the tape deck before recording any parts (see Chapter 7). The sequencer then plays the synthesizers directly along with the recorded parts on tape (see Fig. 22-5). As mentioned previously, the sequencer tracks are often called "virtual tracks" because they are not recorded onto the multitrack tape.

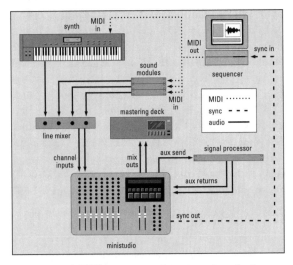

Figure 22-5. A MIDI sequencer plays several synths in sync with the tape tracks. The synths are submixed through a line mixer.

When it's time to mix, the virtual synth tracks are mixed to the master tape along with the parts recorded on the multitrack. Most ministudios don't have enough inputs to accommodate several synths in addition to the tape tracks, which makes it necessary to submix the synths with an external line mixer. A line mixer is simply an external mixer designed to accept line-level instruments such as synths and samplers; line mixers do not have microphone inputs.

The relative levels and pan positions of the virtual synth tracks are established with the line mixer. The stereo output of the line mixer is then sent to two free channels on the main mixer. The channels connected to the line mixer are panned hard left and right to maintain the stereo image (see Fig. 22-5). The input selector on these channels should be set to

"line" rather than "tape." The levels of these two channels affect all the synth parts together and should be adjusted to blend properly with the tape tracks.

In the Can

Mixing is a dynamic process that often requires many passes before you get it right. Be sure to listen periodically at a very low volume to make sure you can hear everything. Once the mix is finished, wait a few days and then play a copy on a home or car stereo to listen under "normal" conditions. If you notice that your mix does not sound clear or punchy in these environments, it's probably an indication that you should try remixing the song.

Always strive for a clean, clear sound in which all parts are audible without getting into each other's way. The key to a good mix is experimentation, so don't be afraid to try different things. You're bound to find your own unique "sound" in the process, which can only help you realize the potential of your music.

PREMASTERING

One of the many things you must keep in mind while mixing is the end product: the CDs or cassettes that will be sold to untold millions of fans. The process that takes your music from mixdown to duplicated CDs or cassettes is called mastering, and it behooves all engineers to understand this process as they mix.

Masters of the Universe

Mastering has two goals. The first is to make your music sound as good as possible before it is duplicated. This includes making it sound like a smoothly flowing whole, rather than a disjointed series of disparate tunes. Listeners shouldn't have to adjust the volume and tone controls on their stereos from one tune to the next. The second goal is to put the entire program in the correct format for duplication in the selected medium.

The entire process goes something like this. First, you mix the recorded tracks and sequenced parts (virtual tracks) to a 2-track format, usually DAT or open-reel analog. (For fidelity reasons, you should avoid mixing to cassette if possible.) The product of this step is sometimes called the premaster.

You don't necessarily have to mix the tunes in the order you intend for the final product. The order in which they are mixed depends on many factors, including which tunes are ready for mixing, what mood you're in that day, and so on. So the second step of the mastering process is putting the mixed tunes in the desired order and separating them with the desired length of silence. This step is called the sequence and assembly phase of mastering, and it results in the project master. The entire process of going from the main mix to the project master is known as premastering.

Next, you send the project master to a mastering studio, where a mastering engineer may perform additional processing (such as EQ) to prepare the project for CD replication, after which he or she transfers the project master to what is called the master. A copy of the master is sent to you for approval, after which the master is transferred to a production master, which is used to duplicate the project to the selected medium. (If you're lucky enough to live in a major metropolitan area with a local mastering house, you can take your project master to the engineer in person, listen to it together, and discuss what the engineer might do before creating the master.)

Mixdown

As you mix your tunes, there are a few things you should keep in mind. First, strive for consistency between selections; you generally don't want a wildly different balance of instruments or different peak levels from one tune to another. One way to accomplish this is to mix each selection with respect to a common reference tone. At the beginning of each mixing session, record a 1 kHz sine wave from a tone generator, synth, or reference CD at 0 VU for 30 to 45 seconds at the beginning of the tape. This will help you maintain a consistent overall level from one tune to the next.

(Time out for a quick, shameless, self-promoting plug. The *Mix Reference Disc, Deluxe Edition* contains a wide variety of quality test tones designed for checking levels, diagnostics, and calibrating equipment. It's available for $39.95 from Mix Bookshelf; [800] 233-9604.)

If your selections have individual problems, try to fix them in the mix instead of taking them to the mastering engineer. For example, if the vocals are overly sibilant, use a de-esser on those tracks during mixdown (see Chapter 20). A good mastering engineer can help fix such problems, but it is far easier to fix them during mixdown.

In particular, avoid problems that require opposite solutions in the same frequency range. For example, suppose you have a dull snare and a harsh, sibilant vocal occurring simultaneously. If the mastering engineer tries to fix the snare by applying EQ to the entire mix, it will make the vocal problem worse. This is much more easily solved by equalizing the tracks separately during mixdown.

Although it might seem too obvious to mention, avoid distortion. The mastering engineer can't do much about it other than cut the frequency at which it is the most prominent. After you mix some tunes, listen to them in several different environments

(home stereo, car, etc.). Consider remixing if the sound isn't good in those environments.

If you mix to DAT, use a sample rate of 44.1 kHz. This is the rate used on CDs, so you avoid unnecessary sample-rate conversion if you are aiming for that medium. Besides, the improved fidelity of 48 kHz is not generally noticeable. However, if you already have some selections mixed at 48 kHz, stick with it. It's better to have a consistent sample rate than different tunes at different rates.

Finally, document everything, including all settings on the mixer, synths, and outboard processors. This becomes critical if you ever have to go back and remix.

Processing

Following the generally accepted rules of recording, you should apply as little processing as possible to individual tracks as they are recorded. In most cases, it is better to process tracks as you mix; this lets you try again if something goes wrong. Typically, effects such as reverb, delay, chorusing, and flanging are applied to each track via the mixer's aux sends.

However, there are several effects that can be applied to the entire mix. To accomplish this, route the main stereo signal to the desired processors and back into the mixer for final level control via the main-bus insert points (see Fig. 22-6). From the insert return, the signal flows to the main mix outputs and on to the 2-track mixdown deck.

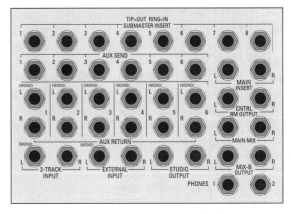

Figure 22-6. The ¼-inch jacks in the master section of a Mackie 8•Bus mixer include insert points for the submaster (top) and main (upper right) buses. Inside these jacks, the tip connector sends the signal out of the mixer and the ring connector accepts the signal returning from one or more external processors.

Many mastering engineers complain that project masters often include an overly wide dynamic range with large peaks. Some engineers recommend keeping the peaks no more than 10 dB above the average level of the rest of the program. Of course, the mastering engineer can apply a bit of compression to the entire mix, but so can you (see Chapter 20). Try a compression ratio of 2:1 and vary the threshold until you hear the best results.

Compression also adds "punch" to your mix, tightening the bass and making the whole sound meatier. However, it also tends to color the sound, which some people like, depending on the type of music. Compression is particularly important when mixing for radio airplay, because radio stations compress everything as it is broadcast.

If you are mixing to DAT, you must not exceed the DAT's "digital zero" level. If you exceed this level, the signal will be digitally clipped, resulting in audible, nasty distortion. (Note that this level is not necessarily equivalent to 0 VU on the DAT's meter. As mentioned earlier, some manufacturers set 0 VU to be less than digital zero so you can record above the 0 VU level as you would on an analog deck and still avoid clipping.) Using a limiter prevents the signal from going beyond the preset level.

Mastering engineers use EQ to improve the sound of the project master. You can try this technique by inserting a stereo graphic or parametric equalizer into the main bus. However, using less than the best EQ with limited knowledge and experience might cause more problems than it solves.

If a particular track needs tonal help beyond the capability of the mixer's channel EQ, try connecting an outboard equalizer to that channel's insert point. For example, a vocal track might be buried even though its fader is all the way up. Selectively boosting certain frequencies in the 4 to 7 kHz range can greatly enhance the vocal's intelligibility. In addition, an inserted EQ can be bypassed without changing its settings, unlike the EQ in some mixers.

An increasing number of mixing engineers insert a 3-D processor into the main stereo signal path during mixdown (see Chapter 21). This can also be done at later stages of the entire mastering process, instead. Spectral enhancers are more common (see Chapter 19). These devices are particularly useful for commercials and other promotional material that must reach out and grab the listener.

Finally, many mixing engineers insert a single-ended noise-reduction unit at the end of the stereo signal path (see Chapter 21). Double-ended processes, such as Dolby and dbx, require a decoder during playback; single-ended designs, such as a downward expander or dynamic filter, require no decoding at playback, making them ideal for reducing noise in your premaster. However, they must be used with care to avoid unpleasant audible side-effects. Be sure to place noise reduction at the end of the chain so it reduces noise from all other devices. Devices such as the dbx 296 incorporate spectral enhancement with single-ended noise reduction.

Of course, few engineers insert all the processors mentioned here into the main signal path (see Fig. 22-7). Each device in the signal chain adds noise and degrades the signal quality to one degree or another. Most engineers recommend that you insert only those devices that are absolutely essential. In general, I suggest a compressor followed by a spectral enhancer and a single-ended noise reduction unit. However, some would legitimately argue that if you have your dynamics and electrical noise under control in the first place, you don't need any inserted processing during mixdown.

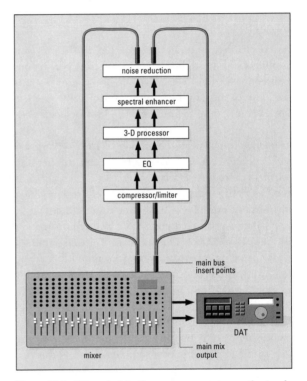

Figure 22-7. Although this diagram goes way over the top in terms of total processing, it illustrates how different processors are connected to the main bus insert points. After returning from the processors, the signal proceeds to the main outputs and on to a DAT or other 2-track medium.

Sequencing and Assembly

Once your premaster is done, it's time to sequence and assemble the tunes onto the project master. This can be done in your studio or the mastering studio. Traditionally, the selections on an open-reel analog premaster are physically cut apart, arranged in the desired order, and spliced together with leader tape, which separates the tunes by the desired amount of time.

Unfortunately, physical splicing is impractical with a DAT premaster. You can digitally transfer the tunes one at a time from one DAT to another, but this can be tricky. Unless you use a DAT machine with assembly-editing or insert-editing capabilities, the subcode data is broken wherever recording is stopped and started, which looks like an error to the DAT machine during playback. Depending on the playback machine, this can result in noise or momentary muting. Even if it sounds fine on your machine, it might not on a different machine during mastering.

If you attempt this procedure, make sure to allow a couple of seconds between putting the machine in Record and starting each selection. After you have finished sequencing and assembling the selections, make a continuous digital transfer of the tape to another DAT, listening carefully for any problems during or between selections. Use the continuous copy as the final project master, keeping the original assembled tape as a backup.

Better still, digitally dump each premaster selection into a computer-based hard-disk recorder and do the sequencing and assembly there. Depending on the system's capabilities, you can normalize the selections' gain to assure consistent levels, and you can apply compression, EQ, soundstage enhancement, spectral enhancement, and noise reduction. You can also specify the fades in and out of each selection. If you have enough hard-disk storage, you can sequence and assemble the entire project within the system and digitally transfer it to DAT in one pass. Otherwise, you must prepare the selections and transfer them to the project-master DAT one at a time.

Leave the first 30 to 60 seconds of the final project-master DAT blank because this is where any tape damage is likely to occur. Following this blank space, record 30 to 45 seconds of a 1 kHz reference tone at 0 VU. (For analog project masters, record reference tones at 100 Hz, 1 kHz, and 10 kHz for high- and low-frequency bias adjustments.) Follow the reference tone with 30 to 45 seconds of silence as a courtesy to the mastering engineer, who might need the time to complete the adjustments.

The selections on the project master should be indexed with sequential start IDs: Number 1 should be the first tune, not the reference tone. If extra IDs were recorded in the sequencing and assembly process, erase them and renumber the remaining IDs.

Finally, prepare detailed documentation of the project master. This should include the length of blank space at the beginning, location and length of reference tones, locations and titles of the selections, individual and cumulative timings, and maximum level readings.

To the Mastering Studio

Now you are ready to send or take your project master to a mastering studio. If you can't visit the studio in person, you might talk with the engineer on the phone to discuss what he or she is planning to do. In this case, you should receive an approval copy of the master before the final production master is made.

If you can visit the studio in person, consider taking your DAT machine with you. Even though DAT is a standard format, discrepancies exist between different machines, particularly professional and consumer decks, which can lead to interchange problems. Listen to the project master with the mastering engineer and discuss what can be done to improve the sound, such as EQ or spectral enhancement. Then let the engineer take over and prepare your project for duplication. Soon, you will have hundreds or thousands of copies of your work, which should make you feel pretty good. Then all that is left for you to do is to sell them.

CHAPTER 23

Manufacturer Mumbo Jumbo

I've always found it amusing to ponder the meaning of product model numbers, so I wrote a humorous (but accurate) article about it for the April 1993 issue of *EM*. A related (and extremely frustrating) topic is the use of different terminology by various manufacturers to describe essentially the same thing for marketing purposes. I try to sort out some of these terms in the second section of this chapter.

ALPHANUMERIC SOUP

Have you ever wondered how electronic-music gear manufacturers come up with model numbers? Sure, some seem clear enough, but others are straight out of left field. Perhaps those letters and numbers don't mean anything, and the manufacturers are just trying to drive us crazy.

And why are products identified with letters and numbers instead of regular names we have some chance of remembering? Some generational products simply add letters and numbers to an already cryptic moniker, and others sport a completely new name altogether. You can't even tell the players anymore without a score card. It's time to unravel the name puzzle.

What's in a Name?
Clearance presents a big problem. Names like Spatializer or Eliminator are easy to remember, but companies that have used a particular name for a product often register trademarks for the name and take a dim view of seeing it on something else. After all, they don't want potential customers to buy a super-soaker water gun called The Eliminator after seeing an ad for a synthesizer of the same name.

The clearance problem is bad enough in the U.S., where it prohibits similar products from using the same name. In Japan, however, the law applies to *all* products. When Korg was trying to come up with a name for the 01/W, they considered the name Genesis. But the Japanese clearance search was so frustrating that Korg gave up on using a real name and opted to use letters and numbers.

Real names were more common in the early days. Remember the Moogs (Mini, Poly, and Memory)? Lovely family. There are even a few instruments that use real names today, such as E-mu's Emulator, Proteus, and Vintage Keys; Korg Wavestation; and Waldorf MicroWave (Is dinner ready yet?). Some instruments avoid the clearance problem by using made-up or creatively spelled names, such as the Oberheim Xpander and E-mu Emax, Proformance, and Procussion. Another instrument to sport a real name was the Ensoniq Mirage. It began shipping in 1984, but the final clearances for the name in all world markets were not obtained until 1989.

Many people think the Akai EWI is a small, flightless bird from New Zealand.

The story of Roland's J-series of instruments begins over 2,000 years ago. According to Roman mythology, Jupiter was the most powerful god and the ruler of heaven, and Juno was his wife. If you're old enough, you might remember that Roland once used the name Jupiter for their most powerful instruments and Juno for the lower end of the line, following long-standing gender roles. Although these instruments have long since vanished, the legacy of their names lives on in model numbers based on the letter "J."

Sometimes, a model number actually reflects a fundamental aspect of the instrument. Many of Roland's model numbers have followed this idea. For example, the DEP-5 is a Digital Effects Processor with five different effects. Their Synchronization BoXes are designated by the letters SBX. The DM-800 is an 8-track Digital Multitrack hard-disk recorder (although the use of the number 800 instead of 8 is somewhat mysterious). Ensoniq also adopted this concept with the DP/4, which stands for Dynamic Processor with four independent effects processors. (The official product designation is Parallel Processor, but the model number PP/4 wasn't a viable option.)

Manufacturers often use internal code names for new products before they are introduced to the public. Although they generally aren't used outside the company, some find their way into the public eye. Anyone who follows the computer industry won't soon forget the code name IBM used on their first laptop before it was released: Clamshell. Ensoniq has used the names of cities in the Southwest as code names for some of their new products. For example, the TS-10 derives its handle from its internal code name, Tucson.

The Next Generation
The idea of evolution and generations within a product line is mind-boggling. What do they do, breed instruments in the back room? One of the most complex family instrument trees comes from Ensoniq (see Fig. 23-1), which has three major branches: samplers, low-end synths, and high-end synths. The naming conventions in this tree follow two completely different philosophies: names that mean something and names that don't. In general, the samplers have meaningful acronyms, while the synth names might or might not mean something.

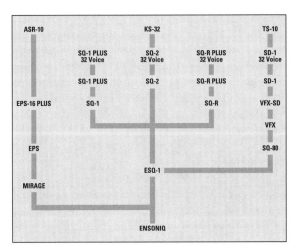

Figure 23-1. Ensoniq's synth and sampler family tree.

The sampler that followed the Mirage was the EPS, which stands for Ensoniq Performance Sampler. The next generation was the EPS-16 Plus, so called because it used 16-bit resolution and included a

bunch of other new features. In the next generation, Ensoniq decided to change the family name to ASR-10, which maintains the tradition of meaningful acronyms. ASR stands for Advanced Sampling Recorder, while the number was selected because it's nice and round. However, people began to ascribe meaning to the number after the fact; the instrument was made during Ensoniq's tenth-year anniversary, the onboard sequencer has eight tracks in addition to two audio inputs for processing external signals, and so on. Ensoniq representatives just smile and say, "Yep, that's what the number means, all right." With the ASR-88, the number indicates that the instrument sports an 88-key, weighted keyboard.

Roland named its Jupiter and Juno analog synths, including the Jupiter-8 shown here, after the Roman pantheon's first family.

The low-end synth line started with the ESQ-1. The letters ostensibly denote the fact that this Ensoniq instrument included a Synthesizer and seQuencer. Yamaha had already begun to associate the letter Q with sequencers in their QX line of hardware MIDI recorders, and Ensoniq decided to maintain that convention. Coincidentally, ESQ evokes the company name quite well.

The ESQ-1 evolved into a higher-end instrument called the SQ-80 (synth and sequencer; no meaning in the number), which led to the VFX (cool combination of letters, absolutely no meaning). This high-end branch of the tree grew to include the VFX[SD], which indicated the addition of a sequencer and disk drive. Apparently, they abandoned the convention of denoting sequencers with the letter Q. Otherwise, the instrument would have been called the VFX[QD], which would have quickly been dubbed the VFX-Cutie throughout the industry. To avoid the trap of ridiculously long model numbers, the next generation was called the SD-1, followed by the SD-1 32 Voice. (It's getting long again.) The following generation established a new family name, TS-10, with a nice, round number.

Meanwhile, the low-end product line was discontinued for a while and then later resurrected with the SQ-1 keyboard and SQ-R rack-mount instruments. The next generation included the SQ-2, SQ-1 Plus, and SQ-R Plus, all of which included improved piano samples among other enhancements. As technology marched inevitably onward, all of these models added the designation "32 Voice" to their already lengthy monikers to indicate their increased polyphony. The next member of this line was called the KS-32, which avoids the tangled web of model numbers while continuing to indicate 32-note polyphony. Perhaps KS stands for keyboard synthesizer, or maybe the code name for the instrument was Kansas City.

I've always wondered how the Korg 01/W got its name; most electronic music products start with letters followed by the numbers. It turns out that the model number M10 was one of the top candidates for the new instrument. This makes sense, considering it represented the next generation of M1 technology. But there was dissension among the ranks; not everyone liked the idea. In a flash of creative insight, the founder of Korg, Tsutomu Katoh, turned the model number upside down, and the 01/W was christened.

The evolution of the Yamaha DX7 also can be traced by the numbers. Unfortunately, Yamaha seems to avoid spaces and hyphens like the plague, sometimes resulting in model numbers like DX7IIFD (translation: second-generation DX7 with a floppy disk drive). The low end of the second generation was the DX7s, making it impossible for journalists to write about the instrument in the plural. ("There were seven DX7s on stage.") The second generation of the Kawai K1 is called the K1II, which creates all kinds of confusion, especially if the font exhibits little difference between "1" and "I."

Model Number Derby

Regardless of their meaning (or lack thereof), some letters and numbers are used more often than others. I'd wager that X is the most common letter. What's so special about X? I suppose it suggests power, mystery, and adventure (Malcolm X; X marks the spot). Consider Yamaha's long line of products with model numbers that begin with DX, KX, QX, RX, and TX, not to mention Roland's JX models, Ensoniq's VFX, Korg's Wavestation EX and 01/W Pro-X, and Peavey's PCX 6. Unused X-based model numbers are becoming scarcer than hen's teeth!

Apparently in response to this trend, Casio decided to use the letter Z as the primary letter for their pro products. This included the AZ-1 strap-on keyboard controller, CZ and VZ synths, DZ MIDI drum kits, FZ samplers, and RZ sampling drum machines. Meanwhile, Yamaha moved on to the letter Y, with model numbers that started with SY, RY, and QY.

What about numbers? Unless they're related to

a specific aspect of the product, most numbers are multiples of 10, 100, or 1,000. Why is this? Perhaps these numbers convey a greater sense of importance. People place greater emphasis on decade birthdays, and just wait till you see the parties on Dec. 31, 1999 (and the hangovers on Jan. 1, 2000).

Interestingly, Yamaha has a long history of using odd numbers; many of their newer numbers are odd multiples of eleven and five. Why has Yamaha consistently bucked the trend of numbers ending in zero? Could it be that they are counting on the psychologically dynamic quality of odd numbers?

The family lineage of the Yamaha DX7IIFD is clear enough, but the model number is among the longest without a space or hyphen.

My favorite model numbers form interesting words. Of course, there's the Akai EWI; many people think I'm talking about a flightless bird from New Zealand or small, furry creatures dancing in their treehouses on a distant planet after the Empire's Death Star was destroyed by rebel forces. Korg's SQD-1 sequencer always gives me a chuckle. How can you find the disk drive amongst all those tentacles? Mr. Potato Head loves banging on the Roland SPD-8 percussion controller, and Peavey's CH8FD keyboard controller requires application of a topical ointment to reduce chafing. This model number would make the perfect license plate for a keyboard-playing dermatologist.

Outta Here

In general, I'm sure manufacturers try to come up with model numbers that mean something germane to the products whenever possible. Otherwise, they try to use something that is memorable, looks nice, and speaks well. Ultimately, products succeed or fail based on what they are and how well they work, not what they're called. But the importance of model numbers and names must not be underestimated. After all, where would we be without the Aphex Aural Exciter Type C^2 with Big Bottom?

Most people are probably familiar with the story of the Tower of Babel (Genesis 11:1-9), which explains why there are different languages among the peoples of the Earth. According to the Bible, shortly after the Great Flood of Noah, "The whole Earth had one language and few words." But when the people started building a tower "with its top in the heavens," God disapproved and said, "Behold, they are one people, and they have all one language; and this is only the beginning of what they will do; and nothing that they propose to do will now be impossible for them. Come, let us go down, and there confuse their language, that they might not understand one another's speech." (I assume God was talking to the angels.) God then scattered them across the face of the Earth, and they stopped building the tower. The abandoned city became known as Babel, a word that apparently comes from the Hebrew *balal*, meaning confusion.

I'm reminded of this story every time I learn how to operate a new synthesizer. It seems that every instrument has its own language, often using different terms for the same thing. Of course, some parts of a particular synth are truly new or unique and require their own name. But much of the nomenclature is nothing more than marketing hype designed to impress the consumer. Unfortunately, it can be more confusing than enlightening.

Foundation

Take the various types of synthesis. Most modern synths make noise in a similar manner, sending sampled sounds and electronically generated, harmonically rich waveforms through various types of filters that reduce or remove certain harmonics. Generically, this is known as sample-based, subtractive synthesis. Although they could use this term, most manufacturers seem determined to invent new names for the same basic process.

E-mu came up with a surprisingly meaningful term for the type of synthesis used in the Morpheus: Z-Plane Synthesis. The instrument sends a sampled sound through a filter that "morphs" smoothly between two or more independent filter settings in real time. Filter morphing can occur along three axes in a 3-D depiction, i.e., between two filter settings on the X axis, that pair and two other filter settings on the Y axis, and those four and four other settings on the Z axis.

Ensoniq used the term Crosswave Synthesis in their SQ-80, in which sampled attack transients are combined with sustained waveforms before proceeding through a subtractive signal path. They switched to the term Dynamic Component Synthesis for the VFX and subsequent synths. In this scheme, instru-ment sounds and effects are integrated, and the effects can be dynamically controlled in real time. For example, an LFO can modulate the pitch of a sound to simulate vibrato while also modulating the amount of reverb applied to the sound. More recently, Ensoniq has turned away from giving new names to synthesis technologies. Huzzah!

For the M1 and its offspring, Korg uses the term Advanced Integrated (AI) Synthesis, meaning sample-based subtractive synthesis with onboard effects such as reverb, delay, and so on. This was a relatively new feature when the M1 was introduced. The 01/W and its offspring use AI² Synthesis, which enhances the AI scheme in various ways (see Fig. 23-2). In particular, it adds the ability to control and modulate effects in real time. Does this sound familiar?

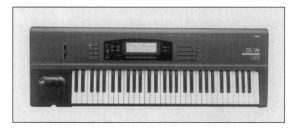

Figure 23-2. The Korg 01/W was one of the first synths to use AI² synthesis. Multisamples are called "Multisounds," and LFOs are dubbed "Modulation Generators" or "MGs."

The term Vector Synthesis is used by several manufacturers (starting with the Sequential Circuits Prophet VS) to indicate the ability to combine several sound elements, such as different timbres or effects, in varying amounts by moving a joystick or other 2-dimensional controller in real time. (In mathematics, a vector is a quantity that is specified by a magnitude and a direction, so the term is used appropriately in this context.) Korg's Wavestation instruments use Advanced Vector Synthesis, in which the movement of the joystick can be recorded and played back. The joystick can also be used to pan sounds and control the effects. The Yamaha SY22 and SY35 use Dynamic Vector Synthesis, which also includes programmable, repeatable joystick movements.

Kurzweil came up with a meaningful term for their K2000 and K2500 synths: Variable Architecture Synthesis Technology (VAST). Even the acronym is appropriate. This is more than sample-based subtractive synthesis; the normal filter in the signal path is joined by many other available sound modifiers. You can select one of 31 different algorithms (which determine the signal flow through the instrument), then assign various digital signal processing (DSP) functions to "black boxes" in the signal path.

Roland is no stranger to techno terminology.

Their early digital pianos use Structured Adaptive (S/A) Synthesis. In this process, sounds are painstakingly created by hand from individual harmonics, which is generically called additive synthesis. Roland does not use this technique anymore.

Roland's D-50 and its offspring use Linear Arithmetic (L/A) Synthesis, in which analog synth parameters are digitally generated. These are combined with sampled transient attacks and sustained waveforms, then sent through a relatively traditional filter/amplifier chain or a more complex signal path. This is not unlike Crosswave Synthesis in the Ensoniq SQ-80. Like Ensoniq, Roland has recently shied away from inventing new names for synthesis techniques, simply calling their new models multitimbral synthesizers.

One of the few companies to avoid the sample-based subtractive approach (at least until recently) is Yamaha. In 1986, they introduced Frequency Modulation (FM) Synthesis in the DX7 and its offspring. In this process, the frequency of one oscillator is modulated (varied up and down) very quickly by another oscillator, which produces a wide range of timbres, depending on the relationship between the frequencies and amplitudes of the oscillators.

The SY77 and its progeny use Advanced Frequency Modulation (AFM), in which the original FM process was refined and enhanced. These instruments also include sample-playback capabilities. Yamaha's sample format was originally called Advanced Wave Memory (AWM), which later became Advanced Wave Memory 2 (AWM2). Sounds generated by both techniques are combined and sent through sophisticated digital filters. The result is Realtime Convolution Modulation (RCM) Synthesis. This term actually has more meaning than you might think, as it refers to the mathematical process by which the filters operate.

Yamaha's VL1 and its descendants use Virtual Acoustic Synthesis (VAS). This departure from sample-based subtractive synthesis doesn't use samples at all. This is an example of physical-modeling synthesis, in which the physical properties of acoustic instruments are simulated directly using DSP technology.

Architecture

Most modern synths use a "building-block" approach to create sounds. At the lowest level of the hierarchy are individual samples. In the case of drums and percussion, there is usually a single sample of each instrument. However, most melodic and harmonic instruments are sampled playing several different notes. These samples are assigned to the appropriate keyboard ranges to form multisamples, which let you play the instrument throughout the entire musical range without sounding too unrealistic.

Samples and multisamples are combined in var-

ious ways to create the basic sound entity that you call up on the front panel and play from the keyboard. This entity is generically called a patch, program, voice, or preset. In many cases, a small number of patches can be combined to create split or layered sounds across the keyboard; these constructs have no common generic name. In multitimbral instruments, programs can be combined into larger entities (again, with no common generic name). These larger multitimbral entities are normally used to play different sounds on different MIDI channels.

At the bottom of the hierarchy in E-mu's Proteus synth line are multisamples E-mu calls Instruments. Up to two Instruments are combined to form Presets, the basic playable entity. In the UltraProteus and Morpheus, up to sixteen Presets can be combined into HyperPresets. Multitimbral entities are formed by assigning Presets and HyperPresets to MIDI channels in a MidiMap.

The hierarchy in Ensoniq synths starts with multisamples called Waves, which include several custom-built Transwaves. These Transwaves consist of several different samples, placed end to end, that you can sweep through with a modulator such as the mod wheel or an envelope generator. Applying various parameters to a Wave or Transwave creates a Voice. Up to six Voices are combined to form a Program or Sound (depending on the specific model), which is the basic, playable entity. Multitimbral groups of Programs or Sounds are called Performance Presets.

Korg came up with some interesting terms to describe the hierarchy of the M1 and its progeny. Multisamples are called Multisounds (egad!), which are combined to form Programs (nothing unusual there). Programs are combined in various ways to form several types of Combis; the multitimbral variety is called a Multi Combi! In the Wavestation, multisamples are called Waves, and up to four Waves are combined to form a Patch. The basic playable entity is called a Performance, which consists of up to eight Patches assigned to Parts. The multitimbral construct is called a Multiset, which includes up to sixteen Performances.

The hierarchy of the Kurzweil K2000 includes many levels. Individual Samples are assigned to different areas of the keyboard in a Keymap to form multisamples. A Keymap is sent through a VAST algorithm to form a Layer. Up to three Layers are combined to form a Program, the basic playable entity; a special type of Program, called a Drum Program, can include up to 32 Layers. Up to three Programs can be combined to form a Setup of split or layered sounds. The K2000 is always in multitimbral mode, so there is no particular multitimbral entity. All these items are examples of Objects, a name applied to anything and everything that can be named, saved, edited, or deleted within the instrument.

Roland instruments are awash with hierarchical nomenclature, so hold onto your hat. In the D-50, the bottom of the hierarchy is called a Partial, which includes its own sample-playing oscillator, filter, and amplifier. Each Partial is like a complete sample-based subtractive synth. Two Partials are combined to form a Tone, and two Tones are combined to form a Patch, the basic playable entity. In more recent synths, Roland dispensed with Partials; each Patch consists of four Tones. For multitimbral applications, each Patch is assigned to a Part, which includes its own assignable MIDI channel. Parts are then combined into a Performance.

The Roland Sound Canvas and its progeny conform to the General MIDI (GM) specification, which standardizes the program numbers of different kinds of sounds. For example, an acoustic-piano sound is always Program Change 1 (see Chapter 7). Roland's version of General MIDI is called GS; these letters mean nothing according to the official company line, but rumor has it they stand for General System. GS includes all 128 GM sounds and then some, because the original Sound Canvas predated the final GM specification.

The hierarchy of these instruments starts with Samples, which are controlled with various parameters to form Tones, the basic playable entity. There are two types of Tones: Capital Tones and Sub-Capital Tones. Capital Tones include the 128 standard GM sounds, while Sub-Capital Tones are variations of the Capital Tones. Tones are assigned to Parts, sixteen of which form a multitimbral Performance.

The Yamaha SY77 and its direct descendants start with Elements, which can be either AFM sounds or AWM samples. In the VL1, an Element is a specific physical model. Depending on the instrument, two or more Elements are combined to form a Voice, the basic playable entity. In these instruments, a Voice can be split or layered with different Elements. (In the SY85 and TG500, split and layered sounds are created with several Voices in a Performance.) Multitimbral entities are called Multis.

Tools

Within each synth, there are many functions, parameters, and components with their own names. Although I can't cover them all here, let's take a look at a few of the more interesting examples.

Some instruments offer the capability to play a sequence of samples, one right after another. Generically, this is called wave sequencing, a term that was invented by Korg for their Wavestation. In the Ensoniq TS-series synths, it's called Hyper-Wave.

When they first appeared, digital filters were limited in their ability to vary over time. Roland soon overcame this limitation, calling their digital filters TVFs (Time-Varying Filters); Korg calls theirs VDFs (Variable Digital Filters). Similarly, digital amplifiers (which control the volume of the final sound) are called TVAs by Roland and VDAs by Korg.

Some companies like to obfuscate the obvious. Roland calls their oscillators Wave Generators (WGs), while Yamaha calls their FM oscillators Operators. (This actually has some meaning: operators are oscillators with their own dedicated envelope generators.) Korg calls their LFOs Modulation Generators (MGs).

Some instruments include a Quick Edit function, which provides several sliders or other controls on the front panel. By moving one slider, you can edit several related parameters at once. For example, a slider labeled "Brightness" might change several filter and envelope parameters. This makes it easy to quickly and intuitively change the nature of a sound without having to enter the dreaded edit mode. The Yamaha SY85 and TG500 call this function Quick Edit (amazing!). In the Korg M1 and its progeny, this function is called Performance Editing. The Korg Wavestation calls each group of related quick-edit parameters a Macro.

The Roland D-70, JX-1, and ∂Juno also include a Quick Edit function, with several sliders called a Palette on the front panel (see Fig. 23-3). The Roland JD-800 and all current synth models also have a Palette, but it serves an entirely different purpose. Four sliders edit the last selected parameter for each of the four Tones. This makes it easy to edit the same parameter for all Tones, but it has nothing to do with editing several related parameters with one slider.

Figure 23-3. The Palette on the front panel of the Roland D-70 lets you edit several related parameters by moving one slider.

Amen

If you're confused by the bewildering array of terms and phrases used by the manufacturers of synthesizers and samplers, you're not alone. Although this might not be a problem of biblical proportions, it does tend to impede the creative process, and many consider creativity to be divine. Perhaps manufacturers will contemplate this when they sit down to design the next generation of instruments from which heavenly music will emanate.

Internet Glossary

The explosive growth of the Internet has spawned a whole host of new terms, acronyms, and phrases to learn. It is important for electronic musicians to understand this new lexicon if we are to make our way past the infobahn's pitfalls and potholes. So here are many of the terms that all netnauts must know—from slang to technospeak—along with their definitions. Internet terms used in these definitions are themselves defined elsewhere in this glossary. Happy surfing!

A

address A string of characters that identifies the location of a site on the Internet. This term often refers to the destination of an e-mail message. The first part of an address is the user name, or handle, followed by an "at" symbol (@) and the domain name of the service that maintains the e-mail account. For example, my e-mail address is srwilkinson@att.net.

agent A type of software program designed to autonomously perform specific tasks in the background. For example, an agent might search the Internet for references to a particular subject you wish to study.

Archie A software program that resides on a host computer for finding specific files available from FTP sites.

ASCII Acronym for American Standard Code for Information Interchange. A cross-platform, standard code in which numbers are assigned to represent letters, numbers, punctuation marks, and common symbols. This allows different computers and applications to read each other's text.

attached file A program, document, or other file that is linked to and sent with an e-mail message. The attached document does not appear within the e-mail message; instead, it is linked to the message and sent along with it. Both sender and receiver must use an e-mail program that supports attachments.

B

bandwidth A measure of the amount of information that can flow through a connection or device. In telecommunications applications, bandwidth is typically expressed in bits per second (bps), kilobits per second (Kbps), or megabits per second (Mbps).

binary file Any file, such as a program or graphic document, that is not in ASCII format.

BinHex A method of encoding binary files so they contain nothing but ASCII characters. After encoding, binary files can be sent via e-mail without having to be an attached file. The receiving computer must have software that can decode a BinHex file back into its original format.

black hole On the World Wide Web, a hyperlink to a document that has been erased or moved.

browser A software program that lets you surf the World Wide Web, browsing for interesting information. Most current browsers can display graphic information, but a few (especially older ones) support text only. Popular examples include Netscape's *Navigator* and Microsoft's *Internet Explorer*.

C

channel A particular topic of discussion within IRC. Your computer must have IRC client software to participate in real-time chats, or you must be proficient in the use of a UNIX shell account.

client software A software program that resides in your computer and lets you access various Internet resources.

compression A means of reducing the amount of data needed to represent a file. Files on the Internet are often compressed to reduce download time or allow real-time playback over the phone lines.

cookie A file maintained by your browser that contains information about who you are and what hyperlinks you have followed as you surf the World Wide Web. Also called a "magic cookie."

cyber A prefix indicating a computer-oriented concept. For example, "cyberspace" is a term that generally refers to the Internet.

D

daemon A software program that manages requests for various types of files. Daemons are found on host and local computers.

decryption The process by which an encrypted message is decoded.

dialup access A means of connecting one computer to another (or to a network such as the Internet) using a modem to dial a certain phone number.

domain name The name used by organizations and individuals to identify their location on the Internet. In the United States, most domain names end with one of several 3-letter extensions: .com (commercial), .edu (educational), .gov (governmental), .net (network), and .org (organizational). In Europe, most domain names end with an extension that indicates the country, such as .uk (United Kingdom).

download The process of requesting and receiving a file from a remote computer via modem or terminal adapter.

E

e-mail Short for electronic mail. The process by which messages are sent over a network such as the Internet. Internet e-mail messages can include attached files (see Fig. G-1).

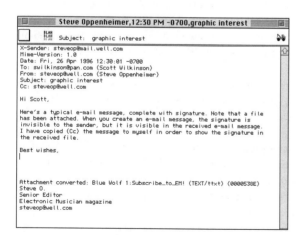

Figure G-1. This e-mail message was created and mailed using Qualcomm's _Eudora Pro_ 2.1.3. An attached file has been converted, as indicated above the signature. Eudora is also available in a shareware version.

emoticon A set of ASCII characters that form a sideways face. For example, :-) might mean "I'm happy," and :-(might mean "I'm sad." Also called a "smiley."

encryption The process by which a message is encoded so that no one other than the intended recipient can read it. This provides some security from hackers.

F

FAQ Acronym for Frequently Asked Questions. Most newsgroups and mailing lists include a FAQ file for newbies to catch up with the topics under discussion so they don't ask questions that have already been dealt with.

finger An Internet utility residing on a host computer or your local computer that lets you obtain information about anyone with an e-mail address. This information is stored in a "finger file" maintained by each user's Internet service provider (ISP) and normally includes the user's name, street address, and other information, such as a list of log-on dates and times. Some ISPs let you establish a "plan" file, which includes any information you wish to make available to anyone who fingers you. Some ISPs refuse finger requests in the interests of their customers' privacy.

firewall A form of security that restricts outside access to a host or server.

flame An e-mail or newsgroup message that includes abusive or inflammatory language often sent in response to a rave or spam.

FTP Acronym for File Transfer Protocol. A set of rules that determine how files are transmitted over the Internet. To use FTP, you must have FTP client software that lets you upload and download files to and from an FTP server. Examples include _Anarchie_ and _Fetch_ (see Fig. G-2) . Many browsers also include FTP client functions. In some cases, you must log in with a password to exchange files with the server, but many servers include files that are available to anyone through a procedure called "anonymous FTP."

FTP archive A directory of files available using FTP. Sometimes called an "FTP site."

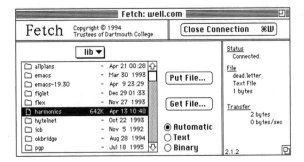

Figure G-2. *Fetch* 2.1.2 is a simple, shareware File Transfer Protocol (FTP) client program that lets you upload and download files.

G

Gopher A software program that uses a menu system to help you find files, software, documents, and other resources. Many host computers include this program, and there are also versions for your local computer. This search method is somewhat outdated.

H

hacker A person with in-depth programming knowledge. Internet hackers often try to break into computer systems for either benign or nefarious purposes. Such people are also called "crackers."

handle The name you use as the first part of your e-mail address. For example, my handle is srwilkinson.

helper program In a browser, a supplementary program that handles multimedia files, such as animation, video, and audio. Most browsers do not include helper programs, which must be downloaded from the Internet and configured for your browser.

home page The point of entry into a Web site that links to other pages and documents on the World Wide Web.

host Any computer that makes files and applications available to users of the Internet.

HTML Acronym for HyperText Markup Language. This is a set of conventions used to prepare documents for display on the World Wide Web. In conjunction with HTTP, it allows Web authors to embed hyperlinks in Web documents.

HTTP Acronym for HyperText Transfer Protocol. This is a standard that supports the exchange of files on the World Wide Web. In conjunction with HTML, it allows Web authors to embed hyperlinks in Web documents.

hyperlink In hypertext, an underlined or otherwise emphasized word, phrase, or other object that displays another, related document when selected (e.g., by clicking with a mouse).

hypertext A document in which certain words, phrases, or other objects are underlined or otherwise emphasized. Selecting these words or phrases opens a related document. Hypertext is created using HTML and HTTP.

I

Internet A worldwide system of interconnected computer networks based on the UNIX operating system and including millions of computers and users. Also called the "infobahn" or "information superhighway."

IRC Acronym for Internet Relay Chat. A chat service that lets you communicate with other users in real time on the Internet by typing on your computer. Various topics are discussed on different IRC channels. You must have IRC client software on your computer to use this service or access it directly with a shell account.

ISDN Acronym for Integrated Services Digital Network. A phone system that allows digital information to be transmitted directly. Basic ISDN provides two data channels (called "B" or "Bearer" channels), each of which can carry up to 64 Kbps. Primary ISDN provides up to 23 channels, each with 64 Kbps bandwidth. To use this system, you must have an ISDN line installed and a terminal adapter. In addition, your ISP must provide ISDN access to the Internet.

ISP Acronym for Internet service provider. A commercial enterprise that offers direct connection to the Internet.

J

Java A programming language developed by Sun Microsystems. Java lets programmers develop small applications called "applets." Because these applets are hardware-independent (i.e., they can run on any type of computer, at least in theory), they are ideal for the Internet.

Jughead A function within *Gopher* that lets you search for key words that appear in directory titles, not menu items.

L

LAN Acronym for Local Area Network. A network that connects computers over relatively short distances, typically within a single building.

lurk To read newsgroup or mailing list messages without posting any of your own. This is a good way to become familiar with a newsgroup before participating.

M

mailing list A service that compiles information on a specific topic. After you subscribe to a particular mailing list, you regularly receive e-mail on that topic. Some mailing lists are managed with a program called *Listserv*.

modem Short for modulator/demodulator. A device that converts (modulates) digital signals from a computer into analog form so they can be sent on standard telephone lines. It also reconverts (demodulates) these signals back into digital form at the receiving end of the line.

moderator The person who oversees a newsgroup discussion or mailing list and tries to keep it on topic.

N

netiquette A set of informal rules that define reasonable behavior on the Internet. For example, typing a message in all caps is considered shouting and should be avoided except in the most extreme cases.

netnaut Someone who uses the Internet.

newbie Someone who is new to a particular newsgroup or mailing list (or the Internet in general). Newbies should lurk for a while and read any available FAQ files before sending messages of their own.

newsgroup An online discussion group devoted to a particular topic, such as *Star Trek*, the Grateful Dead, etc. Members of a newsgroup contribute to the discussion by posting messages. See usenet.

newsreader A client software program that lets you subscribe to newsgroups. Many browsers include newsreader client software.

O

online Of or related to the Internet. Also, to be connected to a remote computer.

online service A commercial enterprise that offers news, encyclopedias, airline reservations, and many other forms of information to users who connect to the service with their computers and modems. Most online services also provide access to the Internet. Examples include America Online and CompuServe.

P

POP Acronym for Point of Presence. A geographical area in which it is possible to access a wide-area network (WAN) or online service with a local phone call.

post To send a message to a mailing list or newsgroup. Also, a posted message.

POTS Acronym for Plain Old Telephone Service. The standard phone service in most areas of the world.

PPP Acronym for Point to Point Protocol. One of two standards for connecting computers directly to the Internet. The other standard is SLIP. PPP is newer than SLIP, and it incorporates superior data negotiation, compression, and error correction.

R

rave To carry an argument beyond reason in a newsgroup, mailing list, or e-mail. Considered a breach of netiquette.

S

search engine A service that helps you find information, particularly Web sites, on the Internet. Examples include Yahoo (www.yahoo.com), Lycos (www.lycos.com), and Alta Vista (www.altavista.digital.com; see Fig. G-3).

server A computer that offers various documents and resources to users of the Internet. Examples include FTP and World Wide Web servers.

shell account An inexpensive but limited type of dialup access to a UNIX computer. Once you are logged on, you must use the UNIX command-line interface to invoke various Internet applications, such as Telnet, *Gopher*, and IRC.

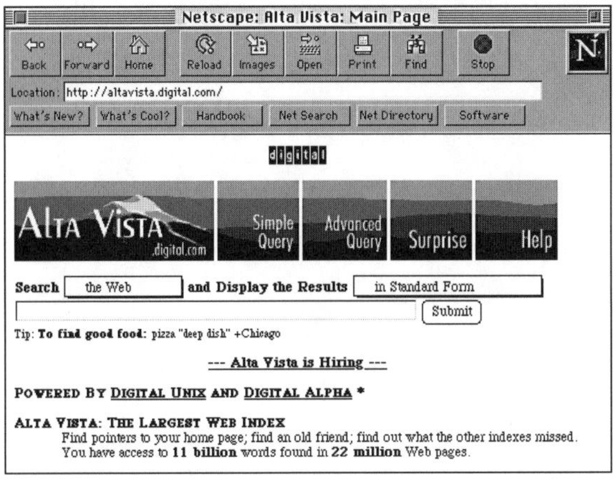

Figure G-3. Alta Vista (shown in Netscape's Navigator 2.0 Web browser) offers one of the most powerful search engines on the Web.

signature A short note at the end of e-mail, mailing list, or newsgroup messages that typically includes the sender's name, organization, and e-mail address.

site A specific location on the Internet.

SLIP Acronym for Serial Line Internet Protocol. One of two standards for connecting computers directly to the Internet. The other standard is PPP.

spam To post the same, often irrelevant, message to many newsgroups, mailing lists, or e-mail recipients at once. Also, to post the same message many times to the same newsgroup, mailing list, or e-mail recipient. (Spam is very annoying, and it's an example of bad netiquette.) Also, a term referring to self-promoting messages and junk mail.

spider A type of software program that prowls the Internet looking for any specified information. New resources are added to a database that users can comb with a search engine.

stream The process of sending audio and/or video signals over the Internet in real time. For example, a Web site might send streaming audio to your computer when you connect to it, letting you hear the audio as you visit the site.

subscribe To add your name and e-mail address to a newsgroup or mailing list you wish to join.

surf To wander the Internet.

T

T1/T3 Two types of high-bandwidth digital phone lines. T1 can carry up to 1.544 megabits per second (Mbps); T3 can carry up to 44.21 Mbps. Both of these types of phone lines are much faster than ISDN.

TCP/IP Acronym for Transmission Control Protocol/Internet Protocol. These standards, or protocols, allow data to be transmitted from one computer to another over the Internet.

Telnet An Internet function that lets you connect to other computers on the Internet, even if they don't support TCP/IP. This provides a text-only interface to the remote computer. You must have Telnet client software on your computer to use this function. Examples include *NCSA Telnet* and *Comet*.

terminal adapter A device that connects to a computer and sends and receives digital data on an ISDN phone line. This serves essentially the same function as a modem, but it doesn't convert digital messages to analog form.

thread A chain of messages that relate to a single subtopic within a newsgroup or mailing list.

troll To post a facetious message containing an obvious error within a newsgroup in the hopes of causing a gullible person to respond and point out the error.

U

UNIX The operating system software used by most Internet host computers.

upload The process of sending a file from a remote computer to a server via modem or terminal adapter.

URL Acronym for Uniform Resource Locator. A string of characters that identifies a particular Internet site, usually a World Wide Web, FTP, or newsgroup site. All Web site URLs begin with "http://" followed by the site's domain name and any directory paths. URLs for FTP sites begin with "ftp://" and URLs for newsgroup sites begin with "news:"; otherwise, these are identical to the URLs for Web sites.

usenet The conglomeration of newsgroups on the Internet. Most newsgroups fall into one of eight basic categories, based on the topics they address: alt (alternative), comp (computer), misc (miscellaneous), news, rec (recreation), sci (science), soc (society), and talk (controversial topics). Each usenet site includes some but not necessarily all newsgroups.

uucode A process whereby a binary file is encoded into an ASCII file, which can then be sent as e-mail or posted to a newsgroup or mailing list. The receiving computer must decode the message to restore the binary file. The specific UNIX programs to accomplish this are called "uuencode" and "uudecode." This is similar to BinHex.

uucp Acronym for UNIX-to-UNIX cp (the UNIX copy command). A utility that lets UNIX computers exchange files, e-mail, and newsgroup articles.

V

Veronica A function within the *Gopher* software program that lets you search for key words that appear in directory titles and menu items.

virtual Of or relating to computer-based entities. For example, a computer-generated environment is called "virtual reality."

virus A software program designed to wreak havoc with computers. These programs are often distributed clandestinely over the Internet.

W

WAN Acronym for Wide Area Network. A network that connects computers over much longer distances than local-area networks (LANs) allow. Some WANs, such as Tymnet and SprintNet, provide local dialup access to online services and the Internet.

Web page One screen or document within a Web site.

Web site A particular location on the World Wide Web that offers information and downloadable files.

World Wide Web A global hypertext system that uses the Internet to transfer information. It is often abbreviated as Web or WWW.

Z

zine Slang for online magazine (as well as other, non-electronic magazines).

Index

¼-inch TRS (Tip-Ring-Sleeve) phone plugs 125
¼-inch TS (Tip-Sleeve) phone plugs 124
2-way speaker 159
3 dB down points 135, 178
3-way speaker 159
3-D audio processors 191
5-pin DIN 50
5-way binding posts 156
5.1-channel format 194
50-pin SCSI connector 117
A weighting 36
A/V-capable hard disk 104
acoustic drum triggers 83
acoustic suspension speaker 160
active crossover 160
active electronics 136
active sensing 54
active termination 119
Adaptive Differential Pulse Code Modulation (ADPCM) 104
ADAT Optical (Lightpipe) 128
additive synthesis 9
AES/EBU 127, 128
Aftertouch 14, 51
algorithm 18
aliasing 42
All Notes Off (ANO) 52
All Sound Off 52
alpha scale 7
alternate noteheads 111
alternating current (AC) 21, 23
ambience 191
Ampere, Andre 21
amperes 21
amplifier 9, 11
amplitude 4, 180, 191
        envelope 12
        modulation 175
analog audio signals 21
analog-to-digital converter (ADC) 40
anti-aliasing filter 42, 46
anti-imaging filter 44
anvil 36
apex 37
articulation 112
assembly editing 203
attack 185
attack parameter 184
Audio Engineering Society (AES) 127
audio isolation transformers 28
audition 109
auditory nerve 37
Auto Track Finding (ATF) 142
auto-wah 174
AutoLink 108

autolocator 143
automatic accompaniment software 115
automatic modulators 11
aux return 148, 149, 164
aux send 147, 149, 164
aux send/return 199
aux signal 147
average access time 104
average data rate 116
azimuth 191
Bach, J. S. 6
back plate 133
back-electret condenser 133
balanced
        cables 26, 125, 130
        power 28
banana plugs 126
band-reject filter 11
bandpass filter 11
bandwidth 128, 178
        audio 42
        digital 42
        filter 11
Bank Select 51, 87
banks 108
barrier strips 156
base 30
basic channel 52
basic tracks 196
basilar membrane 37
bass reflex speaker 160
Baudot, Marie-Dominique 19
beaming 111
Bel 31
Bell, Alexander Graham 31
Benade, Arthur 17
biamping 158, 160
bias 141
binary number system 40
binaural recording 192
bipolar transistors 154
birdies 46
bits 40, 97
blackout 28
BNC connector 127
boost 176
bouncing 197
boundary microphone 133, 134
breathing 189, 190
brickwall filter 42
brownout 28
Bundle 109
bytes 40, 97
calibration 141
capacitors 154
capstan 140
capsule 130
cardioid microphone 131

Carlos, Wendy 7
CD-Recordable (CD-R) 105, 107
CD-Rewritable (CD-RW) 105
center frequency 11
cents 5
channel 51
        fader 147
        inputs 146
        mode 53
        mode messages 52
        path 150
        pressure 51
        voice messages 51
channelization 65, 93
chase 68
chassis ground 27
checksum 99
chord symbols 112
chords 5
chorusing 173, 175
chromatic mode 80
chunks 69
Circle of Fifths 5, 6
circuit 21, 24
Class
        A 155
        AB 155
        B 155
        G 155
        H 155
clefs 111
clipping 155, 183
clock 54, 67
        signal 126
closed loop 95
Coarse Tuning 54
coaxial 128
        speaker 159
cochlea 36
coercivity 145
combi mode 15, 58
common-mode rejection 28
compact disc (CD) 105
compact reference monitors 158
companding 188
compression
        audio 202, 203
        digital 44
        lossless 44
        lossy 44
compressor 183
computer-aided instruction (CAI) 113
concha 36
condenser microphone 133
conductive losses 36
cone diaphragm 159
Continue command 54, 67
continuous power 156, 161

Control Change (CC) 51, 53
        continuous 51
        switched 51
control input, 186
control responses 96
control voltage 186
controller 94
controller mapping 77
Cook, Perry 18
count-in 64
CP-340
        Type I 127
        Type II 128
cross-platform transfers 70
cross-staff beaming 111
crossfades 106
crossover 160
crosstalk 140, 188
current 21, 23, 32
current limiter 155
cut 176
cut-and-paste 65
cutoff frequency 10
cycle 3
cycles per second 3
daisy chain 50, 116
damping factor 157
DAT 141
data bytes 52
data compression 104
Data Decrement 54
Data Entry 54
Data Increment 54
data transfer rate 104
data-path width 116
DB25 connector 116
dbx 188, 189
        Type I 189
        Type II 189
DC offset 157
de-emphasis 141, 189
de-essing 187
decay time 165, 166
decibels (dB) 30, 31, 33, 130
        dBm 32
        dBu 33
        dBV 33
defragmentation 107
delay 167
        multitap 168
        ping-pong 168
        single 167
        slapback 169
        time 168
delta modulation 45
delta-sigma modulation 45
delta-time value 69
demagnetizer 144
denormaled 152

density (reverb) 166
depth (LFO) 13
detuning 169
diaphragm 158
differential
coding 45
SCSI 117
diffusion (reverb) 166
digital audio workstation
(DAW) 103
digital signal processing
(DSP) 47
digital signal processor (DSP) 16
digital-to-analog converter
(DAC) 16, 44
direct box 134
direct current (DC) 21
direct outs 148, 149
direct-injection (DI)
box 126, 134
directional mic 131
discrete speaker 159
distance 191
distortion 124
dithering 44, 45, 46
dithering down 47
Dolby 188, 189
A 190
B 190
C 190
Digital 194
Pro Logic 193
S 190
SR 190
domains 138
dome tweeters 159
Doppler effect 174
double-ended noise
reduction 188
downward expansion 190
drill-and-practice format 113
driver (speaker) 158
drop frame (SMPTE) 68
drum brain 82
ducking 186
dynamic filtering 190
dynamic headroom 156
dynamic mics 132
dynamic phase-shifting 181
dynamic range 34, 43, 132, 183
dynamic voice allocation 59
dynamics 112
dynamics processor 183
E-mu
HyperPresets 208
Instruments 208
Presets 208
ear canal 36
ear training 114
eardrum 36
early reflections (reverb) 166
echo 63
edit buffer 110
edit decision list (EDL) 106
edit mode 15
edit/compare button 15

editor/librarian 107
effects 199
efficiency (speaker) 161
EG Velocity sensitivity 14
electret condenser 133
electromagnetic interference
(EMI) 27, 188
electromotive force (EMF) 21
Electronic Industries Association
(EIA) 156
Electronic Industries Association
of Japan (EIAJ) 127
elevation 191
End of Exclusive (EOX) 53
enharmonic equivalents 5
Ensoniq
Hyper-Wave 209
Performance Presets 208
Program 208
Sound 208
Transwaves 208
Voice 208
Waves 208
envelope generator (EG) 12
EQ 199, 202, 203
⅓-octave graphic 178
defeat switch 147
dynamic 181
graphic 177, 179
parametric 178, 179
quasi-parametric 179
semiparametric 179
shelving 147, 177
sweepable 179
sweepable mid 147
equal temperament 6
equal-loudness curves 35
equalization (EQ) section 147
equalizers 176
erase head 138
European Broadcasting Union
(EBU) 127
event list 65
expander 185
exponents 30
expression pedal 14
external terminator (SCSI) 118
fade ins 106
fade outs 106
far field 159
Faraday shield 135
fast winding 140
faux 168
Federal Trade Commission
(FTC) 156
feedback
audio 179
delay 168
figure-eight microphone 132
filter 9, 10
filter EG 13
Fine Tuning 54
fixed disk 104
flanger 175
flanging 173
Fletcher, Harvey 35

Fletcher-Munson equal-loudness
contours 35
FM synthesis 9, 13
foot controller 77
footswitch 77
force-sensing resistors (FSRs) 81
formants 5, 16, 17, 171
format converter 128
Fourier, Jean Baptiste Joseph 4
fragmentation 107
frames per second (fps) 68
free field 162
Freed, Adrian 19
FreeMIDI 102, 108
frequency 3, 10, 21
frequency LFO 13
frequency modulation 9
frequency response 34, 130,
157, 161
Frequency Shift Keying (FSK) 67
frequency-dependent gating 187
fretboard controllers 78
fundamental 4
gain 33, 34
mistracking 189
pot 146
game format 113
gap width 140
gate time 82
gating 185
General MIDI (GM) 73, 74, 209
General Purpose (GP)
Registers 96
General Purpose Controllers 54
glitching 86
global effects 59
grace notes 111
granulation noise 46
graphic editing 65
ground 24
ground lifter 27
ground loops 27
ground point 24
ground-lift switch 28, 136
group buses 148
group jacks 149
group-assign buttons 148
half-normaled 151
half-track tape decks 139
hammer 36
handshaking 95, 98, 108
harmonic 4
hard-disk recorder (HDR) 103
computer-based 103
modular 103
harmonic components 4
harmonic generation 180
harmonic restoration 181
harmonic series 4
harmonic spectrum 4, 180
harmonic synthesis 180
harmonization 85
head-related transfer functions
(HRTFs) 192
header 69
headroom 161

heads out 144
heat sink 155
helical recording system 141
hertz (Hz) 3
hex pickup 79
hexadecimal 97
high-frequency damping 167
high-frequency power supply 155
high-Z mics 132
highpass filter 10
hiss 188
hold mode 85
hot wire 24
hyperacusis 37
hypercardioid microphone 132
hypersensitivity 37
idler 140
imaging 161
impedance 22, 23, 124, 128,
132, 161
impure intervals 5
in-line connector 164
in-line mixer 150
inches per second (ips) 140
incus 36
individual pads 82
induction 27
Information Fields 96
inner ear 36
input control 164
input gain 183
input impedance 22
insert cable 176
insert editing 203
insert points 147, 149
insertion effects 59
instrument level 124
integrated controllers 82
integrated sequencers 63
intelligent pitch shifter 170
intensity 4, 34
intermodulation (IM)
distortion 157
intervals 5
inverse-square law 4
jackfields 150
Jaffe, David 19
Japanese MIDI Standards
Committee (JMSC) 50
jitter 126, 128
Joule's Law 23, 25, 30, 31, 33
Joule, James 23
just intonation 6
key follow 13, 14
key input 186
key signature 111
keyboard action 77
keywords 109
kilohertz (kHz) 3
kinetic energy 21
knee 184
knee frequency 177
Korg
Combis 208
Macro 209

Modulation Generators (MGs) 209
Multi Combi 208
Multiset 208
Multisounds 208
Patch 208
Performance 208
Performance Editing 209
Programs 208
VDAs (Variable Digital Amplifiers) 209
VDFs (Variable Digital Filters) 209
Waves 208
Kurzweil
Drum Program 208
Layer 208
Objects 208
Program 208
Samples 208
Setup 208
last-note priority 59
layering 10
least significant bit (LSB) 47
least significant byte (LSB) 53, 87
legato mode 81
length parameter 69
lesson format 113
level 33, 34, 198
LFO 13
libraries 109
limiting 184
line conditioning 28
line level 124
line mixer 200
line regulator 29
linear sequencers 63
load 22
local control 52
localization 191
logarithms 31
loudness 34
low-bit conversion 44
low-frequency damping 167
low-frequency effects (LFE) channel 194
low-frequency oscillators (LFOs) 11
low-Z mics 132
lowpass filter 10
lyrics 111
Macintosh Audio Compression/Expansion (MACE) 104
Macintosh Enhanced SCSI Hardware (MESH) 119
magneto-optical (MO) removable media 105
makeup gain 183
mallet controllers 82
malleus 36
manual modulators 11, 13
mapping 93
master 201
master aux-send controls 149

master clocking 127
master controller 50
master module 148
mastering 196, 200
matching transformer 132, 137
maximum data rate 116
maximum output level (MOL) 145
meantone temperament 6
Melco 129
merge 65
meta-events 70
Metal Oxide Semiconductor Field Effect Transistor (MOSFET) 154
metronome 64
mic level 124, 125
mic pre 125
mic preamp 125
mic/line switch 146
micro DB50 117
micro DB68 117
microphone 130
microtuning 5
mid-side 131
middle ear 36
MIDI 50
bias 93
conversion 94
delay 93
feedback 93
filtering 93
implementation 56
interface 92, 102
limiting 93
merger 92
offset 93
patch bay 93
processor 92
reverse 94
scaling 93
MIDI Clock 54
MIDI Implementation Chart 56
MIDI In 50
MIDI Machine Control (MMC) 55, 94, 143
MIDI Manufacturers Association (MMA) 50
MIDI Out 50
MIDI Show Control 55
MIDI Thru 50
MIDI Time Code (MTC) 55, 68, 94, 96, 106
MIDI Time Code (MTC) Quarter Frame 53
MIDI Tuning Standard 7, 55
midrange drivers 159
MiniDisc 105
Ministudio 141
mixdown 198
mixer's insert points 176
mixers 146
in-line 149
split 149
mixing 196
models 15

modular digital multitrack (MDM) 141, 143
modulation 9, 51
modulation effects 173
modulation pedals 14
modulation wheel 14, 77
modulators 11
monitor mix 197
monitor path 150
monitors 158
Mono mode 80
guitar controllers 80
Mono On 52
MOSFET (Metal Oxide Semiconductor Field Effect Transistor) 155
most significant byte (MSB) 53, 87
Motion Control Process (MCP) 95
Motion Control States (MCS) 95
moving-coil mic 132
MS mic 131
Mu-Metal 135
mult 151
multi mode 15, 58
Multichannel Audio Digital Interface (MADI) 129
multiplex 41
multiplexing 128
multiport MIDI interface 63, 102
multisamples 208
multitimbral 10, 58
Multitracker 141
Munson, W.A. 35
music notation 110
music theory 114
music-education software 113
musicianship 114
mute button 147
near-field reference monitors 158
neural-network technology 79
neutral wire 24
nibble 40
noise floor 188
noise modulation 189
noise reduction 141, 185, 188, 203
noise shaping 48
noise-induced loss 37
non-drop frame (SMPTE) 68
non-normaled 152
Non-Real Time Universal SysEx 55
Non-Registered Parameter Numbers (NRPNs) 54
normaled connection 151
normalization 106, 203
notch filter 11
Note On/Off 51, 53
notes 111
Nyquist frequency 42, 46
Nyquist, Harry 42
Oersted, Hans Christian 145
oersteds 145

off-axis 131
offline processing 106
Ohm's Law 23, 30
ohms 22
omni mode 52
omnidirectional mic 131
OMS 102, 108
on-axis 131, 159
open loop 95
open-loop transport 140
optimization 107
organ of Corti 37
oscillator 9, 10
ossicle chain 36
outer ear 36
output control 164
output gain 183
output impedance 22
output power 156
output transistors 154
oval window 36
overdubbing 64, 196
oversampling 42
overtone 5
overtone series 4
pad switch 132
page view 111
pan 51
pan pot 148, 150, 199
panic button 52
parallel interface 126
parallel mode 85
parent/child relationship 109
pass-through terminator 118
passive crossover 160
passive termination 119
patch 9, 208
patch bays 150
patch cord 151
patch points 150, 152
pattern-oriented sequencers 63
PCM samples 9
peak power 156
peak-power rating 161
pedals 14
Pelog 7
performance mode 15
phantom power 133
phantom-power switch 146
phase 173
phase response 135, 136
phase shifter 174
phon 35
phone plug 124
phono plug 125
physical modeling 16
pickup pattern 131
piezo triggers 81
pinch roller 140
pink noise 179
pinna 36
pitch bend 51
Pitch Bend Sensitivity 54
pitch correction 170
pitch EG 13
pitch shifters 169

pitch wheel 77
pitch-bend range 14, 80, 81
pitch-bend wheel 14
pitch-to-MIDI converter 78, 79
pitch-to-MIDI converters
    (PMCs) 83, 84
platforms 102
play mode 15
playlist 106
plug-ins 106
pointers 106
polar graph 131
poly mode guitar controllers 80
Poly On 52
poly pressure 51
polyphony 10, 58
Porcaro, Nick 19
portamento 14
Portastudio 141
ported speaker 160
position 199
postfader aux send 148
PostScript 112
potential difference 21
potential energy 21
power 23, 31
power acoustic 34
power amplifier 154
power bandwidth 157
power factor 23
power transformer 154
power-supply rails 154, 155
powered monitors 160
pre-emphasis 141, 189
predelay 166
prefader aux send 147
prefader listen (PFL) 147
premaster 200
premastering 196, 201
premix 149
presence peak 131
presets 9, 208
pressure
    keyboard 14
    MIDI 51
Pressure Zone Microphone
    (PZM) 133
primary 28
primary coil 134
print-through 144, 188
production master 201
program 9, 208
program blending 110
program change 51
program mode 58
programmable harmonization 85
project master 201
propagate 2
proximity effect 131
pulse-code modulation (PCM) 41
pulse-width modulation
    (PWM) 46
pulses per quarter note
    (ppqn) 61
pumping effect 189, 190
punch blocks 150

punch in 144
punch out 144
pure intervals 5
Pythagorean comma 6
Pythagorus 6
Q 11, 178
quality factor 178
quantization
    digital audio 43
    distortion 46
    error 43, 46
    grid 66
    groove 66
    noise 43, 46
    sequencing 66
    value 40, 45
quarter-track tape decks 139
Quick Edit function 209
radio-frequency interference
    (RFI) 27, 157, 188
random access 105
random patch generation 110
rate (LFO) 13
ratio
    compression 183
    expansion 185
RCA plug 125
reactance 22
Real Time Universal SysEx 54
record head 138
redithering 47
reference level 32
regeneration 168
Registered Parameter Numbers
    (RPNs) 54
relative phase 174, 180
release 185
release parameter 184
removable cartridges 105, 107
repro head 138
Reset All Controllers 52
resistance 22
resolution 45
    digital audio 43
    sequencing 61, 72
resonance 11
resonance modes 16
resonant synthesis 19
rests 111
retentivity 145
Return to Zero (RTZ) 143
reverb 165, 175
    cathedral 166
    chamber 166
    gated 166
    hall 166
    nonlinear 166
    plate 166
    reverse 166
    room 166
    spring 166
    time 166
    type 166
reverberation 165
reverse (digital audio) 106
RFI/EMI filtering 28

rhythmic resolution 111
ribbon controller 77
ribbon microphone 133
Rich, Robert 7
ripple effect 178
rise time 157
Roland
    Capital Tones 209
    GS 74, 89, 209
    Palette 209
    Partial 209
    Parts 209
    Patch 209
    Performance 209
    Samples 209
    Sub-Capital Tones 209
    Tones 209
    TVAs (Time-Varying
        Amplifiers) 209
    TVFs (Time-Varying
        Filters) 209
    Wave Generators
        (WGs) 209
rolloff 177
root mean square (RMS) 22
rotary speakers 175
rotary-speaker simulato 175
rotating head 141
safety ground 24
sag 29
Sample Dump Standard 55
sample-and-hold circuit 40, 42
sample-and-hold waveform 13
samples 208
sampling period 41
sampling rate 41
saturation 145
saturation distortion 145
Scandalis, Pat 19
Scholz, Carter 7
scratch vocal 196
scroll view 111
SCSI Connect Auto-Magically
    (SCAM) 118
secondary 28
secondary coil 134
seek time 104
segmentation 94
self clocking 127
self-oscillation 11
semi-weighted action 77
semicircular canals 36
sensitivity 66, 132, 161
sensory-neural hearing loss 37
sequence and assembly 200, 202
sequencer 61
sequencing
    real-time 64
    step-time 64
Serial Copy Management
    System (SCMS) 142
serial interface 126
shelving frequency 177
shield 26, 124, 130
shift 65
shock mount 130

short circuit 24
sidechain design 180
sidechain input 186
sidechain output 186
sight reading 114
signal ground 26
signal-to-noise ratio (S/N)
    34, 140, 157, 188
sine waves 4
singer's formant 5
single in-line packages (SIPs) 118
single mode 15
single-ended noise
    reduction 190, 202
single-ended SCSI 117
slave 50
Slendro 7
slew rate 157
sliders 14, 77
Small Computer System
    Interface (SCSI) 116
    extenders 119
    Fast 117
    Fast-20 117
    Fast-40 117
    Fast-80 117
    ID 117
    initiator 116
    narrow 117
    repeaters 119
    SCSI-2 117
    SCSI-3 117
    switchers 120
    termination 118
    terminator power 119
    Ultra 117
    Ultra2 117
    Ultra3 117
    wide 117
Smart FSK 68
Smith, Julius 18, 19
SMPTE 106
SMPTE generator/reader 68
SMPTE offset 68
SMPTE time code 68
Society of Motion Picture and
    Television Engineers
    (SMPTE) 157
soft-knee compression 184
software plug-ins 164, 171
software sequencers 63
solo button 147
solo in place 147
solo mode 81
Song Position Pointer 53, 67
Song Select 53
Sony 9-pin 97
Sony Digital Interface Format
    (SDIF2) 129
Sony/Philips Digital Interface
    Format (S/PDIF) 128
sound 2
Sound Controllers 54
sound pressure 35
sound pressure level
    (SPL) 35, 130

sound wave 2
sound-pressure level decibel 4
soundstage 161, 191
soundstage enhancement 203
source noise 188
spade lugs 126
speaker cable 126
speaker level 124, 126
spectral enhancement 203
spectral enhancers 180
spectral restoration 181
speed (LFO) 13
speed of sound 3
spikes 28
Spiral of Fifths 6
splicing 202
splitting 92
stand-alone sequencers 63
standard conditions 3
standard guitars 79
Standard MIDI Files
    (SMFs) 69, 111
        Type 0 72
        Type 0 files 69
        Type 1 72
        Type 1 files 69
        Type 2 72
        Type 2 files 69
standard musical notation 65
standing wave 16
stapes 36
Start command 54, 67
Start IDs 142
status byte 52
staves 111
Stilson, Tim 19
stirrup 36
Stop command 54, 67
strength 66
strip chart 65
stripe 68
striping 67
subcode data 142
subgroups 148
submix 149, 200
subtractive synthesis 9
supercardioid microphone 131
supply reel 140
surge/spike protector 28
surges 28
swing 66
switch pedals 14
switching power supply 155
sync converter 67
synthesis 9
    Advanced Frequency
        Modulation (AFM) 208
    Advanced Integrated
        (AI) 207
    Advanced Vector 207
    Advanced Wave Memory
        (AWM) 208
    Advanced Wave Memory 2
        (AWM2) 208
    AI^2 207
    Crosswave 207

Dynamic Component 207
Dynamic Vector 207
Frequency Modulation
    (FM) 208
Linear Arithmetic
    (L/A) 208
Realtime Convolution
    Modulation (RCM) 208
sample-based
    subtractive 207
Structured Adaptive
    (S/A) 208
Variable Architecture
    Synthesis Technology
    (VAST) 207
Vector 207
Virtual Acoustic Synthesis
    (VAS) 208
Z-Plane 207
synthesizers 9
System Common 53
system damping 158
System Exclusive (SysEx)
    53, 54, 97, 108
System Real Time 53, 54
System Real Time messages 67
System Reset 54
tails out 144
takeup reel 140
Tap Tempo 169
tape 149
tape counter 143
tape formulation 145
    chrome 145
    ferric 145
    metal 145
tape lifter 140
tape noise 188
tape speed 140, 142
TEAC Digital Interface
    Format (TDIF) 129
telescoping shield 28
temperament 6
tempo map 61
temporary threshold shift
    (TTS) 37
tension arm 140
thermal recalibration 104
thermal runaway 155
thermal-overload protection 156
thinning 93
third harmonic distortion
    (THD) 145
throughput 104
thru 63
timbre 176, 191
time alignment 136
time signature 111
timing 191
tinnitus 37
tonal correction 179
tonal matching 179
tone 9
toroidal transformer 154
Toslink 128

total harmonic distortion
    (THD) 156, 157
Track Bitmap 96
track chunks 69
track width 140, 142
tracking 78, 196
tracking delay 79
transducers 158
transformers
    1:1 135
    step-down 134
    step-up 134
    turns ratio 135
transposition 65, 171
transverse-mode rejection 28
tremolo 13, 174
triamping 158, 160
trigger signal 82
trigger-to-MIDI converter 82
trim pot 146
true earth ground 24
truncation 47
TT jacks 151
Tune Request 53
Tuning Bank Select 54
Tuning Program Select 54
tweeters 159
two's-complement 40
tympanic membrane 36
type parameter 69
unbalanced cables 26, 124
uninterruptable power
    supply (UPS) 29
unity gain 186
universal ed/libs 107
Universal System Exclusive
    (Sysex) 54, 94
unweighted action 77
VAC 21, 22
Van Duyne, Scott 19
VDC 21
velocity 13, 51, 53
velocity curves 81
velocity follow 14
velocity mixing 82
velocity switching 82, 94
vibrato 13, 174
Virtual Acoustic Synthesis
    (VAS) 17
virtual tracks 106, 197
voice allocation 59
voice coil 132, 158
voice mode 15
voices 9, 10, 208
Volta, Alessandro 21
voltage 21, 23, 32
voltage regulator 29
voltage-controlled amplifier
    (VCA) 186
volts 21
volume 4, 33, 34
volume (MIDI) 51
volume unit (VU) 34, 138
VRMS 22
wah-wah 13, 174
Watt, James 23

watts 23
watts RMS 23
wave sequencing 209
waveform 4, 10, 13, 21
waveform (LFO) 13
waveguide synthesis 18
wavelength 3
weighted action 77
weighting 35
Werckmeister, Andreas 6
wet/dry control 164
wind controllers 83, 84
woofer 159, 160
word clock 126
word length 43
words 40
write-once-read-many
    (WORM) 105
XLR 125, 130
Yamaha
    Elements 209
    Multis 209
    Operators 209
    Voice 209
    XG 75, 90
    Y2 129
zoning 77
µLaw audio compression 104

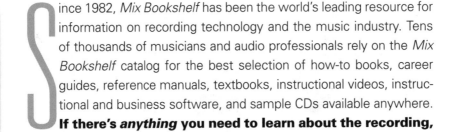